Protect Yourself At All Times

## Books by Thomas Hauser

### General Non-fiction

Missing
The Trial of Patrolman Thomas Shea
For Our Children
(with Frank Macchiarola)
The Family Legal Companion
Final Warning: The Legacy of Chernobyl
(with Dr. Robert Gale)
Arnold Palmer: A Personal Journey
Confronting America's Moral Crisis
(with Frank Macchiarola)
Healing: A Journal of Tolerance and Understanding
With This Ring (with Frank Macchiarola)
Thomas Hauser on Sports
Reflections

### Boxing Non-fiction

The Black Lights
Muhammad Ali: His Life and Times
Muhammad Ali: Memories
Muhammad Ali: In Perspective
Muhammad Ali & Company
A Beautiful Sickness
A Year at the Fights
Brutal Artistry
The View From Ringside
Chaos, Corruption, Courage, and Glory
I Don't Believe It, But It's True
Knockout (with Vikki LaMotta)
The Greatest Sport of All
The Boxing Scene
An Unforgiving Sport
Boxing Is . . .
Box: The Face of Boxing
The Legend of Muhammad Ali
(with Bart Barry)
Winks and Daggers
And the New . . .
Straight Writes and Jabs
Thomas Hauser on Boxing
A Hurting Sport
A Hard World
Muhammad Ali: A Tribute to the Greatest
There Will Always Be Boxing
Protect Yourself at All Times

### Fiction

Ashworth & Palmer
Agatha's Friends
The Beethoven Conspiracy
Hanneman's War
The Fantasy
Dear Hannah
The Hawthorne Group
Mark Twain Remembers
Finding the Princess
Waiting for Carver Boyd
The Final Recollections
of Charles Dickens
The Baker's Tale

### For Children

Martin Bear & Friends

# Protect Yourself at All Times

*An Inside Look at Another Year in Boxing*

By Thomas Hauser

The University of Arkansas Press
Fayetteville
2018

Manufactured in the United States of America

ISBN: 978-1 68226-074-6
e-ISBN: 978-1-61075-648-8

22 21 20 19 18 5 4 3 2 1

♾The paper used in this publication meets the minimum requirements of the AmericanNational Standard for Permanence of Paper for Printed Library Materials Z39.48-1984.

Library of Congress Cataloging-in-Publication Data:

Names: Hauser, Thomas, author.
Title: Protect yourself at all times : an inside look at another year in boxing / by Thomas Hauser.
Description: Fayetteville : The University of Arkansas Press, [2018] | Includes bibliographical references.
Identifiers: LCCN 2018002606 | ISBN 9781682260746 (pbk. : alk. paper) | ISBN 9781610756488 (e-ISBN)
Subjects: LCSH: Boxing.
Classification: LCC GV1133 .H3444 2018 | DDC 796.83--dc23
LC record available at https://urldefense.proofpoint.com/v2/url?u=https-3A__lccn.loc.gov_2018002606&d=DwIFAg&c=7ypwAowFJ8v-mw8AB-SdSueVQgSDL4HiiSaLK01W8HA&r=4fo1OqKuv_3krqlYYqNQWNKNaWxXN20G1PCOL-2ERgE&m=DcsnrTqO6VBhSNgvZVZ_uQZUBSQRbsxpXzVdNL4N-s0&s=OCVP0Q2JKCNWuJlJz2W8sxnzEXX7AKmBGPqRG9aIb30&e=

*The first time I was in a fighter's dressing room prior to a fight was when Billy Costello granted me access while I was researching The Black Lights. Since then, numerous fighters—some of them from boxing's elite, others club fighters—have allowed me to spend the hours before and after a fight in their dressing rooms prior to my writing about them. It's a privilege that I never take for granted.*

*I often ask myself what it would have meant to history if someone had been in Joe Louis's dressing room before he fought Max Schmeling, writing down what happened and what was said. In Sugar Ray Robinson's dressing room. Or Jack Dempsey's.*

*This book is dedicated to the fighters who've granted me that access. I'd like to thank them by name: Roy Jones Jr, Evander Holyfield, Manny Pacquiao, Miguel Cotto, Jermain Taylor, Kelly Pavlik, Bernard Hopkins, Gennady Golovkin, Canelo Alvarez, Sergio Martinez, Tim Bradley, Chad Dawson, Paulie Malignaggi, Ricky Hatton, James Toney, John Duddy, Shannon Briggs, Nikolai Valuev, Jarrell Miller, Vinny Maddalone, Samuel Peter, Michael Grant, Anthony Ottah, Seanie Monaghan, Kevin McBride, Hector Beltran, Ernest Johnson, Kevin Burnett, Katie Taylor, and Billy Costello.*

# Contents

## Fighters and Fights

## Curiosities



## Issues and Answers

# Author's Note

*Protect Yourself at All Times* contains the articles about boxing that I authored in 2017. The articles I wrote about the sweet science prior to that date have been published in *Muhammad Ali & Company*; *A Beautiful Sickness*; *A Year at the Fights*; *The View From Ringside*; *Chaos, Corruption, Courage, and Glory*; *I Don't Believe It, But It's True*; *The Greatest Sport of All*; *The Boxing Scene*; *An Unforgiving Sport; Boxing Is*; *Winks and Daggers*; *And the New*; *Straight Writes and Jabs*; *Thomas Hauser on Boxing*; *A Hurting Sport*; *A Hard World*; *Muhammad Ali: A Tribute to The Greatest*; and *There Will Always Be Boxing*.

# Fighters and Fights

*Cus D'Amato once said, "To see a man beaten, not by a better opponent but by himself, is a tragedy."*

# Jermain Taylor vs. Kelly Pavlik: Ten Years Later

On September 29, 2007, Kelly Pavlik knocked out Jermain Taylor at Boardwalk Hall in Atlantic City in one of the most dramatic fights I've ever seen. It was a particularly emotional experience for me because of a bond I shared with both men.

Jermain Taylor and his team gave me full access during fight week for both of his battles against Bernard Hopkins and also his fights against Winky Wright and Kassim Ouma. Team Pavlik accorded me the same privilege for Pavlik's two confrontations with Taylor and, later, his fights against Gary Lockett, Bernard Hopkins, and Sergio Martinez.

Taylor and Pavlik were enormously talented, likable young men. I was with them in their greatest moments of triumph and also for heart-breaking losses. I sat with them in hospital emergency rooms when they were being stitched up after victories and defeats.

When things start to fall apart for a fighter, it's hard to put the pieces back together again. Taylor and Pavlik wound up as roadkill in a brutal sport. Each man had his demons, as most fighters do. Ten years after their historic first encounter, their story is a cautionary tale.

Taylor grew up poor in Little Rock, Arkansas. There was a down-to-earth, wholesome, almost gentle quality about him. His father abandoned the family when Jermain was five, leaving Jermain, his mother, and three younger sisters behind. The children were raised in large part by their maternal grandmother, who was murdered by her own son (Jermain's uncle).

"He had a bad drug problem," Taylor told me years ago. "He wanted money and she wouldn't give it to him, so he cut her throat and killed himself. I was at the Goodwill Games when it happened. They told me about it when I got home. I heard what they were saying, but it wasn't real. Then I went into her bedroom. There was blood all over the sheets, all over the floor, and I realized that what they were saying was true. I'd won a bronze medal at the games. At the funeral, I put it in her casket."

Taylor won a bronze medal in the light-middleweight division at the 2000 Olympics and turned pro under the aegis of promoter Lou DiBella. Pat Burns, a former Miami cop with an extensive amateur coaching background, was brought in to train him. Under Burns's tutelage, Taylor won his first twenty-three pro fights. On July 16, 2005, he challenged Bernard Hopkins for the undisputed middleweight championship of the world.

Hopkins derided Taylor at every turn during the pre-fight promotion.

"As a child, I had a real bad speech problem," Taylor said when it was his turn to speak at the final pre-fight press conference. "I stuttered a lot. I still do it some, so it's hard enough for me to talk without trying to talk trash. Bernard Hopkins might out-talk me, but I'm gonna out-fight him."

"The early rounds belonged to Taylor," I wrote after the fight:

> Jermain advanced behind his jab, while Bernard slowed the pace by retreating and keeping his right hand cocked to discourage forays by the challenger. Taylor was faster. Hopkins minimized the number of encounters by moving around the ring and did his best work while punching out of clinches with sharp punishing blows. Fifty seconds into round five, the fighters clashed heads and an ugly wound pierced Taylor's scalp just above the hairline to the bone. Blood flowed freely and would for much of the night. In round nine, the challenger seemed to tire and the roles of predator and prey were reversed. The champion began his assault. A right hand hurt Taylor in round ten. More punishing blows followed. Round eleven was the same. Then came a moment that will forever define the career of each fighter. There was a minute left in round eleven. The momentum was all with Hopkins. Taylor was backed against the ropes, in trouble. Hopkins landed a big right hand. And in his darkest moment, Jermain summoned the strength to fire three hard shots with lightning speed into Bernard's body. Rather than continue the exchange, Hopkins stepped back. No one knew it at the time, but that was when Jermain Taylor established himself as a champion.

Taylor won a razor-thin split decision.

There was a parade in Little Rock to honor Jermain's accomplishment. Thousands of fans attended a rally at the end of the route. "That was the best feeling I ever had," Taylor said afterward. "It was amazing that all those people came out just for me."

Then came a trip to New York for a meeting with fellow Arkansan Bill Clinton. "Anywhere I go," Jermain said, "restaurants, clubs, wherever; they don't charge me. Of course, when I was broke and needed it, no one gave me anything for free."

Hopkins pressed for an immediate rematch. He thought he'd figured Taylor out in the second half of Hopkins-Taylor I and also that Jermain would come in soft after celebrating his win.

Hopkins was wrong. In their December 3 rematch, Taylor prevailed on a unanimous decision.

"Jermain Taylor has charisma," HBO commentator Larry Merchant proclaimed. "There's something about his look and bearing that gets your attention."

"I was impressed," Showtime Boxing analyst Al Bernstein says, looking back on that time. "I thought Jermain was the new star that boxing had been waiting for, that he might be one of those great middleweight champions who are remembered forever."

But a corrosive factor was at work.

A Little Rock resident named Ozell Nelson had played a pivotal role in Taylor's early life. Jermain had grown up without a father, and Nelson had filled the void. He'd even taught Jermain the rudiments of boxing. Now Nelson and Pat Burns weren't getting along.

After each Taylor-Hopkins fight, there had been sniping that Burns had a "white slavemaster mentality" and wasn't a top-notch trainer despite his having overseen Jermain's transformation from a raw amateur to middleweight champion of the world. There was a lot of money to be made off Taylor now that he was a champion, particularly if Burns's salary were to become available for redistribution.

Taylor owed much of his success as a fighter to Burns. But in his mind, Nelson had saved his life.

Dennis Moore is a Little Rock police detective who has known Taylor since Jermain was in sixth grade. In many ways, he has been like a big brother to Taylor.

"Jermain was in a good place after he beat Hopkins," Moore says. "Then some people got in his ear and pulled him away from Pat Burns and things changed. I'm not saying Pat was perfect. But Pat is a hands-on guy who runs a tight ship. He ran training camp the way it should have been run in terms who was allowed in, the things Jermain did and didn't do in his free time, and giving Jermain life advice. Ozell did some wonderful things for Jermain when Jermain was young. But there came a time when the money became a factor and Ozell did some things that hurt Jermain."

After the second Taylor-Hopkins fight, Burns was replaced by Emanuel Steward and Nelson was given an expanded role in training camp.

Steward was a legendary trainer, and deservedly so. He fit into that small group of men who are able to teach and strategize before a fight and then motivate and counsel adjustments in the heat of battle. One doesn't have to debate the issue of whether Steward was a better trainer than Burns. It's enough to say that Burns was a better trainer for Taylor.

Steward brought Taylor to the Kronk Gym in Detroit to train and introduced him to a lifestyle that wasn't a good fit.

"The people who took over didn't have Jermain's best interests at heart," Moore says. "When those guys got involved, his life took a turn for the worse. Jermain was a never a social drinker. I remember his saying to me once, 'What's the point of drinking if you're not going to get drunk.' Even when things were going well, Jermain would drink after fights. When he was with his new team, he started drinking more heavily.

"Then they started introducing him to women," Moore continues. "Jermain wanted to be a good family man. He was family first. But because of his upbringing, he'd never had anyone to teach him certain things and he was easily influenced. After that, he got into drugs. Jermain is a really good person inside. But when drugs are involved, he's not. Nobody made Jermain do it. He was an adult. But he was susceptible, and he chose the wrong way. They sucked him dry. And where are they now?"

There's a time-honored maxim in boxing that holds, "if a fighter isn't getting better, he's getting worse." In the three fights immediately after Burns's departure, Taylor's performance declined. On June 17, 2006, he was held to a draw by Winky Wright. Six months later, he was unimpressive in decisioning Kassim Ouma. On May 19, 2007, Taylor was awarded what many thought was an undeserved split decision over Cory Spinks.

That set the scene for Taylor-Pavlik.

Pavlik grew up in Youngstown, Ohio's blue-collar, beer-drinking bar culture. His father was a steelworker who later worked as an insurance agent. His mother was a cook at Hardee's.

Kelly started fighting at age nine at the Southside Boxing Club, where Jack Loew, who sealed asphalt driveways for a living, taught children to box. He worked odd jobs in high school to get the money to travel to amateur tournaments. More often than Pavlik cares to remember, he was busing tables when classmates came in for something to eat after a school dance.

Pavlik turned pro at age eighteen. He had a thin, muscular frame, power in both hands, a solid chin, and knew only one way to fight: going forward, punching. After thirty consecutive wins, he was offered a fight on HBO against knockout artist Edison Miranda. Most of his team cautioned against it.

"Make the fucking fight," Pavlik told his manager, Cameron Dunkin. "If I can't beat him, I'll get a job."

Pavlik knocked Miranda out in the seventh round.

The odds on Taylor-Pavlik were even in the days leading up to the fight. The "smart" money was on Taylor and the Youngstown money was on Pavlik. On fight day, the professional money came in, making Taylor an 8-to-5 favorite.

Each man had a fervent hometown fan base that made its way to Atlantic City for the fight.

Taylor came out aggressively in round one. He was quicker than Pavlik and his hands were faster. Midway through round two, Jermain timed a right hand over a sloppy jab. The blow landed high on Pavlik's head. Kelly staggered backward, and the champion followed with a fifteen-punch barrage that put the challenger on the canvas.

Pavlik rose at the count of two, but there were eighty-eight seconds left in the round.

"I was shaky," Pavlik admitted later. "That right hand hurt. I'd been knocked down before but there was never a buzz. It had always been a balance thing. This time, there was a tingle and my legs weren't so good. I was there mentally but my legs were gone. All I could think was, 'Hold on, get through this round.' He hit me with some more hard shots, but I got through the round."

After round two, the Taylor fans were celebrating like the fight was over.

In Hopkins-Taylor I, Jermain had walked through fire. Now Pavlik had to do the same.

In the corner after round two, Kelly managed a weak smile. "I'm okay," he told Jack Loew. But he was bleeding from the nose and mouth.

Then, incredibly, Pavlik won round three. The punches that Taylor had thrown in the second stanza seemed to have taken more out of him than out of Pavlik.

Dennis Moore, who was in Taylor's corner that night, recalls that, after round four, Jermain walked back to his corner and told Emanuel Steward, "Coach, I have nothing left."

"All the things that Jermain had done wrong in Detroit caught up to him," Moore says.

The die was cast. Taylor was faster. He was ahead on points throughout the fight. But inexorably, Pavlik was beating him down. The champion found himself having to punch his way out of corners. When the fight moved inside and one of Pavlik's hands was tied up, Kelly fought with the other hand rather than clinch. He made Taylor fight for every second of every round.

"Jermain has a chin," Pavlik said afterward. "I hit him with some punches, flush, right on the button early, and he didn't budge. But then he started to wear down. In the fifth round, I thought I hurt him a bit against the ropes. But he came back with a right hand that came close to putting me in trouble again, so I reminded myself to be careful. In the seventh round, I hit him with another good right hand and his reaction was different. I saw his shoulders sag. There was that little buckle in his knees, and I knew I had him."

The right hand backed Taylor into a corner again. Pavlik followed with a barrage of punches, and Jermain went limp. He was defenseless. Referee Steve Smoger stepped between the fighters. Kelly Pavlik was the new middleweight champion of the world.

"Oh, man," Pavlik says, looking back on that moment. "I remember it like it was yesterday. The excitement. The feeling inside. I started fighting when I was nine years old. For sixteen years, that had been my dream. Everything was a blur. Running to the corner, putting my arms in the air.

Everyone grabbing at me and hugging me. 'Do you know what you've done?' Yeah, I knew what I'd done. I was champion of the world."

It was an important night for boxing. Millions of fans had seen the fight because it was on HBO, not pay-per-view. Pavlik had put on a show reminiscent of Arturo Gatti's enthralling, never-say-die, action style. And he had Gatti's blue-collar, ethnic appeal.

"That night," Jim Lampley, who called the fight for HBO, says, "I thought that Kelly Pavlik was on the verge of becoming the face of American boxing."

When Pavlik returned to Youngstown after the fight, his SUV was met at the Ohio border by a caravan of police cars and fire trucks that escorted him home.

The perks kept coming.

Pavlik threw out the ceremonial first pitch before game four of the American League Championship Series between the Cleveland Indians and Boston Red Sox. He sat beside the legendary Jim Brown after presiding over the coin toss before a Cleveland Browns home game against the Miami Dolphins and addressed the Ohio State Buckeyes before the Ohio State-Michigan football game. A congressional resolution praised him for his commitment and continuing loyalty to Youngstown and the state of Ohio.

"It's weird," Kelly said at the time. "One day, I was ignored. And the next day, people are calling me a savior. I haven't changed, but a lot of people are treating me different. Go figure. I'm just doing my job."

Five months after dethroning Taylor, Pavlik won a unanimous decision in a Las Vegas rematch. But there were warning signs on the horizon.

Jack Loew says that Pavlik drank beer and occasional shots while training for both Taylor fights.

"But Kelly didn't start drinking at age twenty-five," Loew says. "He was drinking when he turned pro at eighteen, and it only got worse. He was going to be Kelly Pavlik whether it ruined him or not. I tried to stop it. But Kelly wouldn't listen. He'd say, 'Come on, Jack; you drink too.' And I had a choice. I could deal with it as best I could or walk away. I'd been in boxing a long time. I'd had one fighter I made a lot of money with. I'd been with Kelly since he was a kid. For most trainers, a fighter like Kelly comes along once in a lifetime. And that's if they're lucky. So I put up with it. I became part of the let's-be-quiet-about-it team. Kelly wasn't going to change. Not when he'd become a world champion and a millionaire doing things his way. In Kelly's mind, there was no problem."

After beating Taylor twice, Pavlik had an easy title defense against an overmatched Gary Lockett. Then, on October 18, 2008, he stepped up in weight to fight Bernard Hopkins at a contract weight of 170 pounds.

Once again, Pavlik drank during training camp. Worse, in the days prior to the fight, he suffered from bronchitis with a fever as high as 101 degrees and had taken Mucinex, penicillin (one shot on Wednesday night), and ciprofloxacin (500 mg twice a day through the day of the fight).

Hopkins dominated en route to a unanimous-decision triumph.

At that point, the once-adoring local media turned on Pavlik. There were reports of heavy drinking and blaring headlines: "Pavlik Fights Off Rumors About His Personal Life."

"People were killing each other on the streets in Youngstown," Mike Pavlik, Kelly's father, recalls. "You had young men and women dropping dead from heroin every day. And the media fixated on every little stupid mistake that Kelly made."

"The calls started coming in," Cameron Dunkin remembers. "'Kelly was out late last night, drinking. Kelly was out last night. He was drunk.' I'd ask him, 'How are you doing, Kelly?' And he'd say, 'I'm doing great.' But you knew he wasn't. In a boxing ring, Kelly was as tough, physically and mentally, as a person could be. But in real life, he was weak."

After losing to Hopkins, Pavlik returned to 160 pounds and he successfully defended his title in lackluster outings against Marco Antonio Rubio and Miguel Angel Espino. On April 17, 2010, he was dethroned by Sergio Martinez.

Soon after, Pavlik entered a treatment program at the Betty Ford Clinic in Rancho Mirage, California, but left before completing the program. He returned for a longer stay in the autumn of that year. But he still wanted to do what he'd always done, and that included drinking.

Four victories over pedestrian opposition followed. Pavlik entered the ring for the last time on July 7, 2012. "If you don't have it anymore, whatever the reason, boxing is a dangerous hobby," he says. "I didn't have it anymore, so I got out."

But the drinking continued. Since retiring from boxing, Pavlik has pleaded guilty to a series of criminal charges including assault, breaking and entering a foreclosed house (that was known locally as a "haunted" house), and disorderly conduct. In April 2017, he was given a six-month suspended sentence after pleading guilty to charges related to shooting a man with a pellet gun. Meanwhile, Taylor's life was also spiraling downward.

Emanuel Steward was dismissed after the knockout loss to Pavlik, and Ozell Nelson took over as lead trainer. In November 2008, Taylor won a lethargic decision over a diminished Jeff Lacy. Then he entered Showtime's 168-pound "Super Six" tournament. Brutal knockout defeats at the hands of Carl Froch and Arthur Abraham followed.

More seriously, Taylor sustained a brain bleed in the Abraham fight.

Andrew Meadors is a Little Rock financial planner who helped Taylor manage his money during the glory years.

"It will be interesting now to see how Jermain does personally," Meadors said after the Abraham fight. "We're telling him he has a whole new life. He needs to find new things to do every day that don't cost a lot of money. Hunting, fishing, family life, church groups, charity work. He'll feel lost for a while because boxing is such a routine. I hope he doesn't do what many young men do who are upset about their lives: engage in alcohol abuse with loser-type people who want to drink all the time. That would make me very sad. Jermain has a choice now on how his life goes. The final chapter of his life has yet to be written."

Eventually, Taylor returned to the ring and won four fights against low-level opposition. Pat Burns was back in his corner, but it was too late. The ceiling was caving in.

On August 26, 2014, Taylor was arrested and charged with first-degree domestic battery and aggravated assault after shooting his cousin in the leg. On the night of the shooting, the cousin had appeared uninvited at Jermain's home with a second man, who had recently been released from jail. Taylor ordered them off his property. They wouldn't leave, so Jermain took a gun and fired several warning shots in the air, at which point the cousin said that Jermain didn't have the guts to shoot him.

The day after his arrest, Taylor was released on $25,000 bail. There was one last fight, an October 8, 2014, decision over forty-one-year-old Sam Soliman that brought Jermain a bogus championship belt.

Then, on January 19, 2015, Taylor was arrested again, this time on charges of aggravated assault, endangering the welfare of a minor, and possession of marijuana after he fired a gun during a parade in Little Rock honoring Martin Luther King Jr. His bail was revoked.

While Taylor was in jail, family tragedy added to his troubles. A brother who suffered from seizures died. Then Jermain's mother was diagnosed with brain cancer and died while he was incarcerated. Jermain wasn't allowed to attend the funeral. But the judge overseeing his case let prison guards escort him to the funeral home so he could have some quiet time with her.

"That hurt," Pat Burns says. "It hurt a lot, not being there for his mother at the end."

On December 1, 2015, Taylor pleaded guilty to charges related to three separate incidents: (1) shooting his cousin; (2) threatening a family and shooting his gun in the air after the Martin Luther King Jr Day parade; and (3) assaulting a fellow patient while in a court-ordered rehabilitation program. On May 20, 2016, a Pulaski County circuit judge imposed a six-year prison sentence that was suspended on the condition that Taylor stay out of trouble, submit to drug testing, and perform 120 hours of community service.

Taylor will be thirty-nine in August. He and his wife, Erica, had four children together. In 2014, she filed for divorce and her petition was granted.

"Jermain and I talk on the phone from time to time," Pat Burns says. "He has a lot of regrets. The divorce was the right thing for Erica and the kids, but that's not what Jermain wanted to be. He wanted to be a good husband and a good father. He's hurting a lot over some of the things he did."

And the money is gone. Burns says that Taylor is working part-time now as a personal trainer. But he'll need to get a steady job.

Dennis Moore will always be in Jermain's life.

"Jermain is trying his best now to stay clean and stay out of trouble," Moore reports. "I think he's on the right road to living a normal life, but it will be a struggle."

"As far as I know, Jermain has been clean and sober for a year now," Andrew Meadors says. "He understands that one mistake could put him in prison for a long time. I'm hoping for the best. I'll do whatever I can to help him. But like a lot of people, my fear is that, someday, he'll be in the newspapers again for the wrong reason."

Taylor has worked his way back into good physical shape since his incarceration. He talks from time to time about fighting again. That would be unfortunate.

Dr. Margaret Goodman (one of the most knowledgeable advocates for fighter safety in the United States) says it's possible that brain trauma from boxing contributed to Taylor's problems. "With CTE [chronic traumatic encephalopathy]," Dr. Goodman explains, "you see extreme personality and mood changes. But you wouldn't know whether that's the case here without a lot of tests."

The most reliable tests for CTE are conducted post-mortem.

Efforts by this writer to contact Taylor in conjunction with this article were unsuccessful.

Pavlik, who's thirty-five, appears to be better positioned for the future than Taylor. Kelly has money from his ring career, a reasonably strong family support system, and no signs of CTE. He and his former wife, Samantha, divorced but are now living together again with their daughter and son, ages eleven and eight.

"I'm not a materialistic person," Pavlik recently told this writer. "I don't need expensive things. I saved my money and I have some investments. I'll never have to throw a punch or punch a time clock again. I'd like to have my own gym someday, but I want to do it right. I'll need knowledgeable people working for me, and I'd have to be there every day."

Like Taylor, Pavlik is subject to random drug and alcohol testing as part of his sentence. He's in a supervised diversion program and can't drink or leave Ohio without court permission for one year. If he gets in trouble, he goes to jail. He now weighs 235 pounds after making a commitment to power lifting, "Solid, all muscle," Kelly says. "I enjoy lifting. It makes me feel good."

Years ago, Pavlik acknowledged, "I honestly wouldn't wish fame on anybody. There are a lot of perks that come with it. But there's a lot of bad and a lot of stress that comes with fame, too."

He still feels that way.

"Some of the stuff I did was childish," Pavlik admits. "I put myself in stupid situations. My dad told me again and again, 'You're in the spotlight now. Watch what you do.' But I wanted to be me. That was my thing. I figured I'd succeeded at my job, so why should I change? But things came with being champion that I hadn't expected. You're supposed to go to the gym. Bust your butt. Go home. Fight. But I was also supposed to be a role model. And do this charity. And please, visit this dying kid in the hospital. It would mean so much to him. And the next day, it's an old man who's dying or I go see children with mental disabilities. I didn't have time to do everything people wanted me to do. There were times when I was overwhelmed by it all. And if you don't do everything that everyone else wants you to do, all of a sudden you're an asshole. I didn't change. But after I became champion, everything around me did. Then you start hearing, 'Kelly is in a bar. He's here drinking.' Well, I'd just busted my ass in training for two months and fought twelve rounds. If I want to play darts and drink beer, which is what I did before I became champion, why can't I? Besides, if what I'm doing is so bad, what are you doing here drinking with me? You've got a wife and kids and you're drinking your whole week's pay away? I never said I had a halo over my head. I never thought I was better than anyone else. I made some bad decisions. There were times when I was out of training and overdid it. I wanted to have fun. But if you look at all the incidents, they wouldn't have been news if it wasn't Kelly Pavlik. People say, 'Oh, you're Kelly Pavlik. You got off because of your name.' No! It got blown up because I was Kelly Pavlik.

"The BB-gun incident was misreported and blown out of proportion," Pavlik continues. "No one writes that this guy was doing work on my property and living in my home at the time; that we were taking turns shooting at targets; that he stayed in my house the night after it happened and, the next day, brought his kids over to go swimming. Or that he pressed charges against me so he could get a settlement. I'm minding my p's and q's now. I'm more careful about the situations I put myself in. No more kid stuff. It's been over a year since I've had a sip. I'm still playing in dart leagues. I'm still having fun. But it's a different kind of fun than I had before."

"When Kelly was sober," Jack Loew says, "he was as much fun to be around as any young man I've known. If he doesn't go back to drinking, he'll be okay."

"Do you miss drinking?" Pavlik is asked.

"No. Not now."

"Will you drink again when the year is up?"

"That's a good question," Kelly answers. "I don't know."

There's a self-sabotaging mechanism that comes with alcoholism and drug addiction. If a person is motivated and gets in a good treatment program, he learns where the problem comes from and how to deal with it.

I had the opportunity to watch Kelly Pavlik and Jermain Taylor under the most intense circumstances imaginable. I saw them in moments of celebration and also in bitter defeat. Each time, they handled what came at them on fight night with courage, dignity, and strength. I believe that these qualities are at their core.

"We were champions," Pavlik says, reflecting on his ring rivalry with Taylor. "No one can ever take that away from us. The only two guys I lost to will be in the Hall of Fame someday. And Jermain beat one of the guys who beat me."

"I have a lot of respect for Jermain," Pavlik says in closing. "I like him. He's a good person. He was at the top before I was. I'd like to sit down with him someday and trade old fight stories. Not just about our fights, but about the times he beat Bernard Hopkins. Both of us fell down. But when a fighter gets knocked down, he gets back up and keeps fighting."

*Shortly before fighting Danny Garcia, Keith Thurman told me, "I had long hair when I was young. People used to say to my mom, 'You have a very pretty little girl.' So when I was four, I cut it. Then, in sixth grade, I went back to long. In the amateurs when I was knocking everybody out, they called me 'Samson'. I think about cutting it off from time to time, but I like what I know. Braids will do."*

# Keith Thurman: "If You Can Beat Me, Beat Me"

On March 4, 2017, *Showtime Championship Boxing on CBS* featured the highly anticipated WBC-WBA welterweight championship fight between Keith Thurman and Danny Garcia.

Thurman is one of the more intriguing personalities in boxing today. And that statement could be amended to extend beyond the sweet science.

Dan Birmingham, who trains Thurman, said last year, "I've known Keith since he was kid. I've been working with him since he was fifteen. And I still don't really know him. He's very opinionated. He has an opinion about everything. And he reminds me of a hippie from the sixties. Outside the ring, Keith is all peace and love. He's a giver. He plays the flute, guitar, and a little piano. He would have done well at Woodstock. But when the bell rings, he'll rip your head off."

Thurman's mother was a telemarketer. His father worked, among other things, as a nursing care assistant. They divorced when Keith was young, and his father had three more children in a subsequent marriage.

"There's no blueprint for being a perfect parent," Thurman says. "But both of them tried. My father always talked to me like a young man, not a little boy. My mother raised me as a single parent, which was hard, and I probably made it harder because I was rambunctious at times. I have my own home now. But when I started making money, I kept living at home and helped my mother pay off the mortgage. I'm grateful for everything they taught me."

Thurman has strong self-belief and a personalized faith. "I'm more spiritual than religious," he explains. "I believe that the Creator knew what He was creating and that there's harmony amidst the chaos. I believe that human beings were created to love and respect each other. I was raised as a Christian, but I don't practice a specific religion because of the structure. My connection to my Creator is personal. I've read a lot about the world's religions and studied them in my way. I look for what they have in common rather than their differences. Religion can help you understand how to build character in yourself and in others.

"It's important to me to always be growing as a person," Keith continues. "I was a high school dropout, but I like to learn. Part of me has always wanted to go to college."

Thurman likes to talk. He has a preference for hip-hop and rhythm and blues, but says, "Good music is good music, whatever kind it is." Then, in the next sentence, he acknowledges, "I have a love-hate relationship with music. Songs tend to seep into your subconsciousness, and it interferes with my meditation. Sometimes, when I'm meditating, it feels like I'm turning on the radio."

He also has thoughts to offer on government and politics:

- "I'm proud to be an American. I have a lot of opinions on a lot of subjects. One of the best things about being an American is the right to have opinions and speak openly about them."
- "I'm a boxer. I know how to take a punch. America is the strongest nation in the world. But after 9/11, America didn't know how to take the punch. Go to war in Iraq? What was that for?"
- "Life is hard. There's no easy way of going about it. Sometimes the government makes life easier. Sometimes it makes life harder."
- "I like to break down words. Like politics. 'Poly' means many. Ticks are blood-sucking parasites. So it's there, right under your nose."

Thurman is articulate, thoughtful, and complex. But none of that matters in a boxing ring unless a fighter can fight.

Thurman can fight. His first mentor in boxing was Ben Getty, who trained Keith from a young age. Getty died in 2009, leaving his charge in Dan Birmingham's hands. To this day, Thurman quotes Getty on aspects of life ranging from finance to Frank Sinatra. But most of the quotes are on boxing:

- "Ben Getty always said, 'Smart fighters win and dumb fighters lose.'"
- "Ben Getty always said, 'You can't wait on a rematch. You have to make adjustments now.' There's no reason that someone should be able to hit you again and again with the same punch. If he hits you more than twice with the same punch, you're doing something wrong."
- "Ben Getty used to tell me, 'It's just around the corner, boy.' If I could have Ben back for a day now, I'd tell him, 'Well, I guess we've reached that corner.'"

"Boxing has been my whole life since I was seven years old," Thurman says. "It's the only thing that has stayed consistent except my mother and father. I've never had a job. I never delivered pizza. I mowed lawns from time to time when I was a kid to pick up some extra change, but that's all. I don't know how to do an oil change. I don't know calculus. But I know boxing.

"Boxing brings happiness and excitement to me," Keith continues. "I had difficulty with team sports. I didn't like relying on others for victory. Not everybody can be a boxer. It's a whole other kind of sport. You need a special mentality and some very special qualities to be a boxer. But I love the sport. It's more than a source of income for me. I love being tested. If you can beat me, beat me."

Thurman sees himself as a boxer first and a puncher second, explaining, "Every training camp, I focus on a new technique. I want to be able to adapt to anything that comes my way." But he's quick to add, "Not one opponent ever got in the ring with me and said afterward, 'Keith Thurman can't hit; his power is overrated.' People used to say about me, 'Man, this kid can punch. Wait till he gets his man strength. He'll be at his strongest by age twenty-eight.'"

Thurman smiles: "Well, I'm twenty-eight now."

Thurman–Garcia shaped up as an attractive fight. Each man turned pro in November 2007 and is in his prime.

Thurman brought a 27–0 (22 KOs) record into the bout and was the reigning WBA 147-pound champion. His signature win was a 115–113, 115–113, 115–113 decision victory over Shawn Porter at Barclays Center last year.

Garcia (33–0, 19 KOs) is one year older than Thurman. He rose to prominence with a fourth-round upset knockout of Amir Khan in 2012, won several 140-pound belts, and claimed the vacant WBC 147-pound crown last year with a unanimous decision win over Robert Guerrero.

Thurman was a 2-to-1 betting favorite.

Ever since Luis Collazo doubled him over with a body shot (Keith stayed on his feet), the naysayers have said that Thurman doesn't like it when an opponent goes hard to the body. Eighty years ago, the naysayers said the same thing about Joe Louis and Louis responded, "Who do?"

"I know how to handle being hurt," Thurman said in the build-up to Thurman–Garcia. "Danny has power. If he lands right, he can hurt me. But he's not going to match me in power. I'm bigger; I'm stronger. Danny's resume isn't a welterweight resume. It's knockdown power versus knockout power. He's dangerous, but I'm more dangerous. Round by round, minute by minute, second by second, the truth will be revealed."

But Garcia had faced similar odds in overcoming Lucas Matthysse and more daunting ones against Amir Khan.

"At the end of the day," Danny said at the final pre-fight press conference, "all 'underdog' means is that there's a bunch of people who don't know what I can do." To which Angel Garcia (Danny's father and trainer) added, "Thurman beat guys he was supposed to beat. Danny beat guys when people didn't think he'd win."

That brings the narrative to Angel Garcia.

Angel gives the impression of being tightly coiled, physically and mentally. Even on good days, there's a lot of anger bubbling just beneath the surface. He talks with his hands and tends to get in people's space when he talks to them, often jabbing them with a finger to make his point. When Danny was young, Angel spent several years in prison for drug-related offenses.

At a January 18 press conference to announce Thurman vs. Garcia, Angel hurled racial epithets at Thurman (who is African American) and ranted about "motherfucking immigrants [who] come from another country." Thereafter, there was talk that the New York State Athletic Commission might deny Angel a license to work his son's corner on fight night.

Thurman wanted Angel in Danny's corner. At the time of the tirade, Keith told reporters, "Danny knows how to deal with his father. He was raised by his father. He knows what to expect from his father. At the end of the day, crazy Angel doesn't get to do anything but run his mouth. He can't punch for Danny. He can't take the punches for Danny. What they do in the ring is what matters. I care about the fighter, not the fighter's father."

Also, Thurman reasoned that, if Angel were denied a license, Team Garcia would try to tarnish a Thurman victory by claiming that Danny was disadvantaged by his father's absence.

It was all moot. The New York State Athletic Commission as presently constituted doesn't upset applecarts when the applecart is owned and operated by powerful economic interests (e.g. Barclays Center and CBS).

On February 22, Angel met with NYSAC chairperson Ndidi Massay, acting executive director Tony Giardina, and director of boxing Eric Bentley to discuss his transgressions. On March 2, shortly after the final pre-fight press conference ended, the commission issued a terse statement that read, "The New York State Athletic Commission has approved Angel Garcia's license application to participate in Saturday's bout."

Angel wasn't on the dais at the final pre-fight press conference. But he did attend the event and spoke extensively with the media afterward. In these conversations, he was careful to not repeat any of the thoughts that had landed him in hot water. He was also careful not to say anything that could be remotely construed as an apology.

"I had a little meeting with them," Angel said of his sit-down with commission personnel. "But it was nothing. I didn't do nothing [wrong], but I did my part. They told me to do something, and I did it. I completed my half. I did a small video. We do a lot for kids anyway. We donate haircuts and we do things for the kids in the neighborhood [in Philadelphia]. So it ain't nothing new for us to do something like that. So I donated to the Joe Frazier Foundation, money, and then that was it. And then I had to say, if I offended any immigrant or whatever, or refugees. I made a video like that."

The New York State Athletic Commission declined a request for information regarding whether the video referenced by Angel Garcia is available for viewing and how much money Garcia donated to the foundation. A Google search raised questions as to whether such a foundation currently exists.

Then it was fight night.

Barclays Center has shown a commitment to building an ongoing boxing program. The announced crowd of 16,553 constituted an arena record for the sweet science.

Former heavyweight contender Gerry Cooney, who was in attendance, captured the anticipation as the moment of reckoning arrived: "Right now, if you're a fighter, you want the bell to ring. Just ring the bell, baby, and let's fight."

Thurman–Garcia was a great matchup, which is all fans can ask of a promotion. It wasn't a great fight.

Round one was the most exciting of the bout. Thurman came out hard, stunned Garcia with a left hook up top, and followed up nicely. But from round two on, the excitement waned. Thurman was wary of Garcia's counterpunching ("I was impressed with the way he read my punches," Keith said after the fight) and spent long periods of time circling away from his opponent. Meanwhile, Garcia was cautious about engaging and more invested in countering than getting off first. Each man took the other's punches well when they landed. There was drama because of the stakes involved. But the expected fireworks were few and far between. The crowd booed sporadically from the midway point on.

The New York State Athletic Commission had agreed to accommodate CBS by allowing seventy-second rest periods between rounds instead of the standard sixty seconds. That allowed CBS to program its commercials the way it wanted to. There's no way of knowing whether that altered the flow of the bout.

It was a hard fight to score. Each judge gave Thurman the first, fifth, and eighth rounds while leaning toward Garcia in rounds six and ten. The other rounds were up for grabs. In the end, two judges—John McKaie (116–112) and Joseph Pasquale (115–113)—favored Thurman, while Kevin Morgan (115–113) sided with Garcia.

Earlier in the week, Angel Garcia had spoken with the media about Danny and said, "He not my son now. He's my fighter."

At the post-fight press conference, Danny was asked, "How did your dad like the decision?"

"My dad is always upset," Danny answered.

Then Angel, who was a late arrival at the press conference, had his say: "You can't win a fight running, bro. You gotta make contact. You can't just run. You can't be a world champion like that."

At that point, Keith Thurman and Dan Birmingham entered the room and the Garcias walked out. Speaking to the fans' disappointment over the way the fight unfolded, Thurman put the night in context: "Sometimes when you come to a boxing match, you get what you want. You see a fight. And sometimes you get boxing. I finessed my way to victory tonight."

Thurman has his eye on history. "Either you're the best or you aren't," he says. "I want to prove that I'm the best."

However, he's also a practical man, who notes, "Boxers are entrepreneurs, and the life of an athlete is short. You have to ride the wave while it lasts. The goal is to find a way to produce income that will give me a good cash flow for life after I retire from boxing."

Then Thurman adds, "Having money is a job in itself. Growing up, I didn't have much. I'd hear the saying, 'More money, more problems.' And I'd ask, 'How is that so? It seems to me, more money, more solutions.' But I understand that now."

And a final thought . . .

"When you're a kid," Thurman says in closing, "time seems to last forever. And now, time seems so short. But I'm happy to be in this moment. I'm living the life I want to live."

*Jerry Izenberg (the dean of American sportswriters) once said, "In order to be an MMA champion, you need every skill that's outlawed on the planet. The very things we pride ourselves on not doing, these people elevate to an art form." But MMA is a fact of life in sports today and can't be ignored.*

# UFC 208, Holly Holm, and Boxing

For well over a century, boxing was the dominant combat sport in America. John L. Sullivan, Jack Johnson, Jack Dempsey, Joe Louis, Rocky Marciano, Muhammad Ali, and their brethren captured the imagination of the American people. Sugar Ray Robinson was known throughout the land. As American heavyweights fell by the wayside, fighters in lighter weight classes like Ray Leonard, Oscar De La Hoya, and Floyd Mayweather stepped into the void. But in recent years, boxing has suffered from self-inflicted wounds. And with its popularity diminishing, mixed martial arts has stepped into the void.

Mixed martial arts is still a niche sport, but it has a fervent following. In the world of MMA, there's UFC and everyone else. Last year, UFC was sold to a group of investors led by WME-IMG, who were backed by venture capital from Silver Lake, Kohlberg Kravis Roberts, and Michael S. Dell. The sale price was widely reported as between 4 and 4.2 billion dollars. UFC is headquartered in Las Vegas and has almost six hundred employees with offices in London, Singapore, and Toronto.

There are A-sides and B-sides in UFC fights, but everyone is presumed to get a fair shake from the referees and judges, which isn't always the case in boxing. In another departure from boxing, elite UFC fighters are expected to go in tough. As L. Jon Wertheim wrote in *Sports Illustrated* last year, "UFC has an aversion to risk aversion. There are no cagey promoters larding fighters' records by pitting them against tomato cans. There's no swirl of alphabet-soup sanctioning organizations crowning different champs. Fighters can't—and don't want to—duck each other."

Like boxers, mixed martial artists need experience. But UFC isn't the place to get it. Once a combatant reaches the UFC level, there are no gimme fights. Randy Couture's record when he retired from MMA was

19 wins against 11 losses. He's in the Hall of Fame because he went in tough from the start.

UFC's most promising vehicle for achieving mass market acceptance was Ronda Rousey, who was on the verge of becoming a pop-culture icon. Then Rousey was unexpectedly annihilated by Holly Holm in November 2015 and suffered a forty-eight-second blow-out loss to Amanda Nunes in a December 30, 2016, comeback fight.

Rousey's fall from grace was offset to a degree by the 2016 legalization of MMA in New York, which had been the nation's last holdout state. UFC 205, which was contested at Madison Square Garden on November 12, 2016, drew a sellout crowd of more than twenty thousand and generated a $17.7 million live gate (a record for both UFC and the Garden). A December 10 UFC card in Albany followed.

On February 11, 2017, UFC returned to New York City with UFC 208; a ten-bout card at Barclays Center in Brooklyn. In the main event, Holly Holm faced off against Germaine de Randamie for the championship of the UFC's newly created 145-pound woman's division. The primary supporting bout saw forty-one-year-old Anderson Silva return to the Octagon against Derek Brunson.

Holm vs. de Randamie was a title fight and thus scheduled for five rounds. All of the other bouts were scheduled for three.

The eight-sided configuration of the arena at Barclays Center is an ideal physical setting for the UFC Octagon. UFC 208 sold out with an announced attendance of 15,628. That's a smaller number than for boxing at Barclays because the set-up for UFC shows includes four large video screens that hang from the rafters and block the view from some seats. The screens are essential to following the action from certain angles when the combatants are grappling on the canvas.

There's constant—and loud—music that stops only for the fights.

The first bout of the evening was transmitted online at UFC Fight Pass. The next four bouts were televised on FS1. The final five were incorporated into the UFC 208 pay-per-view telecast.

Football fans don't show up for a game in the third quarter. Baseball fans don't arrive by design in the sixth inning. But at most major boxing events, including those contested at Barclays Center, the seats are virtually empty when the first bout starts. That's because boxing fans have come to expect one-sided, who-cares undercard fights.

At UFC 208, the arena was close to three-quarters full by the time the first fight started. Bruce Buffer (Michael's brother) was the ring announcer. His presence for all ten fights rather than just the two featured bouts was a signal to fans that all of the fights mattered.

In its early years, UFC was ignored by the mainstream media. So it bypassed the powers that be and developed a core fan base through the Internet. Overall, MMA media today are younger than their boxing counterparts. Few of them are classically trained, but they're arguably more knowledgeable about their sport than the average boxing writer.

At big boxing events, members of the boxing community and media circulate and interact with one another. The physical set-up at Barclays Center for UFC 208 was such that there was little socializing or free flow of traffic.

UFC personnel were everywhere, working in clearly defined roles. One of them, seated at the edge of the Octagon in the first row of a three-row press section, was Tom Gerbasi.

Gerbasi, age forty-eight, bridges the divide between MMA and boxing. His father was a retired marine who became vice president of operations for a building maintenance company. His mother worked at myriad jobs, ranging from the day shift at a hardware store to the night shift at a home for wayward children. Gerbasi received his early education at Holy Name of Jesus Grammar School in Brooklyn and Xavier High School in Manhattan. He graduated from St. John's College with a degree in athletic administration in 1990, couldn't find a job in sports management and, for the next ten years, worked in building maintenance.

Gerbasi's father was a boxing fan, and Tom followed his lead. He began writing for CyberBoxing.com in 1996—"for free," he ruefully adds. "I was freelancing and would take any job that involved writing about boxing." His breakthrough came when the *Village Voice* hired (and paid him) to write articles about Patty Alcivar and Jill Matthews. That led to freelance publicity work for two more women boxers (Leah Mellinger and Nina Ahlin) and also for Clifford Etienne.

Then Gerbasi was hired to construct Shane Mosley's first website ("I still have a picture of the $600 check that Jack Mosley gave me"). That led to similar projects for Johnny Tapia and David Reid. Meanwhile, Team Mosley had brought in a Californian named Gary Randall to do additional graphic work for its site.

Randall and Doug Fischer had recently founded a website called *House of Boxing*. In May 2000, Randall called Gerbasi and asked how much he was making at his current job as a maintenance worker.

"Thirty-five thousand a year," Gerbasi told him.

"I'll give you ten thousand more and you can work from home," Randall offered.

Gerbasi's responsibilities with *House of Boxing* included editing the recently hired Michael Katz, writing articles of his own, and overseeing the posting of website content. "It was a nice run," he remembers. "The Internet was taking off, and we were like kids in a candy store. We loved boxing. We were out there hustling. We weren't jaded yet. It was a good time."

Then *House of Boxing* was acquired by Worldwide Entertainment & Sports (WWES). There was financial mismanagement and WWES was careening toward bankruptcy. At that point, Gerbasi, Randall, Fischer, and Steve Kim (who was writing for House of Boxing) left the site and founded *MaxBoxing.com*.

Another good run followed. Randall spearheaded a membership program that offered special content to *MaxBoxing* visitors for five dollars a month. This was before free Internet news content was a fact of life. The membership program flourished, peaking in 2002 when Mike Tyson melted down at press conference to announce Tyson versus Lennox Lewis, bit Lewis on the leg, and engaged in a lengthy profanity-filled rant. *MaxBoxing* captured it all on video, which was unusual for that time.

Then the financial model soured. Free Internet video content became the norm. And membership at *MaxBoxing* declined.

In October 2005, Gerbasi got a telephone call from UFC president Dana White, who offered him a job editing the UFC website. For a while, he edited UFC.com and continued writing for *MaxBoxing*. Eventually, a British company acquired *MaxBoxing* and stopped paying the bills (most notably, money owed to Gerbasi). He left *MaxBoxing* in 2009. Since then, while working for UFC, he has continued writing about boxing for *The Ring*, *Boxing Scene*, and *Boxing News*.

Gerbasi's editorial duties for UFC include writing and editing content for UFC.com, writing event programs, and writing the script for fighter videos that are shown in the arena and on television just before each fight.

It's central to the UFC philosophy and essential to Gerbasi's job that he personalize the fighters.

Or viewed another way . . . Imagine being in high school. Two of the toughest guys in your class have a beef with each other and agree to meet in a parking lot after school to determine which one is tougher. That would be riveting for their classmates to watch. Why? Because the other students would know these two guys and be likely to have a rooting interest in the fight. UFC tries to build fan identification for all of its fighters.

"I like MMA," Gerbasi says. "People look at MMA and say, 'This is so violent.' And it is violent, but there's an art to the whole thing. Take all the nuances of boxing. Then multiply that by all the other disciplines you need to know to survive in MMA. And UFC makes an effort to be fan-friendly. Boxing should learn from UFC. Top Rank seems to think that loud music is the UFC fan experience. That's wrong. The UFC fan experience is ten competitive fights on a card, not one or two. At a UFC show, the fights come one after another without long breaks in between. If you don't know who the undercard fighters are, we'll educate you. Boxing isn't going away. I still love boxing. But there's a lot to be said for MMA."

Roy Jones was once asked for his opinion of MMA and answered, "A good fight is a good fight."

That said, the fights at UFC 208 were disappointing. The UFC highlight action promos that fans see on television and online are just that—highlight action clips. Seven of the evening's first eight fights went the distance. The exception was bout number eight, when Tim Boetsch decided at the 3:41 mark of round one that it would be wiser to tap out than have his left arm ripped from its socket by Jacare Souza.

To paraphrase Roy Jones, "A slow fight is a slow fight." During UFC 208, the crowd was often quiet and there were boos from time to time. Five minutes (the length of a UFC round) is long time for a fighter who gets in trouble early. Five minutes is also a long time for fans when nothing much is happening.

Also, championship boxing at its best offers exciting, sustained action at a high level and an ebb and flow for the duration of a fight. In MMA, the action is more likely to come in short bursts without the same building drama.

The ninth bout of the evening—the "co-main event"—saw Anderson Silva take on Derek Brunson. Silva is MMA royalty. Between 2006 and 2012, he was triumphant in sixteen consecutive outings. But Silva entered the Octagon at Barclays Center winless in his last five UFC contests (a 2015 decision victory over Nick Diaz having been changed to "no contest" after Silva tested positive for illegal performance-enhancing drugs). In Silva's prime, he was a devastating counterstriker. He's still a formidable presence, and Brunson seemed intimidated to the point of being reluctant to lead. There was drama in the fact that this was Anderson Silva, but not much more. Silva prevailed on the judges' scorecards by a 30–27, 29–28, 29–28 margin.

Then it was time for Holm vs. de Randamie.

Holm, age thirty-five, is more vibrant and physically imposing in person than she appears to be on television. She began her professional combat sports career as a kickboxer. Then she turned to the sweet science and fashioned a 33–2–3 (9 KOs) record as a professional boxer.

She's a fighter at heart. In 2011, Holm suffered a brutal beating in a seven-round knockout loss to Anne Sophie Mathis. She figured out what she did wrong and, six months later, fought Mathis again, winning a clear-cut unanimous decision.

"I had to shut out a lot of negativity," Holm said later about the Mathis fights. "A lot of friends told me I was crazy to fight her again. I told them, 'That's why you're not doing this and I am.' Could she have knocked me out again? Yes. But I would have had to live with it until the day I died if I didn't try."

Holm turned to MMA in 2011 and had her first fight under the UFC banner on February 28, 2015. Eight and a half months later, she was in Australia to fight Ronda Rousey.

"People were asking me, 'How long do you think you're going to last against her?' Holm recalls. "And I was like, 'I'm not going all the way to Australia to participate. I'm going there to win.'"

Holm stunned the combat sports world by knocking Rousey out in the second round. Asked on media day (three days before fighting de Randamie) about the fringe benefits that flowed from that conquest, Holly answered, "I love John Elway. Who gets to meet John Elway [now general manager of the Denver Broncos] and talk to him during a game? I did."

But Holm was unable to capitalize financially on beating Rousey the way she might have.

Rousey was packaged as a sex symbol. With the right make-up and clothing, Holm, who has attractive features and long blond hair that stretches far below her waist, looks as much the model as Rousey. But she has been packaged differently.

Holm also has a different view of the world and her place in it. "Do you feel like a star?" she was asked on media day.

"No," she answered. "I just feel like Holly."

And more significantly, Holm's championship reign was short. Four months after beating Rousey, she lost her spot on top of the hill by submission to Miesha Tate. Then, on July 23, 2016, Holm extended her losing streak to two fights when she dropped a unanimous five-round decision to Valentina Shevchenko.

"I know I'm coming off two losses in a row," Holm said. "It's a sore spot in my heart. It's sour. I was prepared. I just didn't perform well on those nights."

That said, Holm was in danger of moving from being a major story in mixed martial arts to a footnote. On media day, more than one writer suggested that she might be remembered as "the Buster Douglas of MMA." And Holm herself seemed anxious.

"It's the biggest high of your life when you win," she said. "I'm always chasing that. But sometimes I hate it, this hurt in your gut. You have this day that's getting closer and closer. When I was waitressing, I had this dream sometimes that I was serving drinks and all I had on was my bra. Then I'd wake up and say, 'Thank God, that wasn't real.' Now I have this dream that I have a fight coming up. I wake up and it's fight day. It's real."

Holm was favored to beat the thirty-two-year-old de Randamie. Germaine was 46-and-0 with 30 knockouts as a Muay Thai kickboxer and is a strong puncher. But after transitioning to MMA in 2008, she'd suffered three losses in nine fights, including a first-round knockout defeat at the hands of Amanda Nunes.

Also, Holm (who fought Rousey at 135 pounds) had fought as a boxer at weights ranging from 138 to 151 pounds. It was generally believed that the 145-pound weight limit would suit her. And she'd fought better UFC competition than de Randamie had fought.

Then came the fight. De Randamie was the early aggressor and won the first three rounds, landing the harder, more-damaging blows. Every punch she threw came with bad intentions. Holm, by contrast, kept circling away. And many of her assaults—kicks and punches—seemed to be of the "stay away from me" variety.

At the close of the second round and again after the third, de Randamie landed a punch after the horn sounded. The first of these illegal blows shook Holm and seemed to call for a one-point deduction. But referee Todd Anderson let the infractions pass. In the fourth and fifth rounds, Holm tried to take the fight to the mat to neutralize de Randamie's punching power, but de Randamie stayed on her feet. The crowd booed sporadically throughout. All three judges scored the fight 48–47 in de Randamie's favor.

Dana White represents UFC's economic interests. But he's also an advocate for the fans. When the show was over, White acknowledged, "Not one of our better events. I always feel that, if we come into a place, you're going to have at least a few good fights that are going to get you up out of your seat. We didn't have any of those. I was hoping that the main event would deliver and erase most of the rest of the night. That didn't happen. It's been a long time since we've had a bad show. It happens." White then unloaded on Todd Anderson and the New York State Athletic Commission (which, in recent years, has been plagued by incompetence and corruption).

"I feel like the ref from New York shouldn't be reffing a main event fight," White said. "They don't have enough experience. He should not have been in there. But again, we don't make those decisions. The commission does. That was a bad decision by them. If that guy takes a point for hitting after the bell, it's a draw. Everybody was blowing me up on the phone. 'What's wrong with this ref?' and 'What's wrong with this ref?' What's wrong with this ref is, he doesn't have big fight experience. None of these guys do in this state yet. They should have had one of the experienced MMA refs in there reffing that main event."

Meanwhile, although Tom Gerbasi now works for UFC, boxing still owns a piece of his heart. That's clear when he reminisces about what he calls "my first and only sanctioned amateur fight."

"It was on February 5, 1997, in the novice division of the *New York Daily News* Golden Gloves," Gerbasi recalls. "The same tournament that produced Sugar Ray Robinson and Riddick Bowe. If there had been a novice novice division, I would have been in it."

Gerbasi was twenty-eight years old at the time, six feet tall, 217 pounds (down from 235 when he began training).

"It started on a whim," he recounts. "I was writing for CyberBoxing and said to myself, 'Let me see what this is like.' I'd been in the gym for less than three months before the fight, and I didn't have what you'd call a Spartan training ethic. I'd been stung a few times in sparring but had never been hurt. I figured, if I get hit, I'll fight through it and come on strong at the end. Looking back on it all, it was pretty stupid."

"The opponent was a guy named Diesel 'Truck' Means," Gerbasi continues. "The fight was at Blessed Sacrament Church in Brooklyn. All the fighters were in one room before we went out to fight. I can't see without my glasses. All I could see was shapes. When I looked across the room at the guy I was fighting, his arms looked as thick as my legs. My trainer came over and told me, 'Your opponent looks slow.' I was slow too. I had no speed, no power, and as it turned out, no chin.

"I remember touching gloves," Gerbasi says, concluding his saga. "The next thing I remember is being in an ambulance with two guys telling me, 'Don't worry. You'll be okay.' Later on, I learned that the referee gave me a standing eight count and then I got knocked down face first like John Tate against Mike Weaver. It was over in sixty-three seconds. If you're being kind, you'll write 'one minute three seconds.' It sounds longer that way."

So. . . . Does Gerbasi have misgivings about his fistic adventure?

"Not at all," he says. "Over the years, that night has come up in conversations I've had with some of the greatest fighters in the world. It's not a sore topic with me. I don't regret doing it. Years ago, I was in Atlantic City and met Roberto Duran. Duran was my idol when I was young. His son translated for us. I told him about my fight. He laughed a kind of wicked laugh and hugged me. To a man, when I talk about it with fighters, they tell me, 'Hey, you got in there. You did it.'"

*Two months before retiring from boxing, Paulie Malignaggi acknowledged, "A lot of times, fighters go into boxing from bad circumstances. Then they make their life better. And then they wind up back where they started. That's always been my nightmare. Don't wind up back where you started. Don't wind up with the problems you had at the beginning of your career, when you're wondering where you go from here and how do you pay your bills and all this stuff."*

# Paulie Malignaggi: "No More Coming Back Now"

Paulie Malignaggi got knocked out by a body shot in round eight of his March 4, 2017, fight against Sam Eggington in London. The image of Malignaggi lying on the canvas in agony, unable to rise, wasn't pretty.

When Malignaggi was in his prime, Eggington wouldn't have been able to hit him with a handful of rice. But Paulie is far removed from his prime. On March 4, he looked as out of place in the ring as a fifty-year-old man dating a twenty-year-old woman.

I like Paulie. I've always liked Paulie. I met him when he was twenty years old and chronicled his career in boxing as he moved from infancy to an old man as a fighter.

I was glad the Eggington fight ended on a body shot and not a concussive blow to the head. But punches to the liver add up, too.

On December 11, 1981, Muhammad Ali fought Trevor Berbick in the last bout of The Greatest's illustrious ring career. By that time, Ali was a shell of his former self. Maryum Ali, Muhammad's oldest child, later told me, "I wanted him to lose. I wanted him to win but I didn't because, if he won, he'd keep fighting and I didn't want him to fight anymore. I was in the last row of the first level of the stadium that night. I remember saying to myself, 'If he loses, he won't fight again, and I'll be happy. But if he wins, he'll go on and on.'"

Those were my sentiments when I turned on the television to watch Malignaggi versus Sam Eggington.

Paulie understood the folly of what he was doing. In May 2016, he sat for an interview I conducted for a documentary entitled *Ali: A Life* and told me:

> Ali, Sugar Ray Robinson, Joe Louis; they all fought long past their prime. I think the message in that is, no matter how much greatness you achieve, it will pass and so you have to learn to let it go. Sometimes you want to hold on to it so tight and it has to be ripped from you. The same ego that made you great can also cost you. The ego is the reason you become great. It's what drives you. But it's also what makes you stay around too long, and there has to be a way to release it gracefully as opposed to having it ripped from you and shredding you in the process. Trust me; it's easier said than done. But when you've seen it right in front of you in the cases of those great fighters, it doesn't become any more reality than that.
>
> There are situations where you have achieved so much and it's hard to walk away. And there are situations where you might have achieved enough but want more. When you have achieved greatness like Ali, you become addicted to the fame. You become addicted to the power it gives you. You become addicted to the success. Then there are situations like with myself where I've achieved a lot, but I feel like I could achieve just a little bit more and maybe my name will get a little bit more respect in history. You start to believe that you can summon this out of you if you really, really believe in it because your self-belief is what got you there in the first place. Obviously, it's not the case. Nature is nature. We all get old, so both situations present a very harsh set of circumstances, a very harsh set of decisions you have to make that will make your head spin. They really will make your head spin because, when you go, you're never coming back. And the way you felt last year, you can never feel like that again. The way you felt two years ago, you will never feel that again. You're only getting older and you're only going to feel less good.

Over the years, I kept writing this-is-the-end columns about Paulie. And I always had to write another. "There's still a bit of coming to grips with the fact that you're not going to fight any more," he told writer Tom Gerbasi. "People think you're weird that you can't come to grips with something that to them is so simple. But in reality, it's not so simple. You want to dream for just a little bit longer. The sun's coming up, though. It's almost time to stop dreaming."

All of us take risks in varying degrees. We don't eat as well as we should. We don't exercise enough. We indulge in alcohol or recreational drugs. Paulie exposed himself to the risks inherent in continuing to fight because he craved the high he got from fighting.

"I don't need the money," Paulie explained in a piece that aired last year on Showtime before he fought Gabriel Bracero. "I don't need the fame. But I still need to fight. Even my friends think I'm a little crazy, and maybe I am. I know fighters don't age gracefully. I know fighters get hurt. But I also know in my heart, I've got to fight at least one more time. Why? Love. Not the normal kind. More like a bad girlfriend. She's broken my heart; she'll do it again. And I keep coming back for more. My mind knows better; my heart doesn't. You see, boxing loved me when no one else would. I was a kid from Sicily, a high school dropout. Boxing gave me things I couldn't imagine. Boxing let me dream. That's what I want. That's what I'm fighting for. That chance to dream again."

But the losses continued to mount, and the purses got smaller. After Malignaggi lost to Eggington, my fear was that, several months from now, Paulie would say, "I can't end my career on the canvas. I want to go out a winner. All I want is one more fight against a guy who doesn't pose much of a threat. Then I'll quit; I promise."

Part of me is still afraid that will happen. But two days after losing to Eggington, Paulie sent me an e-mail that read, "I will most definitely focus on commentating now. No more coming back."

Later that day, he officially announced his retirement.

I'm still worried. Paulie is an expert boxing analyst for Showtime and Sky Sports, one of the best in the business. But every blow to the head he took in fights and in sparring had the potential to cause incremental brain damage. That's boxing's often-unspoken fear. One doesn't have to reference Muhammad Ali to make the point. Go to a big fight and there are reminders everywhere. Former fighters, including more than a few world champions, who slur their words and don't connect their thoughts as well as they once did.

Meanwhile, let's celebrate what Paulie accomplished. He won thirty-six professional fights and held both the IBF 140-pound and WBA 147-pound titles. So many of today's fighters talk tough and disappear when it's time to sign a contract. Paulie didn't talk tough, but he went in tough. Look at the fighters who beat him before Eggington: Miguel Cotto, Ricky Hatton, Juan Diaz, Amir Khan, Adrien Broner, Shawn Porter, and Danny Garcia. Paulie fought all of them when they were in their prime.

So give Paulie credit for his ring skills and heart, his fighting through the pain of a broken orbital bone and multiple broken hands. Smile when you think of his ever-changing hair and sense of style. Appreciate his honesty and self-deprecating sense of humor.

"The good thing," Paulie told me not long ago, "is that I'm in some historic boxing highlight reels that people will watch forever. The bad thing is that I'm getting knocked out."

*In today's world, having a belt doesn't necessarily mean that a fighter is a champion. Gennady Golovkin is a champion.*

# Golovkin–Jacobs: A Bigger "Drama Show" Than Expected

On March 18, 2017, Gennady Golovkin and Danny Jacobs met in the ring at Madison Square Garden in a middleweight title-unification bout. It was supposed to be an orderly coronation for Golovkin. But fights are unscripted, and this one unfolded in defiance of expectations.

Outside the ring, Golovkin is one of the least-imposing elite fighters imaginable. His face is largely unmarked. His body language is laid-back. He looks like a computer geek with a quiet, placid demeanor. He turned pro after winning a silver medal on behalf of Kazakhstan as a middleweight at the 2004 Athens Olympics, compiled a 36–0 (33 KOs) professional record, and claimed the WBC, WBA, IBF, and IBO 160-pound titles.

In the minds of many, the only thing standing between Golovkin and greatness was the absence of elite opponents on his record. Sergio Martinez, Miguel Cotto, and Canelo Alvarez all steered clear of him when they held one version or another of the middleweight crown.

Whoever Golovkin fights—tall guys, short guys, finesse boxers, big punchers—Gennady says, "No problem." He delights in giving fans what he calls "big drama show" and came into Madison Square Garden to fight Jacobs riding a string of twenty-three consecutive knockouts.

Jacobs entered the bout with a 32–1 (29 KOs) ledger and was the "regular" (or phony) WBA middleweight champion. He's a good fighter whose career as a boxer has been defined more by his ring failures than his ring triumphs.

Now twenty-nine, Jacobs amassed a 137-and-7 record as a much-decorated amateur. But he lost twice unexpectedly to Shawn Estrada in the 165-pound division at the trials for the 2008 Beijing Olympics. The first time he was matched tough as a pro (against Dmitry Pirog in 2010), he crumbled and was knocked out in the fifth round.

But those losses were overshadowed by Jacobs's inspirational return from being stricken with cancer to fight again at a world-class level. That chapter of Danny's life began in 2011, when he felt numbness in his legs and began having difficulty walking. The diagnosis was osteosarcoma: a life-threatening form of bone cancer that had wrapped a tumor around his spine.

Jacobs underwent surgery and returned to the ring after a nineteen-month layoff. For the rest of his life, he'll have titanium rods in his back. It's difficult to overstate the magnitude of his accomplishments and courage.

There was mutual respect between the fighters in the build-up to Golovkin-Jacobs.

"He's a very good guy," Golovkin said of his opponent. "I've watched a couple of his fights. He looks good. He looks strong. And he looks very focused. I think he is the best that I have been up against in my career. I'm very excited to fight Daniel Jacobs. He is world-class and will be a big test for me."

Jacobs responded in kind, saying, "I'm a fan of the sport. I like to watch Triple-G too. I've watched him his whole career. He's a great fighter. He has power. He cuts the ring off well. His jab is good. He's not the hardest guy in the world to hit, but he takes a good punch. I'm honored to share the ring with him."

Golovkin-Jacobs represented a huge opportunity for Jacobs. In boxing, one win or one loss can dramatically alter the trajectory of a fighter's career. Everything was aligned for Danny to become a star if he beat Golovkin. With that in mind, Jacobs declared, "I want to go and tackle greatness. I want to go into Madison Square Garden and see my family and see my friends and see everybody there for me. I'm ready for my fans to be in my corner and everyone standing up and cheering when that first bell rings. It's a big opportunity for me, and I'm looking forward to it. Winning this fight will take everything to the next level."

But Jacobs wasn't just an underdog. Many insiders thought that he had virtually no chance. From the day the fight was announced until fight night, Jacobs had to smile through people wishing him luck at the same time they were thinking, "Poor Danny. He has no idea what Gennady will do to him."

Golovkin's most notable wins had been against Kell Brook, David Lemieux, Martin Murray, Curtis Stevens, and Matthew Macklin. That's not Marvin Hagler and Carlos Monzon, but it's better than the best that Jacobs could offer (Peter Quillin and Sergio Mora).

Also, there were questions about Jacobs's ability to take a punch, largely because of his loss to Pirog.

"I'm a far better fighter now than I was then," Jacobs said of that defeat. "I'm stronger. I'm smarter. I'm a complete 180 from the fighter I was then. Mentally, physically, all across the board in any way you can possibly grow, I've grown from that fight. This whole question about my chin; I'm not saying it's absurd, but it's a little far-fetched."

However, Abel Sanchez (who has trained Golovkin for nineteen fights in a row) added fuel to the fire.

"In forty years," Sanchez proclaimed, "I've never had a fighter that hits as hard as Gennady. Jacobs is a sharp puncher with a good right hand. But he won't go twelve rounds."

Curtis Stevens and David Lemieux had each been knocked out by Golovkin at Madison Square Garden. Asked what advice he might have for Jacobs, Stevens was marginally encouraging, saying, "Danny's an excellent boxer. He can win as long as he stays away, but it's hard to stay away for twelve rounds. We've gotta see if his chin holds up. I'm not trying to be mean and I'm not taking anything away from him. But we all know his chin is a little suspect."

Lemieux was less sanguine. "I have no advice for him," David responded. "He can do what he wants. I don't think he's gonna win."

Still . . . there's a long list of fighters who've said in the past that they wanted to fight Golovkin but didn't. They've talked the talk but disappeared when given the opportunity to walk the walk. Jacobs genuinely wanted to fight Golovkin. And he was looking forward to the encounter as his coming out party.

"I know this guy has a reputation," Jacobs said. "He's the number one guy at the moment. I can't deny that. You have to give respect where respect is due. But I think I'm the better fighter. I'm bigger; I'm faster. I have power and a good boxing IQ. Whatever he does, I'll be ready for it. Just because he has A-plus or A-minus power and I have B-plus or B-minus power doesn't mean both guys can't go down or both guys can't get hurt. I have to be careful, but so does he. I know what I'm capable of. I know what I'm good at. It's all about putting it in sync on fight night. So many people are doubting me. There's nothing better than fulfilling your dreams and proving all the doubters wrong in the same night."

Madison Square Garden was buzzing on fight night, with an announced crowd of 19,939. Golovkin was a 6-to-1 betting favorite and 4-to-1 favorite to win by knockout. Gennady is so efficient and methodical in the ring that people tend to forget his fights are unfolding in real time, that he's flesh and blood, not a machine, and that anything can happen in a prize fight.

Both men fought cautiously at the start. Golovkin was stalking but not as aggressively as he has in recent fights. Jacobs was content to box from the outside.

In round three, Golovkin began to close the gap and dictate the distance between Jacobs and himself. That paid dividends in round four, when Gennady caught Danny against the ropes and landed a jab followed by a straight right hand that put Jacobs on the canvas.

At that point, the assumption among most onlookers was, "Okay; here we go. The fight is over."

Not . . .

In round five, counterintuitively, Jacobs began fighting effectively as a southpaw, which he did thereafter for long stretches of time. That seemed to slow Golovkin. Then Danny started letting his hands go a bit more.

Golovkin was never able to find his rhythm. He never put punches together in a way that landed more than one effective blow at a time. For much of the night, he looked ordinary. Other times, he looked old.

In round nine, Jacobs appeared to tire a bit. He got sloppy and over-reached on several punches, enabling Golovkin to tag him with a solid right uppercut. But otherwise, Gennady failed to capitalize on the few mistakes that Danny made.

The fight seemed to be up for grabs in the final two rounds. The crowd sensed an upset. But it wasn't to be. The decision could have gone either way, and the judges ruled in Golovkin's favor by a 115–112, 115–112, 114–113 margin.

Writing for the *Independent*, Steve Bunce put the night in perspective when he declared, "It is far too simple to dismiss the odd performance of Gennady Golovkin on Saturday night as the start of the end for the fighting maestro. But that is exactly what it looked like at times. Golovkin looked weary, lacked precision, and was too predictable. After nearly 400 amateur fights and 36 in the paid ranks, he might just be, at 34 and after a life devoted to boxing, getting old."

Then, referencing round four when Golovkin knocked Jacobs down, Bunce added, "Golovkin was expected to finish the fight then, provide his 'big drama show,' and end the night for Jacobs. But there was no Golovkin finish. And that was odd for a man who has ruined so many fighters and has never allowed a hurt fighter the time to survive."

Gennady Golovkin is still a very good fighter. But the aura of invincibility that enveloped him is now gone.

*By 2017, Wladimir Klitschko, like most aging boxers, had a face that reflected the journey of a veteran fighter.*

# Anthony Joshua vs. Wladimir Klitschko: The Future is Now

On April 17, 1860, in Farnsborough County west of London, England's Tom Sayers and John Heenan from the San Francisco Bay area fought to a bloody forty-two-round draw in what was then called "The Fight of the Century."

Sayers-Heenan ended in chaos without a winner being declared. Heenan was fighting blind in one eye with the other eye rapidly closing. Sayers was barely able to defend himself. At that point, the ropes on one side of the ring were cut, either to save Sayers from defeat or (if the alternative version is accepted) to prevent the Englishman from being strangled to death by Heenan, who allegedly was pressing Sayers's neck against the top strand and pushing down with all his might on the Englishman's head.

On April 29, 2017, England was again at the center of the boxing world. This time, Wladimir Wladimirowitsch Klitschko and Anthony Oluwafemi Olaseni Joshua did battle at Wembley Stadium in London.

It was a massive event, and boxing's most anticipated heavyweight title fight since Lennox Lewis vs. Mike Tyson fifteen years ago. It was generation versus generation, with the past meeting the future in the present. Two men vying for the right to be called the best heavyweight on the planet on a night that the ninety thousand fans who were in attendance will always remember.

Wladimir Klitschko is a man of intelligence and grace. He won a gold medal in the super-heavyweight division as a representative of Ukraine at the 1996 Atlanta Olympics and embarked upon a pro career that has spanned more than two decades.

Entering the Joshua fight, Klitschko's record stood at 64 wins against 4 losses with 53 knockouts and 3 KOs by. His sojourn through the professional ranks began with 24 consecutive victories, all but one by knockout. Then, in 1998, Klitschko fought Ross Puritty, a journeyman from Oklahoma who traveled to Ukraine with 13 losses on his record. Klitschko beat up on Puritty for ten rounds. But in round eleven, Wladimir crumbled from physical and mental exhaustion.

Sixteen Klitschko victories followed that defeat with only one opponent going the distance. In 2000, Wladimir annexed the WBO heavyweight crown with a unanimous-decision triumph over Chris Byrd. But three years later, South African Corrie Sanders knocked Klitschko down four times en route to a second-round blowout. In 2004, Wladimir dominated Lamon Brewster early, but once again faded and was unable to come out of his corner after the fifth round.

At that point, Klitschko reconfigured his fighting style under the tutelage of trainer Emanuel Steward, won twenty-two fights in a row, and earned recognition as the dominant heavyweight in the world. At various times, he held the WBA, IBF, and WBO crowns. His nine-year championship reign came to an end on November 28, 2015, when he turned in an embarrassingly lackluster effort en route to a unanimous-decision defeat at the hands of Tyson Fury.

When Klitschko lost to Fury, he was dismissed as a has-been by some and a never-was by others.

Adam Berlin wrote, "Klitschko deserves praise for carrying himself like a champion outside the ring. He is respectful. He is articulate. But inside the ring, Klitschko has never been great. He has fought carefully, relying on his physical attributes to wear his rivals down. He has made leaning on smaller men an art. It's a rational style. It's a logical style. It's a careful style. And while a methodical approach to boxing can lead to success, it never leads to greatness.

"Wladimir Klitschko," Berlin continued, "was very good during an era when the rest of the heavyweights were less than very good. Most fighters cement their legacy with a win. Klitschko's legacy is cemented with this loss. In this loss, he didn't even fight. It wasn't age. It wasn't a bad night. It was Wladimir Klitschko being Wladimir Klitschko. That's who he is. That's who he'll always be. That's how he'll go down in history."

Frank Lotierzo concurred, declaring, "After twelve rounds of inept boxing, two things are clear. Wladimir Klitschko won't fight and Tyson Fury can't fight, at least not at the championship level. Fury was very lucky to have been in with a fighter like Klitschko, who has gone back physically as a fighter and, on this night, demonstrated that, when he doesn't own every physical advantage conceivable over his opponent, he is very limited and physically handcuffed by his mental trepidation."

That was the biggest knock on Klitschko: his mental state. Older brother Vitali (who reigned first as WBO and then as WBC heavyweight champion for five years) was universally perceived as the tougher Klitschko. As Tom Gerbasi wrote, "Vitali finds a way to win. Wladimir finds a way to lose. That's the difference."

Years ago, I had breakfast with the Klitschko brothers and asked each one whether he was more nervous when he or his brother was fighting. Wladimir answered first: "When Vitali fights, I am more nervous than he is." Then Wladimir added with a smile, "And when I fight, I am more nervous than he is."

Anthony Joshua was born in England. His parents are from Nigeria, where Anthony spent part of his early childhood with his mother, who was trying to establish a business in her native land.

Joshua was six years old when Klitschko won his Olympic gold medal. One day before Anthony turned eleven, Wladimir won his first world championship belt. In 2012, sixteen years after Klitschko accomplished the feat in Atlanta, Joshua won a gold medal in the super-heavyweight division at the London Olympics.

Prior to meeting Klitschko in the ring, Joshua had eighteen knockout victories in as many professional fights. He'd claimed the IBF heavyweight belt by knocking out Charles Martin on April 9, 2016. Next, he successfully defended his title against Dominic Breazeale and Eric Molina. Everyone agreed that Joshua had a great deal of potential. But prior to facing Klitschko, he'd never fought a world-class fighter.

Eighty thousand tickets for Joshua-Klitschko went on sale in January and quickly sold out. Later that month, municipal officials approved the sale of an additional ten thousand tickets, raising the stadium capacity to ninety thousand. That broke the previous Wembley record set by the 2014 rematch between Carl Froch and George Groves and equaled the British attendance record for boxing established in 1939 when Len Harvey successfully defended his British and Commonwealth light-heavyweight titles against Jock McAvoy in London.

Joshua-Klitschko was televised on pay-per-view in the United Kingdom by Sky Sports. There was a delay in finding a TV home in the United States due to what Bart Barry called "a hundred-day catfight between HBO and Showtime that may be a plot to drive the last fifty thousand committed boxing fans in our nation to pirated streams but it probably isn't."

Ultimately, HBO and Showtime shared TV rights.

The promotional narrative was keyed to Joshua. The fight would be "epic . . . a stepping stone toward greatness . . . a pivotal moment in boxing history."

The fighters conducted themselves with sportsmanship and dignity throughout the promotion.

In a reference to erratic past behavior by Tyson Fury and Shannon Briggs, Klitschko began a January 31 press conference for Joshua-Klitschko in New York with the observation, "I'm used to fighters throwing tables or wearing Batman costumes or chasing me in a speedboat. So this is very nice for me."

Referring further to the Fury fight, Klitschko added, "What happened was a great experience for me. I always think that, as one window closes, another opens. Something came out of me and I have tremendous motivation and I'm obsessed with the goal of getting the titles back."

But Wladimir sounded a bit pensive when talking about the past ("It's good to be young and ambitious"). And he conceded, "It's strange to be the B-side. I'm not used to that."

Joshua, for his part, was respectful toward Klitschko ("He's the real deal. He's proved it. He's lived it. He's walked it"). But Anthony was forthright in saying, "I'm going for the knockout. That's what I do. This is my gold-medal fight all over again."

Joshua was a clear betting favorite. His team wouldn't have taken the fight if it hadn't believed that the oddsmakers were right. But most predictions as to the outcome were qualified with a "but." That uncertainty was crucial to the promotion.

"This is the perfect time for the fight because of the risk," promoter Eddie Hearn said. "It's a gamble. If it wasn't a risk, if it wasn't a gamble, do you think we'd break pay-per-view records? Do you think we'd have 90,000 in Wembley? To make a great fight, the timing has to be perfect and there has to be risk on both sides. Anthony Joshua can lose and that's exciting."

Thirty months earlier, Joshua had served as a sparring partner for Klitschko prior to Wladimir's 2014 knockout victory over Kubrat Pulev. Now those sparring sessions were scoured for clues.

"I didn't go to try to prove anything with the sparring," Joshua told the media. "I mainly went to see how a champion sets up his training camp."

Pressed for more, Anthony added, "Wladimir is technical. He will try to maneuver you with his left hand to put you in position to throw his right hand. He's patient. He was trying to set me up so he could throw his shots. That's what I got from sparring with him."

Klitschko also had memories of their time together.

"There are up to fifteen sparring partners in every camp," Wladimir recounted. "People are coming and going, and some of them I don't remember. But I remember Joshua. He impressed me with his attitude. He was very raw, but he carried himself well. I liked his attitude. He was in the background, learning. Sometimes you need to be quiet and just watch. He was observing everything. That is unusual. I've had Olympic champions and former world champions in my camp, but his attitude was totally different. He was not trying to impress anybody. He was sitting on the side, not talking too much. He was watching, learning, asking questions. He was very polite. He was different from the others. We got a feeling for each other. We sparred fifteen or twenty rounds together."

But that was in 2014. Joshua had gotten better since then. Klitschko had gotten older. And sparring isn't fighting.

The case for a Joshua victory on April 29 rested in part on the age differential between the fighters. Wladimir is forty-one. Anthony is twenty-seven. Earlier in Klitschko's career, he'd shown a tendency to fade as fights progressed. At forty-one, he was expected to tire if pressured by Joshua.

Moreover, Klitschko has compiled an impressive body of work. But the names on his ring ledger have been lacking, particularly in recent years.

Since the start of 2012, Wladimir had beaten Jean Marc Mormeck, Tony Thompson, Mariusz Wach, Francesco Pianeta, Alexander Povetkin, Alex Leapai, Kubrat Pulev, and Bryant Jennings, and lost to Tyson Fury. His last impressive performance had been against Povetkin four years ago.

Luis Ortiz's 2015 knockout of Bryant Jennings (who'd gone the distance against Klitschko seven months earlier) cast further doubt on Wladimir's standing

And Klitschko hadn't fought since November 2015, when he lost to Tyson Fury. The seventeen-month layoff was the longest of his career. Would Wladimir come back against Joshua rested and strong or would he come back old?

Rob McCracken has trained Joshua since Anthony's days as an amateur. McCracken was deferential toward Klitschko in the build-up to the fight, saying, "He's a very good fighter. He's a former Olympic champion, been hugely successful as a heavyweight, been champion for a decade or so. Can box, can spoil, can punch, very experienced, very tricky. If you let Klitschko get going and he gets that jab going, he starts pushing and shoving and looking for the right hand, then he's a real handful and difficult hard work. He's been a tremendous fighter and he still is."

But McCracken added, "As great a fighter as Klitschko has been, Father Time is a terrible person when he shows up. And he's already shown up."

Joshua sounded a similar note, saying, "Boxing is a young man's sport. It's my time now."

Ricky Hatton concurred, noting, "Klitschko seems to have been around forever. And none of us go on forever."

Still, Wladimir was a live underdog. Joshua's chin was suspect. And Klitschko can punch.

"What does Anthony do when he gets hit again and again?" Wladimir asked at the New York press conference. "What does he do if he has to go backward? Is he the new Lennox Lewis, or is he the new Frank Bruno?"

Tyson Fury had been able to neutralize Klitschko's power because he circled constantly and used side-to-side movement to keep Wladimir turning. That's not Joshua's style.

Also, the other side of the age coin is experience.

Klitschko had fought sixty-eight times as a professional and gone into the tenth round or later on thirteen occasions. Joshua had logged a total of 103 minutes 27 seconds of ring time in his entire professional career and fought into the seventh round only twice (against Dillian Whyte and Dominic Breazeale). Each of Joshua's other fights had ended inside of three rounds.

"A. J. has lots of energy," Klitschko observed. "He's young. He wants to show it. He has those big muscles that give him confidence. But did you hear about boxing? It's the sweet science. Experience is something that you cannot buy in a shop. You gain it over the years. It is an advantage."

"It's hard to pick a winner," Lennox Lewis said. "Anthony is a great young fighter. I have a lot of respect for him. He has worked hard and dealt with things well. But as far as experience goes, he is lacking a bit. You can go in there and knock out eighteen guys straight, but what have you learned? So you've got Joshua, who is young and strong. And you've got Klitschko, who is old but with so much knowledge and experience. That's why it's so intriguing."

British boxing writer Gareth A. Davies framed the issue as follows: "It's all about timing. Either Joshua and his team have got it spot-on and will feast on a great champion's carcass; or Klitschko will delve into his memory bank, roll back the clock, get that jab pumping again, drain Joshua in clinches, and re-emerge as The Man, having taken a raw novice to school. Has the jump in class been carefully measured and timed to perfection or will the difference in levels be Joshua's undoing?"

"Until you step into the ring with someone, you don't know what you're facing," Joshua acknowledged.

"The question is out there," Klitschko said. "Do I still got it, or is it too late?"

Then Wladimir put the fight in perspective in a way that suited him best: "Please excuse me as this may sound arrogant. But a parallel. Mount Everest, the highest mountain in the world. It's been there for a long time and will be there for a long time. You can climb it during a certain period of time, during two weeks in April, I believe. You can get to the top and say, 'I conquered Everest!' Then you've got to run down because it's going to take you down if you miss the time. A lot of people died there. Some made it back. But Mount Everest is still there. Is Mount Everest defeated? It's still there and it's going to take another life this April."

★ ★ ★

The scene on fight night as Anthony Joshua and Wladimir Klitschko walked to the ring at Wembley Stadium seemed otherworldly, like something out of *Star Wars*. Lights were flashing. Music was blaring. Ninety thousand fans were in a frenzy. There was a WOW factor to it all.

Joshua was a better than 2-to-1 betting favorite. He'd weighed in at 250 pounds, one pound more than his previous high. Klitschko weighed in at 240¼, his lowest since fighting Ruslan Chagaev at the same weight eight years ago.

As the fighters waited for the opening bell, Joshua looked relaxed and focused. "I knew the significance of this fight before I took it," he'd said three days earlier. "If I didn't want to deal with this pressure. I would have taken another route."

Early in the promotion, Klitschko had told the media, "It's a perfect time for us to fight. In three years, Anthony will be too good, and I will be too old."

Joshua was already too good. And Klitschko was already too old.

Klitschko fought tentatively in round one, and Joshua was cautious. In the second stanza, Anthony moved into aggressor mode. For the next few rounds, his confidence increased, and he appeared willing to fight for three minutes a round while Klitschko wanted only sporadic engagements.

Because of Joshua's size and ability, it was one of the few times in Wladimir's career that he was unable to manhandle his opponent in clinches.

Round five was a time-capsule round reminiscent of round ten in the first fight between Evander Holyfield and Riddick Bowe. Joshua jumped on Klitschko at the opening bell, bounced a glancing right hand off Wladimir's ear, followed with a hook up top, and unloaded a barrage of punches.

Klitschko had been on the canvas eleven times as a pro. Twenty-seven seconds into round five, it was twelve.

Wladimir rose on unsteady legs with a nasty cut above his left eye. But he fought back, and, halfway through the round, landed a hook of his own that staggered Joshua and turned the tide. Now Joshua was holding on. Anthony made it to the bell and won the round on the judges' score-cards because of the knockdown. But he looked exhausted. Klitschko had gotten the better of him in those three minutes.

Klitschko's newfound dominance continued in round six, escalating at the 1:07 mark when he drilled Joshua with a straight right hand.

"He got hit with the biggest punch of his career," Rob McCracken acknowledged afterward.

Joshua went down with a thud and got up slowly. He looked like a swimmer who was about to drown. Now he was the fighter struggling to survive.

For the remainder of round six, Klitschko kept trying to measure Joshua with his jab preparatory to throwing a fight-ending right hand. If he'd focused more on hitting Joshua with the jab, Anthony might not have been standing for long.

Klitschko was the aggressor again in round seven, with Joshua still in survival mode. But like Anthony in round five, Wladimir couldn't finish his man.

In round eight, the pendulum swung back in Joshua's favor. Klitschko was tiring. Minute by minute, Joshua was working his way back into the fight.

"Boxing is about character," Anthony said afterward. "When you go into the trenches, that's when you find out who you really are."

And equally important, as Joshua later noted, "As the rounds went on, I was learning things about Wladimir."

By round nine, Joshua was in control again and Klitschko was starting to look like an old fighter.

Round ten was more of the same.

At the start of round eleven, Joshua came out aggressively and landed a right hand that put Wladimir in trouble. But Anthony had learned from his near-death experience in round five. This time, his assault was more measured.

Klitschko has never fought well on the inside. Over the years, his inside game has consisted largely of clinching to immobilize opponents and leaning on them to tire them out. In earlier rounds, Joshua had been able to go inside and punch to the body more effectively than Wladimir's previous opponents were able to. Now he went inside again.

One minute ten seconds into round eleven, a vicious right uppercut followed by a left hook up top dropped Klitschko hard. A minute later, Wladimir was down again, courtesy of another right uppercut and left hook. He pulled himself to his feet with an assist from the ring ropes and was being pummeled in a corner when referee David Fields intervened with thirty-five seconds left in the stanza to spare him from further punishment.

"Two gentlemen fought each other," Klitschko said afterward. "The best man won. Anthony was better today than I. It's really sad that I didn't make it tonight. But all the respect to Anthony."

It was the sort of fight that boxing needs more of. A grand stage, high stakes, good fighters, and a dramatic ebb and flow that made it special. The fact that Joshua was forced to climb off the canvas made his triumph more memorable and, in some ways, more impressive than if he'd ended matters more easily in round five.

Joshua showed that he's mentally strong. He didn't crumble when a lesser fighter would have. He fought through adversity after suffering a hurting knockdown and prevailed; something that many fighters, including Mike Tyson, were unable to do. He's an exciting fighter. He can hurt an opponent with either hand at any time. In some ways, he's reminiscent of the young Riddick Bowe. A big heavyweight with power who has a mean uppercut and knows how to fight on the inside.

One can argue that Klitschko at his best would have beaten this version of Joshua. But if Anthony continues to improve, he may well become a better fighter than Wladimir ever was. It will be interesting to see how much better Joshua gets and whether he'll be able to sustain that level of excellence over an extended period of time.

"I'm only going to improve," Joshua said after conquering Klitschko. "I'm not perfect, but I'm trying. I'm learning so much and I've got ten years left in this game. So we'll have fun together."

As for the significance of Joshua-Klitschko; prior to the fight, the promotion kept throwing around numbers like Wladimir wanted to win this number belt and that number title fight. Boxing fans were told that beating Joshua would make Klitschko a "three-time world heavyweight champion," separating him from the likes of Ruslan Chagaev, Nikolai Valuev, John Ruiz, Chris Byrd, and Herbie Hide (each of whom had only two "championship" reigns). There was a lot of talk about "passing the torch" from one champion to another.

But Klitschko didn't have a torch to pass. Tyson Fury took it from him seventeen months ago. Joshua didn't beat the reigning heavyweight champion. He beat a former champion who hadn't won a fight in more than two years. And forget the belts. In today's world, they're marketing tools, not much more. On paper, Joseph Parker is also a "world heavyweight champion."

What's important is that Joshua-Klitschko was contested for the right be called the best heavyweight in the world. With his triumph, Joshua moved from being a belt holder to a champion. Right now, he's the number one heavyweight in boxing.

Prior to the bout, Vitali Klitschko said of his brother, "If Wladimir wins, it's a huge celebration. If Wladimir loses, it's the time to think about stopping and not fighting anymore."

Let's hope that Joshua-Klitschko was a retirement party for Wladimir with a multimillion-dollar payday instead of a gold watch as the sendoff.

Meanwhile, boxing is flourishing in England.

"British boxing is booming at the minute," Joshua said shortly before Joshua-Klitschko. "People said, 'You have to go to America to be respected.' Not anymore. You come here. You come and fight us. It's amazing how the tables have turned."

Further to that point; Joshua-Klitschko served as a reminder of how important venue and crowd can be in energizing the sweet science. The much-publicized fact that ninety thousand fans attended the fight contributed enormously to spreading the buzz far beyond London.

The boxing world is just starting to know Anthony Joshua. He's a talented, immensely likable young man who has been a winner throughout his time in the spotlight and would be an excellent standard-bearer for the sweet science.

Gareth A. Davies recently wrote, "There is no more watchable, marketable, or important heavyweight in the world right now."

And that was before Joshua beat Klitschko.

*Lennox Lewis once told me, "When I was boxing, I stayed away from thinking about fighters from other eras. But I'd have to say—if I could have fought all the great heavyweights—the greatest challenges for me as I see it would have been Muhammad Ali, George Foreman, Jack Johnson, and Larry Holmes."*

# Ranking Boxing's Greatest Heavyweight Champions

In the past, I've overseen fantasy round-robin tournaments in various weight divisions that matched great fighters from different eras against each other with the results of each fight being predicted by a panel of boxing-industry experts.

The heavyweight division doesn't lend itself to this format. The size differential between fighters from different eras is too great. To draw an analogy to another sport, some of pro football's greatest linemen from the past weighed 240 pounds. They'd be thrown around like rag dolls today. But they were great.

Also, previous polls in this series were limited to fighters from boxing's modern age (roughly 1940 to date). That's because there isn't enough film footage of fighters from earlier eras to properly evaluate how they'd perform against one another and also because boxing technique has evolved considerably since the days of Joe Gans.

To offer another analogy: Babe Ruth is widely regarded as the greatest baseball player who ever lived and, with the possible exception of Ted Williams, baseball's greatest hitter. But if Ruth had been forced to contend with sliders, cutters, screwballs, forkballs, two-seam fastballs, four-seam fastballs, and the like, he might have been less dominant.

This heavyweight poll has different criteria from previous exercises. Rather than match champions against each other in a round-robin tournament, the electors were asked to rank them in order of greatness. This is more than who would have beaten whom. Other considerations are involved.

The poll evaluated twenty champions dating back to the dawn of gloved heavyweight championship fights. The fighters, listed chronologically, are John L. Sullivan, James Corbett, Bob Fitzsimmons, James

Jeffries, Jack Johnson, Jack Dempsey, Gene Tunney, Joe Louis, Rocky Marciano, Sonny Liston, Muhammad Ali, Joe Frazier, George Foreman, Larry Holmes, Mike Tyson, Evander Holyfield, Riddick Bowe, Lennox Lewis, Vitali Klitschko, and Wladimir Klitschko.

"Great" is a hard word to define, and "greatness" is subjective. It was up to each panelist to quantify greatness.

A fighter's skill level is important. But so, too, is that fighter's skill level within the context of his times.

How great was each fighter within his era? Was he the best of his era? Dominant in his era? How many other great heavyweights fought in his era? Great rivalries make great fighters. Did he fight the other great heavyweights of his time? Which elite fighters who were in their prime did he beat? One fight can go a long way toward defining a fighter's legacy.

A great fighter needs great competition. That doesn't necessarily translate into a pristine record.

There was an inclination on the part of the panelists to make pound-for-pound comparisons, thereby elevating fighters like Jack Dempsey and Rocky Marciano above today's much larger champions.

Some fighters were more feared than others. Opponents went into the ring against Joe Louis, Sonny Liston, and Mike Tyson in their prime fearing for their lives.

And the panelists factored in toughness. Some of the fighters on this list had a bit of quit in them. In the eyes of several electors, that was where Mike Tyson came up short.

And then there are fighters like Muhammad Ali, Joe Frazier, Larry Holmes, Evander Holyfield, and Rocky Marciano. "You could have shot those guys ten times with a gun," posits one panelist, "and they still wouldn't have quit."

In weighing greatness, the electors also considered intangibles and how important the heavyweight championship of the world was once upon a time.

Heavyweight champions have resonated in the culture. In that regard, Lennox Lewis (one of the panelists and also one of the champions being evaluated) observes, "A champion's contribution to the sport is more than how great a fighter he was. It's also about what he did outside the ring and what we're left remembering about him."

Each generation wants its own great heavyweight champion. Some generations have him. Some don't. How important was a fighter in his era? What impact did he have on his time?

To what extent does the mythology that enshrouds a fighter factor into his greatness?

Mike Tyson foreshadowed today's social media world, where fame often counts for more than character. Thirty years after Tyson ascended to the heavyweight throne, a Google search for "Mike Tyson" reveals 9,760,000 results. A similar search for Joe Louis turns up 426,000. For some electors, the magnitude of a fighter's fame was worthy of consideration. For others, it wasn't.

For some, character mattered. But one panelist opined, "For what we're doing now, I don't care that Joe Louis was a better citizen than Sonny Liston."

In sum, the criteria diverged significantly from elector to elector. But lurking in the back of many minds was the question: "Which of these fighters took boxing to a new level in terms of skills, societal importance, or both?"

There were thirty panelists.

Trainers: Teddy Atlas, Pat Burns, Virgil Hunter, and Don Turner

Matchmakers: Eric Bottjer, Don Chargin, Don Elbaum, Bobby Goodman, Ron Katz, Mike Marchionte, Russell Peltz, and Bruce Trampler

Media: Al Bernstein, Ron Borges, Gareth A. Davies, Norm Frauenheim, Jerry Izenberg, Harold Lederman, Paulie Malignaggi, Dan Rafael, and Michael Rosenthal

Historians: Craig Hamilton, Steve Lott, Don McRae, Bob Mee, Clay Moyle, Adam Pollack, and Randy Roberts

Lennox Lewis and Mike Tyson also participated in the poll. Neither fighter ranked himself. Instead, a weighted average from the other panelists was assigned to their respective slots on their ballots.

Several electors didn't feel comfortable rating John L. Sullivan, James Corbett, Bob Fitzsimmons, James Jeffries, or Jack Johnson because there's virtually no film footage of Johnson in action and none of the other four. Once again, a weighted average of the rankings from the other electors was used to fill the void.

One elector stated a preference for replacing Vitali Klitschko and Bob Fitzsimmons on his list with Max Schmeling and Sam Langford. Klitschko and Fitzsimmons were assigned a position behind the other eighteen fighters on his ballot.

A weighted average was also employed for Steve Lott with regard to Mike Tyson because of their friendship and close working relationship during the glory years of Tyson's career.

In previous polls (which used the who-beats-whom formula), most electors were confident in the choices. This time, a repeated refrain was, "I could do this again tomorrow and, except for the top few guys on my list, I might have a different order."

But in the end, a consensus emerged.

If one of the fighters had been ranked first on all thirty ballots, he would have had a perfect score of thirty. If a fighter was ranked number twenty on each ballot, his score would have been six hundred. Muhammad Ali's score was forty-six, which, when divided by the thirty electors, equaled a 1.53 "power ranking." That put Ali in first place.

The final rankings are:

| | | | |
|---|---|---|---|
| 1 | Muhammad Ali | 1.53 power ranking | 46 points |
| 2 | Joe Louis | 2.00 | 60 |
| 3 | Jack Johnson | 5.30 | 159 |
| 4 | Rocky Marciano | 6.57 | 197 |
| 5 | Larry Holmes | 7.23 | 217 |
| 6 | Jack Dempsey | 7.67 | 230 |
| 7 | George Foreman | 7.80 | 234 |
| 8 | Joe Frazier | 9.70 | 291 |
| 9 | Mike Tyson | 9.93 | 298 |
| 10 | Sonny Liston | 10.10 | 303 |
| 11 | Lennox Lewis | 10.93 | 328 |
| | Evander Holyfield | 10.93 | 328 |
| 13 | Gene Tunney | 11.60 | 348 |
| 14 | John L. Sullivan | 12.63 | 379 |
| 15 | James Jeffries | 14.70 | 441 |
| 16 | Wladimir Klitschko | 15.47 | 464 |
| 17 | Vitali Klitschko | 15.67 | 470 |
| 18 | James Corbett | 15.87 | 476 |
| 19 | Riddick Bowe | 16.60 | 498 |
| 20 | Bob Fitzsimmons | 17.77 | 533 |

Some of the finishes were by a razor-thin margin. In one instance, there was no margin at all. Lennox Lewis and Evander Holyfield tied for eleventh place with 328 points each.

Jack Dempsey (#6) barely edged out George Foreman (#7) by four points.

Joe Frazier (#8), Mike Tyson (#9), and Sonny Liston (#10) finished in that order separated by a total of twelve points. If the electors were asked to vote again, the order of these three might be different.

The same is true of Wladimir Klitschko (#16), Vitali Klitschko (#17), and James Corbett (#18), who were also separated by twelve points.

Nineteen of the thirty electors ranked Ali first. Nine chose Joe Louis. Two voted for Jack Johnson. Fourteen of the nineteen electors who ranked Ali first ranked Louis second. Seven of the nine electors who ranked Louis first ranked Ali second.

One elector ranked Ali as low as fourth. One ranked Louis fifth.

As illustrated by the chart below, Ali and Joe Louis tied for first place in the ranking by trainers. Ali finished alone in first place in the rankings by media, matchmakers, and historians. Louis finished second in these latter three categories. Johnson finished in third place in the minds of the media and historians. Marciano finished third among the trainers. Foreman finished third among the matchmakers.

| Name | Trainers | Media | Matchmakers | Historians |
|---|---|---|---|---|
| Ali | T-1 | 1 | 1 | 1 |
| Louis | T-1 | 2 | 2 | 2 |
| Johnson | 4 | 3 | 5 | 3 |
| Marciano | 3 | 5 | 4 | 4 |
| Holmes | 5 | 4 | 8 | 6 |
| Dempsey | T-9 | 7 | 6 | 5 |
| Foreman | T-7 | 6 | 3 | 8 |
| Frazier | 6 | 10 | T-9 | T-14 |
| Tyson | 12 | 12 | T-9 | 7 |
| Liston | T-7 | 11 | 7 | 12 |
| Lewis | 11 | T-8 | 13 | T-14 |
| Holyfield | 13 | T-8 | 11 | 13 |
| Tunney | T-9 | 13 | 14 | 10 |
| Sullivan | 15 | 15 | 12 | 9 |
| Jeffries | 14 | 19 | 19 | 11 |
| W. Klitschko | 18 | 14 | 16 | 18 |

| Name | Trainers | Media | Matchmakers | Historians |
|---|---|---|---|---|
| V. Klitschko | 17 | 16 | 15 | 19 |
| Corbett | 16 | 18 | 18 | 16 |
| Bowe | 19 | 17 | 17 | 20 |
| Fitzsimmons | 20 | 20 | 20 | 17 |

In some instances, the panelists offered commentary with regard to their rankings. We'll come back to Muhammad Ali and Joe Louis later. A composite of comments with regard to the other fighters follows.

## #3. Jack Johnson

Jack Johnson was ahead of his time in so many ways. He had advanced skills for his era. Impeccable defense. Underrated offense (he carried many opponents). He was the first heavyweight in history to truly master boxing.

Despite being black, Johnson refused to meet the best black contenders while he was champion. There was no interest from the American public in two black men fighting for the heavyweight title. But he'd already beaten most of these men on his rise to the championship.

What fighter today would get in the ring in front of tens of thousands of people who hated his guts and literally wanted to kill him and talk trash to the guy he was fighting and beat him?

Jack Johnson was the father. He was black America's first black hero.

## #4. Rocky Marciano

Nobody ever got more out of what he had as a fighter than Marciano. No one came into a fight in better shape than Marciano. He could punch. He could take a punch. He learned some rudimentary techniques to accentuate his physical gifts and compensate for his limitations. He was relentless and had a will of iron.

Consider the competition that Marciano beat. Walcott and Charles are derided now as old men when he fought them. But watch the film. They were great fighters who were nowhere near shot. Charles was thirty-two years old in the first Marciano fight. Walcott was thirty-seven, but he out-boxed Marciano for most of their first match. Carmine Vingo, Rex Layne, Roland LaStarza; Marciano beat real fighters on his way up. He did lose (Ted Lowry was robbed in their first match). But when his character was tested, nobody was better. I loved his response when someone asked him what he was thinking when Walcott knocked him down in their first fight: "Gee, this fellow hits hard. I might have to get up a couple of times before I knock him out."

Marciano wouldn't be rated as high as he is without his "O." But he has the "O," and none of the other fighters on this list do. He'd be too small for guys like Ali and Foreman. But he took a better punch and was tougher than all of them.

### #5. Larry Holmes

Holmes did what he had to do to win. Getting off the floor the way he did against Earnie Shavers and Renaldo Snipes, coming back and knocking those guys out; that showed a special kind of greatness.

What a jab! Larry Holmes could knock you out with his jab.

### #6. Jack Dempsey

The Dempsey who fought Jess Willard was a stone-cold killer. He learned his craft and perfected his style over years of fighting. He wanted to end fights as quickly as possible. And his power was no myth. He changed the way guys fought.

Dempsey and Babe Ruth were America's two most important sports figures in the "Roaring Twenties" when sports became an integral part of the culture. He was wildly popular. He brought a whole new audience to boxing. In a golden age of sports, he made boxing popular and respectable.

### #7. George Foreman

A lot of people who are serious about boxing think George Foreman is one of the most underrated fighters ever. He fought his share of soft opponents. But he's also one of the toughest men to ever box (watch the Lyle and Moorer fights). He's one of the hardest hitters ever. And after being heavyweight champion, he came back more than a decade later to do it again.

Foreman was a much better boxer the second time around. He was older and slower, but he'd learned to study his opponents and take advantage of what he saw.

Ali fought Joe Frazier three times and Ken Norton three times. He didn't mess with Foreman again after he beat him.

### #8. Joe Frazier

On March 8, 1971, Joe Frazier could have competed with anybody.

Frazier, like Marciano, was pure fighter. But he lost some of his desire before he retired. And when your biggest asset is desire, that's not good.

Did some of Ali's greatness rub off on Joe? Absolutely. And some of Joe's greatness rubbed off on Ali.

### #9. Mike Tyson

Tyson was the legitimate heavyweight champion of the world for more than three years. That's a long time in boxing. And he has captivated the public's imagination for three decades.

Mike Tyson is looked at now as a bully who folded when things got tough. But Tyson in his prime would have been competitive against anyone.

Tyson was the greatest six-round heavyweight of all time. But if he couldn't take an opponent out in six rounds, he started to fall apart.

When Mike Tyson got discouraged, he wasn't the same fighter. Joe Louis would have discouraged Tyson real fast. A lot of guys on this list would have discouraged Tyson real fast.

### #10. Sonny Liston

Sonny Liston was the best heavyweight in the world for five years. His left hand—jab and hook—was beyond frightening. If he'd been allowed to fight for the championship when he deserved it, all those fights against Cleveland Williams, Eddie Machen, and Zora Folley would have been successful title defenses.

If Cassius Clay hadn't come along, Liston would have had more time at the top.

Sonny Liston was the baddest man on the planet. Compared to Liston, Mike Tyson was a choirboy.

### #11. (tie) Lennox Lewis

Olympic champion. A giant who fought with finesse. He beat every available contender. He came back to beat the only two fighters who beat him in the pros. And this myth that Lennox had no chin. He got up from that bomb McCall hit him with, and I still think the fight was stopped prematurely. The punch Rahman hit him with in South Africa would have KO'd anyone, and there was the issue of altitude in South Africa. Lewis corrected things with Rahman in the rematch.

Lennox carried himself with dignity and grace for his entire career. That should count for something.

### #11. (tie) Evander Holyfield

Holyfield, like Ali, fought everyone. He beat four other guys on this list: Tyson, Bowe, Holmes, and Foreman. Except for Bowe, they weren't in their prime when Evander beat them, but that's still an impressive accomplishment.

Holyfield was bigger than Dempsey and Marciano, but he couldn't punch like them. And when you're fighting, punching means a whole lot.

### #13. Gene Tunney

Tunney is another fighter who learned his craft well over years. A better version of Corbett. But Tunney never fought a black man. He was the only heavyweight champion after Sullivan without a man of color on his record.

Tunney caught Dempsey at the end of Dempsey's career and after Dempsey had been out of the ring for three years. He was able to play the matador to an aging Jack Dempsey's bull. I doubt that he could have done that against Marciano. Marciano would have beaten Tunney down. In fact, a young Dempsey might have beaten Tunney down.

### #14. John L. Sullivan

Sullivan was America's first mass-culture hero and the most idolized athlete who had lived up until his time. He stood out as a fighter the way Joe Louis did in his era.

Sullivan fought for thirteen years, the last ten of which he was a full-blown alcoholic. Drinking nearly killed him in 1888, yet he whipped the next-best (white) man a year later in a bare-knuckle match that lasted more than two hours. It took Corbett twenty-one modern rounds to stop Sullivan when Sullivan was thirty-four years old, had been inactive for three years, and was drinking constantly. This to me is mind-boggling and tells me that Sullivan, in his prime, would have whipped Corbett.

## #15. James Jeffries

Jeffries was a superior athlete who won the heavyweight championship as a virtual novice. That's quite an accomplishment.

Forget about Johnson-Jeffries as a measure of Jeffries as a fighter. It was enormously important as a social event. But as a fight, it was like Ali–Holmes. One guy was a once-great fighter who was shot. The other guy was a great fighter in his prime.

## #16. Wladimir Klitschko

We can't be too American-centric. Boxing is a world sport.

The Klitschkos are two big, well-conditioned guys fighting in an era when the best big guys are going into sports other than boxing.

Give Wladimir credit for staying the course.

Wladimir never seemed to have his heart in it.

## #17. Vitali Klitschko

Vitali didn't have the resume or talent of his brother. But if they fought, I'd pick Vitali. And his role as a serious player in Ukrainian politics adds to his stature.

## #18. James Corbett

Corbett was one of the first successful scientific fighters of the gloved era. Give him credit for that. But he fought for seventeen years and had only eighteen fights. He beat an old drunk (John L. Sullivan) for the title, defended it once against an aging British middleweight (Charlie Mitchell), and lost it to another aging British middleweight (Bob Fitzsimmons).

## #19. Riddick Bowe

Bowe was a super talent and a super waste. He had one great fight; the first fight against Evander Holyfield. Then he got lazy. Riddick had the potential to be much higher on this list but never got there. He was a disappointment. When you squander talent like that, you don't deserve to be ranked high.

## #20. Bob Fitzsimmons

Bob Fitzsimmons won championships in three weight divisions. But he was getting his ass kicked in the Corbett fight until he hit Corbett with a body shot.

★ ★ ★

All of the fighters on this list were great. But Muhammad Ali and Joe Louis stand separate and apart from the rest.

There's a fight that's bigger than boxing.

Certain champions touch an entire generation.

Put symbolism aside for a moment. Joe Louis was a better fighter than any fighter the world had seen before. He was the best ever up until his time.

People remember how good Ali was when he was young. They've forgotten how good Louis was when he was young. Louis had everything. Power, speed, stamina, a textbook style. He lost one fight in the early years of his career, to a very good Max Schmeling (who Louis took lightly and didn't train for properly). When they met again with the championship on the line, Louis knocked Schmeling out in the first round.

That night changed the experience of being black in America. Jack Johnson might have been black America's first black hero. When Louis (the symbol of American democracy) knocked out Schmeling (Adolph Hitler's favorite fighter), Louis became white America's first black hero. In 1951, at the end of Louis's storied ring career, A. J. Liebling wrote, "Joe Louis looks like a champion and carries himself like a champion, and people will continue to call him champion as long as he lives."

Muhammad Ali had incredible physical gifts, skill, determination, and heart. He fought more great heavyweights than anyone and never ducked a challenge. And let's not forget; Ali was past his prime when he beat Joe Frazier and George Foreman.

Ali wasn't always a good sportsman. Joe Frazier and Ernie Terrell can attest to that. But as David Halberstam noted, "He knew how to play the role of champion, inside and outside the ring. God, he knew how to play that role."

Like Louis, Ali changed what it meant to be black in America.

Louis inspired America. Ali inspired the world.

In the end, Ali's edge over Louis in this poll was that many electors felt he was simply the better fighter.

So . . . Are we talking about boxing's greatest heavyweight fighter or boxing's greatest heavyweight champion?

As a symbol, Louis meant as much in his time as Ali did in his; maybe more.

My own preference is to rank Ali number one and Louis 1A.

Given Ali's generosity of spirit, I don't think he'd mind sharing the number-one spot . . . As long as he's the one without the "A."

*The making of most fights is dictated by economic considerations. Canelo Alvarez vs. Julio Cesar Chavez Jr was no different.*

# Canelo Alvarez vs. Julio Cesar Chavez Jr

Boxing is on the ropes in the United States. Self-inflicted wounds coupled with external forces have made it a niche sport. But there are places where the sweet science is healthy and has a fervent fan base.

In England, ninety thousand fans gathered on April 29, 2017, to watch Anthony Joshua defend his heavyweight title against Wladimir Klitschko.

Mexican boxing fans also exude a passion for the sport that transcends geographic boundaries. On May 6, 2017, Saul "Canelo" Alvarez of Guadalajara faced off against Julio Cesar Chavez Jr from Culiacan at the T-Mobile Arena in Las Vegas. The son of an ice cream vendor fought "The Son of the Legend" in one of the most anticipated intramural matchups in Mexican boxing history.

Alvarez was a child prodigy who fought professionally for the first time at age fifteen. He's now twenty-six and a veteran of fifty-one fights with a 49–1–1 (34 KOs) record. The draw came in his fifth pro bout when he was fifteen years old. The other blemish on his record was a 2013 loss by decision to Floyd Mayweather, who befuddled Canelo over the course of twelve long rounds.

The knock on Canelo, if there is one, is that he has beaten faded fighters (Shane Mosley and Miguel Cotto), smaller fighters (Liam Smith and Amir Khan), stylish boxers (Erislandy Lara and Austin Trout), and punchers (James Kirkland and Alfredo Angulo). But he has yet to beat a complete fighter in his prime. That said, he's a world-class fighter.

Julio Cesar Chavez Sr was more than a world-class fighter. He's widely regarded as Mexico's greatest champion. His son, Julio Jr, entered the ring for the first time at age seventeen, armed with his father's name and not much more.

Junior is now thirty-one. Having begun boxing as a curiosity, he developed into a pretty good fighter, but has regressed to being a curiosity again (albeit a less interesting curiosity than before). At one point, he won a faux 160-pound world title, courtesy of the World Boxing Council (which arranged for him to fight Sebastian Zbik for a belt in 2011 and then defend it against Peter Manfredo Marco Rubio, and Andy Lee). That party came to an end on September 15, 2012, when legal maneuvering forced Chavez into the ring against Sergio Martinez.

Martinez treated Chavez like a heavy bag and dominated him for 11½ rounds. The second half of round twelve was different. Writing soon after, I recounted the drama as follows:

> Chavez started slowly in round twelve, moving forward with his hands held high. His left eye was swollen shut. His right eye was ringed by abrasions and his lips were puffy. Martinez kept circling, jabbing. Twenty-eight seconds elapsed before Julio threw his first punch of the round, a tentative stay-away-from-me right hand. Ten seconds later, he offered a meaningless jab. Both punches missed. One minute into round twelve, Chavez had thrown three punches and landed none. Then with 1:28 left, Julio scored with a sharp left hook up top that hurt Sergio. Two more hooks landed flush. Suddenly, with 1:23 left in the fight, Martinez was on the canvas and in trouble. There was pandemonium in the arena. Martinez crawled to the ropes and lifted himself up at the count of six. Referee Tony Weeks beckoned Chavez in. Julio had seventy seconds to finish the job. Sergio, too dazed and weak to tie Chavez up and with his legs too unsteady to move out of danger, hurled punches back at his foe. With one minute left in the fight, Martinez tried to clinch and Julio dismissively threw him to the canvas. Sergio staggered to his feet. Weeks, appropriately, chose not to give him extra time to recover and ordered that the action resume immediately without wiping Sergio's gloves. Fifty-two seconds remained. But now, Chavez too was exhausted. At the final bell, both fighters knew that Martinez had won.

The last round of Martinez-Chavez saved Julio from being branded a fraud. But his reputation was soon in tatters.

Trainer Freddie Roach complained that Chavez had refused to train properly for the Martinez fight. WBC president Jose Sulaiman alleged that Julio had a serious gambling problem that had resulted in millions of dollars lost at the gaming tables. Then the Nevada State Athletic Commission announced that, in a post-fight drug test, Chavez had tested positive for marijuana.

Three years earlier, a Chavez victory over Troy Rowland had been changed to "no contest" because Julio tested positive for furosemide (a diuretic sometimes used as a masking agent). For that offense, the NSAC suspended Chavez for seven months and fined him $10,000. After the Martinez fight, the commission fined Julio $100,000.

Chavez's career foundered thereafter as he continued to slack off in training and struggled to make weight. The World Boxing Council jumped through so many hoops for him that it was suggested the sanctioning body establish a new weight division known as "Chavezweight." The Chavezweight championship would be awarded for whatever weight Julio could make at the weigh-in, and the WBC would present Julio with a special championship belt emblazoned with medallions honoring Burger King and McDonald's.

In the fifty-eight months prior to facing Canelo, Chavez had only four wins (two over Brian Vera, and one each against Marcos Reyes and Dominik Britsch). He'd quit on his stool in a loss to Andrzej Fonfara. Putting matters in further perspective, Julio had fought only one round at an elite level (round twelve against Martinez) since beating Andy Lee in mid-2012.

It's hard being a professional fighter. Whatever his limitations—and there were many—Chavez did get in a boxing ring fifty-three times and had compiled a 50–2–1 (32 KOs) record. But he was dogged by the belief that he's more sizzle than steak and, worse, by the accusation that he lacks heart.

One gets the impression that Canelo fights because he likes to fight and the money is good. One gets the impression that Chavez fights because the money is good.

After considerable negotiation, Canelo–Chavez was made for a contract weight of 164.5 pounds. That was 9.5 pounds more than Alvarez had previously weighed in for a fight and less than Chavez had weighed in five years. The penalty for missing weight would be $1,000,000 for each pound or fraction thereof that a fighter weighed in over 164.5.

Chavez chose to train with Nacho Beristain. Once again, Canelo worked with Eddy and "Chepo" Reynoso.

The promotion had a buzz from the start and showed that boxing's sanctioning bodies are unnecessary at a certain level. Canelo–Chavez wasn't for an alphabet-soup belt. It was for bragging rights in Mexico. Among intramural Mexican rivalries, only the three fights between Erik Morales and Marco Antonio Barrera and, possibly, the four encounters between Israel Vazquez and Rafael Marquez, engendered passions of this magnitude.

"Titles are very important to me," Canelo said. "But this goes above any title. It's for honor, for pride."

Tickets quickly sold out. Early pay-per-view numbers were encouraging. Canelo's previous three bouts had made it clear that he needs a dance partner to engender massive pay-per-view buys. Taken chronologically, the opponents in those fights had been Miguel Cotto (nine hundred thousand buys), Amir Khan (five hundred thousand), and Liam Smith (three hundred thousand).

Now Canelo had a marketable dance partner, albeit one he disrespected.

"He was never a dignified representative for Mexico," Canelo said of Chavez. "I can't respect him because, for me personally, he hasn't done anything. He has shamed his country with what he has done with his career. My fans know that I started from nothing, from the bottom up, from zero, and have worked my way up with a lot of sweat and sacrifices. He has his fans, as well. But I think a lot of his fans are more his father's fans than his."

"I feel I've been over-criticized because I am Senior's son," Julio responded. "All the good I do, I feel it counts for half. And any of the bad is doubled."

In the days leading up to the fight, Alvarez seemed more confident and stronger at his core than Chavez. One got the sense that Canelo embraced the idea of his honor being tested before all of Mexico, while Chavez was a bit intimidated by it.

The prevailing view was that Canelo would go to the body, break Chavez down, and take away his heart.

But a case could be made for a Chavez victory.

Canelo is faster than Chavez. He's a better boxer. Everyone understood that Julio had been given this opportunity in large part because of his father's name. But Chavez is bigger than Canelo. Much bigger. And because of the size differential between them, some knowledgeable observers thought Julio had a good chance to win.

Canelo scoffed at that notion, saying, "I've been fighting professionally since I was fifteen years old, so I've been fighting bigger and stronger guys."

But not lately. As Chavez noted, "He won the title, and then it was pick anybody. He picked smaller guys, so he got used to being the bigger man. And now there's me."

There was also an emotional factor to consider.

The fight offered Chavez a chance for redemption. It was the equivalent of a life preserver being thrown to a drowning man. A victory over Canelo would wipe away every past failure on Julio's ring ledger.

"This fight has created a lot of passion in me, a lot of enthusiasm," Chavez told the media. "That's the difference in this. You're going to see a different Julio that's excited. I can lose to a lot of people. I cannot lose to Canelo."

Sean Gibbons has helped guide Chavez during his sojourn through boxing.

"People talk about Julio's past," Gibbons said. "But that's the past. For a long time, Julio wasn't interested in boxing the way a fighter has to be if he's going to be great or even very good. Then, for four years after he lost to Martinez, Julio hated boxing. But Julio is more into boxing for this fight than I've ever seen him."

Two days before the fight, Canelo was a 6-to-1 betting favorite. There were questions as to whether Chavez would make the 164.5 pound weight limit before rehydrating. And if he did, would he be dead at the weight? Then Canelo and Chavez each weighed in at 164 pounds. A half-pound under. By fight night, the odds had dropped to 4-to-1.

But an elite fighter isn't built in four months after long stretches of lethargy. It takes years of discipline, training, and hard work. Chavez simply wasn't up to the task.

It was hard to imagine Canelo–Chavez not being an entertaining, fan-friendly fight. But it wasn't.

Both men fought cautiously in round one, with Alvarez applying the greater pressure. Chavez could have forced exchanges but chose not to. In round two, Julio opened up a bit but seemed wary of Canelo's punching power. By round three, they were clearly hunter and prey, with Canelo stalking and landing hurting blows. Blood began dribbling from Chavez's nose. Whatever plan Julio might have had before the fight, he was now trying to outbox a man who was quicker, faster, and a better boxer.

From that point on, Canelo beat Chavez down. He was relentless, methodical, patient, and professional en route to a 228-to-71 advantage in punches landed.

In round five, Chavez's left eye began to close, and one began to wonder whether his spirit or body would break first.

In round six, Alvarez went to the ropes, as he would do several times during the fight, in the hope of drawing Chavez into a more vigorous exchange of punches. "But he wouldn't do it," Canelo said afterward. "I thought he was going to fight. He just wouldn't throw punches."

There were times when Chavez accepted Canelo's invitation to trade, but they were few and far between. Almost always, when Canelo fired back, Julio disengaged. He preferred to stay at as safe a distance as possible and never used his size in an effort to rough Canelo up on the inside.

One wondered what might happen if Chavez were able to land a hard overhand right flush on the jaw. But Canelo was boxing too well to find out. And Julio was largely in survival mode.

At the start of the proceedings, the 20,510 fans in attendance had been evenly divided. Whether Canelo won the Chavez fans over or Julio lost them is open to question. But there were fewer Chavez fans in the arena when the final bell sounded.

All three judges scored the bout 120–108. It would have been hard to arrive at a different tally.

"Canelo beat me," Chavez acknowledged afterward. "He is very good, and he beat me. He's fast and he's consistent. The speed and the distance was the key."

Or as writer Tom Gerbasai noted, "The shoes were always going to be too big to fill. Maybe Julio Cesar Chavez Jr knew it from the start."

Meanwhile, Canelo's next fight is scheduled for September 16, 2017, against Gennady Golovkin and is the most anticipated fight of the year. If Canelo beats Golovkin, it will elevate him to "Chavez-like" status in Mexico.

*When Errol Spence was asked about going to England to fight Kell Brook, he answered, "I don't think of it as fighting in England or the United States. We're fighting in a boxing ring that could be anywhere."*

# Errol Spence Has Arrived

These are heady times for British boxing. Four weeks ago (on April 29, 2017), Anthony Joshua knocked out Wladimir Klitschko in front of ninety thousand screaming fans in London to solidify his hold on the heavyweight division. On May 27, 2017, the scene shifted to Sheffield, where twenty-seven thousand partisans gathered in a soccer stadium to watch another Brit—thirty-one-year-old local hero Kell Brook—defend his IBF 147-pound title against Errol Spence.

Standard operating procedure in boxing today is for fighters to call out King Kong, Godzilla, and Darth Vader and then fight Pee Wee Herman, Mickey Mouse, and Donald Duck.

Give Brook (36–1, 25 KOs) credit for going in tough. He won his IBF belt three years ago by decisioning Shawn Porter at the Stub Hub Center in California. Then, after three defenses against less-than-stellar opposition, he went up in weight and challenged unified middleweight champion Gennady Golovkin.

Golovkin beat Brook down. The fight was stopped in the fifth round. But Kell had his moments and was incrementally ahead on the judges' scorecards (39–37, 38–38, 38–38) when the end came.

Spence (21–0, 18 KOs), age twenty-seven, posed another enormous challenge. Errol turned pro after losing a 16–11 decision to Andrey Zamkovoy of Russia in the third round of the 2012 Olympics. Now living in Texas, he entered the Brook fight with the look of a possible future pound-for-pound king. Yes, his opponents had been carefully chosen. They were either too old (forty-two-year-old Leonard Bundu), too slow (Alejandro Barrera), or lacking in power (Chris Algieri, 8 KOs in twenty-four fights). But the way Errol devastated them was impressive. He entered the Brook fight as a 2-to-1 betting favorite.

Brook's backers made the point that Shawn Porter, who Kell beat, was far more formidable than anyone Spence had fought to date. They also pointed to a possible chink in Errol's armor: his chin. There have been rumors that Spence gets hurt more, and more often, in sparring than his team would like.

Paulie Malignaggi referenced that issue, when he told a Sky Sports audience, "Errol is a terrific body puncher with solid hand speed, and he knows how to open you up. But he's untested at this level. The question mark is what happens when Brook hits him, because he hasn't been hit a lot. He hasn't fought anybody like Kell and hasn't been hit a lot by the level of opposition that he's fought. Kell doesn't just hit. He really hits. And he hits with sharp power."

But Spence is very good. He's a southpaw, which makes him even harder to beat. And Brook came into the fight with considerable wear and tear on his body.

In September 2014, Brook suffered serious leg and arm wounds after being attacked by a man with a machete. His thirty-seven pro fights included the aforementioned wars against Golovkin and Porter. And equally problematic, Kell, who has long been a "big" welterweight, fought Golovkin at 160 pounds. There was a question as to how his body would react to shrinking down to 147 pounds again.

Brook-Spence was contested in Sheffield in the wake of the May 22 terrorist bombing in Manchester that took twenty-two lives and injured scores more. Security for the bout was tight.

In boxing, the better fighter usually wins. Spence was the better fighter.

Spence fought a bit tentatively in round one as Brook advanced behind an aggressive jab. In the second stanza, Errol began moving forward, but was still reluctant to let his hands go. That changed in round three, when Spence started fighting more confidently. There was spirited back-and-forth action in rounds four through seven, with Errol getting the better of it and going effectively to the body. His punches strayed low often enough that referee Howard Foster could have made an issue of it but didn't.

After seven rounds, Brook's left eye was closing, and he looked like a tired fighter. At that point, Spence pressed the action. By round nine, Brook was fighting to survive, and Spence was fighting to knock him out.

"When you can't see, there's nothing you can do," Brook said afterward, referencing the damage (later diagnosed as a broken orbital bone) inflicted around his eye.

Forty seconds into round ten, an accumulation of punches put Brook on the canvas, the consequence of what might have been a decision to regroup by taking a knee. Kell fought back valiantly toward the end of the stanza, landing his best blows of the night. Then, midway through round eleven, Brook sought sanctuary on the canvas again, kneeling and signaling to Foster that he no longer wished to fight.

Spence was ahead on the judges' scorecards at the time of the stoppage by a 97–92, 96–93, 95–94 margin. According to Compu-Box, he had a 246-to-136 advantage in punches landed. And Errol showed a chin. Brook hit him often enough but couldn't change the flow of the bout.

After his victory, Spence said he wants to fight WBC-WBA 147-pound champion Keith Thurman next: "I've been calling Keith Thurman out for a long time. So Keith Thurman, come on. Come out."

However, Thurman hasn't sounded like a man who's anxious for that particular fight. Not now, anyway. Earlier this year, Keith was asked about fighting Spence, and replied, "I'm tired about being asked this fucking question. I see greatness in him. Has he been fully tested yet? No. Four years ago, I was Errol Spence and everybody, including Floyd, was ducking me. Build it up and I'll fight him."

At the moment, it's academic. Thurman will be out of action until the beginning of 2018 because of recent elbow surgery. And Shawn Porter (who Keith has already beaten once) has been designated by the WBC as his mandatory challenger.

In an ideal world, Spence would fight Porter next with the winner to face Thurman. Porter would pressure Spence in ways that Brook couldn't. But the ideal rarely happens in boxing.

Meanwhile, let it be noted that Brook came to America to take the title from Porter, and Spence went to England to get it back.

England is a time-honored place for a coronation.

*Don Turner has trained fighters for decades and notes, "It's a lot easier to outbox a guy if you can hurt him."*

# Ward–Kovalev II: Andre Ward Makes a Statement

In an earlier era, the June 17, 2017, rematch between Andre Ward and Sergey Kovalev would have been a can't-miss promotion: two of the best fighters in the world reprising a 2016 encounter that ended in controversy with Ward prevailing on the judges' scorecards by a razor-thin margin. But this is 2017. Instead of galvanizing boxing fans, Ward-Kovalev II was symbolic of boxing's problems.

There was a rematch clause in the contract for Kovalev–Ward I, but Team Ward balked at moving forward with the sequel. Andre seemed ambivalent. And Roc Nation Sports (his promoter) stood to lose several million dollars on the promotion because of its contract with Ward. Meanwhile, Kovalev and Main Events (Sergey's promoter) desperately wanted the rematch; Kovalev for competitive and monetary reasons, Main Events as a financial imperative.

In the end, the fact that the Kovalev–Ward I contract contained a binding rematch clause was dispositive of the issue. But to get Ward-Kovalev II off the ground, Main Events CEO Kathy Duva ceded control of the venture to Roc Nation.

"They wanted to control the promotion," Duva said. "They wanted to set the tone. They specifically used those words. They were going to do things the Roc way. So this is the Roc way."

Kovalev–Ward I was one of the most anticipated fights of 2016. The rematch was close to stillborn.

Roc Nation Sports was founded by Shawn Corey Carter a.k.a. Jay Z in 2013 and has made inroads in numerous sports, most notably with the signing of NBA star Kevin Durant and the NFL's Dez Bryant. But in two and a half years, it has failed to show that it can promote boxing at a world-class level without losing money.

There are a lot of moving pieces that have to be assembled into a well-oiled machine for a big fight to be properly promoted. Roc Nation has yet to show that it has mastered this discipline. It's two flagship fighters—Miguel Cotto and Andre Ward—have been cash drains for the company because of unrealistically large guaranteed purses. Cotto and Roc Nation Sports parted ways earlier this year. Industry insiders wouldn't be surprised if Roc Nation left boxing shortly.

Michael Yormark (president and chief of branding and strategy) is Roc Nation Sports's most visible management figure. But many crucial decisions in areas where Roc Nation's boxing program is intertwined with the company's larger mission are heavily influenced by Desiree Perez.

Perez has been criticized as having an abrasive management style reminiscent of the Queen of Hearts in *Alice in Wonderland*. As reported by the *New York Daily News*, she was arrested in New York in 1994 for possession with intent to distribute thirty-five kilograms of cocaine. Federal authorities charged that she was part of a major drug-distribution ring, and she faced spending well over a decade in prison. But she cooperated with authorities and, after pleading no contest to criminal charges, served fourteen months in prison followed by ten years' probation. Thereafter, she turned her life around and has become one of the most trusted members of Jay Z's inner circle.

Regardless of who is making the decisions at Roc Nation Sports, Ward-Kovalev II struggled financially from the start. And before long, the atmosphere turned toxic.

Kovalev was already bitter about the judges' decision in Kovalev–Ward I.

"I had no emotions," Sergey said of the moment when the verdict was announced. "I was empty. I was just killed by decision. I couldn't change something. I just understood that I was robbed, and I don't have any more belts now. I just have one goal: to beat Andre Ward and beat all shit from him because he doesn't deserve the belt and the status of a champion. I lost respect for him, the way he acts. I don't like him. I want to punish him because he puts his nose really up. I know only one thing: I want to destroy him. I want to punish him and get my belts back."

Ward took the high road in response, saying, "It's a climate right now where there's a lot of talking. Guys don't do what they say they're going to do. They don't perform, and then they find excuses on why they didn't perform. There's only a handful of guys in history that talked and then backed it up. We don't have a lot of that today. It's not a video game. It's real life, and you've got to live it out.

"Anytime there's a close decision you're going to have opinions either way," Ward noted. "I've never refuted the fact that it was a close decision. I respect Kovalev as a champion. I won't call him a former champion. He's the real deal."

But then Andre tarnished his good-guy image by leaving town early and blowing off an edition of *Face-Off* that was scheduled to be recorded by HBO in Las Vegas on May 7, one day after Canelo Alvarez vs. Julio Cesar Chavez Jr. That didn't hurt Andre financially because Roc Nation had guaranteed him an oversized $6,500,000 purse for the fight. But it hurt Kovalev, Main Events, and Roc Nation, all of whom were dependent on pay-per-view buys as their primary revenue stream from Ward-Kovalev II.

Things deteriorated further from there.

Prior to Kovalev–Ward I, Team Ward had tried to sow discord in the Kovalev camp by floating the idea that Sergey was being underpaid by Main Events. In truth, based on the economic realities of the fight, Andre was being overpaid by Roc Nation, which has never been able to balance its boxing economic balance sheet.

In the build-up to Ward-Kovalev II, the Ward camp sought to drive a wedge between Sergey and his trainer, John David Jackson. Both James Prince (Ward's manager) and Josh Dubin (Andre's lawyer) claimed that Jackson had reached out to them about the possibility of working with Ward and Virgil Hunter in preparation for the rematch. "We thought about it strongly," Prince said. "That's why we were conversating with him, because we felt that he could be somewhat of an asset. But at the end of the day, it was an asset that we really didn't need."

Meanwhile, there seemed to be even more enmity between Main Events and Roc Nation than between the fighters. In an interview posted on Twitter, Michael Yormark declared, "They've done nothing to promote this fight. Kathy [Duva] really has done nothing. Sergey has done nothing. Let's be honest. Sergey has no following. Main Events has had him for five, six years. What have they done with him? Nobody knows who he is. He has no following. He can't sell tickets. He can't sell pay-per-view."

The problem with these attacks was that the promotional message was all wrong. It was focusing on personal insults rather than the merits of what was expected to be a very good fight.

Kovalev had started strong in Kovalev–Ward I, knocking Ward down in the second round before fading late.

"I've never had to come from behind like that in a professional fight," Ward said afterward. "I don't want to be there, and I don't feel like I should be there. But you prepare for those moments long before fight night."

In addition to questioning the judges' decision in Kovalev–Ward I, many people (this writer included) felt that referee Robert Byrd had interpreted the rules in a way that allowed Andre to lead with his head and grapple rather than box for much of the fight. However, Sergey put that issue to rest during the kick-off press tour for Ward-Kovalev II when he said, "The referee was good. I have no problems with the referee in the fight."

Kovalev also said the reason he faded late in Kovalev–Ward I was that he'd overtrained for the bout. But that seemed like rationalization. And in any event, Ward contributed significantly to making Sergey tired.

"I'm not here to prove anything although, obviously, my goal is to win in a more definitive fashion," Ward said as Ward-Kovalev II approached. "It's my job to pick up where we left off. There's adjustments that need to be made. But at the end of the day, I just have to be me and being myself is going to be enough. I fought this man for twelve rounds. There's nothing scary about him. He didn't knock me down in the ninth or tenth round and have me holding on to survive. He knocked me down in the second round, and I came back from it. Everybody wants to talk about the knockdown. Did you see the next ten rounds? June 17 won't be any different except I'll start a little earlier."

The fight was contested at the Mandalay Bay Events Center in Las Vegas.

Kovalev's "grand arrival" at Mandalay Bay was not so grand. Meeting with the media, Sergey declared, "Ward and his team are liars. He said that he gave me this rematch as a present for the boxing fans. Don't lie. It was in the contract that you must give me this or you retire. When I see his face, I want to punch it. I am very happy for this opportunity to smash his face. I don't like this guy."

At the final pre-fight press conference on Thursday, Kovalev spoke and then left the dais with the rest of his team before Ward was introduced.

Most promotions grow larger in the public consciousness as a fight approaches. Ward-Kovalev II seemed to shrink as the hour of reckoning neared.

Ward was a 7-to-5 betting favorite. Many media personnel who thought Sergey won the first fight were picking Andre in the rematch.

It was assumed that the bout would be interesting but not necessarily entertaining. That was the kiss of death. Few fans wanted to see rounds four through twelve of Kovalev–Ward I all over again. But the expectation was, that's what they would get.

"The first fight," Bart Barry wrote, "ended in a way that anticipates a predictable result the next time, no matter how many mean sentences the combatants speak about one another. Kovalev's best chance of beating Ward happened ten rounds ago. Every moment since then has made a Kovalev victory less probable. As this fight nears, interest dwindles."

Roc Nation did a good job of selling sponsorships. But pay-per-view buys were tracking at a dismally low level. Kovalev–Ward I had generated roughly 165,000 buys, which was a disappointing number. A source close to the promotion of Ward-Kovalev II says that, initially, Roc Nation maintained in marketing strategy sessions that, with proper promotion, Ward-Kovalev II could engender as many as three hundred thousand buys. In the end, the rematch fell short of the pay-per-view numbers for their first fight.

On Wednesday of fight week, tickets for Ward-Kovalev II were posted on Groupon at a thirty-two percent discount with an additional discount of fifteen dollars per order. Papering the house with "freebies" and selling tickets at discount is not uncommon in boxing. But usually, it's quietly done. Selling tickets on Groupon is a public announcement that anyone who paid full price is a sucker.

Also on Wednesday of fight week, Floyd Mayweather vs. Conor McGregor was announced. That further marginalized Ward-Kovalev II in terms of media coverage and conversation among fans. On the morning of the Ward-Kovalev rematch, the *New York Times* sports section devoted most of its front page and much of page four to Mayweather–McGregor. The *Times* wouldn't have devoted that space to Ward-Kovalev II under any circumstances. But it symbolized the latter bout's plight.

Ward and Kovalev each weighed in at 175 pounds.

Kovalev was the aggressor in round one and did enough to win the stanza since Ward was in stay-away-from-me mode. In rounds two and three, Sergey continued moving forward. But Andre blunted his aggression with movement, kept Kovalev from getting off the way he wanted to, tied him up when Sergey got inside, and landed occasional punches that were hard enough to get Kovalev's attention. Ward also began letting his hands go more (including a hook that landed below the belt and earned a warning from referee Tony Weeks).

By round five, Kovalev appeared to be tiring. He was still the aggressor, but it had become ineffective aggression. He was losing his edge and seemed frustrated by his inability to land cleanly on Ward. More significantly, in a precursor of things to come, Ward landed two hurting body shots at the two-minute mark of round five. That was followed by a left hook up top in round six that was better than anything Kovalev had landed so far.

By round seven, Kovalev seemed to be just going through the motions and Andre was becoming dominant. One minute into round eight, three body blows (at least one of them low) doubled Kovalev over and sent him back against the ropes. More body shots softened him up further. A straight right hand staggered him badly. Now Sergey was struggling to survive. There were more body shots, two of them flagrantly low . . . And referee Tony Weeks stopped the fight.

Ward was ahead 67–66 on two of the judges' scorecards at the time of the stoppage and trailed 68–65 on the third.

Controversy followed.

Paulie Malignaggi was at ringside covering the fight for SKY-TV and said afterward, "I thought the stoppage was terrible. It wasn't like he was hurt to the point where you had to stop the fight. You see guys get that hurt a lot of times in fights and you don't even think about stopping the fight. Ward was hurting Kovalev to the body. But give the fight the proper ending. What's going on? What was with that stoppage? All of a sudden, he stopped the fight. I wasn't even sure what he was doing. I thought maybe he was calling a low blow. The last thing on my mind was that he was stopping the fight."

Kathy Duva asked Nevada State Athletic Commission executive director Bob Bennett for an immediate video review of the blows that led to the stoppage, which is legal under Nevada law. But Bennett declined and later explained, "The only way we can look at an instant replay is under one condition: when a punch or kick terminates the bout and the referee isn't sure whether it's a legal or illegal blow. I asked Tony Weeks, 'Do you want to look at the instant replay?' And he said, 'No. I'm satisfied they were on the beltline.'"

Kovalev didn't object immediately when the fight was stopped. But grasping the full reality of the situation, he soon proclaimed, "He hit with four low blows. The ref didn't call them. I felt I could have continued. This is bullshit."

Main Events quickly sent out a press release headlined "Sergey Kovalev TKO'd by Low Blows." And Duva declared, "I'm still having a hard time processing what I just witnessed. I saw someone who should have been disqualified get his hand held up. Sergey got hit with three low blows, four actually, in the last round. We'll file a protest on Monday."

The view from here is that Tony Weeks should have given Kovalev five minutes to recover from the low blows and deducted a point from Ward (who'd been previously warned for going low). Most likely, it wouldn't have made a difference. Kovalev looked to be finished. But the same could have been said of Anthony Joshua after six rounds against Wladimir Klitschko. And boxing fans know how that turned out.

Meanwhile, controversy over the ending shouldn't overshadow the fact that Ward turned in an impressive performance.

Andre was an Olympic gold medalist. He has fought and beaten more than a few top-tier fighters in their prime. His talent warrants his being regarded as a superstar. But as Larry Merchant recently noted, talent isn't enough. Being a superstar requires that the public feel a connection to a fighter and be moved by him. Ward's style of fighting is too clinical, and he's perceived as too aloof for that connection to occur.

Or as Matthew Swain wrote, "Ward is calculated precisely at every moment. In the ring, he uses balance, timing, and range to make the fight exactly as he wants it to be. It's like a symphony that you know is technically perfect but lacks anything emotive. Ward is much the same in person. Every phrase, every facial movement, every appearance is controlled to room temperature."

Ward views things differently.

"I'm boring because I don't act a certain way on 24/7?" Andre asks rhetorically. "What's that about? I'm understated. That's my lane and I'm comfortable in it. I can't go into a fight thinking about its entertainment value. I just need to do me, execute the game plan, and get my hand raised at the end of the fight."

And in a June 7 media conference call, Ward elaborated on that theme, saying, "Everybody has to be careful when they say 'the fans,' because they don't speak for all the fans. It amazes me that you'll have one person speak for all boxing fans all over the world. If you love boxing, yes, you may have a certain style that you favor. But when I look at the sport of boxing, the guys that were on top for ten years, eight years, seven years, they could do it all. They could bang with you when it was to their advantage. They could outbox you when it was to their advantage. And if you love boxing, you love it all. I appreciate the boxer. I appreciate the boxer-puncher. I appreciate the brawler, who maybe doesn't have the skill to box. I think it's really selfish to just act as if one style is the only style that all fans across the world want to see and that everybody else is not worth watching. I think that's inaccurate, and I don't think that's the way the sport should be represented."

*I could agree with the judges who decided Manny Pacquiao vs. Jeff Horn. But then we'd all be wrong.*

# Age, Bad Judging, and Jeff Horn Beat Manny Pacquiao

On Sunday, July 2, 2017 (Saturday night in the United States), Manny Pacquiao and Jeff Horn met in the ring at Suncorp Stadium in Brisbane, Australia, before 51,052 fans to battle for the WBO welterweight title.

Pacquiao, who entered the contest with a 59–6–2 (38 KOs) record, is no longer the force in boxing that he once was, either as a fighter or a commercial attraction. Five years ago, Juan Manuel Marquez left him lying face-down on the canvas. One punch in a fight that Marquez was losing turned Manny's world upside down.

Pacquiao has had seven fights since then, highlighted by an embarrassingly lethargic outing against Floyd Mayweather in 2015. The last knockout he scored was thirteen bouts and eight years ago. Still, entering the ring to face Horn, Pacquiao was widely regarded as a quality fighter. He was good enough last year to outclass Tim Bradley and Jesse Vargas en route to unanimous-decision triumphs.

The 29-year-old Horn (16–0–1, 11 KOs) wasn't seen as much of a threat to Pacquiao. He'd never fought professionally outside of Australia and New Zealand. The only recognizable names on his record were Ali Funeka and Randall Bailey, both of whom were years removed from their prime and have not won a fight since Horn fought them.

There was the usual pre-fight hype. Freddie Roach (Pacquiao's trainer) told the media, "I have not seen this Manny Pacquiao in seven years. He reminds me of the old days, of the Manny who fought Ricky Hatton, just destroying them."

Pacquiao, for his part, declared, "In all my years of boxing, I have never been as motivated and fired up as this fight."

That led to the question of why Manny was more "motivated and fired up" to fight Jeff Horn than to fight Floyd Mayweather. But no one was taking his comments seriously.

Meanwhile, Horn's trainer, Glen Rushton, told the media that he had a "secret ten-point plan" to beat Pacquiao.

"I can get the job done if I follow it one hundred percent," Horn assured those who were listening.

Pacquiao was a 5-to-1 betting favorite.

The night began on an inauspicious note for ESPN (which televised Pacquiao-Horn in the United States). A Major League Soccer game ran longer than expected and delayed the start of the telecast by four minutes.

Joe Tessitore, Teddy Atlas, and Tim Bradley called the action from ringside backed in the studio by Steve Levy and Stephen A. Smith.

ESPN's telecast opened with Shane Mosley Jr. (10–1, 7 KOs) vs. David Toussaint (10–0, 8 KOs). Suffice it to say for the moment that Shane Mosley Jr is to Shane Mosley as Frank Sinatra Jr was to Frank Sinatra. Toussaint won a narrow split-decision victory in a boring fight.

Next up, Irish Olympian Michael Conlan (2–0, 2 KOs) was matched against Jarrett Owen (5–4–3, 2 KOs). The five guys Owen beat had a composite ring record of 4 wins in 30 fights, and he'd been knocked out by a fighter named Haruki Noma (who never won another fight). In other words, the result of Conlan-Owen was preordained. Owen entered the ring expecting to lose and did, on a third-round stoppage.

IBF junior-bantamweight champion Jerwin Ancajas (24–1–1, 16 KOs) vs. Teiru Kinoshita (25–1–1, 8 KOs) was the third televised fight of the evening. Tessitore trumpeted the fact that Kinoshita had won his most recent three bouts by knockout. He neglected to tell viewers that the three opponents Kinoshita knocked out in these fights had a composite ring record of 0 wins and 9 losses. Ancajas won on a seventh-round knockout.

That set the stage for Pacquiao-Horn.

Horn came to win, not just survive. He fought aggressively in the early going, abetted by the fact that Pacquiao is now thirty-eight years old with the wear and tear of a twenty-two-year ring career on his body.

Manny's reflexes have slowed. Against Horn, his timing was off. He no longer commits to the straight left hand like he used to and was unable to counter effectively for most of the night. He cut Horn near the corner of the right eye in round three and did some good body work from time to time. But that was all he did in the first half of the fight, which looked to be even after six rounds.

Meanwhile, Pacquiao's blood was flowing. He suffered a deep cut on the hairline from an accidental clash of heads in round six and another deep cut above the right eye from a second clash of heads in round seven, cuts that required nine and eight stitches respectively to close after the fight.

By round eight, both fighters were tiring and beginning to lose form in what had become a sloppy bloodbath. But Pacquiao was getting the better of it.

The action peaked in round nine, when Pacquiao pummeled Horn around the ring, prompting referee Mark Nelson to visit Horn's corner during the one-minute break before round ten and threaten to stop the fight.

But Pacquiao was unable to close the show.

Then came the judges' decision: Waleska Roldan 117–111, Chris Flores 115–113, and Ramon Cerdan 115–113 . . . all for Horn.

It was a bad decision. Scoring off of television (not as good a view as the judges had), this writer saw it 115–113 for Pacquiao. If one gave all the close rounds to Horn, those numbers arguably could have been reversed. But it would have been a stretch. And 117–111 was beyond the pale of reason.

Teddy Atlas, sitting at ringside, was apoplectic when the decision was announced. "They gave Horn a trophy for trying hard," Atlas raged. "You're not supposed to get it for trying hard. You're supposed to get it for winning."

Then, after considering his thoughts more fully, Atlas said of Roldan's scorecard, "It's only one of two things. It's either incompetence or corruption. When you see 117–111, I don't think anyone could be that incompetent. I'm sorry. If you know the sport, you watch the sport, you can't be that incompetent. So what else could it be? Corruption."

However, Atlas's reaction was calm compared to that of Stephan A. Smith.

"It was a bogus decision," Smith told viewers. "The thing that I'm depressed about right now is that I don't have the three names and a mug shot of each of those officials for the crime that they committed of robbing Manny Pacquiao tonight. There is no excuse for a decision like this."

Here it should be noted that Roldan was party to a similar miscarriage of justice three years ago when hometown favorite Heather Hardy was awarded a horrible split decision over Jackie Trivilino at Barclays Center in Brooklyn on the undercard of Ruslan Provodnikov vs. Chris Algieri. That decision was so bad that Hardy's hometown crowd erupted in boos when it was announced.

More recently, Roldan was one of the judges involved in the injustice visited upon Roman Gonzalez when she scored his March 18, 2017, fight against Srisaket Sor Rungvisai a draw. The other two judges were even more off base, scoring that bout for Rungvisai.

As for Pacquiao, his age is showing.

Tris Dixon recently wrote of Manny, "We judge him by the standards he has set. And they are incredibly high."

But Pacquiao can no longer meet those standards.

*Mikey Garcia is fond of saying, "Anybody can get hurt with the right punch. But there's more to boxing than power."*

# Mikey Garcia: Too Small, Too Slow, Too Good

Adrien Broner vs. Mikey Garcia at Barclays Center on July 29, 2017, was an intriguing matchup and a significant opportunity for both fighters.

Broner (33–2, 24 KOs) turned twenty-eight one day before the bout. Early in his career, he blew through a series of overmatched opponents and looked great in the process. But he has struggled against more credible competition and, in his two step-up fights prior to facing Garcia, lost to Marcos Maidana and Shawn Porter.

Broner also postures so obnoxiously, says so many silly, self-aggrandizing things, and has been in trouble with the law so often that it's easy to forget the skills he has and how hard it is to do what he does well in the ring.

Shortly after Broner–Garcia was announced, Adrien criticized boxing fans and the media, saying, "I just feel like they don't put enough respect on my name. I'm the one the kids wanna be now. Coming up, everybody wanted to be like Floyd that's my age. Now, coming up, all the kids wanna be like Adrien Broner."

Not . . .

Still, Broner–Garcia offered Adrien a chance to reestablish his credibility as a world-class fighter.

Garcia (36–0, 30 KOs) is one year older than Broner and has met every challenge he has faced in the ring. But because of contractual problems with his former promoter (Top Rank), he'd fought only eight rounds in the preceding forty-two months.

Broner–Garcia wasn't for a world title, but no one cared. It shaped up as the most important fight to date in Garcia's career and an opportunity for him to take a big step forward in terms of public recognition and marketability.

Blue collar vs. gaudy bling.

Garcia opened as a 6-to-1 betting favorite, which seemed like ridiculously long odds.

Broner isn't an easy out. The fighters he'd lost to—Maidana and Porter—were naturally bigger men who'd beaten him with roughhouse tactics and unremitting pressure, which isn't Garcia's style.

Also, Broner–Garcia would be contested at a contract weight of 140 pounds. That represented a new high for Mikey, while Adrien had fought between 140 and 147 pounds on six occasions.

"I'm still a lightweight," Mikey said when the fight was announced. "I feel that my best division right now is at 135."

Meanwhile, Broner has a long history of blowing off contractual weight requirements but told the media he'd "make weight easy."

"I've gotten older and I'm getting more wise," Adrien said. "This next half of my career, I'm focusing more on doing everything the correct way. The first half, I tried to do everything my way. It worked but I could have been better, so I want to try to do everything correctly. I haven't made weight lately. For what? Now I got a reason to make 140. I ain't giving nobody half of one million dollars."

That was a reference to the reported $500,000 penalty that awaited Broner if he failed to make weight.

Then, not only did Adrien make weight; he came in at 138¾ pounds, safely under the contract limit and twelve ounces lighter than Garcia.

The pre-fight buzz had been, "For Broner to win, he has to show up in shape and bring his heart." Now it appeared as though, at the very least, Adrien would show up in shape. By fight day, the odds had dropped below 2-to-1. People were starting to focus on the fact that Broner was naturally bigger than Garcia, faster than Garcia, and better than anyone Mikey had fought.

There were 12,084 fans at Barclays Center on fight night. Rau'shee Warren (14–2, 4 KOs) won a twelve-round decision over McJoe Arroyo (17–1, 8 KOs) in an IBF title-elimination bout. 2016 Irish Olympian and gold-medal winner Katie Taylor (5–0, 3 KOs) outclassed Jasmine Clarkson (4–8) in a mismatch that represented a step down from Taylor's most recent opponents and ended in three rounds.

Then the heavyweights took center stage.

Jarrell "Big Baby" Miller (18–0–1, 16 KOs), age twenty-nine, is one of boxing's more intriguing prospects. He has a huge personality and is touted as having a punch to match. But his work ethic is suspect, and he'd been out of action since August 2016 because of a contractual dispute with his promoter, Dmitry Salita.

Gerald Washington (18–1–1, 12 KOs), despite sporting a record comparable to Miller's, was the designated "opponent." But he wasn't a pushover. In his most recent fight, Washington had been even with Deontay Wilder on two of the three judges' scorecards when he was stopped in the fifth round. And he'd fought better fighters than Miller had fought.

Heavyweights are fun to watch. Miller is fun to watch and listen to. Among the thoughts "Big Baby" uttered in the days leading up to the fight were:

- "I never had to go to a Plan B or a Plan C because nobody can get past Plan A."
- "Gerald Washington is not a bum, but I don't see nothing too special about him. Deontay fought him and it took him five rounds to get him out. So I would definitely like to get him out earlier than Deontay to prove a point."
- "I've never seen anybody go five rounds, get knocked out, and get praised for that. Where I come from, we call that an ass-whipping."

At the final pre-fight press conference, Washington said simply, "I came here to shut that big mouth up."

One day before the fight, Miller weighed in at a personal high of 298.8 pounds. Washington registered a more svelte 248.

The fight began with Washington jabbing and throwing occasional right hands while Miller walked him down with his own hands held high in a protective posture. In round two, Jarrell started going to the body with both fists, and Washington started to slow down. By round three, both men looked tired, which was a testament to Miller's body attack and also his own lack of conditioning. By round five, both fighters looked like they were moving in slow motion. Washington started round six with new-found vigor and landed some good right hands. But Jarrell finished the stanza strong in the manner of a slow-moving avalanche.

After eight rounds, Washington's corner had seen enough and stopped the fight. Two judges had Miller ahead 79–72 and 77–75 at the time of the stoppage. John Stewart's scorecard was inexplicably even at 76–76.

The next bout matched former IBF 154-pound champion Jermall Charlo (25–0, 19 KOs) against Jorge Sebastian Heiland (29–4–2, 16 KOs).

Charlo had scored impressive victories over Julian Williams and Austin Trout in his two most recent fights and is a very good fighter.

Heiland had a 2014 knockout win over a faded Matthew Mackin on his resume but not much more. The four men Sebastian had fought since then have a total of sixty-six losses on their combined ring records. Yet that had been enough for Heiland to be ranked number one by the WBC, which qualified him to fight Charlo (number two) in a middleweight "title elimination" bout that was all but certain to eliminate Heiland. Charlo was a 20-to-1 betting favorite.

Charlo-Heiland was as one-sided as people thought it would be. Midway through round two, Jermall dropped Sebastian with a right uppercut followed by a vicious pounding that referee Benjy Esteves seemed vaguely aware of but was loath to interrupt. At that point, it was clear that Heiland was going to get beaten up until the fight was over, which was in round four.

After the bout, Heiland said he turned his left knee in the first round and that the injury hampered him during the fight. The available evidence strongly suggests that his knee was injured before the fight. More on that later in this book.

That set the stage for Broner–Garcia.

The fight began with Garcia trying to close the gap between them and Broner trying to widen it. Or phrased differently, Mikey was seeking to engage in violent confrontation while Adrien was seeking to avoid it.

Broner likes to lay back and counter until he has worn his opponent down. But countering like that is almost impossible to do against Garcia.

Timing can beat speed. Garcia dominated the first eight rounds fighting a disciplined fight, mixing punches to the head and body, and surgically carving Broner apart. Adrien shook his head so often to indicate Mikey's punches weren't hurting him that, after a while, one could be forgiven for fearing he'd get whiplash.

Broner's best chance to win was to engage. It was clear that he couldn't out-box Garcia. And it seemed that he was more likely to hurt Mikey with one punch than the other way around.

In round nine, Adrien began coming forward and enjoyed his best three minutes of the fight as a consequence of several clean hooks to the head and body and two more that looked low. But he never went for broke, and Garcia reestablished control.

Garcia was technically brilliant and gave Broner a boxing lesson, outlanding him by a 244-to-125 margin over the course of twelve rounds. The judges scored the bout 117–111, 116–112, 116–112 in Mikey's favor. Very few other people in the arena thought it was that close.

After the fight, Garcia declared, "This is definitely one of my best performances ever. I was the superior fighter tonight."

He was right on both counts.

Broner talked the talk. Garcia walked the walk. There's a difference.

*As 2017 progressed, Top Rank had two of the best pound-for-pound fighters in the world on its roster. But it was struggling with the issue of how to showcase and monetize them.*

# Top Rank—ESPN—Lomachenko —Crawford

Three years ago, the eyes of boxing were on Premier Boxing Champions and what Al Haymon was (or wasn't) going to do. Now the talk is about Top Rank and ESPN.

On August 9, 2017, The Walt Disney Company unveiled plans for an ESPN over-the-top streaming subscription video service that will debut in 2018. In 2011, ESPN was in one hundred million homes. Since then, that number has dropped to 87 million as more and more customers cut the cable cord. Each lost home represents the loss of eight dollars a month in cable fees paid to ESPN by local cable companies. Thirteen million homes times eight dollars a home comes to more than $100 million a month in lost revenue for ESPN. Fewer homes also translates into fewer viewers, which means the amount ESPN can charge for commercials drops.

Meanwhile, the July 1, 2017, bout between Manny Pacquiao and Jeff Horn marked the start of a new undertaking by Top Rank (Pacquiao's promoter) and ESPN. No formal announcement of long-term plans has been made. But reports suggest that Top Rank fights will be televised in the United States exclusively on ESPN, ABC, and the new ESPN streaming video channel.

ESPN has televised two Top Rank cards since Pacquiao-Horn.

First, an August 5, 2017, telecast featured WBO 130-pound champion Vasyl Lomachenko (8–1, 6 KOs) vs. Miguel Marriaga (25–2, 21 KOs) with Raymundo Beltran (33–7, 21 KOs) vs. Bryan Vasquez (35–2, 19 KOs) in the opening bout.

The telecast began more than an hour late because ESPN chose to stay with the NFL Hall of Fame induction ceremony (which ran long) and ESPN2 was occupied with what the network considered more important programming. Finally, Beltran-Vasquez began on ESPN2. Lomachenko-Marriaga was aired on ESPN after the Hall of Fame ceremony ended.

Beltran won a majority decision over Vasquez.

Lomachenko completely outclassed Marriaga, outlanding him 186 to 45 en route to a corner stoppage after seven rounds. That was predictable, since Vasyl is high on most pound-for-pound lists and ranked number one at 130 pounds by ESPN, while Miguel wasn't ranked anywhere in any weight division by ESPN.

On August 19, Top Rank returned to ESPN with a three-bout offering headlined by WBC-WBO 140-pound champion Terence Crawford (31–0, 22 KOs) vs. WBA-IBF 140-pound champion Julius Indongo (22–0, 11 KOs).

In the telecast's opening bout, 2016 Olympic silver-medalist Shakur Stevenson (2–0) boxed rings around David Paz (4–3–1) but showed a troubling lack of power. In Paz's most recent outing, he'd lost to an opponent with 3 wins in 13 fights.

Next, Oleksandr Gvozdyk (13–0, 11 KOs) knocked out 30-to-1 underdog Craig Baker in the sixth round. Gvozdyk won a bronze medal for Ukraine at the 2012 Olympics and is a world-class fighter. Baker entered the ring with a manufactured 17–1 record. He'd stepped up in class once before, against Edwin Rodriguez in 2015, and been knocked out in the third round.

That set the stage for Crawford-Indongo.

The twenty-nine-year-old Crawford is near the top of most pound-for-pound lists, and deservedly so. He's an accurate puncher with power and speed, who looks better and better with each fight.

Indongo, age thirty-four, had won belts in his last two fights, journeying both times to his opponent's hometown: Glasgow for Ricky Burns (WBA) and Moscow for Eduard Troyanovsky (IBF). All of Indongo's other fights had been in Africa.

Top Rank wanted to put Crawford-Indongo in Terence's hometown of Omaha. But Lady Gaga had booked the CenturyLink Center for August 19, so the fight wound up in Lincoln, Nebraska.

Without the belts, Indongo would have been a ho-hum opponent. Depending on where one looked, Crawford was listed as a better than 10-to-1 favorite. But the fact that all four major sanctioning body titles were on the line gave the bout a certain cachet.

Top Rank president Todd duBoef did a nice job of hyping the fight.

"This is not an outlier," duBoef said of Indongo at the final pre-fight press conference."This is what happens with boxing. This is no different than Azumah Nelson coming over on ten days' notice and getting in the ring and making a name for himself in the United States. People can change the tide very quickly in the sport of boxing. Indongo is a very talented fighter who has worked figuring out how to master a trade. The door of opportunity opens and he steps through it, and that is the story of boxing. People take advantage of those opportunities, and suddenly a diamond in the rough is discovered."

Indongo built on that theme, telling the media,"I have been in boxing for a long time and not many people know me. I believe this is the time for me to show the world that a boxer from Africa, from Namibia, can beat a guy fighting in his home in front of his people. I know that my country and Africa is on my shoulders. I will travel the world with the four titles. I will take them back to Africa, to my country. I am going to be very very happy."

But fighting Crawford is starting to look like running a race against a gazelle or getting into a one-on-one eating competition with a hungry lion. It didn't take long for Indongo's dream to turn into a nightmare. Crawford dropped Julius in round two and closed the show with a highlight-reel straight left to the body at 1:38 of round three.

"He hit me hard to my body," Indongo said afterward. "I couldn't breathe, it hurt so bad.When he hit me that hard, not only did it hurt, it took my mind away. I couldn't think."

So . . . Where do Top Rank, ESPN, Lomachenko, and Crawford go from here?

The three-hour Pacquiao-Horn telecast averaged 3.1 million viewers on ESPN and ESPN Deportes (including streaming). It was ESPN's highest-rated boxing telecast since 1995 and the highest-rated boxing telecast on cable television since 2006.The main event averaged 3.9 million viewers and peaked at 4.4 million.Those are good numbers.

By contrast, Lomachenko-Marriaga drew an average audience of 728,000 viewers.That's 104,000 fewer people than watched Lomachenko one fight earlier against Jason Sosa on HBO. In that regard, keep in mind, ESPN is available in approximately 87,000,000 homes while HBO is available in only 32,000,000.

Crawford-Indongo attracted an average of 1,200,000 viewers. That's slightly more than Crawford's most recent fight on HBO, a less attractive matchup against Felix Diaz.

As for future opponents; when asked who he might fight next, Lomachenko responded, "For me, it doesn't matter. My job is to work my best boxing in the ring. I will fight anybody. I want to fight, and I want to unify titles."

Unlike many boxers, Lomachenko seems to mean it when he says he'll fight anyone. That puts the ball squarely in Top Rank's court.

As for Crawford, after beating Indongo, Terence declared, "Belts matter. I'm the only one who can be labeled a champion at 140, and that's a big deal to me."

But given the state of world-sanctioning-body politics, it's unlikely that the 140-pound titles will be unified for long unless it's through the mechanism of "super" world championships and other nonsense. Also, the 140-pound division is weak at the moment. However, seven pounds to the north, the welterweight division is loaded. The hope is that Top Rank will find a way to match Crawford against one of boxing's elite 147-pound fighters instead of putting him in one or more meaningless mandatory title defenses.

And by the way, Jeff Horn is not an "elite" 147-pound fighter.

Top Rank has two legitimate candidates for the pound-for-pound throne in Lomachenko and Crawford. The challenge now is to put them in fights that matter. Over the decades, Bob Arum has developed some great fighters and given the world some great fights. But there are times when, fortified by a network output deal, he has presented fans with mismatches and predictably boring contests. Boxing fans aren't stupid. They know the difference.

The ESPN-Top Rank alliance represents another golden opportunity for boxing. Time will tell whether Top Rank delivers the goods or falls short of the mark.

*A prizefight is a violent chess match that can end at any time.*

# The Barclays Buzz

The first fight card at Barclays Center was contested on October 20, 2012, and featured four world-title fights: Danny Garcia vs. Erik Morales, Paulie Malignaggi vs. Pablo Cesar Cano, Devon Alexander vs. Randall Bailey, and Hassan N'Dam N'Jikam vs. Peter Quillin. For good measure, Danny Jacobs, Luis Collazo, Dmitriy Salita, Eddie Gomez, and Boyd Melson were on the undercard.

Barclays is still waiting for The Big One, the megafight that will raise its profile in boxing to a new level. But it has established a pretty good boxing franchise with a nice buzz on fight nights.

October 14, 2017, marked the twenty-fifth fight card at Barclays Center over the past five years. Most of these cards have involved Al Haymon fighters with DiBella Entertainment as the promoter of record. That was the formula on Saturday night, when three 154-pound titles were at stake.

The first of these bouts was Jarrett Hurd (20–0, 14 KOs) vs. Austin Trout (30–3, 17 KOs).

Hurd, age twenty-seven, seized the vacant IBF 154-pound throne when he knocked out Tony Harrison earlier this year.

Trout, now thirty-two, held the WBA 154-pound title several years ago but lost it by decision to Canelo Alvarez. His other defeats, also by decision, were to Erislandy Lara and Jermall Charlo (Jermell's twin brother). His signature victory was a 2012 decision over Miguel Cotto.

"Everybody knows that he's the undefeated champion for reasons," Trout said of Hurd during an October 4 media conference call. "So you can't smack on a kid like that. But we see holes in his game. It's just going to end up being me and him and we have to punch through those holes."

"I've accomplished something that all fighters dream of and that's to win a world title," Hurd responded. "And I don't feel like this is where my legacy ends. This is only the beginning."

Hurd was a 5-to-2 betting favorite.

Erislandy Lara (24–2, 14 KOs) vs. Terrell Gausha (20–0, 9 KOs) was also on the card.

Lara, age thirty-four, is a former Cuban amateur star who worked his way through a series of "interim" titles and vacancies to claim the WBA 154-pound belt. There are some recognizable names on the victory side of his ring ledger, but no big ones. His losses were by decision to Paul Williams and Canelo Alvarez.

Gausha, age thirty, has been carefully matched throughout his career and had never faced a quality opponent as a pro. Lara was a 15-to-1 betting favorite.

Jermell Charlo (29–0, 14 KOs) vs. Erickson Lubin (18–0, 13 KOs) was the third title bout on the card and the one that intrigued fight fans the most.

Like Hurd and Lara, the twenty-seven-year-old Charlo became a 154-pound belt holder by virtue of a vacancy when he defeated John Jackson for the WBC's empty chair. Lubin, twenty-two, is considered a prospect with a bright future in boxing. The question was whether the future is now.

Lubin was a mandatory challenger, which didn't sit well with Charlo.

"I didn't win my first world title until I was twenty-six," Jermell told the media. "So how the fuck is this kid getting an opportunity like this? It's been rough on my mind. I'm thinking, 'Hey, why is this motherfucker fighting me?' I feel like it should have been more of a tournament mode to get a chance to fight me. If you don't have a name, you shouldn't even be in the ring with me."

Lubin responded in kind:

- He's a fool if he thinks I'm not ready for this type of fight. I'm better than anyone he has ever faced, and I'm gonna show that October 14th. This is the fight that's gonna make me into a superstar and this is the fight that's gonna break him. Some might say I haven't been challenged yet, or some might say I've fought nobodies. But realistically, I just make them look like nobodies. I wouldn't be surprised if I do the same on October 14th."
- "I know I'm ready, I came into this game and I fought no opponents with a losing record. Everybody I fought had a positive record. Some undefeated guys, some guys who had just one loss. I won

pretty much every amateur tournament out there. I've been undefeated since I was thirteen years old. I'm glad they put this opponent in front of me, where I can showcase my talent."

- "I'm ready to change the lives of the people around me. I'm ready to change the lives of my parents. My son was born in July, and I just want to make sure he's set for life; for school, for college, for everything. I'll get a house at just twenty-two years old, get the cars that I always wanted that I never had. I'm definitely gonna keep my circle tight and keep the people I've got around me. But it's gonna change my life for good."
- "It's not about what he does. It's about what I do. I believe in my skill. I'm very talented. I think I'm a star already. Everybody loves me."

For all intents and purposes, Charlo-Lubin was the main event.

"That's how I look at it," Lou DiBella said. "And that's how I'm promoting it. Showtime dictates the order of the fights it televises, so Lara-Gausha will go on last. But Charlo-Lubin is the fight that everybody wants to see."

Charlo was a slight 6-to-5 betting favorite.

At the final pre-fight press conference, five of the six title-bout contestants thanked God and Al Haymon. Erislandy Lara just thanked Haymon.

All six fighters made weight.

The announced attendance on fight night was 7,643.

As is often the case at Barclays Center fight cards, the smell of weed wafted through the arena. That gave rise to the suggestion that the Barclays buzz is, at least in part, about being buzzed.

Hurd-Trout was a very good fight. This writer's notes, taken as the action unfolded, read as follows:

Round 1: Hurd the aggressor. Trout counterpunching. although he's more effective when he gets off first.

Round 2: Trout taking Hurd to school.

Round 3: Spirited action. Both guys getting hit. Trout seems to be slowing down a bit.

Round 4: Constant pressure from Hurd. But he doesn't move his head enough. Too often, after Hurd punches, he waits for a receipt. So Trout hits him.

Round 5: Hurd keeps coming forward, trying to break Trout. He's forcing the fight and willing to trade at all times.

Round 6: Trout's punches have lost their snap. Hurd forcing a slugfest. Both guys landing cleanly, but Trout seems to be getting hurt more.

Round 7: Hurd badly cut over the left eye by an accidental head butt, but still teeing off. A good action fight. More and more, Trout is throwing stay-away-from-me punches. Hurd is throwing to do damage.

Round 8: Trout is game but he's getting clobbered. Hurd is stronger and hits harder. When Trout lands, Hurd just keeps coming forward.

Round 9: Hurd comes out for every round applying non-stop pressure and looking to exchange. Trout has very little left. His right eye is closing. This is the worst beating he has taken as a pro.

Round 10: A methodical beatdown. Hurd is showing no respect for Trout's power, maybe because there's none left. Hurd shaking Trout with power punches. [Referee] Eddie Claudio should think about stopping the fight.

In the corner after round ten, Louie Burke (Trout's trainer) appropriately told ring doctor Nitin Sethi that he wanted the bout stopped.

Charlo-Lubin was up next. Most of the first round was a feeling-out process with little action. Two minutes into the stanza, Lubin ducked low and Charlo stung him with a chopping right hand. Thirty seconds later . . . BOOM!

Lubin ducked low again, and Charlo fired a twisting right uppercut that landed flush on Erickson's cheek. Lubin went down hard, his arms and legs unnaturally twisted, shaking spasmodically. At the count of six, referee Harvey Dock stopped the fight. Astonishingly, Erickson somehow made it to his feet before ten seconds elapsed. But the bout was already over.

"I'm fine," Lubin said afterward. "He caught me with a blind shot. I didn't see it coming. It's boxing; it happens."

The crowd thinned out after Charlo-Lubin and continued to do so as the final fight of the evening—Lara vs. Gausha—unfolded. Lara boxed his way to an uninspiring 117–110, 117–110, 116–111 win in what was essentially a walk-out bout.

As for what happens next, Charlo was adamant in demanding, "Give me another title. I want Hurd. Hurd just won. Give me Hurd."

Charlo–Hurd would be an interesting fight. I'll take Charlo.

*Deontay Wilder's career has been aided enormously by creative matchmaking. But as 2017 neared an end, even Wilder's critics conceded that he had become a dangerous fighter.*

# Deontay Wilder vs. Bermane Stiverne: No Surprises

WBC heavyweight champion Deontay Wilder (now 39–0, 38 KOs) has one-punch knockout power. How much power is unclear since, for the most part, he has steered clear of opponents with sturdy chins. And he has gravitated away from big punchers because his own chin is suspect.

Wilder's ring skills have also come under attack.

"I fight with my heart," Deontay has said in response to the criticism. "I fight with my will. Forget skills. Skills ain't got me nowhere in life."

In an effort to silence his critics, Wilder signed to fight Luis Ortiz (27–0, 23 KOs) on November 4, 2017, at Barclays Center in a bout to be televised by Showtime. Ortiz a thirty-eight-year-old Cuban expatriate now living in Florida, looked his best in demolishing Bryant Jennings on a seventh-round knockout two years ago. But he hadn't done much since then, and the prevailing view was that age might be catching up with him.

There was the usual smack-talking after the fight was announced.

"Somebody better endorse the bottom of Ortiz's shoes," Wilder advised the media, "because he'll be on his back, staring at the ceiling, and they'll be seeing both of them at the end of this fight."

And of course, the usual hyperbole.

"Deontay Wilder versus Luis Ortiz is the best heavyweight championship fight that was makable this year," promoter Lou DiBella proclaimed.

That left open the question of where Anthony Joshua vs. Wladimir Klitschko (which drew ninety thousand fans and was televised by two American premium cable networks) ranked in DiBella's thought processes. But the matter became moot when Ortiz tested positive for chlorothiazide and hydrochlorothiazide (both of which are banned under the World Anti-Doping Agency code) and Wilder–Ortiz was cancelled.

Then, in place of Ortiz, the promotion substituted Bermane Stiverne.

Fighting largely against the usual suspects, Stiverne had compiled a 25-and-2 (21 KOs) record. He won the WBC heavyweight belt by knocking out a badly faded Chris Arreola in 2014 and lost it to Wilder in his next outing. His other loss was a knockout defeat at the hands of a 11-and-15 fighter named Demetrice King. Stiverne is thirty-nine years old. He'd fought only once since losing to Wilder (a controversial win by decision over Derric Rossy two years ago). Somehow, that qualified him to be the mandatory challenger for Wilder's WBC title.

WBC president Mauricio Sulaiman told reporters at the final pre-fight press conference, "Whoever thinks this is not the best championship fight that can be made in the heavyweight division is wrong."

But in truth, Wilder–Stiverne was a fight that no one except Team Stiverne and the WBC had much interest in seeing.

Wilder has voiced resentment in recent months over the fact that the American public hasn't gotten behind him the way that the Brits support Anthony Joshua and other nations supported Vitali and Wladimir Klitschko.

"I'm the best, hardest-punching, most feared heavyweight in the world," Deontay declared at an October 14 media sit-down. "I don't have to put punches together. It's one punch, goodnight. Tell your favorite fighter to come see me."

Wilder also referenced the hardships of boxing, observing, "A lot of people say what I can't do, but they're not me. They don't train. They don't bust their ass every day in the gym, lay in the bed and you can't really get a good position to sleep because your body is so sore."

The promotion sought to infuse drama into Wilder–Stiverne by noting that Stiverne was the only opponent who'd gone the distance with Wilder. Bermane, in turn, said he'd lost to Deontay the first time around because of unspecified health issues. That led Wilder to reply, "People don't want to hear excuses. They want a winner and they want a loser. The facts are the facts. The person that loses, nobody wants to hear the reason. They just want to hear you say, 'Hey, I admit it. I lost, but I'm gonna try my best the next time.' People respect that. People don't like a loser that contradicts themselves. One minute, you're good, you're healthy. You're talking so confidently. And then, when the time to fight happens, all of a sudden something just so dramatically happens in the ring."

Then Stiverne upped the ante, telling the media at the final pre-fight press conference, "One thing that really caught my attention—and I don't really pay attention to social media and all that stuff—is that he said that he fears for my life." At that point, Stiverne turned to face Wilder. "You fear for my life, man? You fear for my life? I don't fear for your life because I'm a killer! If that's what it takes for me to take that title, that's what I'm gonna do. And I'm gonna walk away with a smile on my face."

"I don't have to say what I'm gonna do because I'm gonna show him," Wilder responded. "It will be a show-and-tell on Saturday night. Like my daddy said; I'll whup you because I love you."

Most of the excitement in the pre-fight promotion was supplied by Don King.

King sightings in boxing are rare these days. But DK has a promotional interest in Stiverne (and also in Eric Molina, who'd been brought in as an opponent for Dominic Breazeale in an undercard fight).

King turned eighty-six in August 2017. His hair is no longer thick enough to rise dramatically toward the heavens. His frame is a bit stooped and he walks more slowly than before. The custom-made "Only in America" jacket he wears is fraying and discolored at the cuffs. But he remains a man of remarkable energy and vitality. His booming voice and high-pitched laugh still pierce the air. He commands attention wherever he goes. King might not look seventy anymore, but he doesn't look eighty-six either.

"God has sent Bermane Stiverne to do His work," King proclaimed at the final pre-fight press conference. "Bermane is going to do what Donald Trump did and triumph against all odds."

The announced attendance on fight night was 10,924, but that included a lot of giveaway tickets.

Once upon a time, King would have had both fighters in the main event and controlled the undercard as well. Now he was on site with a 15-to-1 underdog (Stiverne) and a 7-to-2 long-shot (Molina).

Breazeale stopped Molina in eight rounds.

In the first Showtime bout of the evening, Sergey Lipinets (12–0, 10 KOs) and Akihiro Kondo (29–6–1, 16 KOs) battled for an IBF 140-pound belt of questionable provenance. Three of Kondo's opponents during the past two years had records of 0–0, 0–1, and 0–0 at the time he fought them. Lipinets decisioned Kondo by a 118–110, 117–111, 117–111 margin in a fight that was closer than the scorecards indicated.

Next, Shawn Porter (27–2–1, 17 KOs) took on Adrian Granados (18–5–2, 12 KOs).

Porter came out on the short end of razor-thin decisions in his two biggest fights (against Kell Brook and Keith Thurman) and had scored victories over past-their-prime former champions Andre Berto, Paulie Malignaggi, Devon Alexander, and Adrien Broner. He's a volume puncher whose mauling, brawling style and chin make him a tough out for anyone. If Shawn shortened his punches and placed them more judiciously, they'd be more effective.

Granados was an opponent for young fighters on the rise until 2015, when he upset an applecart by knocking out Amir Imam. That got him a fight against Adrien Broner in which he acquitted himself well but lost. Now he's an opponent again.

This was a stay-busy fight for Porter while he waits for Keith Thurman to heal, have a comeback bout against a soft opponent, stay healthy, and then (maybe) fight Shawn again.

As expected, Porter mauled and brawled for most of the fight. Granados fought with heart and a measure of skill. But Adrian's defense is porous, and he had nothing to keep Shawn off. Porter dominated the first ten rounds before an injured left hand led to his avoiding contact in the final two stanzas. That cut his margin of victory to 117–111, 117–111, 117–111.

Then it was time for Wilder–Stiverne.

Bermane was never svelte. He turned pro twelve years ago at 233 pounds and has entered the ring as high as 258. For his most recent outing against Derric Rossy, he weighed in at 254. Facing Wilder two years ago, he tipped the scales at 239.

For Wilder redux, Stiverne weighed in at an unsculpted 254¾ pounds. One could imagine Don King arguing, "Bermane is in shape. Round is a shape."

Wilder weighed in at 220¾.

This time against Stiverne, Wilder came out behind an aggressive jab and Bermane did nothing. More than a minute passed before the challenger threw his first punch, a meaningless stay-away-from-me jab that fell far short of the mark. That was followed twenty seconds later by a tentative jab in the direction of Wilder's midsection.

Just past the two-minute mark of round one, Wilder jabbed and followed with an uncharacteristically (for him) straight right that landed smack in the center of Stiverne's face. Bermane went down hard and rose unsteadily. Every punch Deontay threw after that seemed to come in as wide an arc as was anatomically possible. But they landed often enough and hard enough to do damage. Referee Arthur Mercante halted the carnage after the third knockdown at 2:59 of the round. CompuBox credited Stiverne with throwing four punches. He landed none.

★ ★ ★

Boxing is very much a "what have you done for me lately" business. That said, something that happened at Barclays Center on Saturday night troubled me.

Seanie Monaghan is an honest, hardworking fighter and a thoroughly decent man who has been a fixture on the New York boxing scene for years. In his last fight, he suffered the first loss of his ring career, a knockout defeat at the hands of Marcus Browne.

Monaghan began his comeback on Saturday night in an eight-round bout against Evert Bravo. One day prior to the fight, DiBella Entertainment (the promoter of record) advised Team Monaghan that Seanie's fight might be a "swing" bout. Monaghan and company weren't happy about it but were told they had no choice.

DiBella Entertainment didn't control the bout order. That was decided by Showtime in conjunction with Al Haymon. Showtime didn't care when Monaghan–Bravo was contested because it wasn't a TV fight. The decision was made by Haymon, who had a financial stake in most of the other undercard fighters, but not in Monaghan.

P. J. Kavanagh (Monaghan's manager) told this writer on the morning after Seanie's fight, "We got to Barclays when they told us to, which was six o'clock. At first, we were on the list as the sixth fight of the night. Then they told us that we weren't going on until after the Wilder fight.

Seanie took it like a professional and didn't complain. All he said was, 'Let's stay positive.'"

Monaghan didn't glove up and start warming up until Wilder began his ring walk. Then, after the Wilder fight, the powers that be put another swing bout on before Monaghan–Bravo.

Here, one might add that, unlike most undercard fighters, Seanie is a good ticket seller. His team sold hundreds of tickets in bars and other outlets for his comeback fight. And that's not counting the tickets his fans bought at the box office and online.

The bell for round one of Monaghan–Bravo didn't ring until 12:22 a.m. The fight went the full eight rounds and ended at 12:53, with Seanie winning a unanimous decision.

"It's the hand we were dealt and we played it," Kavanagh says. "And Lou DiBella has been good to us. But we've gotten a lot of complaints from fans who felt that they and Seanie were disrespected."

Seanie Monaghan has earned the right to be more than a walk-out bout and to know in advance what time he's fighting. He and his fans deserved better.

*Thomas Edison once observed, "Opportunity is missed by most people because it is dressed in overalls and looks like work."*

# "Big Baby" Takes a Baby Step Forward

Boxing's heavyweight division is wide open. Anthony Joshua and Deontay Wilder—two exciting but flawed fighters—are at the top. After that, it's anyone's ballgame. Twenty-nine-year-old Jarrell "Big Baby" Miller (now 20–0–1, 18 KOs) wants the ball.

Miller has a massive torso, huge arms, and thighs that conjure up images of giant oak trees. Fast-twitch muscle fiber isn't his thing. Think clubbing, heavy-handed blows.

Miller projects BIG. Big personality, big mouth, 6-feet-4-inches, close to 300 pounds of big. In 2015, he was fighting at 255 pounds. In July of this year, he weighed in at 299 to fight Gerald Washington.

Jarrell's frame hasn't filled out as much as it's overflowing. He's built more like an NFL offensive lineman than what we're accustomed to seeing in an elite fighter. But viewers don't walk away from the TV screen and go to the kitchen to make a sandwich when Miller is fighting. He has charisma. He hits and gets hit. He's making noise in boxing, not just with his mouth but with his fists.

On November 11, 2017, Miller fought Mariusz Wach (33–2, 17 KOs) in the middle bout of an HBO tripleheader at Nassau Veterans Memorial Coliseum. Eddie Hearn, who promotes Joshua and has built Matchroom Boxing into the most powerful promotional company in the United Kingdom, was the man in charge. Hearn is planning to open an office in New York in 2018. This was a trial run of sorts.

Danny Jacobs (32–2, 29 KOs) vs. Luis Arias (18–0, 9 KOs) was styled as the main event. At the start of this year, Jacobs's ring career was defined by two fights: a July 31, 2010, knockout defeat at the hands of Dmitry Pirog, and a first-round KO of Peter Quillin on December 5, 2015.

Then, at Madison Square Garden on March 18, 2017, Jacobs came out on the short end of a razor-thin decision in a middleweight-championship bout against Gennady Golovkin. One should be wary of over-evaluating fighters based on a loss. But in losing to Golovkin, Jacobs forced a reevaluation of his skills and chin, which had been questioned since the loss to Pirog.

Arias, an 8-to-1 underdog, worked hard in the pre-fight promotion to raise his profile above that of a fungible opponent.

"I'm the young kid from Wisconsin that nobody knows," Arias told the media. "Everyone thinks I'm coming in to lose. But if you look at his record, there's nobody there that he beat. You can build a fighter up and make him look a lot better than he really is. You keep him away from punchers. You keep him away from boxers. You keep him away from legitimate threats. The tough fights that I see, he lost. This is a mixture of me being underrated and him being overrated. Daniel Jacobs is going to be in a dogfight, a very hard fight. I'm going to rough him up and be in his face all night. I want a war."

"It's kind of hard to listen to him," Jacobs said in response. "He can talk a good one. But at the end of the day, it's about what you do inside the ring. People aren't praising me for going twelve rounds with Gennady Golovkin. Let's not get that confused. If they're praising me, they're praising me for the fact that they believe that I won the fight. Talk outside the ring is good for promotion. But then the fight starts and there are levels to this game. I'm on a much higher level than Arias."

Meanwhile, Miller–Wach shaped up as the most intriguing fight of the night.

Miller has lived for most of his life in Brooklyn, which has led him to proclaim, "Brooklyn has a pedigree, the homestead for some of the world's greatest heavyweight boxers. You've seen Riddick Bowe. You've seen Mike Tyson. You've seen Shannon Briggs. I'm next in line."

Jarrell also advised the media, "I'm the Big Baby, but I'm going to give Wach the pacifier and put him in the crib. There is nothing like Big Baby. No one throws as many punches. And I knock people out. Trust me, I'm not worried about him. I'll make it easy on him and get him out quick. Wach is going to be just another guy that I crush."

That said, Wach was a good measuring stick for Miller. Mariusz's only losses were a decision defeat at the hands of Wladimir Klitschko in 2012 and a stoppage on cuts against Alexander Povetkin in 2015. He's not a big puncher, but he's big (268 pounds), tall (six feet, seven inches), and durable.

"This is a big night in Jarrell Miller's career," Eddie Hearn said two days before the fight. "If he beats Wach, he can be a world-class heavyweight. If he destroys Wach, he can be an elite heavyweight. We'll see what's real and not real on Saturday night."

Dressed in black, Jarrell Miller entered his dressing room at Nassau Coliseum on fight night at 7:50 p.m.

The room was small and irregularly shaped, fifteen feet wide and a bit longer. It looked more like a renovated studio apartment than a fighter's dressing room.

Four cushioned, folding metal chairs were lined up on a finely sanded hardwood floor. Two Formica-topped credenzas would serve as seats for most of Team Miller, including Jarrell, in the hours ahead. There was a small sink, a refrigerator, a faux fireplace, and a large TV monitor. Several framed lithographs graced the light-gray walls. A large mirror was mounted above a faux-marble vanity table at the far end of the room.

Jarrell posed for smartphone photos with several team members, sat on top of one of the credenzas, and opened a bottle of Muscle Milk protein shake.

Then he began texting.

The HBO telecast was scheduled to start at ten o'clock with Cletus Seldin vs. Roberto Ortiz in the opening bout. Miller had been told to be ready to walk by 10:15 in the event of a quick knockout.

A New York State Athletic Commission inspector led Jarrell from the dressing room to a medical tent for his final pre-fight physical. While the fighter was gone, rap artist Leonard Grant (better known as Uncle Murda) entered and took a seat. Later, he would lead Jarrell to the ring.

Jarrell returned, sat on the credenza, and resumed texting.

Trainer Harry Keitt left to watch Wach's hands being wrapped.

There was quiet conversation. Music played intermittently depending on Jarrell's mood of the moment. Occasionally, he sipped from a bottle of water. Just before nine o'clock, he lay down on the credenza, using his leather groin protector as a pillow, and closed his eyes.

Keitt returned.

Jarrell rose from the credenza and sat on one of the folding chairs. Assistant trainer Aureliano Sosa began taping his hands, right hand first. Ten minutes later, the task was done. Jarrell lay down on the credenza again, alternately texting and relaxing with his eyes closed.

David Fields, who would referee Miller–Wach, came in to give Jarrell his pre-fight instructions.

Eddie Hearn and Dmitriy Salita (Miller's co-promoter) paid their respects.

At 9:40 p.m., Jarrell rose from the credenza like a man getting out of bed, took off his black track suit, and put on his boxing shoes.

Curtis Jackson (a.k.a 50 Cent) entered. Jarrell jumped to his feet and embraced the rap impresario. Then, as long as he was on his feet, he shadow-boxed for thirty seconds before sitting down on the credenza again. Shortly before ten o'clock, he stretched briefly on the floor before putting on his groin protector and trunks.

Harry Keitt gloved him up.

Jarrell hit the pads briefly with Aureliano Sosa, shouting as he punched.

"Nobody beats me!"

"No chance!" the chorus responded.

"Nobody beats me!"

"No chance!"

"What time is it?" Keitt demanded.

"Miller time!"

"What time is it?"

"Miller time."

Seldin–Ortiz ended on a third-round stoppage.

Jarrell's friend and publicist Alvina Alston led the group in prayer.

Miller put on his robe, walked the length of the room, and examined his image in the mirror above the vanity table.

It was time.

The fight itself was a disappointment for Miller's partisans. Jarrell had weighed in at 283.4 pounds, which led them to believe that he was in better shape than he'd been for his knockout victory over Gerald Washington fifteen weeks earlier. But he didn't look like an elite heavyweight.

Wach gave away his advantage in reach and height, allowing Miller to fight at close quarters for most of the bout. Jarrell went to the body throughout, which is a commitment he usually makes. But Mariusz takes a good punch. And Jarrell has clubbing power, not one-punch knockout power, which enabled Wach to stay on his feet.

As in past fights, Miller's defense was flawed. But he showed a good chin. And when Wach landed, Mariusz didn't have the power to exploit Jarrell's defensive limitations.

Midway through the bout, Wach injured his right hand. From round seven on, he was a one-handed fighter. One minute into round nine, New York State Athletic Commission chief medical officer Nitin Sethi appropriately intervened to stop the fight. Miller outlanded Wach in every round en route to a 204-to-95 CompuBox advantage.

After the bout, much of the attention in Jarrell's dressing room was focused on the TV monitor that showed Danny Jacobs doing battle against Luis Arias. On paper, Arias hadn't posed much of a threat to Jacobs. In the ring, he didn't either. Jacobs cruised to a unanimous-decision triumph.

"I expected more from Jarrell tonight," Harry Keitt said. "But he did what he had to do."

Miller's self-evaluation was similar.

"Nobody looks good against Wach," Jarrell offered. "And I didn't either. I was a little sloppy in there; I know that. I never really found my rhythm. And I hurt my elbow in training camp, so it was hard for me to snap my jab. It is what it is. A win is a win."

As for what comes next; it's expected that Miller and Jacobs will fight again on an HBO card in April 2018, most likely at Barclays Center. After that, who knows?

How will Jarrell do when he steps up to the next level of opposition? There are things he has to improve upon, and it's no secret what they are.

Miller is slow. There's not much he can do about that. He can be outslicked. As he moves up in class, his success will depend to a great degree on his ability to take punches: big ones and the accumulation of small blows. But he has to do a better job of protecting his chin.

Also, Jarrell doesn't get maximum leverage on his punches or put his weight into them as effectively as he might. That's a legacy from his years in kickboxing, which demands that combatants balance their weight differently than conventional boxers do. And while Miller is a huge, strong guy, he's not physical enough on the inside. When he gets inside, he should be leaning on opponents, shaking them, tugging at them, wearing them down.

Some boxing insiders have compared Jarrell to Riddick Bowe, which would be a compliment were it not followed by, "He's the laziest fighter with talent I've seen since Bowe."

Miller weighed in fifteen pounds lighter for Wach than he had for his previous fight. And he made a point of telling the media, "I haven't had a cheeseburger in two months." But that didn't mean he was in better shape.

There's a level of preparation that involves sophisticated nutritional monitoring and grueling, carefully calibrated physical conditioning that can transform a fighter's body into a more effective delivery system for the skills he has. Jarrell has to take himself there.

In that regard, it wasn't reassuring that, in the dressing room after the Wach fight, Miller declared, "I felt I was stronger and performed better when I was heavier."

There's a line that separates confidence from complacency and foolishness.

And finally, there's a nagging issue that dates back to 2014, when Miller was suspended by the California State Athletic Commission after testing positive for methylhexanamine following a Glory 17 kickboxing event. More recently, he was removed from the WBC rankings because of his refusal to participate in the WBC's Clean Boxing Program supervised by the Voluntary Anti-Doping Agency. The WBA now appears poised to institute its own drug-testing program with VADA, which could endanger Jarrell's top-ten ranking with that organization.

At the kick-off press conference for Miller–Wach, Jarrell told the assembled media, "If you know anything about the streets and boxing, you know it takes a long time to get to where I'm at."

It would be foolish for Jarrell to blow things now by giving less than his best effort when he's so close to success.

*Promoter Kathy Duva is sometimes referred to as "the first lady of boxing." But she gets competition from Rosie Perez.*

# Rosie Perez on Muhammad Ali

January 17, 2017, marked the seventy-fifth anniversary of Muhammad Ali's birth. To celebrate the occasion, Epix televised an original documentary entitled *Muhammad Ali: A Life.*

I was involved in the making of the documentary, both as a talking head and on the production end. One of the pleasures that came with the job was working with Rosie Perez.

Perez is best known as an actress whose breakthrough films were *Do the Right Thing* and *White Men Can't Jump*. She has been nominated for an Academy Award and three Emmys. She's also a community activist, a choreographer, and a serious boxing fan.

Rosie participated in *Muhammad Ali: A Life* and is on camera throughout the documentary. Some of what she had to say is in the final version; some isn't. The quotes below are from Rosie and reflect her personal experiences as well as some of her insights regarding Ali and boxing.

★ ★ ★

"I was subjected to a lot of beatdowns. I grew up rough. I knew what it felt like at seven years old to get hit in the face."

"When I started in my career, people were like, 'Why do you have to talk with such a strong accent?' And I go, 'Because I have a strong accent.' A former agent said to me, 'You know, you could pass.' I go, 'For what?' I knew exactly what she was trying to say. She goes, 'Tone down the accent.' I told her, 'It's beyond insulting that you said that to me. You're fired.' Everyone thought I was crazy because nobody was trying to represent me, and that person represented me, and I was very thankful for it. But I wasn't going to bow down for it. I said, 'No, I will not.' Even when I got nominated for an Oscar, it was still told to me over and over and over again. And I didn't have the personality that Ali had that could make light of everything. I was very, very angry. My accent has lessened since then because I stepped off the blocks of Bushwick and I've gone out into the world. But it was organic; it wasn't premeditated. It wasn't something I did for my career. And when Ali said, 'I will not apologize for who I am,' it had a huge effect on me. That set the path to give me the encouragement to say, 'You know what? I can do it differently.'"

On Ali's womanizing: "It's not right for me to judge. I cheated on a boyfriend. I really was not proud of that. I swore to myself I would never cheat again, and I never have. I would judge Ali if he had cheated in the ring. If he had cheated in the ring, I would judge him harshly because that's for us. What you do in the ring, you do, not only for yourself and your career as an athlete, but you do it for the fans. You cheat us when you cheat. I have a big issue with that. And it's a very dangerous sport, so you could put someone else's life in jeopardy because of that. But in regards to Ali's personal life, I have certain feelings about what Ali did still to this day. But it's not right for me to judge. We all fall short."

"I saw the Thrilla in Manilla in a theater. We snuck in. We couldn't afford those tickets; we wanted to see the fight, so we snuck in. Even as little girls, we knew how to do it. We made friends with the security guy at the back door. You slip him a dollar or you sit there and crack jokes. Then he opens the door and you slip in. I'm so glad I got to see it. But when I went back to school and said I saw the fight, nobody believed me."

"I cried when I saw him fight Frazier in Manila. I was like, 'He just didn't give up. This is the greatest man ever.' Other people were saying, 'What a fool.' They actually said that. 'What a fool. He should have thrown in the towel. They both should have. This is stupid.' But what I saw was determination and grit, never say never, I won't give up. And for me, a child who was a victim of poverty and of child abuse—kids used to make fun of me—I was like, 'I'm going to be great.' I used to say stuff like that. That's what I saw in him. That's what I saw in that fight. It changed me as a person."

"I was disappointed in Muhammad Ali in the way he treated Joe Frazier. As a person that had dealt with racism and prejudice and bigotry at a young age, I thought that it was really bad seeing my hero inflict that upon someone else who was of his own race. I felt bad for Joe; I really, really did. That hurt me. That hurt me a lot. Ali was such a big hero, and he was using that language and just verbally and mentally and emotionally beating this man down. I understood that it was a tactic. I got all that. But even as a young kid. I was like, 'It's just too far.' When you're a kid and you're treated differently because of the color of your skin, you know how that feels. And what was really strange was that there were a lot of kids of color who were defending Ali. They defended Ali. And I was one of the few kids to say, 'That's wrong.'"

"People ask me, 'Why do you love going to the fights?' It's not just the fight itself. It's the whole thing. It's waiting on line to get into the arena. It's finding your seats. It's saying hello to your boxing friends. It's saying, 'Look, over there. There goes Bernard Hopkins. Oscar De La Hoya is right there. There's Bob Arum. The first time I said hello to Bob Arum, he didn't know who I was. I'm like, 'Hey, Bob Arum; how are you doing?' He looked at me like I was insane. The second time I saw him was at Madison Square Garden. I said, 'Hey, Bob Arum.' He goes, 'Hello, young lady. I know who you are.' I said, 'You do?' He says, 'Yeah. Very nice to meet you.' It's fantastic. It's fun. You want more of it and you can't wait to go to another fight. A fight in Vegas, I just love it. I like to go there the day before and just kind of settle in. I stay in the hotel, go downstairs, meet everybody, shake hands, talk and BS. I just love it."

"In some sports, you have predominantly this set of people, predominantly that set of people. I'm not just talking about race either. There is a certain class of people that go and watch a tennis match. There is a certain class of people that watch NASCAR. Football is a little more mixed. But with boxing, there are no color lines. There are no socio-economic lines. It's just people."

"When I watch a boxing match, a strange thing happens in my heart. It's as if I'm fantasizing that that's me in the ring. The Danny Garcia versus

Paulie Malignaggi fight. Paulie is a friend of mine. Every punch that Paulie absorbed, I felt. I've been in those situations. Not on a prize-fight level, not on a professional-athletic level. But I've been in those situations where, 'My gosh, someone is beating the crap out of me. What am I going to do?' I didn't have that stamina that Paulie had. I didn't have that power that Danny Garcia had. But they have it, so I get to experience that level of greatness. I get to see it and I get to sit ringside. I get to cheer for them and I get to cry for them, and that's why I love boxing. It's things that I experienced as a child that didn't play out the way I wanted them to play out. But here are two prizefighters who are going to give me that opportunity every single time, over and over again. I root for them. I root for the winner and I root for the loser. I really do."

"I always dreamed of the day. I always believed in my heart and soul that, one day, I would meet Muhammad Ali. One day, I'm invited to this party by a certain athlete. I go to the party, got real cute, having a great time at the party. That certain athlete's wife comes over to me and says that I must leave. She wasn't very nice. Actually, she was very rude and very mean about it. The group of people that I was sitting with who were kissing up to me turned on me in an instant. I was in shock, I couldn't believe what was happening. A group of people circled around the athlete's wife and were saying, 'That's right. Tell her to leave. That's right.' I was like, 'What?' She wanted me to leave because she believed that I was having an affair with her husband, which I wasn't. I didn't even know that's what she thought at the time. Everyone was closing in on me. I got paranoid. I felt extremely threatened and I was extremely embarrassed. My emotions were rising up in me. This one particular person, who was a celebrity, who will remain nameless; she got close to my face and told me, 'Nobody wants you here. You better leave.' Brooklyn jumped out of me. Bushwick came out in full force. I turned to the woman and I said, 'If you don't get the fuck away from me, I'm going to punch you in your fucking face and I'm going to punch you in your big fucking fat titty.' Everyone went, 'Huh?' My girlfriend, Rhonda, was with me. She was a VP at a record company at the time and she got just as ghetto as I'd gotten. She said, 'We'll take all you motherfuckers on.' Then I feel a big hand on my shoulder, and I'm thinking it's security. I turn to say, 'Get the fuck off of me.' And it was Muhammad Ali. In an instant, I was the seven-year old girl that dreamed, one day, I was going to meet the champ. I cried like a baby. My face turned bright red. The tears just started flooding down my eyes. My mascara was down in streaks. Lonnie was with him. She said, 'That's all right; that's all right. You don't have to go anywhere. Come on, let's go sit over there. Sit with us.' I said, 'No.' I was mortified. I was extremely embarrassed. This was not how I envisioned that I was going to meet the champ. Muhammad was pulling me in close and he had his condition and his body was shaking. He gets very, very close to my ear and he whispers in my ear. He says, 'If I was younger . . .' I burst out laughing. And then I started getting hysterical again. I said, 'I didn't want to meet you like this. I don't want to meet you like this. This is not happening.' I didn't join them. I left the party because I just was too embarrassed. I sat in the car on the way home and cried the entire ride back to my house. Rhonda was like, 'Are you okay?' I said, 'No, that's not how it was supposed to go down. I wasn't supposed to meet the champ like that.' It wasn't until years later that I realized that's how it was supposed to go down. He saw me at my worst and he only saw the best of me. He saw me at my worst and put his hand on my shoulder, pulled me in, and told me, 'I've got your back. It's okay. Don't worry about it. Nobody is going to hurt you because I'm here.'"

"Muhammad Ali will always be my perfect flawed hero."

*Muhammad Ali had a face that everyone could love. But there was a lot more to him than his looks.*

# More on the Muhammad Ali Documentary

Robert Lipsyte and Randy Roberts were also featured prominently in the Muhammad Ali documentary referenced in the preceding piece.

Lipsyte covered Ali as a journalist for the *New York Times* and other publications from the early 1960s on. He was present at the Fifth Street Gym when Cassius Clay met the Beatles; at Convention Hall when Clay dethroned Sonny Liston; and at Ali's home in Miami when Muhammad uttered the immortal words, "I ain't got no quarrel with them Vietcong."

Roberts is a distinguished professor of history at Purdue University with books about Jack Johnson, Jack Dempsey, Joe Louis, and Mike Tyson to his credit. Most recently, he co-authored *Blood Brothers: The Fatal Friendship Between Muhammad Ali and Malcolm X*.

The quotes below are from Lipsyte, Roberts, and others in the boxing community who were interviewed for the documentary. Some of these quotes are in the final version of the film; some aren't. All of them offer insight into the extraordinary life of Muhammad Ali.

★ ★ ★

Randy Roberts: "Here is this guy who emerges from the 1960 Olympics with a gold medal in the light-heavyweight division. He wants a tomato-red Cadillac. He wants to be rich. He wants to become heavyweight champion by the time he's twenty-one or twenty-two years old. This is what he stands for. This is what he wants. I don't think there was a whole lot more than that. I don't think he ever saw the direction he was going to go in. He wanted what all great athletes want. Money, riches, fame. But en route to that goal, a life happened."

Robert Lipsyte: "It's instructive to go back to the movie with Will Smith—Ali—which gives the impression that he came out of the womb this man of principle who was going to remake the world. That's not true at all. He was, I think, an intelligent but ignorant and totally uneducated, barely literate kid who, from the age of twelve on, really did nothing but box and was in that tunnel. He evolved into this fighting machine who was totally suggestible on so many levels to his boxing trainers, to the Nation of Islam, to the currents of the society around him. He became Muhammad Ali incrementally over a number of years. The idea that anybody is the picture on the dollar bill at birth is insane. We learn this in sports, where Michael Jordan didn't make his junior high school basketball team. He didn't start in high school until late. He had to work hard and develop. We understand that. Sometimes it's harder to understand how people mature and develop socially, politically, and emotionally."

Randy Roberts: "When he burst on the world stage, it was all about, 'Ain't I pretty? Ain't I the prettiest?' He never said, 'Ain't I handsome?' But he was able to get away with it. Take a look at those early images of him. Very few athletes, if any, look that good. And there have been none that looked that good and were that good."

Robert Lipsyte: "Let's remember that Muhammad Ali came out of an unstable, abusive home. His father was violent. His mother was ineffectual. He lived in a segregated city. When he came back from Rome with the Olympic gold medal in 1960, he still could not go to every restaurant he wanted to go to. But here was a group, the Nation of Islam, that said, 'You're beautiful. Black is beautiful. We are the real people. White people were carved out of us by an evil scientist.' Elijah Muhammad became his surrogate father. He had all these brothers and uncles within the Nation of Islam. He had an enormous support system of people who believed in him in ways that gave him real inner strength."

Randy Roberts [to Lipsyte]: "The reality is that you didn't meet Ali in the 5th Street Gym [in 1964]. He was still Cassius Clay at that time.

Then you started to cover Muhammad Ali. In many ways they are two different figures."

Robert Lipsyte: "I don't think that there were many reporters sitting at ringside [for the first Liston fight] who thought Cassius had any chance. But something kind of clicked in the back of my mind when the bell rang and they came out. I suddenly realized, Cassius Clay is bigger than Sonny Liston. We'd all been writing David versus Goliath. But David was taller, and he was big, and we had to now start re-evaluating a little bit. Then, within the first couple of rounds, it was very clear that Cassius Clay had a script. He was following his script. He was moving faster, and he was taking control of the fight. Except for that moment when he was blinded in the fifth round, he was in total control of the fight."

Teddy Atlas: "He was the first guy that did things wrong in a ring and made it right. It's pretty special that he could write his own textbook."

Robert Lipsyte [on the day after Liston–Clay I]: "This kid who'd been so garrulous and loud and brassy was very subdued and very quiet. I remember the press conference the next morning. He said, 'The fight is over. Now I can just be polite.' All the older reporters were kind of, 'Yeah, I knew it was just an act.' They were all very satisfied because it somehow reaffirmed their conservatism, their idea that we're not really up against something new or different here. It's just some flashy guy who tried to pull the wool over our eyes. But now that he's won the championship, he's going to be like everybody else and show us respect and be calm. They went off to write their stories and left a group of younger reporters. We were dissatisfied. Somehow, we felt betrayed because we had a different idea of who Cassius Clay was. He was the future. He was a revolution. He was different from every athlete who'd ever lived. People kept pressing him. Young reporters kept pressing him. 'So, this was all an act? What about the Muslims? Is there any connection between you and the Muslims?' He kept deflecting and moving. Suddenly, somebody asked, 'Are you a card-carrying Muslim?' That was a very evocative Cold War line because of, 'Are you a card-carrying communist?' Great implications.

'Are you a card-carrying Muslim?' He kind of jumped back and said, 'Red birds stay with red birds, and blue birds with blue birds, and lions with lions, and tigers with tigers, and I'm not going to go any place where I'm not wanted.' Somebody said, 'What about integration? What about the civil rights movement?' That's when he made his declaration of independence. He said, 'I don't have to be what you want me to be. I'm free to be who I want.' That was the story. He said a lot of other things later that have been chipped into the wall of history. But that declaration of independence was very powerful and has resonated up to this day."

Bernard Hopkins: "Muhammad Ali was our face. He gave us a voice to be able to speak boldly and proudly about what we believe we can do. At that time when it was so easy to compromise, so easy to say okay, he stood up."

Paulie Malignaggi: "He was a person that made lot of people believe in themselves when maybe they had a reason not to believe in themselves. He was a person that showed just how mentally strong you can be. He stood for something and he wasn't going to give up what he stood for no matter what the price would be."

Robert Lipsyte: "The use by the media of his name, Muhammad Ali, became a kind of political litmus test. There were some people who just could not say 'Muhammad Ali.' They couldn't give it to him. But by 1965–1966, if you went up to him and said, 'Hey, Cassius,' he wouldn't talk to you. The reporters who couldn't get 'Muhammad Ali' out of their mouth would say, 'Hey, champ.' And he would give them that lizard eye because he knew what that was all about. It took a long time before people were able to call him Muhammad Ali. I know, I had a really hard time getting 'Muhammad Ali' into the *New York Times*. In the beginning, they wouldn't do it. They said, 'Well, unless he changes his name in a court of law.' I said, 'Come on. This is about him choosing his own name. We don't bother Cary Grant and Rock Hudson or John Wayne with what's your real name?' But the *Times* wouldn't do it. After I made enough of a fuss, it was 'Cassius Clay, who prefers to be called Muhammad Ali.' And then, after a while, 'Muhammad Ali, also known as Cassius Clay.' I remember really being embarrassed, writing these stories in which he would refer to himself as Muhammad Ali and the desk would change it to Cassius Clay, which wasn't what he said. Once, I apologized to him. I said, it was out of my control. He patted me on the top of my head and said, 'Don't worry. I realize you're just a little brother of the white establishment.'"

Paulie Malignaggi: "Muhammad Ali versus Cleveland Williams, I don't know of any heavyweight in history who beats that Ali. When I watch that fight, it's the most amazing thing. He's just blitzing him with speed, timing, angles. You don't know where it's coming from and it looks effortless. They took that away from him. They robbed him of what would have been his greatest years in the ring. They robbed us of seeing something so brilliant."

Roy Jones: "He stood up for right. He's the best example of that you'll ever see."

Robert Lipsyte: "There was something almost innocent about Muhammad Ali. Dick Gregory called him the baby of the universe. Even at his vicious worst, there was an innocence about him and kind of an absorption of the ills of the world in his willingness to embrace everyone. There was something glowing about him. He was one of those people to whom we can attach our needs. We need a hero to be brave. We need a hero to have principle. We need a hero to understand us. He seemed to have all those things."

Randy Roberts: "He gave everybody around him the same amount of him. He didn't reserve himself for the rich, the famous, the influential."

Paulie Malignaggi: "When he came back, you now had to respect how mentally strong and how much of a competitor he was. Before, he made it look easy. Now you got to see how badly this guy wanted to win. And when you show how badly you want to win no matter what price you have to pay, that shows character. So we started to learn about the character of the man inside the ring, not just the character of the man outside the ring. This man stood for something and he was willing to fight for it no matter what outside the ring. And then he was willing to fight for what he wanted inside the ring. In both situations, he was willing to accept the consequences no matter what to achieve what he wanted and needed to achieve. That's a rare kind of man."

Teddy Atlas: "It's a paradox. It's a struggle. It's alternating currents as far as what Ali means to me. He means that, if you believe in something, you stick to it no matter what the consequences are. So that's one thing. But then the paradox of it is that sometimes I look at him and he wasn't quite as sparkling as I wanted to believe. He was mean-spirited to Frazier. He did a lot of mean things there, and that went in contrast to what brought me to Ali's side. A guy that loved all people, a guy that believed in remaking the world in the right way. To have the beautiful image that I want to have of him, I have to forget about how he took apart Joe Frazier and how it affected and impacted Joe Frazier with him being so mean towards him."

Randy Roberts: "The language he used [to demean Joe Frazier] was unforgivable, but somehow it was forgiven. If your politics allied with his, you tended to say, 'Well, it's a show.' You know, one of the most mystifying aspects of Ali is, some of the things that he did and some of the things he said were absolutely repugnant. But the love for him seemed unconditional."

Roy Jones: "You got to have courage, but you also got to have faith. If you don't have faith, then you won't have courage, Ali wasn't sure he could beat George Foreman. But he had an idea. He challenged him. He felt he would figure out a way or God would give him a way. That's courage and faith combined, and that's where Ali was best."

Bill Caplan [George Foreman's publicist in Zaire]: "George loves Ali. But at that time, he didn't like him. Ali had this plan of walking around with the crowds, saying 'Ali, Bomaye,' which meant 'Ali, kill him.' You can't really like a guy who was asking the people of Kinshasa to kill you."

Teddy Atlas: "Ali reminds me that there's a price for greatness. And he also reminds me that what makes you great, that great drive, that great ego, that great belief that you can do anything, that nothing is going to stop you; that can wound you if it's not controlled."

Robert Lipsyte: "I talked to George Foreman in the late 1990s. By this time, he was totally lovable. It was a TV interview and I had everything I needed. So I asked, 'How do you feel as Muhammad Ali deteriorates further and further, knowing that you did a lot of the damage to him?' And George said, 'You know, I think about the old veterans of American wars who protected us. They take off their hands or their legs or their eyes that they lost in this war, and all you can do is thank them for what they did for us. And that's the way I think about Ali.' Now George didn't actually answer the question. But I thought that was a beautiful way to think about Ali and to think about his damage now as part of his sacrifice for us."

Randy Roberts: "His whole life is a product of choices. Good choices, bad choices, I don't think he made a whole lot of conscious choices where he went home and agonized, 'What am I going to do?' I don't think there was that cerebral quality of trying to think through choices. I think he made most of his choices ad hoc, and he usually made the right choice. If you go back and look at the big choices—maybe not some of the personal ones—he tended to make the right choice. His position on Vietnam turned out to be the right position on Vietnam. His declaration of independence turned out to be the right declaration. The really big choices that he made, he tended to be on the right side of history."

Robert Lipsyte: "You think of Ali with all the hopes, dreams, aspirations, sentiments that we put on him. He became for us the model, the symbol, the trailblazer of courage, the great hero athlete, the man who sacrifices, gives up for principle. Whatever it is you want him to be in your mind, he can be that. He's such a great love absorber that he can represent all of us in so many different ways. But I think it's what the watcher saw rather than the watched. Do you think that there's less there than we want to believe was there?"

Randy Roberts: "We can criticize Ali in a thousand different ways. But he cared about people. He truly cared about people."

Robert Lipsyte: "His legacy was sanitized, partially by time and partially, I think, by his current wife, Lonnie, who is the curator of his legend and business activities. It's not to anybody's advantage who has a financial stake in him now to remember that, once upon a time, he was threatening and that a great deal of America, black and white, was frightened of him."

Gareth Davies: "Muhammad Ali spoke like a poet. He fought like a warrior. He made black beautiful. He made boxing beautiful. He oozed charisma and was probably the most beautiful man on the planet. He always had time for people. He was a people person, and people loved him. He never ever stopped being a man of the people. He'll be remembered as the greatest character we've had in boxing and, probably, the greatest character in sport."

*Farewell fights in celebration of a great career often go poorly. Anyone who doubts this reality should consult with Bernard Hopkins, who was unceremoniously knocked out of the ring by Joe Smith in December 2016. One year later, the honoree was Miguel Cotto.*

# Miguel Cotto's Last Fight: A Star Says Goodbye

On December 2, 2017, at 7:15 PM, Miguel Cotto walked into a dressing room at Madison Square Garden, preparing to fight for the last time.

Cotto had a lot on his mind. Nine weeks earlier, his Puerto Rican homeland had been devastated by a historic hurricane that shattered the island's infrastructure and killed as many as a thousand people. And more relevant to the hours ahead, the thirty-seven-year-old fighter had pledged that this would be his final fight.

The dressing room was a large, oval enclosure that houses the New York Rangers on game nights. Locker stalls with a plaque bearing the name and uniform number of each player ringed the room. Rolls of tape lay scattered about, a reminder of the team's 5-to-1 victory over the Carolina Hurricanes the night before. Two large sliding doors on a credenza at the far end of the room also functioned as blackboards with a red-and-blue diagram of a hockey rink emblazoned against a white backdrop on each one. Several erasable marker pens lay on a shelf behind the doors.

Cotto was wearing black pants, a burgundy jacket over a white T-shirt, and blue track shoes. His mother, wife, two sons, one of his two daughters, trainer Freddie Roach, assistant trainer Marvin Somodio, cutman David Martinez, strength and conditioning coach Gavin MacMillan, and Bryan Perez (his closest friend) were with him.

Miguel checked his email, put on some music, and sat down on one of two brown leather sofas that had been placed on opposite sides of the room. Over the next 45 minutes, he texted, talked intermittently with Perez, and ate half of a large container of fruit salad. That left Roach with time to reflect on his six-fight tenure with Cotto.

"I'm glad Miguel is retiring on his terms," Freddie said. "That it's not some commission saying, 'You're all washed up, you're done.' I wish more fighters made decisions like that. I know I couldn't do it. I fought five times after I should have quit and lost four of them. The last fight I had was in Lowell, Massachusetts, which was my favorite place to fight. I embarrassed myself. I didn't even try to win. After that, I knew it was time."

In 2009, Roach trained Manny Pacquiao for his brutal demolition of Cotto. Did he feel badly about that, given his fondness for Miguel today?

"No," Freddie answered. "That was my job then. But I'm on Miguel's side now."

Roach paused.

"You know, Miguel and Manny are the two most talented fighters I've had. A trainer is lucky if one fighter like that comes his way in a lifetime. I've had two of them. But this is a must-win fight for Miguel. After everything he's accomplished, he doesn't want to go out on a loss."

At eight o'clock, Cotto left the dressing room and accompanied his family to their seats inside the main arena. After returning, he chatted with Golden Boy matchmaker Robert Diaz and Cotto Promotions vice president Hector Soto before leaving again, this time with New York State Athletic Commission inspector Joe Schaffer for his pre-fight physical examination and to give a urine sample. He returned at 8:40, took off his pants, put on his boxing shoes, and handed his watch and necklace to Bryan Perez for safekeeping. Then he opened a sealed bottle of Fiji water he'd brought with him and began eating the rest of his fruit salad.

NYSAC inspector Ernie Morales informed him that was a problem. If Miguel ate anything more now, he'd have to provide another urine sample. And under NYSAC rules, he could only drink water provided by the promotion which, in this case, consisted of twenty-four bottles of Dasani on a table at the far end of the room.

"But I like Fiji," Miguel protested. "Water is water."

Morales held firm.

Robert Diaz dispatched someone from Golden Boy to buy ten bottles of Fiji water for Cotto and ten more for Sadam Ali (Miguel's opponent) so each camp would be treated equally.

Roach went down the hall to watch Ali's hands being wrapped.

Miguel turned his attention to a large television monitor and stretched while watching an early preliminary fight.

The ten bottles of Fiji water arrived.

Andre Rozier (Ali's trainer) came into the room and watched as Somodio taped Miguel's hands. When the wrapping was done, Cotto lay down on the blue-carpeted floor and Marvin stretched him out. Then Miguel put on his protective cup and trunks, shadow-boxed for a while, and circled the room offering a kind word and physical gesture to everyone there.

Oscar De La Hoya, Golden Boy president Eric Gomez, and director of publicity Ramiro Gonzalez came in to wish Miguel well. They were followed by referee Charlie Fitch, who gave Cotto his pre-fight instructions.

There was more shadow-boxing.

Shortly after ten o'clock, Miguel went into an adjacent room with Perez and Soto for a brief prayer.

Somodio gloved him up.

More shadow-boxing.

Cotto hit the pads with Roach for five minutes, took a minute off, and did it for five minutes more.

Another break . . . More padwork.

Rey Vargas vs. Oscar Negrete (the co-featured fight of the evening) ended.

Miguel put on his robe, left the room, and walked to a boxing ring as an active professional fighter for the forty-seventh and final time.

Miguel Cotto was touted as boxing royalty from early in his pro career. After turning pro in 2001, he moved quickly through the 140-pound ranks with victories over Cesar Bazan, Carlos Maussa, Victoriana Sosa, and Lovemore N'Dou before capturing the WBO crown with a 2004 knockout of Kelson Pinto. A run of successful title defenses and a move up to 147 pounds followed. There were WBA title-fight victories over Carlos Quintana, Zab Judah, Shane Mosley, and others. All that changed on July 26, 2008, when Cotto fought Antonio Margarito and suffered a brutal eleventh-round knockout defeat in a bout in which Margarito's handwraps are now widely believed to have been loaded.

Miguel was never the same fighter again. He was badly beaten by Manny Pacquiao and outslicked by Floyd Mayweather and Austin Trout. As Paulie Malignaggi (who Miguel brutalized in 2006) later observed, "There's always a point in a fighter's career when he starts to lose the ferocity. Every fighter loses that ferocity little by little. You either make too much money or you get a little older and start to not have as much desire."

That seemed to be Cotto's fate. Then Miguel claimed the WBC middleweight title by stopping a physically compromised Sergio Martinez and followed with an impressive fourth-round knockout of Daniel Geale. A loss by decision to a younger, stronger Canelo Alvarez and a decision victory over Yoshihiro Kamegai for a vacant 154-pound WBO belt brought his career to Sadam Ali.

Cotto was at his best when he fought at 140 or 147 pounds, weights at which he was able to impose his size and physical strength on opponents.

Meanwhile, Ali was following a less glamourous path. The twenty-nine-year-old former United States Olympian had been unable to rise to the top as a pro. The biggest win on his pro ledger was a 2014 stoppage of Luis Carlos Abregu that looks less impressive today in light of the fact that Abregu has had only one fight since then and lost it by knockout to a 10-and-8 journeyman opponent.

Last year, Ali stepped up in class to fight Jessie Vargas for the vacant WBO welterweight title and was stopped in the ninth round. Cotto–Ali would be Sadam's first fight at a contract weight of 154 pounds. The contest was for the WBO 154-pound title, but the belt was largely irrelevant to the pre-fight promotion.

The storyline was simple: "This is Miguel Cotto's last fight."

Ali, an 8-to-1 underdog, had been chosen as the opponent on the assumption that he lacked the essentials to pose a serious threat. It would be better to see Cotto go out on a win against a lesser fighter than to leave boxing in the manner of so many great champions who lost badly in the final fight of their ring career.

Sadam himself acknowledged during a November 15, 2017, teleconference call that it was "a little scary" to be fighting "a legend who I grew up watching."

Cotto–Ali was Miguel's tenth fight at Madison Square Garden. Ticket sales were hurt by an attractive slate of televised college football conference championship games the same night. More significantly, the core of Miguel's fan base in New York is the city's Puerto Rican community. And many would-be ticket buyers in that demographic were sending whatever discretionary income they had to relatives on the island who were hard hit by Hurricane Maria.

Still, a better-than-expected walk-up sale, coupled with promotional giveaways, lifted fight night attendance to 12,391.

Cotto had weighed in for the bout at 151.6 pounds, his lowest weight since fighting Manny Pacquiao in 2009. Ali weighed in at 153, his highest weight ever.

Once the bell for round one sounds, there's no room for sentiment in a boxing ring.

In the early going, Ali's hand speed and elusive footwork gave Cotto trouble. Sadam had come to win and was getting off first, while Miguel moved methodically forward but was unable to land effectively.

Cotto was also having difficulty getting out of the way of punches, which happens to fighters when they get old. A sharp right to the ear followed by a right to the temple wobbled Miguel in round two.

Then Cotto began using his jab effectively and landing hooks to the body. By round six, Ali was tiring. There was swelling around Sadam's right eye. And Miguel's bodywork was taking a toll.

One moment can change everything in boxing.

Early in the second half of the fight, most likely in round seven or eight, Cotto tore a tendon in his left biceps.

As Bart Barry wrote long ago, "There's the pain of torn flesh or cramped muscles or wheezing breathlessness. And then there's injury. Injury is a non-negotiable signal sent to the central nervous system. One doesn't make his living in athletics without knowing the difference."

The torn tendon was an injury. It caused acute pain and rendered Cotto unable to effectively jab or hook. After eight rounds, Miguel was leading on two of the judges' scorecards and was even on the third. But he was now a one-armed fighter.

Ali continued to fight a disciplined fight, following the formula of getting off first and not waiting for a receipt. As Sadam's confidence grew, he fought more aggressively and won the last four rounds on each of the judges' scorecards.

Referee Charlie Fitch did a good job of overseeing the bout. And the judges got it right: 116–112, 115–113, 115–113 in Ali's favor.

Sadam might have been a "safe" opponent. But Father Time isn't.

It wasn't supposed to end this way. But boxing is rarely about happy endings.

Cotto was in obvious pain in his dressing room after the fight.

New York State Athletic Commission chief medical officer Dr. Nitin Sethi and Dr. Kevin Wright (an orthopedic surgeon) examined Miguel's left arm and confirmed that he'd suffered a torn tendon in his left biceps. Worse, the tendon had been torn away from the bone. At their suggestion, Miguel agreed to visit the emergency room at Weill Cornell Medicine that night to see if urgent care was needed to stabilize his condition before the surgery that would follow.

It was hard to separate the injury from the outcome of the fight.

"Sadam caught Miguel with a good right hand in the second round," Roach acknowledged. "He was more explosive than I thought he'd be. But Miguel's jab was working well, and he was doing good body work with the hook until he tore his biceps. He came back to the corner with a look on his face like he was in pain. I asked what was wrong, and he told me his arm was killing him. I've see that injury before. It takes your power away. And it hurts like hell."

Meanwhile, Cotto was philosophical about the night's events.

"This was the last chapter of my book on boxing," he said. "Now I have another book to write that will be more about my family."

Bryan Perez was asked if Miguel would miss boxing now that his career as an active fighter is over.

"I don't think so," Bryan answered. "For a while now, boxing has been a job as much as a passion for Miguel. It's his work. And it's hard work."

Andreas Hale recently summed up Cotto's sojourn through boxing with the thought, "Cotto may not have a pristine record like Floyd Mayweather or have rumbled through weight classes like Manny Pacquiao. But he never backed down from an opponent no matter their age, size, or strength. You'll be hard-pressed to find another fighter who faced peak-level opposition like Cotto did. He never waited for the 'right time' to take on an opponent because anytime was the right time. Take a look at his resume for proof. If you wanted to fight Miguel Cotto, Miguel Cotto wanted to fight you. He has given fight fans everything he had and then some."

Cotto's legacy as a fighter is that of a warrior who carried himself with dignity and grace in and out of the ring. His motto was simple: "I do my best every time I fight."

One can argue that there's nothing noble about one man trying to render another man unconscious by inflicting concussive blows to the brain. But Miguel Cotto has ennobled boxing.

*The year 2017 was a challenging one for boxing. Some fights passed the test; others didn't.*

# Fight Notes

The first weekend of note for boxing fans in 2017 saw a Showtime doubleheader featuring Badou Jack vs. James DeGale and Jose Pedraza vs. Gervonta Davis at Barclays Center on January 14.

The card was a hard sell. None of the featured fighters has a significant fan base in New York. The momentum that promoter Lou DiBella established at Barclays the previous year with Keith Thurman vs. Shawn Porter and Carl Frampton vs. Leo Santa Cruz was lost when the New York State Legislature and state athletic commission partnered to impose an irrational insurance requirement that temporarily shut boxing down in New York. And the New England Patriots were playing the Houston Texans in an NFL playoff game televised by CBS opposite the Showtime telecast.

DiBella handled most of the nuts-and-bolts promotional work. But Floyd Mayweather (who promotes Jack and Davis) put considerable time and effort into the promotion. Their efforts were rewarded when 10,128 fans showed up at Barclays Center on fight night.

Pedraza–Davis was the first of the two co-featured fights.

Pedraza (22–0, 12 KOs) entered the ring as Puerto Rico's only reigning world champion, having won the IBF 130-belt in 2015 with a twelve-round decision over Andrey Klimov.

The twenty-two-year-old Davis (16–0, 15 KOs) was recognized as having enormous potential but had been softly matched to get him to his title shot. That raised the question of whether he'd experienced enough of a learning curve to pass the test.

Pedraza was a slight betting favorite.

From round one on—abetted by fast hands, notable power, and the ability to land punches from all angles—Davis evinced an impressive commitment to violence. He went to the body effectively and, over time, raised ugly welts under both of Pedraza's eyes. There were moments when Gervonta bent the rules. But on those occasions, referee Ricky Gonzalez was reasonably effective in reigning him in.

Pedraza fought gamely. When Davis appeared to take the early part of round five off, Jose attacked and it looked momentarily as though the tide might be turning. Then Gervonta resumed his assault. A straight left to the body in round six hurt Pedraza badly. A crushing right hook up top ended matters in round seven.

Pedraza isn't Superman. In his first title defense, he struggled to a split decision verdict over a shopworn Edner Cherry. But he's a reasonably good professional fighter, and Davis overwhelmed him with a dominant performance.

In some respects, Gervonta's skill set is reminiscent of a young Adrien Broner. When Broner was rising in prominence, he looked great against lesser opponents. But as his career progressed, Adrien showed a tendency to look for a way out when things got tough.

Davis looked so good on Saturday night that Badou Jack and James DeGale had a hard act to follow. But follow it they did with a twelve-round bout that evolved into an exciting war of attrition.

Johannes Gabriel Badou Nyberg was born in Sweden, moved to Las Vegas, changed his name to Badou Jack, and has been fighting professionally since 2009. His record before fighting DeGale stood at 20 wins, 1 loss, and 2 draws with 12 knockouts and 1 KO by. The big win on his resume was a 2015 split-decision verdict over George Groves that brought him the WBC 168-pound title. He retained his belt in 2016 with a majority draw against a faded Lucian Bute (who has won only two of his most recent six fights).

England's James DeGale (23–1, 14 KOs) won a gold medal in the middleweight division at the 2008 Beijing Olympics, claimed the IBF 168-pound belt in 2015 with a unanimous decision over Andre Dirrell, and had successfully defended his title twice. He was a 5-to-2 betting favorite over Jack.

DeGale started strong on Saturday night and was the busier fighter in the early going, scoring a knockdown in round one with a straight left hand up top. But Jack fought aggressively and had DeGale in retreat for most of the bout. James flurried effectively at times but didn't let his hands go often enough. And when he landed, he often failed to follow up

At the end of round five, Jack accidentally decked referee Arthur Mercante with a left hook that landed high on Mercante's cheek.

Arthur beat the count. In the following stanza, Jack hurt DeGale with a well-placed body shot and took control of the fight. But DeGale fought back in the late rounds when both men were tired and both men dug deep. Then, in round twelve, Jack dropped DeGale with a solid right hand. James was hurt. He'd already suffered a perforated eardrum and a dental bridge had been knocked out of his mouth in round eight (which necessitated a visit to the dentist one day after the fight). But he finished on his feet.

This observer scored the bout 114–112 in Jack's favor. The judges saw things a bit differently. Glenn Feldman gave the nod to DeGale 114–112. Steve Weisfeld and Julie Lederman scored the bout even at 113–113, leading to a majority draw that allowed each man to keep his title.

★ ★ ★

In touting his network's Jack–DeGale / Pedraza–Davis doubleheader, Stephen Espinoza (executive vice president and general manager of Showtime Sports) rightly declared, "These fights aren't mismatches. They aren't tune-up fights."

The same couldn't be said about PBC's fights on Spike the previous night. Friday the 13th of January saw a PBC doubleheader that featured two 50-to-1 mismatches.

In the opening bout, Anthony Dirrell, who wore a WBC 168-pound belt for eight months before losing it two years ago to Badou Jack, took on Norbert Nemesapati.

Nemesapati lost two fights within the span of eighteen days last summer. Thereafter, he supposedly rehabilitated himself to the point of qualifying as a sacrificial lamb for Dirrell by winning three fights in a row. His opponents in those three fights had a composite ring record of four wins in eighty-three outings.

That's not a typographical error.

In the main event, WBA 154-pound champion Erislandy Lara was matched against a badly faded and hopelessly outclassed Yuri Foreman.

There wasn't one second in Dirrell–Nemesapati or Lara–Foreman when the outcome was in doubt. Nemesapati's corner wisely stopped their man's bout after six rounds. Lara disposed of Foreman with a left uppercut in round four. The only good thing about Lara–Foreman is that it was short, so Yuri was spared a bad beating.

It's inherent in the nature of boxing that some fighters will get beaten up. We saw that at Barclays Center the following night, when three fighters (James DeGale, Jose Pedraza, and Ievgen Khytrov) were taken to a hospital emergency room afterward as a precautionary measure. But when fights are showcased on national television, they should be competitive sporting events, not predictably one-sided beatings.

Lara–Foreman and Dirrell–Nemesapati aren't what PBC was supposed to be about.

★ ★ ★

On February 10, 2017, Bounce TV televised a Premier Boxing champions triple-header. Robert Easter impressively dismantled an overmatched Luis Cruz, and Terrell Gausha looked lethargic in outpointing Luis Hernandez. But the story of the night was the WBA super-bantamweight title fight between Rau'shee Warren and Zhanat Zhakiyanov.

Warren was a heavy favorite. And the odds widened exponentially when he knocked Zhakiyanov down twice in the first round. In round three, the momentum shifted. Zhakiyanov appeared to drop Warren with a pair of right hands, but referee Gary Rosato ruled that Rau'shee's trip to the canvas was caused by a push. Thereafter, Zhakiyanov forced the pace. Warren, bleeding from the nose, had his moments but spent a great deal of time avoiding conflict rather than engaging in it.

The fight was contested at the Huntington Center in Toledo, Ohio. Warren was the house fighter in every sense. He's a favorite of PBC impresario Al Haymon. He's a three-time United States Olympian. And he's from Ohio. It seemed like a foregone conclusion that Rau'shee would get the judges' nod. Zhakiyanov is from Kazakhstan.

Then came the decision: Larry Hazzard Jr, 115–111 for Warren . . . John Stewart, 115–111 for Zhakiyanov . . . Ryan Kennedy, 116–110 for Zhakiyanov.

The wide discrepancy in the scoring was similar to the gap that existed in 2016 when Warren lost a split decision to Juan Carlos Payano. On that occasion, two judges scored the fight 113–111 for Payano while the third judge had it 115–109 for Warren.

Kudos for the honest scoring that boxing fans saw in Warren's fights.

★ ★ ★

Good judging was the takeaway from the February 10, 2017, PBC card in Toledo. Bad refereeing was the takeaway from the February 18 card featuring PBC fighters in Cincinnati Ohio.

Showtime televised the featured bouts. In the opener, Marcus Browne and Thomas Williams squared off in a light-heavyweight contest. Sixty-eight seconds into round two, Browne scored a flash knockdown, dropping Williams with a stiff jab. Then, with Williams defenseless and clearly on the canvas, Browne whacked him with a vicious left to the side of the head.

This isn't the first time that Browne has punched an opponent who was on the canvas. He also did it in his most recent fight before this one, an April 16, 2016, outing against Radivoje Kalajdzic at Barclays Center in Brooklyn. In that bout, midway through round one, Kalajdzic visited the canvas on what was clearly a slip. And Browne hit Kalajdzic with a jolting straight left when Kalajdzic was down. Instead of warning Browne for his transgression and deducting one or more points, referee Tony Chiarantano mistakenly called the incident a knockdown and ignored the foul.

Referee Ken Miliner was no better in overseeing Browne–Williams. Williams was badly hurt by the illegal blow. Browne should have been disqualified for a flagrant foul. Instead, Miliner counted Williams out. Then a light went on in the referee's head, and he deducted a point from Browne while allowing Williams five minutes to recover. But that missed the point.

Williams was in no condition to continue after being knocked woozy by an illegal punch. He staggered and seemed a bit disoriented when he rose. He was not allowed to sit, nor was he examined by a doctor during the recovery period. He was knocked down twice more and counted out in the sixth round.

To repeat: Browne should have been disqualified for a flagrant foul.

Miliner also evinced an embarrassing lack of familiarity with the rules of boxing. Just before the action in Browne–Williams resumed, the referee was overheard on a Showtime microphone saying several times that the fight would pick up with the start of the third round rather than continuing the interrupted second stanza.

In the main event, Adrien Broner took on Adrian Granados. The contract weight was 142 pounds. But Broner had trouble making weight and Granados was advised—take it or leave it—that the new contract weight was 147 pounds.

Broner isn't the only fighter with a history of blowing off weight requirements. Julio Cesar Chavez Jr comes quickly to mind, among others. But Broner has raised the practice to an art form with no repercussions to date. That tarnishes the integrity of the competition.

Broner–Granados was scheduled for ten rounds. Ernie Sharif was the referee. Unfortunately, Sharif allowed Broner (who was the house fighter and hometown favorite) to foul throughout the bout.

In round three, Broner rocked Granados with a combination that consisted of an elbow to the nose followed by a head butt that opened a cut on the bridge of Granados's nose. That was followed by more elbows, more head butts, forearms to the throat, and other maneuvers that might be acceptable in mixed martial arts but are illegal in boxing.

Sharif looked on as a somewhat interested spectator might throughout it all.

It was a difficult fight to score. I gave the nod to Granados by a 96–94 margin. The judges awarded Broner a split-decision victory, which led Granados to complain during a post-fight interview, "They were playing with me. We had to change the weight. They're just playing all types of fucking games. That's bullshit. Give me a fair go. You all are treating me like I'm a dumb ass. Come on, man. That's bullshit."

Broner has lost both times he went in tough (against Marcos Maidana and Shawn Porter). He fights like a man who's looking for shortcuts and, in recent years, has regressed as a fighter. He should be fighting at 140 pounds but appears to lack the discipline to make that weight.

★ ★ ★

In all three of PBC's February 25, 2017, fights on FOX, the referee stopped the bout with the loser still on his feet. Each stoppage was appropriate.

In the first televised bout of the evening, heavyweights Dominic Breazeale and Izuagbe Ugonoh engaged in an unartful slugfest that was more brawling than boxing. But it was fun while it lasted.

Breazeale was knocked out by Anthony Joshua in seven rounds in June 2016. In that outing, he showed toughness and courage but not much more. Ugonoh was born in Poland to Nigerian parents, fought his first nine pro contests in Poland, and then moved to New Zealand, where he had eight more bouts.

Ugonoh was the aggressor in rounds one and two and landed reasonably often as Breazeale plodded stoically forward. But in round three, Izuagbe got careless, found himself on the receiving end of a right hand, and acquainted himself with the canvas. He rose to stagger Breazeale before the round was done. Then, after the bell, Breazeale landed a thudding right hand to the kidney, and Ugonoh sank to the canvas in pain. Referee Jeff Dodson let the matter pass without warning, as he'd done when Breazeale tackled Ugonoh earlier in the stanza.

In round four, two overhand rights wobbled Breazeale. This time, Dominic missed the open-field tackle and stumbled to the canvas. But in round five, Breazeale turned things around, winding up with two overhand rights that everyone in the arena except Ugonoh could see coming. That put Ugonoh down for the second time. He beat the count but was being pummeled when the referee intervened to save him from further punishment at the fifty-second mark.

Next up, Jarrett Hurd battled Tony Harrison for the vacant IBF 154-pound belt. Both fighters had beaten the usual suspects. But Harrison was knocked out in the ninth round when he stepped up in class in 2015 to fight Willie Nelson.

In the early rounds of Hurd–Harrison, Hurd was the more confident, more aggressive fighter. Harrison fought cautiously, picking his spots and throwing enough counterpunches to keep Jarrett honest. In round three, Harrison found a groove, becoming busier and more effective than before. In part that was because Hurd didn't know how to cut off the ring (or if he did, he couldn't implement the strategy). And in part it was because Hurd seemed mystified by a counterpuncher.

Then, in round eight, Harrison began to tire, and one wondered if the Willie Nelson fight was in the back of his mind. If it wasn't, it should have been. Two minutes and eight seconds into round nine, a straight right dropped Harrison to the canvas. He rose, looked disoriented, spat out his mouthpiece, and referee Jim Korb stopped the fight.

That set the stage for Deontay Wilder vs. Gerald Washington.

Since winning his WBC heavyweight belt twenty-five months ago against Bermane Stiverne, Wilder had faced Eric Molina, Johann Duhaupas, Artur Szpilka, and Chris Arreola. That's low-level competition.

Washington, age thirty-four, is a former college football player who played defensive end, mostly as a backup, for the University of Southern California. He had fourteen amateur fights and didn't turn pro until four months after his thirtieth birthday. Prior to attending college, he was a helicopter mechanic in the United States Navy.

In an effort to hype Wilder–Washington, the promotion kept talking about what a "great athlete" Washington is. The same was said about former college football player Michael Grant before he was knocked out by Lennox Lewis, Dominick Guinn, Jameel McCline, Carlos Takam, and Manuel Charr. Grant was a better athlete than Washington and also a better fighter.

Wilder defended the choice of Washington as an opponent, citing his own seven-month layoff due to a broken hand and torn biceps before adding, "We all know boxing is a business first. No matter what fans want to see, no matter what anybody wants to see, boxing is a business."

Fighting in Birmingham as a native son of Alabama, Wilder was the local hero and a 12-to-1 betting favorite.

The first few rounds of Wilder–Washington saw Wilder do next to nothing while Washington tried to establish his jab. But Washington fights with his feet spread so far apart that he pushes his jab rather than stepping into it. Worse, Washington leans in when he throws the jab and brings it back low and slow. That's a no-no in boxing and raised the question of what would happen when Wilder got around to timing Washington's jab and dropped a right hand over the top. The answer came in round five: KO 5. At the time of the stoppage, one judge had Wilder ahead 39–37. The other two judges had the fight even at 38–38. That was hometown scoring.

Later in the evening, Wilder got into another fight. This one was against Dominic Breazeale in the lobby of the Westin Birmingham Hotel, where the fighters and their respective camps were staying.

Wilder had signaled bad blood toward Breazeale at the post-fight press conference, telling the media, "He had an altercation with my little brother. You don't mess with my little brother. If you have a problem, you come to me and we can handle it. We can deal with it accordingly. So with that, I've got a problem with him. And it ain't no problem that I wanna see him in the ring. So I'll see him."

See him, Deontay did. The fight spilled out onto the street and police intervention was necessary to restore order.

On Sunday morning, Breazeale posted a statement on Instagram that read, "I want to address the fact that Deontay Wilder and a mob of about 20 people unprovokedly attacked my team and my family in the lobby last night. My coach and I were blindsided by sucker-punches and my team was assaulted as well, all in front [of my] wife and kids. This cowardly attack has no place in boxing and, believe me, it will not go unpunished."

Wilder had a previous run-in with the law when he was arrested in 2013 after an incident in a Las Vegas hotel room and charged with domestic battery by strangulation. According to a police report, the woman in question had a possible broken nose, swelling around her eyes, a cut lip, and red marks on her neck. Wilder's attorney later said that Deontay was apologetic and had mistakenly thought the woman was planning to rob him. The matter was settled out of court.

But returning to in-ring combat . . . Wilder can whack with his right hand. The chopping punch to the temple that dropped Washington would cause problems for any heavyweight. However, a good heavyweight might be experienced enough to not get hit by it. And Deontay has flaws as a fighter. Lots of them, including the fact that he pulls straight back from punches instead of slipping them. At present, he's an intriguing contender, not a champion.

★ ★ ★

It was the kind of knockout that boxing fans love and hate.

On March 11, 2017, *HBO Boxing After Dark* featured David Lemieux (36–3, 32 KOs) vs. Curtis Stevens (29–5, 21 KOs) in a scheduled twelve-round bout from Turning Stone Resort Casino in Verona, New York.

Lemieux–Stevens shaped up as an exciting fight.

Lemieux, age twenty-eight, was being groomed against soft opposition when he went in semi-tough against Marco Antonio Rubio in 2011 and was knocked out in the seventh round. His ship sank further when he lost a decision to Joachim Alcine in his next outing. Since then, Lemieux had won eleven of twelve fights, most notably against Fernando Guerrero, Gabriel Rosado, and Hassan N'Dam N'Jikam. But he was obliterated when he stepped up in class to fight Gennady Golovkin in 2015.

Stevens, age thirty-two, turned pro in 2004 and was expected to rise steadily through the ranks. But he has run hot and cold during his career, losing fights he should have won (versus Marcos Primera) and also fights he was expected to lose (against Golovkin and Andre Dirrell). Curtis can be formidable, even heroic. Or he can stink out an arena (as he did in disappointing efforts against Jesse Brinkley and N'Dam N'Jikam).

Both Lemieux and Stevens made the 160-pound contract weight one day before the fight. But because their encounter was for a pair of very minor sanctioning-body belts, they were required to weigh in again at 170 pounds or less on Saturday morning. Stevens did so, weighing in at 167¼ pounds. Lemieux blew off the second weigh-in, leaving him ineligible to compete for a faux title that virtually no one in or out of boxing cared about. On fight night, according to the "unofficial HBO scale," Lemieux entered the ring at 177 pounds and Stevens weighed 170.

There was considerable trash-talking between the fighters in the build-up to the fight. Lemieux was the primary provocateur, but Stevens gave as good as he got.

"I am who I am, seven days a week," Curtis said during a media conference call. "If I've got something to say about you, I say it to you. The difference between me and David is, David says it to the camera and I say it to directly to his face."

Later, Stevens added, "This is boxing. Everyone has a turn to get hurt."

On Saturday night, it was Curtis's turn.

Lemieux pushed the action from the opening bell. Round one saw hard-punching, non-stop exchanges that could have been taken from a movie script, with Lemieux dishing out more than he took. Round two featured Stevens throwing hard left hooks up top that missed and hard left hooks to the body that hurt. In round three, Stevens continued to meet Lemieux's aggression with aggression. Then . . .

Lights out!

Both fighters threw left hooks, with Lemieux pulling the trigger first. Stevens was unconscious before he hit the canvas. He lay there for a disturbingly long time and was taken from the ring on a stretcher after regaining consciousness. Later that night, he underwent a CT scan at a local hospital as a precautionary measure and was responsive and well in the early hours of Sunday morning.

The knockout brought back memories of November 4, 2005, when Jaidon Codrington—a super-middleweight who was once considered a "can't-miss" prospect—brought a 9–0 (9 KOs) record to Oklahoma to fight Allan Green.

Stevens and Codrington were friends who trained together at Brooklyn's Starrett City Boxing Club. Because of their all-knockout records, they were known in boxing circles as "The Chin Checkers."

Seconds into Codrington–Green, Green fired a left hook to the temple that landed in a freakish way, leaving Jaidon senseless but still standing with his arms frozen upright. Green then landed several more blows and Codrington pitched forward face-first into the ropes, where he was entangled on the bottom two strands. Several spectators pushed him back into the ring. His body looked lifeless and his neck was twisted grotesquely so that his head was tucked beneath his torso. He was carried from the ring on a stretcher.

"I thought he was dead," Showtime boxing analyst Steve Farhood, who was at ringside, later admitted.

Codrington recovered and resumed his pro career. But he was never the same fighter again.

Boxing isn't a video game. And the stakes go far beyond the money involved.

★ ★ ★

I know this flies in the face of conventional wisdom. But I think one reason pay-per-view shows have engendered poor buy numbers lately is that boxing fans feel cheated by, and have grown weary of, colossally boring undercard fights. It's hard to remember the last time a pay-per-view undercard gave fans a "water-cooler fight."

That changed on March 18, 2017, when Roman "Chocolatito" Gonzalez defended his WBC 115-pound title against Srisaket Sor Rungvisai (a.k.a. Wisaksil Wangek) on the undercard of Gennady Golovkin vs. Danny Jacobs at Madison Square Garden.

Gonzalez (46–0, 38 KOs) was at or near the top of most pound-for-pound lists.

Rungvisai (41–4–1, 38 KOs, 2 KOs by) had fought four times since 2015. His two most recent opponents were making their pro debut when he fought them and, according to *BoxRec.com,* haven't fought since. His other two opponents last year had records of 12 and 19 and 3 and 5 (with 14 losses by knockout between them).

Chocolatito was a step up in competition for Rungvisai (which was thought to be like saying the iceberg the *Titanic* hit was a step up in competition from an ice cube in the vessel's cocktail lounge).

Gonzalez vs. Rungvisai turned out to be an enthralling savage, brutal fight.

Boxing fans knew they were in for the unexpected when Rungvisai dropped Gonzalez with a hard right to the body in round one. An accidental clash of heads in round three opened a horrific gash on Gonzalez's right eyebrow. Chocolatito appeared shaken by another clash of heads in round six, after which referee Steve Willis deducted a point from Rungvisai.

Blood streamed down the right side of Gonzalez's face throughout the bout, leaving him at a significant disadvantage.

Round after round, the two men traded blows with abandon, fighting as though it would be an affront to their honor to slip a punch. A purist might have quibbled that defense is also part of boxing. But there were twelve rounds of non-stop "oohs" and "aahs." Each man fought beyond what can be reasonably expected of a professional fighter.

Imagine Arturo Gatti versus Arturo Gatti, and you have Gonzalez versus Rungvisai.

At the final bell, the crowd rose and paid tribute with a standing ovation. Both fighters were taken to the hospital afterward. In addition to the many blows that they took to the head, Gonzalez had possible eye damage and there was considerable blood in Rungvisai's urine.

Most members of the media (including this writer) thought that Gonzalez won the fight, many by a comfortable margin. The judges saw things differently, giving the nod to Rungvisai on a 114–112, 114–112, 113–113 majority decision that elicited vociferous boos from the crowd.

According to CompuBox, Gonzalez out-landed Rungvisai by a 441 to 284 margin with a 372-to-277 edge in "power punches." The judges might have been scoring blood rather than punches landed.

★ ★ ★

The latest installment of "Brooklyn Boxing" was contested at Barclays Center on April 22, 2017. The main fight of the evening was a WBC "elimination" bout between Shawn Porter (26–2, 18 KOs) and Andre Berto (31–4, 24 KOs) to determine the mandatory challenger for Keith Thurman's 147 crown.

In a co-featured bout, WBC 154-pound title-holder Jermell Charlo (28–0, 13 KOs) squared off against Charles Hatley (26–1–1, 18 KOs).

The key figure in it all was Porter.

Asked to describe himself, Porter says, "I think I'm a good guy. I believe in positive energy. I'm always positive. I'm always respectful. I work hard. I follow the rules. I hang out with the right people. I'd rather play Monopoly with my friends than hang out at a nightclub all night. I like looking good, but I don't like looking like anyone else, so there's some of that in my style. I love the competition in boxing and being in the moment. When I'm in the ring, I love hearing the crowd scream. It's exhilarating, an indescribable feeling. And I'm always trying to make other people happy."

Porter is a very good fighter who hasn't quite gotten over the hump. He stepped up to the elite level on two occasions (against Kell Brook and Keith Thurman) and lost a close decision each time.

Berto was a promising prospect who got rich against a string of soft touches during the Kery Davis era at HBO. What Andre didn't do during that time was develop his ring skills to their full potential. He's now thirty-three years old and his best years as a fighter are behind him. Over the past six and a half years, he has won four of nine fights.

"Everybody knows the boxing game," Berto said during an April 13 media conference call. "You're as good as your last performance. They'll write you off quick. That's just how the game goes. I can't sit there and be upset at it. I knew what I was getting into."

As for the co-feature, Charlo-Hatley was Jermell's first fight since he claimed the vacant WBC 154-pound throne with an eighth-round knockout of John Jackson eleven months ago. His twin brother, Jermall, recently held the IBF 154-pound title but announced that he was relinquishing it to move up to 160 pounds.

Hatley was an unheralded challenger. "I'd like a little respect," he said at the final pre-fight press conference. "Once they clean him [Charlo] up off the ground, I'll get that respect."

"Keep running your mouth," Charlo told him.

Jermell was an 8-to-1 favorite.

Round one was a feeling-out stanza. Then Charlo found the right range. Midway through round three, a jab-right combination put Hatley on the canvas. He rose quickly and spent the rest of the round on his bicycle. From that point on, Jermell was the clear aggressor. Thirty seconds into round six, a vicious, picture-perfect, straight right from Charlo landed flush on Hatley's jaw and rendered him unconscious.

That set the stage for Porter–Berto.

Shawn Porter is in his prime. Andre Berto is past it.

Also, Porter is exactly the kind of fighter who's wrong for Berto. A big, strong guy who keeps coming forward throwing punches and can take a punch; a much better version of Jesus Soto Karass, who wore Andre down and knocked him out in the twelfth round three years ago.

At an April 5 media workout, Porter said of Berto, "I've seen him in fights where he goes past the fifth or sixth round and things start to fall apart for him." One week later, Shawn added, "My mindset says, every time we get in the ring, our opponent won't be able to keep up with the pace that I perform at. I do everything I can to be ready for a fight like that. I'm always prepared to fight at the faster pace than the guys that I box."

Against Berto, Porter fought less aggressively than expected in round one, with neither fighter doing much of note. In round two, Shawn went to work. A mauling body attack pinned Andre against the ropes and, just before the bell, a chopping right hand high on the forehead dropped Berto to the canvas.

Round two also saw Porter cut over his left eye from an accidental clash of heads. In round four, another head butt sliced open Porter's right eyelid, and a third accidental clash of heads opened an ugly gash on Berto's left eyelid.

Soon, there was enough blood on the ring canvas that it looked like the beginning stages of a painting by Jackson Pollack.

Meanwhile, Porter was relentlessly forcing the pace, doing his best work when he trapped Berto against the ropes and pounded away with a non-stop body attack. On occasion, Berto responded effectively with uppercuts. More often, he tried to tie Porter up.

It was here that referee Mark Nelson mishandled the fight. There were times when Porter accepted the clinch and breaking the fighters was appropriate. But on more than twenty occasions, Nelson broke the fighters when there was no need to break them.

Sometimes, simply instructing the fighters to "punch out" is the right thing to do.

More troubling, there were many times when Porter pinned Berto against the ropes and, despite Andre's efforts to tie him up, was doing damage with his free hand. Separating the fighters, as Nelson did, interrupted Shawn's momentum and forced him to work his way in all over again.

Nelson also lost control of the fight to the extent that he was unable to put an end to the repeated clash of heads that caused multiple cuts and seemed to leave Berto a bit shaken on several occasions.

Porter took round seven off after dominating the first half of the fight. He resumed his assault in round eight. In round nine, he was teeing off against Berto, who was trapped against the ropes, when Nelson correctly halted the action.

Porter out-landed Berto in every round but the seventh en route to a 175-to-81 advantage in punches landed with a 138-to-60 superiority in power punches. Fifty-one of his 138 power shots were to the body. His late dominance was reflected in the fact that he outlanded Berto 40 to 11 in round eight and 20 to 1 in the abbreviated ninth round.

Porter can now look to the future. His next fight is expected to be a rematch against Keith Thurman in what has been likened to a de facto 147-pound tournament. A real tournament would be better than a de facto one.

As for the Charlo brothers, they're good fighters. It would be nice if they were matched tougher so we can find out how good.

★ ★ ★

Saturday, May 20, 2017, saw a six-hour window with multiple fights on HBO and Showtime, five of which were notable for varying reasons.

First up, twenty-two-year-old Gervonta Davis (17–0, 16 KOs) defended his IBF 130-pound belt against challenger Liam Walsh (21–0, 14 KOs) in London.

Davis, who's promoted by Mayweather Promotions, is an exciting fighter and a good one. He has breakout potential, which he showed in a seven-round demolition of Jose Pedraza earlier this year.

Walsh was a typical sanctioning-body "mandatory" opponent. Before the fight, Mayweather Promotions CEO Leonard Ellerbe likened Davis–Walsh to Floyd's 2005 beatdown of Arturo Gatti. Nothing on Liam's resume suggested that Ellerbe was wrong.

Gervonta blew through Walsh en route to a third-round stoppage.

Who does Davis fight next? There will always be mandatory challengers and beltholders of limited ability he can ply his trade against. Most likely, that's the course his team will follow in the near future. It would be nice if Gervonta were given an opportunity to prove his mettle against stiffer competition now.

Later in the evening at the MGM National Harbor in Maryland, local favorite Gary Russell Jr (27–1, 16 KOs) ran his record to 28–1 with a seventh-round knockout of Oscar Escandon (25–2, 17 KOs) in a WBC 126-pound title bout.

Russell was born in Washington, DC, and lives in Capitol Heights, Maryland. Davis was born and lives in Baltimore. That's a natural geographic rivalry. Russell is older and more experienced. Davis is a shade bigger. Russell could move up four pounds to challenge Gervonta.

One of the reasons Premier Boxing Champions has disappointed to date is that it hasn't promoted enough fights that matter in the larger scheme of things. Gervonta Davis vs. Gary Russell Jr would matter.

Also on Saturday night, WBC–WBO 140-pound champion Terence Crawford (30–0, 21 KOs), defended his titles on HBO against Felix Diaz (19–1, 9 KOs) in the big arena at Madison Square Garden.

The twenty-nine-year-old Crawford is on the short list of the world's best fighters.

Díaz age thirty-three, won a gold medal representing the Dominican Republic in the 141-pound division at the 2008 Olympics. Lou DiBella (Diaz's promoter) beat the drums loudly for his fighter to get the assignment against Crawford (who's promoted by Top Rank).

Diaz is a solid fighter. But his accomplishments in the professional ranks are on the thin side. His best showing to date was a 2015 loss to Lamont Peterson. Most observers felt the judges missed the mark on that one, having been influenced by too much hometown cooking. That said, Felix has been less than scintillating as of late. In his most recent fights, aside from the loss to Peterson, he (1) won seven of ten rounds against Gabriel Bracero (a faded Paulie Malignaggi won eight); (2) decisioned Sammy Vasquez (Luis Collazo knocked Vasquez out); (3) won a questionable majority decision over Adrian Granados; (4) eked out a split decision over Emmanuel Lartei Lartey; and (5) knocked out Levis Morales in the seventh round (Morales has lost 4 of his last 7 fights).

Crawford was a 15-to-1 betting favorite.

One might liken watching Crawford dismantle Diaz to listening to a recording of Luciano Pavarotti sing in an ordinary opera. Whatever the limits of the music, it's still Pavarotti.

Crawford controlled round one with a probing jab that was stiff enough to keep Diaz from working his way inside. In round two, Felix was able to close the gap a bit but was clearly troubled by Crawford's faster hands and better footwork. Then Terence started landing power shots.

Diaz is tough. He kept trying to grind it out, making Crawford work for everything that Terence got. But Felix was totally outclassed. By the middle rounds, Crawford was landing every punch in the book. Meanwhile, Diaz's eyes were starting to close and his punches were getting wilder, which left him increasingly open to counters.

By round eight, Diaz's enthusiasm for battle had waned to the point where he was no longer moving forward aggressively but simply trying to survive. Crawford could have coasted to a decision. Instead, he stepped up his assault.

Diaz had too much heart to quit. But the differential in skill was too great for him to defend against Crawford's onslaught. After ten rounds, trainer Joel Diaz asked referee Steve Willis to stop the beating.

"I didn't want him to take any more punishment," Joel said afterward. "Enough was enough."

Saturday night also saw two moments that highlighted the darker side of boxing.

In one of these bouts, Jonathan Maicelo (25–4, 12 KOs) squared off against Raymundo Beltran (33–7, 21 KOs) in a 135-pound "title elimination" contest.

Beltran was driven to the canvas by a blatant head butt in round one that referee David Fields mistakenly called a knockdown. The blow left Maicelo bleeding from his scalp and Beltran with a cut on his left eyelid.

In round two, Maicelo resumed his assault, landing fifteen punches (fourteen of them "power punches") to Beltran's four. Then, one minute and twenty seconds into the stanza . . . BOOM! ! !

The best revenge for a blatant head butt that opens a cut on a fighter's eyelid and results in an incorrectly called knockdown is a lights-out, highlight-reel, left hook that lands flush on the jaw and renders the head-butter unconscious before the back of his head whacks against the canvas.

Maicelo was unconscious for a disturbingly long time and, after regaining consciousness, was carried from the ring on a gurney. After being taken to the hospital for tests and observation, he was reported to be all right.

The incident served as a reminder that boxing is a violent sport with sometimes deadly consequences.

The other incident was more troubling. In a 168-pound bout that preceded Russell–Escandon on Showtime, Andre Dirrell (25–2, 16 KOs) faced off against Jose Uzcategui (26–1, 22 KOs).

Uzcategui was ahead on the judges' scorecards when, at the end of round eight, he scored with a three-punch combination, the last punch landing after the bell. The foul appeared to be inadvertent. Dirrell indicated that he was unable to continue, and referee Bill Clancy disqualified Uzcategui.

That gave Dirrell the dubious distinction of being a fighter whose two biggest wins have come via disqualification. In 2010, Arthur Abraham was appropriately disqualified for punching Dirrell when Andre was on the canvas. But in Dirrell–Uzcategui, disqualification seemed an unduly harsh penalty since Uzcategui's transgression appeared to be inadvertent. Going to the judges' scorecards (which would have given the victory to Uzcategui) would have been a more equitable judgment. But Dirrell was the house fighter, and the house fighter is often given favorable treatment in boxing.

What happened next was far worse.

Dirrell's trainer and uncle, Leon Lawson, walked across the ring to the opposing corner as though he intended to talk with Uzcategui's trainer.

Then he sucker punched Uzcategui with a vicious left hook that landed flush on the fighter's jaw. Somehow, Uzcategui managed to stay on his feet. A wider in-ring altercation followed.

Lawson's blow was reminiscent of the sucker punch that James Butler unloaded on Richard Grant after losing to Grant in 2001. Going back further in time, it evoked memories of the assault that Riddick Bowe's manager, Rock Newman, visited on Andrew Golota after Golota was disqualified for low blows in a 1996 bout at Madison Square Garden.

Butler was arrested on the spot. He later pled guilty to felony assault, served four months in prison, and was released on five years' probation. In 2004, he bludgeoned Sam Kellerman (the brother of HBO commentator Max Kellerman) to death with a hammer.

Newman's assault sparked a riot that overwhelmed the seventy Madison Square Garden security personnel and fifty ushers who were on site. One hundred fifty New York City police officers were called to Madison Square Garden before order was restored. Fifteen spectators and nine police officers were treated for injuries at local hospitals. There were sixteen arrests.

Following Lawson's unprovoked attack, a charge of criminal assault was filed against him. As of this writing, a warrant for his arrest is outstanding. Incarceration followed by a multi-year suspension from boxing would appear to be in order.

Some observers criticize boxing as barbaric. When things like this happen, they're right.

★ ★ ★

It was a good night for the Nassau Veterans Memorial Coliseum on Long Island in New York but a bad night for fighters from Long Island. That in a nutshell summarizes the fight cards that were televised on July 15, 2017, by HBO and FOX.

Seanie Monaghan and Joe Smith are "throwback fighters." Each man grew up on Long Island and still lives there. In the 1940s, they would have been neighborhood fight-club headliners and local heroes. And they would have been fighting each other, as they did ten years ago, when Monaghan lost a decision that could have gone either way to Smith in the finals of the light-heavyweight novice division of the Golden Gloves.

Instead, on Saturday night, they were in separate cities in separate bouts. Monaghan on FOX at the newly renovated Nassau Coliseum, and Smith on HBO at the Forum in Inglewood, California.

Saturday marked the first sports event at the Nassau Coliseum since it reopened in April after a two-year renovation. It was also the first fight card there since Mike Tyson knocked out Steve Zouski in 1986.

Monaghan (28–0, 17 KOs) was matched against Marcus Browne (19–0, 14 KOs).

Seanie started boxing late. Now thirty-five years old, he has paid his dues and done everything that trainer Joe Higgins has asked of him over the past seven years. But he'd never fought a quality opponent in the pros.

"I'm lucky," Monaghan said as fight night approached. "I've fought in some pretty cool places. Barclays Center in Brooklyn, Boardwalk Hall in Atlantic City, Radio City Music Hall, Foxwoods, the MGM Grand and Thomas & Mack in Las Vegas, the big arena at Madison Square Garden. Up until now, the Theatre at the Garden has been my favorite. I fought there in the finals of the Golden Gloves, which was my first taste of the bigtime. And I've fought there six times as a pro, so it feels like home. But Nassau Coliseum is ten minutes from my gym and twenty minutes from my home. I can see the Coliseum becoming a new home for me."

Browne didn't care about geography. Now twenty-six, he'd represented the United States as a light-heavyweight at the 2012 London Olympics, where he lost in the first round to Australian Damien Hooper. His record stood at 19-and-0 with 14 KOs. He'd been groomed from the start of his professional career as a "prospect" and viewed Monaghan as a stepping stone.

Seanie was aware that some people labeled him as little more than a white Irish guy from Long Island who could sell tickets. For the first time in his pro career, he would be entering the ring as an underdog.

"That just adds fuel to the fire," Seanie warned.

One week before the fight, Monaghan downloaded a photo of Browne to use as the screensaver on his iPhone. "After Saturday, I'll put the picture of my kids back up," he promised.

Browne has good physical gifts, but his heart has been questioned. Monaghan's pre-fight strategy was straightforward. "My job is to turn this into a battle of wills, a grinding kind of fight," he said.

Talent versus heart.

Seanie knew coming in that the early rounds would be hard. But he didn't know they'd be as hard as they were.

Speed kills. Monaghan was a sitting duck for everything that Browne threw at him, and Browne threw every punch in the book. A straight left that landed high on the forehead dropped Seanie in the first minute of round one. A low blow from Marcus halfway through the opening stanza that referee Steve Willis correctly called gave Seanie time to recover. But round two was more of the same. A right hook followed by a barrage of punches had Monaghan in trouble again, and Willis stopped the carnage. The CompuBox stats were 42 to 9 in Browne's favor.

Two more slugfests followed.

When last seen in New York, Artur Szpilka (20–2, 15 KOs) was being scraped off the canvas at Barclays Center after being knocked out by Deontay Wilder. In his only other Big Apple outing, he'd been knocked out by Bryant Jennings. Szpilka's opponent, twenty-eight-year-old Adam Kownacki, had fashioned a 15–0 (12 KOs) record against mediocre opponents and wanted to show that he's more than a club fighter.

In a battle of Polish-born heavyweights, Kownacki, as is his custom, plodded forward aggressively from the opening bell. Szpilka had been out of action for eighteen months and looked flat from the start. Kownacki knocked him down in the fourth round and was beating Artur around the ring when referee Arthur Mercante stopped the slaughter.

The main event matched thirty-four-year-old Robert Guerrero 33–5–1 (19 KOs) against Omar Figueroa (26–0–1, 18 KOs), who's seven years Robert's junior.

Guerrero collected an array of belts as he moved from 126 to 147 pounds. But he has now lost in five of his most recent seven outings. Three of these losses were to Floyd Mayweather, Keith Thurman, and Danny Garcia. But Robert had also lost to David Peralta and Gamaliel Diaz. He's still a tough out, but he's an out. His best days are in the past.

Figueroa is a crowd-pleasing fighter who gets hit too much and has benefited in the past from home-state refereeing and judging in his native Texas. Prior to facing Guerrero, Omar hadn't fought in nineteen months, in part because of chronically injured hands.

Figueroa–Guerrero was contested at 147 pounds. It was an exciting in-close, action fight that at times resembled a barroom brawl.

Whatever Guerrero once had, he doesn't have it anymore. Round one was his. Then, in round two, Figueroa turned things around with a huge left uppercut that dropped Robert for a count of nine. Guerrero came back firing hard, but was knocked down twice more in the stanza. Only the absence of a three-knockdown rule and the bell saved him.

It was a short reprieve. Two more knockdowns in round three ended matters. It's time for Guerrero to think seriously about retiring.

Meanwhile, on the other side of the continent, Joe Smith faced off against Sullivan Barrera.

Smith (23–1, 19 KOs), age twenty-seven, moved onto the radar screen last year with knockout victories over Andrzej Fonfara and Bernard Hopkins. He'd been stopped early in his career after suffering a broken jaw against Eddie Caminero (a career 7-and-9 fighter who lost six fights in a row after beating Smith). But that was in the past.

The thirty-five-year-old Barrera (19–1, 14 KOs) lost a twelve-round decision to Andre Ward in 2016. His most notable victory was a 2015 knockout of Karo Murat.

Smith–Barrera was marked by spirited, mostly one-way action. Joe's moment of glory came in round one (which he was losing) when a left hook to the forehead thrown from an awkward angle put Barrera on the canvas. But Sullivan soon found a home for his uppercut and took Joe to school, helped by the fact that Smith has good power but also has trouble setting up his punches. The final CompuBox numbers were a lopsided 187 to 61 with the judges scoring the fight 97–92, 97–92, 96–93 in Barrera's favor.

★ ★ ★

HBO's triple-header at Madison Square Garden on November 25, 2017, marked the start of a unique fifteen-day period. The current Madison Square Garden opened in 1968. This was the first time ever that the building has hosted boxing in three consecutive weeks.

The November 25 card was built around thirty-two-year-old Sergey Kovalev, who held the WBA, IBF, and WBO 175-pound titles until losing a disputed decision to Andre Ward in November 2016. Seven months later, Ward stopped Kovalev in round eight of a rematch.

Thereafter, Kovalev and trainer John David Jackson parted ways on less-than-good terms. Among the thoughts that Jackson offered on the separation were:

- "Sergey said a couple of things. He's blaming me for the loss. But you can't blame me for your loss when you quit. He quit! Once Andre started hitting him to the body, he was done."
- "Sergey and I have been going through stuff for years because he's a real asshole. All the Russians that I've trained, they're wonderful people. This guy is a complete dick. Sergey started making money, getting big headed, and he didn't want to train hard anymore. Every camp was worse and worse."
- "If he comes back, he's damaged goods. He would probably beat a couple of guys, but now they know your secret. You can't take it to the body. You're in trouble."

Kovalev, for his part, responded, "The whole time I worked with John David Jackson, I got nothing from him except mitts work. I don't want to say any bad words. He's a nice guy, but he's not the coach for me. A coach should help you inside the ring in between rounds when you have one minute for rest. He should say tactics, how to open the target or move to the left or right or back or forward. Because emotions and adrenaline of every fighter inside the ring is very high, fighters don't see a lot of things [trainers] can see from the side."

When Kovalev returned to action on Thanksgiving weekend, it was with a new trainer (Arbor Tursunpulatov) and, he professed, a new attitude.

"Life showed me that I should be more concentrated on my boxing career if I want to do this," Sergey told the media. "I cleaned up my body and I cleaned up my mind from zero. All life is like a lesson for me. Right now, I feel all bad things are gone from my mind."

Asked about what some thought was a premature stoppage in the Ward rematch after Andre hit him with several illegal low blows, Kovalev answered, "Better for me if Ward knocked me out to close the questions. The Ward fight was like a bad dream. Now I am awake again and must go on with my boxing career. What happened happened. Everything is good. I'm ready to get new fights and new belts again."

Kovalev's opponent on November 25, Vyacheslav Shabranskyy, had questionable credentials and a knockout loss to Sullivan Barrera on his ring ledger. Initially, Kovalev–Shabranskyy was scheduled for ten rounds. Then, on September 21, Andre Ward announced his retirement, freeing up the WBA, WBO, and IBF belts. On October 26, the WBO decreed that Kovalev–Shabranskyy would be for its 175-pound title.

The fight was contested in the Theater at Madison Square Garden. The announced attendance of 3,307 included more than a few giveaways. The crowd was flat to begin with. And an interminably long wait before the televised fights began (marked by loud music that didn't appeal to any on-site demographic) didn't help matters.

A super-featherweight matchup between Jason Sosa and Yuriorkis Gamboa was first up on HBO.

A "boring" fight isn't boring to the fighters involved. Their health and economic future are on the line. They're trying to beat another man senseless and, at the same time, trying to survive.

That said, Sosa–Gamboa was boring. The fans in attendance could have been sitting in a movie theater watching a documentary about pottery-making for all the noise they made.

Gamboa was a shooting star who now looks to be shot. The speed and explosive power that once marked his performances are gone.

Sosa is a one-dimensional fighter who reported to training camp thirty pounds above the contract weight and wasn't in shape to push the action for ten rounds. But against Gamboa, Jason did some good body work from time to time and made the fight, such as it was.

Referee Ron Lipton made the correct call in two knockdown situations: first, in round three when Gamboa tumbled to the canvas after being hit by a hook to the body and tripped over Sosa's foot; and again in round seven, when Yuriorkis's glove touched the canvas as a consequence of his having been wobbled by a clean punch.

But Lipton has a tendency to insert himself into fights more than necessary. Gamboa held half-heartedly throughout the bout. Sosa could have punched his way out, which would have kept the action flowing. Instead, again and again, Lipton physically broke the fighters, which meant that Gamboa had more time to regroup and was incentivized to keep holding.

The consensus at ringside was that Sosa was a clear winner by a margin in the neighborhood of six points. Judge Robin Taylor's scorecard was the first to be announced.

94–94.

That elicited a chorus of boos from the few fans who had been engaged enough to actually watch the fight.

Then Michael Buffer read the scorecards of John McKaie (95–93) and Don Trella (96–92).

For Gamboa.

Picture a fastball the bounces in the dirt three feet in front of home plate and is called "strike three" by the umpire. That was the judging in Sosa–Gamboa. The New York State Athletic Commission could have taken three people at random out of the crowd and they would have done a better job.

The next fight— a light-heavyweight matchup between Sullivan Barrera and Felix Valera—was a sloppy, foul-filled affair. Referee Mike Oretega deducted three points from Valera and one from Barrera for low blows. This time, three different judges got it right, scoring the contest 98–88, 97–90, 97–89 for Barrera.

Then it was time for Kovalev–Shabranskyy.

Kovalev was a 12-to-1 betting favorite, for good cause. One minute forty seconds into round one, he dropped Shabranskyy with an overhand right. Vyacheslav rose quickly and, a minute later, was on the canvas again, courtesy of a clubbing right hand followed by a left hook.

Round two was more of the same. Fifteen seconds into the stanza, another right over the top shook Shabranskyy. Just before the two-minute mark, an accumulation of punches put him on the canvas for the third time. He rose. Kovalev pummeled him around the ring some more. And referee Harvey Dock waved off the action at the 2:36 mark.

There are some good fights to be made now at 175 pounds. If boxing were a well-run sport, fans would see a four-man elimination tournament with Kovalev, Artur Beterbiev, Olexander Gvozdyk, and Dmitriy Bivol to determine who's the best 175-pound fighter in the world. Adonis Stevenson, who in recent years has shown no interest in fighting elite opposition, could be the alternate. That way, Stevenson could continue to talk about going in tough and continue to not go in tough.

Boxing is not a well-run sport.

And a closing note on the November 25, 2017, festivities at Madison Square Garden.

Prior to Sosa–Gamboa, Michael Buffer introduced Ron Lipton with the words: "Inside the ring, in charge of the action at the bell, referee Ron Lipton."

Later, in introducing Harvey Dock, who was the third man in the ring for Kovalev–Shabranskyy, Buffer proclaimed, "When the bell rings, the man in charge of the action, your referee, world-championship veteran Harvey Dock."

As Buffer was leaving the arena at the end of the night, Lipton approached him and complained about the introductions, saying, "How could you introduce us like that? He doesn't have my experience. I started refereeing before he did. I've done more championship fights than he has."

Right now, Harvey Dock might be the best referee in boxing.

★ ★ ★

The third fight card in as many weeks at Madison Square Garden was contested at the Theater on December 9, 2017. The promotional hook was the occasion of two two-time Olympic gold medalists facing off in a professional championship fight for the first time.

Vasyl Lomachenko, age twenty-nine, is the reigning WBO 130-pound champion and at or near the top of most pound-for-pound lists. He lost a disputed split-decision to Orlando Salido in his second pro bout (for the WBO 126-pound belt) and has been undefeated in nine fights since then.

By way of comparison, in Floyd Mayweather's second pro fight, Pretty Boy (as Money was then known) fought an opponent named Reggie Sanders who had a 1–and-1 record and ended his career with a 12–47–4 mark.

Guillermo Rigondeaux entered the ring to face Lomachenko with a 17–0 (11 KOs) professional record and was the reigning WBA 122-pound champion.

Amateur records are subject to question. But Lomachenko is said to have compiled an otherworldly amateur mark of 396 wins against a single loss. Rigondeaux reportedly had a 463 and 12 amateur ledger. What's not subject to question is that, representing Ukraine, Lomachenko won

Olympic gold medals in 2008 and 2012. Rigondeaux won gold medals at the 2000 and 2004 Olympics on behalf of Cuba.

Lomachenko is exciting to watch. Rigondeaux has a reputation for being a boring fighter.

Three years ago, Bob Arum was asked whether he thought boxing should go back to fifteen-round championship fights.

"I was against the change to twelve rounds when it happened," Arum answered. "But I don't see any reason to go back to fifteen. Fifteen rounds might be less exciting because the fighters would be pacing themselves more. Besides, it's bad enough watching Guillermo Rigondeaux for twelve rounds. Who wants to watch fifteen?"

More recently—on November 26, 2016, to be precise—Arum was asked about the possibility of matching Lomachenko against Rigondeaux.

"Listen," Arum responded. "I'm building up Lomachenko because of his unbelievable ability to be a superstar. I'm not going to put him in a fight which he'll win easy but will be a snoozer. It will be a shit fight. You can't put him in with Rigondeaux, who will snooze him out. If you want to see an entertaining fight, you don't want to see that fight."

All that changed, of course, when Lomachenko–Rigondeaux became a reality.

"Years from now," Arum proclaimed at the final pre-fight press conference, "when they write about the great matches in boxing history, this will be one of the fights they're talking about."

Lomachenko was a 7-to-2 betting favorite. With good reason. Vasyl might not be (as Arum proclaims) "the best fighter since the young Muhammad Ali." But he's awfully good.

Dressed at the final pre-fight press conference in jeans and a blue plaid shirt and wearing thick-rimmed glasses, Lomachenko could have left Madison Square Garden and walked unnoticed down Seventh Avenue. There's nothing remarkable-looking about him. Until he gets in a boxing ring.

Asked how important the Rigondeaux fight was to him, Vasyl answered, "This fight is important to the fans."

One had the feeling that it was just another fight to him.

Rigondeaux had never fought above 122 pounds before (two weight classes below Lomachenko).

"I went up to 130," Guillermo acknowledged, "because it was the only way I could get this fight made. I would rather it have been at a lower weight."

More significantly, Rigondeaux is thirty-seven years old. Lighter-weight fighters tend to age poorly because their speed diminishes more dramatically than with heavier boxers. Moreover, Guillermo had fought only three rounds in the twenty-four months preceding his outing against Lomachenko. And he was rumored to have "lifestyle" issues.

At a media sit-down prior to the final pre-fight press conference, Rigondeaux had the look of a man who was there to pick up a paycheck. Earlier that day, Lomachenko had been asked, "What's the best thing about being a fighter?"

"The best thing is when you fight for the history and the glory," Vasyl responded.

Now Guillermo was asked, "What's the best thing about being a fighter?"

"Nothing," he answered.

The Theater was sold out with 5,102 fans in attendance.

The first fight of the evening, like too many that followed, was a mismatch. Bryant Jennings (now 21–2, 12 KOs) is Top Rank's current heavyweight resurrection project. Jennings had one win in the previous forty months, a knockout of West Virginia's hapless Daniel Martz. Here, he fought Donnie Haynesworth, who had never fought outside of North Carolina and had beaten one guy with a winning record (forty-nine-year-old Mark Brown). Jennings looked lethargic en route to a third-round knockout triumph.

Later in the evening, in one of four matchups televised by ESPN, Bryant Cruz was KO'd by Christopher Diaz.

United States Olympian Shakur Stevenson stopped a punching bag named Oscar Mendoza in the second round, but was unable to knock him down. Stevenson is a stylish boxer but appears to have Paulie Malignaggi's punching power. Whether or not Shakur has Malignaggi's intangibles remains to be seen.

Also on ESPN, Irish Olympian Michael Conlan won a unanimous decision against a no-hope opponent named Luis Molina. Watching Conlan–Molina was like watching banderilleros stab a bull for eighteen minutes and having the spectacle end without the matador entering the ring for the kill.

The main event was only marginally more competitive. Rigondeaux was an elite fighter. Lomachenko is an elite fighter. There's a difference. And even at his best, Rigondeaux probably couldn't have beaten Lomachenko.

Round one was tactically fought. Rigondeaux was slightly more aggressive than Lomachenko, who seemed to be studying Guillermo to find out what he needed to know.

Whatever it was that Vasyl was looking for, he found it. He established his primacy in round two and ran the table from that point on.

Lomachenko is a creative master when it comes to speed and angles. He isn't a big puncher, but he's a sharp puncher who discourages opponents and, over time, beats them up. Against Rigondeaux, Vasyl kept moving and punching from all angles, mixing shots to the head and body with both hands, piling up points and doing damage.

Rigondeaux tried holding, head-butting, elbowing, hitting below the belt, rabbit-punching, hitting on the break, and every other illegal tactic that referee Steve Willis (who eventually deducted a point for the holding) let him get away with. Nothing worked. According to CompuBox, Guillermo didn't land more than three punches in any round. He quit at the end of round six, claiming an injury to his left hand. X-rays taken after the fight confirmed that there was no tissue tear or break.

"This is not his weight," Lomachenko said afterward. "So it's not a big win for me. It was easy."

Lomachenko is a special talent. Now he needs true inquisitors so boxing fans can learn whether we're witnessing the emergence of a great fighter or the arrival of a very good one.

*"Many of Arturo Gatti's most stirring moments," Carlo Rotella wrote, "resulted from his failure to attend to the rudiments of defense and movement. He was like an outfielder who has to dive to make game-saving catches because he gets a poor jump on fly balls."*

# Intimate Warfare: The Gatti–Ward Trilogy

One of the problems with boxing today is that too many of the fights that fans see are mismatches. The best fighters are often the most protected and reluctant to go in tough.

Arturo Gatti and Micky Ward never appeared on any pound-for-pound lists. Neither man was a great fighter in terms of the skills he possessed. All the heart in the world couldn't make them competitive with elite boxers. But they were good action fighters who never shied away from going in tough. They fought each other three times within the span of thirteen months. Each fight was scheduled for ten rounds. No alphabet-soup belts were at stake. Gatti–Ward II and III were very good fights. Gatti–Ward I was a great fight and the reason why boxing fans talk reverentially about the Gatti–Ward encounters to this day.

*Intimate Warfare* by Dennis Taylor and John Raspanti (published by Rowman & Littlefield) is the story of the Gatti–Ward trilogy.

Ward lived a relatively quiet life outside the ring and had a devoted fan base. Gatti burned the candle at both ends and had a cult following.

Gatti's curriculum vitae included alcohol and drug abuse and numerous arrests for drunken driving.

"I've known a number of fighters who could party really hard," HBO blow-by-blow commentator Jim Lampley observed. "Fighters who were pushing themselves to the limit in that regard the same way they would push themselves to the limit in the ring. And there was nobody like Arturo."

Pat Lynch (Gatti's manager) concurred, saying, "My wife and I would worry if the phone rang at three in the morning, hoping it was just him asking for a few dollars, hoping he wasn't in trouble."

But there was a sweet side to Arturo. In November 2002, I was in Atlantic City for the second Gatti–Ward fight. Paulie Malignaggi (who was relatively unknown at the time) was scheduled to fight Paul Delgado on the undercard. Arturo had just finished a sit-down in a conference room with a small group of media. Paulie had come in to listen and was standing off to the side.

"Arturo is my hero," Paulie told me.

"Have you met him?"

"No."

"C'mon. I'll introduce you."

Gatti had a fight coming up in two days. He was struggling to make weight, which can turn the nicest fighter in the world into an ogre. But he was warm and welcoming to Paulie and talked with him for several minutes.

"That made me feel good," Paulie said afterward. "He treated me like I'm somebody."

As for Gatti and Ward as fighters . . .

"Ward," Taylor and Raspanti note, "was a reliable action fighter of limited ability, who could be counted on by one of the second-tier boxing networks to provide formidable competition for opponents perceived to have a brighter future."

His will was the key to his marketability.

"Everybody's heart is the same size," Ward posited. "It's your will to be able to go through pain and not give up [that counts]. You can't train for it. Either you have it or you don't. Either you're born with it or you're not."

Meanwhile, Gatti fought in a manner that earned him the sobriquet of "the Human Highlight Reel."

"Smash him with a right hand that splits an eyebrow causing blood to pour down his face," Steve Springer of the *Los Angeles Times* wrote. "Crush him with a body shot that caves in a rib. Pound him until his legs become too shaky to support his body. Arturo Gatti will accept all that stoically. He always has, knowing it's part of boxing, the cruel and often painful sport in which he makes a living. Just don't ignore him, dismiss him, or show him a lack of respect. That, he can't accept."

When Arturo fought, Tim Starks noted, "You knew you were going to get a show. Every time."

"You can't give a fighter higher accolades than to say he always gave fans more than their money's worth," promoter Russell Peltz said.

Boxing is the ultimate one-on-one sport. Two evenly matched fighters are necessary for a great fight. When Gatti and Ward met in the ring for the first time, they had sixteen losses between them. Gatti had two competitive advantages over his opponent. He was faster and six and a half years younger. Given the fact that Ward was pushing thirty-seven, that was a significant age differential. But they were well-matched.

Their first encounter, contested at Mohegan Sun on May 18, 2002, was a brutal breathtaking drama.

"Two fighters on a collision course have total faith in their own abilities and their own will to win," Taylor and Raspanti write. "Each believes he possesses a bottomless well of determination that, when it is needed, will be there and be enough when he needs it. Neither man believes he will lose the fight. Yet one of them will."

Ward prevailed on a narrow 95–93, 94–93, 94–94 majority decision.

"I always wondered what it would be like to fight my twin," Gatti said afterward. "Now I know."

Fights II and III took place at Boardwalk Hall in Atlantic City. Each outing was an uphill climb for Ward, who lost unanimous decisions on November 23, 2002 (98–91, 98–91, 98–90) and June 7, 2003 (97–92, 96–93, 96–93).

Ward retired after Gatti–Ward III. Gatti fought on for another four years until other men's fists inflicted damage and pain that was too much for even him to bear.

*Intimate Warfare* consists of alternating chapters on Gatti and Ward until they meet in the ring and their lives are joined. Like its subjects, the book is a solid, workmanlike effort. It summarizes what's already known about both men but doesn't break new ground. The best retelling of Arturo Gatti vs. Micky Ward remains watching a video of their first fight.

The last chapter of *Intimate Warfare* is devoted to Gatti's untimely death in Brazil seven years ago. Depending on which version of events one believes, either he committed suicide by hanging himself from a staircase after a night of hard drinking and quarreling with his wife, or he was murdered by his wife with the assistance of one or more accomplices. Initially, Arturo's wife—a former exotic dancer named Amanda Rodrigues—was arrested and charged with murder. Three weeks later, the charges were dismissed.

Most of Arturo's friends and business associates (including Micky Ward) think he was murdered. They believe that he loved life and his two children too much to commit suicide. I agree with them. For those reasons and one more.

On the day it was announced that Arturo had died, I thought back to a Boxing Writers Association of America dinner that I attended at a hotel in midtown Manhattan. If memory serves me correctly, it was in 2003, when Arturo and Micky were co-honored for having participated in the 2002 "Fight of the Year."

I'm not certain of the date, but I remember one moment from the dinner very clearly. Midway through the awards presentations, I left my seat to go to the men's room. When I got there, an intimidating young man was blocking the entrance.

"You can't go in there," he said.

"Why can't I go in there?"

"It's in use. You'll have to go to another floor."

"What do you mean, it's in use? There are a dozen urinals and toilets in there."

At which point, Arturo staggered out of the men's room, dead drunk, accompanied by a woman who looked very much like a dancer at a not-very-exclusive adult club.

"Blow job," Arturo announced when he saw me.

And he pointed to his fly. Which was still unzipped.

In that condition, Arturo couldn't have walked a straight line, let alone figured out the mechanics of detaching his wife's purse strap, hooking it over a bannister railing, and hanging himself.

But let's end on a more ennobling note.

"Ward and Gatti," Taylor and Raspanti write, "will be remembered as mortal men who, mostly through courage and sheer will, accomplished things before our very eyes that should not have been humanly possible. They pushed themselves beyond those physical limits that the rest of us have come to accept, past the fatigue, the agony, the fear, the nagging desire to give up, rest, and save at least part of themselves for another day. And they did it three times."

They were sportsmen of the highest order, who fought within the rules and treated each other with respect before, during, and after their bloody trilogy.

*Reflecting on his life at the top, Mike Tyson has said, "Living recklessly was exciting, but coming down is hard."*

## Iron Ambition: Mike Tyson and Cus D'Amato

Few fighters have captured the public imagination the way that Mike Tyson did. The primary architect of "Iron Mike," as the world saw him, was Cus D'Amato.

Four years ago, Tyson co-authored an autobiography entitled *Undisputed Truth* with Larry Sloman. Now Tyson and Sloman have reunited to write *Iron Ambition* (published by Blue Rider Press), a biography of D'Amato as viewed through the prism of his relationship with Tyson.

The origins of the Tyson–D'Amato relationship are well known. Simply stated, in Mike's words, "I was a bad kid. Went to institutions. Then I met an old guy who trained fighters. And this guy gave me the blueprint for the rest of my life."

D'Amato was a great trainer, a master motivator who understood the mechanics of boxing and could teach a man to fight. Again, in Tyson's words, "For Cus, boxing was a metaphor for living. He took the weak and made them strong."

In 1980, on one of Tyson's early visits to D'Amato's home in Catskill, New York, Cus told him, "You know, I've been waiting for you. I've been thinking about you since 1969 [when Jose Torres, one of D'Amato's champions, retired]. If you meditate long enough on something, you get a picture. And the picture told me that I would make another champion. I conjured you up with my mind, and now you're finally here."

But life with D'Amato was complicated.

"Everybody thinks I'm up there with this old, sweet, white Italian guy," Tyson recalls. "Cus was a vicious cantankerous beast. He was just a bunch of rage. He was always plotting revenge. That's what I was about, getting him back on top. All of it came out of vindictiveness and bitterness.

I was too young at that time. I didn't understand the nuances. But now I know what was going on. If he could get into any kind of position with leverage, he'd like to hurt his enemies. Cus was very vindictive. He was always in a state of confrontation. He couldn't live without enemies. If he didn't have enemies, he would make one. That's what I came out of. Cus had so many legitimate enemies that he got paranoid that everybody was his enemy. He had a few guns in the house. If we were on the road for a fight, he'd sleep with a knife by his side. In the house, Cus's bedroom was off limits. He had it rigged up with a matchbox that would fall on the floor if someone opened the door."

D'Amato quickly established a psychological hold over Tyson. When Mike was thirteen, Cus told him, "Listen to me, boy. People of royal descent will know your name. The whole world will know who you are. Your family name will reign."

Tyson recounts D'Amato "putting gasoline on a raging fire that was consuming me." He recalls looking at an old copy of *The Ring* record book that Cus gave him like he was "looking at a *Penthouse* magazine." Falling under D'Amato's influence, he watched the first Leonard–Duran fight on television and, "Everything just clicked. I finally understood fighting. People were applauding and going crazy, and my dick got hard."

"Cus wanted the meanest fighter God ever created," Tyson says. "Someone who scared the life out of people before they even entered the ring. Every day, Cus would tell me I'm the most fierce, ferocious fighter the world has known. I used to love it when he said stuff like, 'You remind me of a modern-day Jack Dempsey, you're just so ferocious.' When people began to describe me as a savage, I'd get an erection.

"Cus made me feel that hurting people was noble," Tyson continues. "He showed me the difference between fear and intimidation. Being intimidated prevents you from performing at the highest level you're capable of. Fear can help you ascend to great heights. When you get hit, that's when you gotta be calmest. When you're not being hurt is when boxing becomes fun."

There were times when life with D'Amato was hard beyond the normal demands of boxing.

"Cus believed that, if you didn't take all his shit, you were a bad person. . . . Cus would tell me, 'Don't thank me. This is who you are. I'm just bringing it out of you. I've done nothing.' And then he'd turn around and say, 'There's no way to accomplish this without my direction. You have to listen to me. . . .' Cus wanted to make you better. But in order to make you better, he had to break you. That's a bad process. Sometimes you break people and you can't put them back together."

Yet through it all, Tyson recalls, "I was truly a young man on a tunnel-vision mission. I never felt such a glorious feeling. He made me feel like I was somebody, that I mattered. I held Cus in such high esteem, like a god. And I was like his slave. If he told me to kill somebody, I would kill them. I'm serious. I was a sick fuck. I think about this a lot. It's this old washed-up dude and this fucking slum dweller. This dude is telling me shit and I'm believing it. I think I'm invincible. Cus had me thinking I'm this invincible fucking monster from another galaxy. He thought so highly of me as a fighter, it was like he was worshipping me. And I started worshipping myself. At sixteen years old, I believed that all the heroes and gods of war—Achilles, Ares, all these gods and all the old fighters—were watching me and I had to represent them. I had to be blood-thirsty and gut-wrenching. We were fighting for immortality. Nothing else mattered than being worshipped by the entire world."

*Iron Ambition* is really two books presented to the reader in alternating chapters. The first book is Tyson's recounting of his life with D'Amato. The second is a recounting of Cus's life separate and apart from Mike and, to a degree, how D'Amato's pre-Tyson experiences shaped his relationship with Tyson. Both narratives are presented in Tyson's voice, although the second narrative appears to be largely the product of exhaustive research by Sloman.

Sloman writes smoothly. His research on D'Amato's relationship with organized crime is presented largely from Cus's point of view. Much is made of D'Amato's adversarial relationship with James Norris, Truman Gibson, and the International Boxing Club. But as Tyson and Sloman acknowledge, Cus was also comfortable in the presence of Anthony "Fat Tony" Salerno (who began his career with Lucky Luciano and later became a Genovese family underboss). Sloman and Tyson, to their credit, acknowledge that relationship and quote D'Amato as telling writer Paul Zuckerman in the early 1980s, "I wasn't fighting the mob. I was fighting the IBC. I'd rather you wrote that. I don't want to challenge these people. I got along. I never challenged them."

There's a poignant recounting of Tyson's last conversation with D'Amato, which took place at Mt. Sinai Hospital in New York on November 3, 1985, one day before Cus died.

"Cus was open to facing his own mortality," Tyson explains. "He would always say, 'God, I wish I had more time with you.' I thought Cus would always be around. I never thought he would die. But he always told me that he wasn't going to work my corner. He wanted Kevin [Rooney] and [cutman] Matt Baranski to be there. He didn't want me to come back to the corner one day and he wouldn't be there."

D'Amato died at age seventy-seven, three days after Tyson's eleventh professional fight.

"When Cus died, I lost my spirit," Tyson acknowledges. "I don't think I ever did get over his death. I felt cheated by destiny when he died. With Cus gone, the punches seemed to hurt me more. When Cus died, I started hitting the bottle more. I've been an alcoholic my whole life. I think I'm a drug addict, a cool drug kid. But I'm a fucking sloppy drunk. I drank when I was nine years old in Brownsville and I drank beer when I was doing amateur tournaments. With Cus gone, I began to drink more."

Jimmy Jacobs, who had lived with D'Amato for a decade and (with the financial backing of Bill Cayton) subsidized D'Amato's boxing venture in Catskill, tried to fill the void left by Cus's death. But despite Mike's fondness for Jim, that was impossible.

On November 22, 1986, Tyson demolished Trevor Berbick to claim the WBC heavyweight throne.

"Plotting and scheming with Cus was the best time of my life," Tyson recounts. "Our goal was all about barbarian success and superiority and then, boom, it was there and he wasn't. Now I'm twenty and famous all over the world. You walk outside and you've got a thousand crazed fans within a one-block radius. But I'm just a trained monkey. By the time I won the belt, I was a wrecked soul. I was lost because I didn't have Cus. All I knew was winning the belt for Cus. That was our goal. We were going to do this or else we were going to die. That was the payoff for all that sacrifice, suffering, dedication."

Then, on March 23, 1988, two days after Tyson knocked out Tony Tubbs, Jim Jacobs died at age fifty-eight. In Mike's next bout, he demolished Michael Spinks. But things in the ring deteriorated after that, culminating in Tyson's February 11, 1990, knockout loss at the hands of Buster Douglas.

"People always say that, if Cus had lived longer, he would have worked on my character," Tyson states. "Fuck my character. You know what my character would have been? Putting people in comas and, at the end of the day, saying yes to Cus's decisions."

*Iron Ambition* is the most complete portrait of Cus D'Amato that boxing fans are likely to see for a long time. But like its subject, the book has flaws.

Too often, things D'Amato said that are demonstrably false are treated as true. For example, one factor adding to D'Amato's certainty that Tyson would be heavyweight champion of the world someday was the astrological phenomenon that—in Tyson's words— "I passed Cus's test. I'm a Cancer. Every heavyweight champion was born under only three signs, and Cancer was one of them."

But that's simply wrong. The heavyweight champions from John L. Sullivan through Muhammad Ali were born under nine different astrological signs.

More significantly, there are places where Tyson goes over the line in ascribing powers to D'Amato and others. At one point, he describes a man who can take the sights off a BB gun, put a piece of tissue over the hole in the center of a metal washer, throw the washer in the air, and shoot a BB through the center of the washer. "But the amazing thing," Tyson claims, "was that he could teach anyone to do this within an hour and they'd never miss."

How was this possible? According to Tyson, the man was "training the unconscious mind of his pupils similar to how a Zen monk taught archery."

Tyson also talks about D'Amato developing a system that allowed Jose Torres to throw "a six-punch combination in two-fifths of a second."

Forgive me, but that's nonsense.

There's a sanitized recounting of sexual goings-on in Catskill and elsewhere.

There's very little in *Iron Ambition* about Teddy Atlas, who assisted D'Amato in training Tyson until an explosive falling out.

Steve Lott worked with Bill Cayton and Jim Jacobs for well over a decade, was in Tyson's corner for virtually all of Mike's fights through Tyson–Spinks, and shared an apartment with Tyson for several years. But there's no mention of the role that Lott played in Tyson's life.

In the end, readers of *Iron Ambition* are left with the question of what D'Amato would have thought about the way Tyson squandered his ring talent. Tyson, for his part, now sees things differently from the way D'Amato saw them.

"What was in my mind," Tyson asks, "that made me work so hard and think that I'd cut off a hand for that cheap tin piece-of-shit belt? I loved going through life with Cus then, but it's not like I don't have any resentments now. Why did I have to work so fucking hard that I have arthritis throughout my body. Now I can't walk without pain. I can still work out but I'm a wreck. I broke bones all over my body. I'll probably be crippled later in life. I can't remember shit sometimes. All from fighting for that belt. Cus believed in dying in the ring, dying on your shield. But I realize now, nothing is more important than life. There is no trophy; there is no glory, more important than life and the people you love. I'd be the first to want to die with honor in the ring back then, but not now. That is a sucker's game. And I was probably the biggest sucker who ever came into this game."

And one final note . . .

In 1983, I decided to write a book about the sport and business of boxing: *The Black Lights*. The first two people I interviewed for the book were Bill Cayton and Jim Jacobs.

"If you're going to write a book about boxing," Bill told me, "you have to talk with Cus D'Amato." Bill and Jim also told me about a young man named Mike Tyson who was living with Cus. Mike was seventeen years old at the time. He was going to be the greatest heavyweight champion ever, they said. But more important, under Cus's tutelage, Mike had become a "model citizen."

Bill and Jim arranged for me to spend a weekend in Catskill. I stayed in the house with Cus, Camille Ewald, and the young men Cus was working with, including Tyson. I'll recount my memories of that weekend another time. But I do want to share some thoughts now about Bill Cayton.

At one time, Cayton owned the copyright on the largest collection of fight films in history. His film collection made him a rich man. In 1999, he sold his film library to ESPN and further solidified his personal fortune. Along the way, he helped guide Tyson to stardom as Mike's manager and generated an enormous amount of money for fighters like Wilfred Benitez, Edwin Rosario, Vinny Pazienza, Tommy Morrison, and Michael Grant.

Cayton is trashed repeatedly and bitterly in *Iron Ambition*. The details of his business relationship with Jim Jacobs are inaccurately reported. He's given no credit for having devised the marketing strategy that helped propel Tyson to superstardom.

Bill could be egotistical and condescending. He was also brilliant and honest. There came a time after Jacobs's death when Tyson was lured away from Cayton and fell under the spell of Don King and then Shelly Finkel. Bill was hurt by Tyson's defection. But he refused to blame Mike.

In a way, the situation was analogous to Floyd Patterson's betrayal of D'Amato. Cus guided Patterson to the heavyweight championship of the world. Then Floyd dumped him. Reflecting on what happened afterward, Tyson declares, "The one person who betrayed Cus the worst always got a pass from him. Cus never said anything derogatory about him. He always defended him. Cus said only beautiful things about him. I was jealous of Patterson. Cus loved him so much. Then I realized that the reason Cus always stayed loyal to Floyd, despite all of Floyd's treacherous acts, was that Floyd gave Cus his championship. He gave him that feeling that Cus always wanted. So Cus was indebted to him."

In a similar way, Cayton felt indebted to Tyson.

The way people are remembered is important. Bill died in 2003 and is no longer here to defend himself. But this doesn't mean that Mike Tyson's attacks on his character should go unrebutted. Bill Cayton did right by Mike Tyson.

*It's not necessary to have been a boxer to be a good boxing writer. But it helps.*

# Fighters as Writers

"It's easy to like Las Vegas the same way it's easy to like an honest hooker. Neither one pretends to be anything but what they are. They just flash you a little thigh, give you an honest price, and then screw you. You might blow your paycheck in an afternoon, but you just keep smiling because you're having a good time spending it and you knew you were going to get ripped off when you got there."

That's good writing. It comes from a novel about boxing entitled *Cornered*, written by a former fighter named Rick Folstad.

A small group of fighters have put their experiences into words as writers. This column isn't about boxers whose names were attached to autobiographies that someone else wrote for them. It's about fighters who've done serious writing on their own.

James J. Corbett, who defeated John L. Sullivan in 1892 to claim the heavyweight throne, wrote articles about boxing and an autobiography, *The Roar of the Crowd*. Former light-heavyweight champion Jose Torres was the primary author of books about Muhammad Ali and Mike Tyson and wrote dozens of articles for the Spanish-language press.

One writer reversed the order. Jack McKinney was a respected sports columnist for the *Philadelphia News*. Athletically gifted, McKinney worked out regularly, had more than his share of bar fights, and decided he wanted to have one fight as a pro.

On June 29, 1963, McKinney scored a first-round knockout at St. Mary's Gym in Painesville, Ohio. As befitting an event of that nature, Don Elbaum promoted the card.

"There were five fights that night," Elbaum recalls. "I was the promoter and I also refereed Jack's fight. In those days, they let me do things like that in Ohio. Jack came out like a wild man, throwing punches like crazy, and knocked the other guy down. I counted to ten real fast, like in about four seconds, and that was it."

The identity of McKinney's opponent that night is uncertain. Some accounts say it was a club fighter with an 0 and 4 ring record. Elbaum recalls a different set of circumstances, saying, "The original opponent fell out at the last minute. I think someone might have seen him working out in the gym and decided that he looked a little better than we wanted him to look. So I called Billy Gutz, who managed fighters in Ohio, and Billy sent a last-minute substitute."

According to *BoxRec.com*, the opponent was Alvin Green, a journeyman with a 22–10–3 record. If so, one can be forgiven for suspecting that Green was "doing business" that night. Several years earlier, he'd gone the distance with an aging Ezzard Charles in the final fight of Charles's distinguished ring career.

Tris Dixon was born in 1979 and boxed on and off as an amateur between the ages of sixteen and twenty-six. His literary resume includes a stint as the editor of *Boxing News*, numerous articles, and two books about the sweet science: *The Road to Nowhere* (Pitch Publishing) and *Money: The Life and Fast Times of Floyd Mayweather* (Arena Sport).

"I was a rugby player," Dixon recalls. "Some of the guys I played with said they boxed for fitness and asked if I wanted to try it. I went to the gym with them and, after a few months, the coach asked, 'Do you want to spar?' It's a macho environment, so you don't say 'no.' Then, after a year of sparring, it was, 'How about a fight?' And it's still a macho environment, so you say 'sure.'"

Dixon had twenty amateur fights en route to a 13-and-7 ring record.

"I remember my first fight very clearly," Tris says. "I was quite nervous. I was losing. At the end of the second round, I caught the guy with a right hand. Before the third round, my trainer told me, 'Use the right hand. He's a southpaw.' And I said to myself, 'Oh, yeah. He's a southpaw.' I'd been fighting for two rounds and hadn't noticed he was a southpaw. That's how nervous I was."

"I liked the training," Dixon continues. "I was proud to be a fighter. For me, every waking moment in the month before a fight was about the fight and trying to cope with the pre-fight pressure and pre-fight fear. I read a lot about what Cus D'Amato said about fear. If you've never fought, it's hard to appreciate the fear and pressure involved."

Why did Dixon stop fighting?

"Over time, I stopped caring as much as I had before," Tris answers. "I no longer had the same motivation to go to the gym. I was never massively hurt, but I wasn't very good at it. Sometimes I still go back to it in my mind. But I'm twelve years removed from being an active boxer now, so it's less raw and there's less of an overlap in my mind between being a writer and a fighter than there used to be."

Rick Folstad played football and baseball when he was growing up in Little Falls, Minnesota.

"But I was a terrible basketball player," Folstad recalls, "so there was nothing to do in the winter. One day, I was in a high school play. We were rehearsing in a gym. Duane and Rodney Bobick [American heavyweights who plied their trade the 1970s] were there. And I got interested."

Folstad had sixty amateur fights. In 1974, he journeyed to Denver to compete in the National Golden Gloves.

"My first two fights were pretty easy," Rick recounts. "Then, in the quarter-finals, I fought a guy named Aaron Pryor. I did pretty well in the first round. After the second round, I went back to my corner and asked, 'Who is this guy?' I lost a decision, but I went the distance. I think that's pretty cool. I went the distance with Aaron Pryor."

Folstad turned pro in 1975 and remembers, "When I put on the small gloves [eight ounces instead of ten] for my first pro fight, I said to myself, 'I'm going to be able to really nail this guy with these.' Then I realized, 'Hey, wait a minute! He'll be wearing the same gloves. He'll be able to really nail me.'"

Fighting professionally for four years, Folstad amassed a 20–2 (8 KOs) record. "I loved the one-on-on, being under the lights, seeing my name on posters," he says.

Then he suffered a detached retina and retired as an active fighter.

"Sugar Ray Leonard fought after he'd had a detached retina, but he was making millions of dollars a fight. I couldn't risk losing an eye for twelve hundred dollars."

Then Folstad turned to writing. "As far back as I can remember," he notes, "I always liked writing and I always wanted to be a writer." Now sixty-five, he lives in Florida with his wife (a one-time sportswriter and former features editor for the *Tampa Tribune*). Over the years, he has written for numerous publications and covered two Super Bowls for the

*Rocky Mountain News*. He's at his best when recreating the gritty details of the sport and business of boxing.

"The fact that I was a fighter still defines me," Rick says. "I'm proud that I did it."

Frank Lotierzo writes regularly for *TheSweetScience.com*. *BoxRec.com* lists him as having had one pro fight, a draw in 1982. But he had an impressive amateur career.

Lotierzo fell in love with boxing on the day that Cassius Clay beat Sonny Liston to annex the heavyweight crown.

"From that time on," Frank says, "all I wanted to do was box. My parents hated the idea, but eventually they let me do it. I started going to the Cherry Hill PAL as soon as I got my driver's license. My first trainer was Joey Giardello. After a while, Joey asked me, 'Frank, do you want to be a champ in Cherry Hill or do you want to get better?' I said I wanted to get better. So he told me to go to Joe Frazier's gym in Philadelphia, ask for George Benton, and tell him that Joey sent me."

Lotierzo trained at Joe Frazier's Gym from 1978 to 1982. Frazier was there on a regular basis, working with his son, Marvis. Great fighters like Sugar Ray Leonard, Thomas Hearns, Marvin Hagler, Roberto Duran, and Michael Spinks were always passing through.

Lotierzo remembers, "I hated it when I pulled up to the gym and saw Michael Spinks's silver Corvette parked outside because I knew George Benton would make me spar with him. I sparred over a hundred rounds with Michael starting in 1979. And I sparred with Ray Leonard once. Ray came to the gym to train for a week before he fought Tony Chiaverini. George Benton had trained Benny Briscoe when Benny fought Chiaverini the year before, and Angelo Dundee thought Ray could learn something from Benton. I was in awe of Ray. He was so fast. I was an aggressive fighter, so he had to hit me to keep me off, but he took it easy on me.

"I was in the gym every day," Lotierzo continues. "I loved going to the gym to train, and I was always willing to spar with those guys. In my mind I was telling myself, 'I'm going to be fighting them for real some day.' But the actual fights were something else. Every time I was scheduled to fight, I'd think about a way to get out of it. That was how I handled the pressure leading up to a fight. I'd tell myself, 'If I say I injured this, if

I say I can't fight because there's something else important I have to do that day.' It wasn't until my hands were wrapped and the gloves were on that I said to myself, 'Okay. I have to fight.'"

Fighting at weights from 154 to 175 pounds, Lotierzo compiled a 52-and-2 amateur record and won the 1977 New Jersey Golden Gloves at 165 pounds.

"I was a swarmer," Frank recalls. "Like a 165-pound Ray Mancini. Then I broke my jaw, sparring. I let it heal. It happened again in sparring. I let it heal again. And then I broke it sparring a third time. I didn't have a glass jaw. A glass jaw is when you get knocked out. In all my fights, I was knocked down once and never knocked out. It had to do with the calcium in my bones. That's just the way it was. So I stopped fighting."

Lotierzo had worked as a bartender and bouncer while training at Joe Frazier's Gym. He also attended Camden Community College and Rutgers. Later, he made good money as a stockbroker for Prudential–Bache. He now works for Dun & Bradstreet.

"After I stopped fighting," Lotierzo reminisces, "there were so many thoughts pent up inside me. Then one night, I was having dinner with my fiancée and her sister and brother-in-law. Her brother-in-law said, 'You should write. You have so much to say about boxing.' I'd thought about writing before. That night was when I decided to do it. The first article I wrote was about Joe Frazier. That was around 2001, and I've been doing it ever since. I don't talk much about what I did as a fighter. I never saved my own boxing memorabilia. But I have my memories."

Chris Arreola once declared, "I don't care what the writers say. They don't throw punches. They probably never got punched in the face in their entire life. They don't live my life."

Tris Dixon, Frank Lotierzo, and Rick Folstad have all been punched by men trained in the art of hurting. So what they have to say about boxing is instructive, as are their thoughts on boxing writing.

Dixon: "There are some very good writers out there today. But with the Internet the way it is, things are a bit of a free-for-all. Everybody can have their voice heard. Some of them are incredibly poor writers. Some of them are incredibly good and just need a break. But I don't know how many of them fully appreciate the difficulty of the journey, where the fighters come from and what it takes to get to the top."

Lotierzo: "I don't like it that anyone with a laptop can say they're a boxing writer, and then they go out and write just to say something controversial. So many times, I see someone write, 'He stopped fighting. He stopped throwing punches. He stopped trying to win.' Well, things change when you get hit. When a fighter gets hit, he gets a lot more judicious with his punches."

Folstad: "Most of the boxing media doesn't understand what it means to be a fighter; the demands that boxing puts on you, how much it takes out of you, how intense it is. They criticize fighters without knowing any better. They don't understand what's involved. If the average person gets a bad cut, it's 'Help! Stop everything. Get me to a doctor.' When a fighter gets cut, it's the opposite. You're not worried that you're bleeding. You're not worried about getting to a doctor. You're worried that they might stop the fight. How many people really understand that?"

In other words, boxing looks easier from outside the ring than it does from inside the ropes.

*George Foreman has said, "Muhammad Ali made you love him." But not everyone felt that way.*

# Muhammad Ali: A Life

Important historical figures are like blocks of marble that writers feel compelled to sculpt. More than fifteen thousand books have been written about Abraham Lincoln. Muhammad Ali won't reach that mark, but his life invites exploration.

There will always be a need and a market for good Ali scholarship. The most notable of the recent Ali books is *Blood Brothers* by Randy Roberts and Johnny Smith, an extraordinary recounting of the relationship between Ali and Malcolm X that expands what we know about Ali, Malcolm, and their time. Other books have succeeded in varying degree in recounting a particular facet of Ali's life or his life as a whole.

Some doors close to writers over time. Potential interview subjects pass from the scene. Half of the two hundred people I interviewed while researching *Muhammad Ali: His Life and Times* between 1988 and 1990 have died since then. But other avenues of exploration have opened up as government files are declassified and personal archives become available to scholars.

The latest effort at chronicling the life of Muhammad Ali is *Ali: A Life* by Jonathan Eig (published by Houghton Mifflin Harcourt).

Referencing Cassius Clay on the night of his first fight against Sonny Liston, Eig writes:

> Much of Clay's life will be spent in the throes of a social revolution, one he will help propel, as black Americans force white Americans to rewrite the terms of citizenship. Clay will win fame as the media grows international in scope, as words and images travel more quickly around the globe, allowing individuals to be seen and heard as never before. People will sing songs and compose poems and make movies and plays about him, telling the story of his life in a strange blend of truth and fiction rather than as a real mirror

> of the complicated and yearning soul who seemed to hide in plain sight. His appetite for affection will prove insatiable, opening him to relations with countless girls and women, including four wives. He will earn the kind of money once reserved for oil barons and real estate tycoons, and his extraordinary wealth and trusting nature will make him an easy mark for hustlers. He will make his living by cruelly taunting opponents before beating them bloody, yet he will become a lasting worldwide symbol of tolerance, benevolence, and pacifism.

Thereafter, Eig strips away much of the gravitas that Ali has been clad in over the decades. His work parallels the question asked by journalist Robert Lipsyte: "Do you think that there's less there than we want to believe was there?"

Eig conducted a massive amount of research. His words are polished and flow nicely.

There are some sloppy mistakes. Eig refers to Maryum, Rasheda, Jamillah, and Ibn Muhammad as "Ali's children from his first marriage." But Ali's first wife was Sonji Roi, and they did not have children together. Belinda Ali (Muhammad's second wife, who later changed her name to Khalilah Ali) was their mother.

There's also a lot of hyperbole.

Sonny Liston "pounds the heavy bag so hard the walls shake." As Clay readies to challenge Liston for the heavyweight championship of the world, "There's little debate among the men in the press corps about who will win. The question—the only question in most minds—is whether Cassius Clay leaves the ring unconscious or dead."

Writing about Ali versus Cleveland Williams in the Astrodome, Eig calls the thirty-five thousand spectators in attendance "one of the largest audiences to ever witness a sporting event." That's just wrong. Baseball and football drew larger crowds as a matter of course. And where boxing was concerned, Jack Dempsey and Joe Louis drew larger crowds on at least eight occasions.

But there are larger issues to address in evaluating *Ali: A Life*.

Eig is on solid ground in his interpretation of Ali as a public figure and social force. He's also on point when he writes that, leading into the first Ali–Frazier fight, Ali was "becoming more of a celebrity rebel" than the real thing.

But Eig understates white support for the civil rights movement of the 1960s and sometimes falls into the trap of overgeneralization.

For example, writing of the days after Ali was convicted for refusing induction into the United States Army, Eig states, "White newspaper reporters attacked again."

So did some black commentators. And there were numerous "white newspaper reporters" such as Jerry Izenberg, Robert Lipsyte, and Barney Nagler who vigorously defended Ali.

Also, the platform for Ali's greatness was boxing. And Eig never captures Ali's greatness as a fighter, perhaps because he doesn't understand boxing.

Young Cassius Clay is described by Eig as devastating Allen Hudson at the 1960 Olympic Trials with "a huge right hook." But Clay was an orthodox fighter. He didn't throw a "right hook."

Similarly, Eig writes that, in their 1963 fight at Madison Square Garden, Doug Jones "bashed Clay's head with a right hook that sent Cassius toppling into the ropes." Again, it wasn't a right hook. And Clay didn't "topple into the ropes." Then Eig writes, "When the final bell rang, the audience exploded with approval, convinced that their man Jones had won. The TV announcers said they thought the fight might have been a draw. But to the judges and referee, the fight wasn't close. They awarded Clay the victory in a unanimous decision."

In that era, fights in New York were scored on a round-by-round basis. Referee Joe LoScalzo inexplicably scored Clay–Jones 8–1–1 for Clay. But judges Frank Forbes and Artie Aidala gave Clay the nod by a 5–4–1 margin. You can't get much closer than that.

Writing about Ali's 1966 bout against George Chuvalo, Eig states, "At one point in the opening round, Chuvalo banged fourteen consecutive right hooks to the same spot on Ali's left side" and adds that, over the course of fifteen rounds, "He gave Ali a vicious beating."

Again, they weren't "right hooks." The fighters were in a clinch, Ali had immobilized Chuvalo's left hand, and Chuvalo was pumping his free right hand to the body. More importantly, Chuvalo did not inflict a "vicious beating" on Ali. And Muhammad won the decision in the Canadian's home country by a lopsided 74–62, 74–63, 73–65 margin.

Too often, Eig denigrates Ali's boxing skills. Everyone who follows boxing understands that Ali was diminished as a fighter as his career went on. But there are times when Eig doesn't give Ali full credit for his ring skills when Muhammad was near his peak.

Eig raises the possibility that both Liston fights were fixed. He repeats a claim George Foreman has made intermittently over the years that Foreman's own manager-trainer, Dick Sadler, drugged George in Zaire. Then, later in the book, Eig recounts a press conference in Chicago when promoter Don King announced Ali's upcoming fight against Chuck Wepner.

"Why was Dick Sadler, manager to George Foreman, standing by King's side?" Eig asks. "In the months ahead, Sadler and King would work together promoting Ali's fights, and Sadler would work at Deer Lake as an assistant trainer for Ali. Was this Sadler's reward for poisoning George Foreman? The answer may never be known."

This lends more credence to an ugly, unsubstantiated allegation than it deserves.

Eig also travels down a rabbit's hole with the use of recently compiled CompuBox statistics.

Long before CompuBox turned its attention to Ali, Bill Cayton and Steve Lott ran punch counts on some of Ali's fights. Two decades ago, Cayton summed up their findings as follows:

> When Muhammad was young, he was virtually untouchable. The two hardest punchers he faced in that period were Sonny Liston and Cleveland Williams. There was no clowning around in those fights. The last thing Ali wanted was to get hit. In the first Liston fight, if you throw out the round when Ali was temporarily blinded, Liston hit him with less than a dozen punches per round; most of them jabs. In the second Liston fight, Liston landed only two punches. When Ali fought Cleveland Williams, Williams hit him a grand total of three times the entire night. But if you look at the end of Ali's career; in Manila, Joe Frazier landed 440 times and a high percentage of those punches were bombs. In the first Spinks fight, Spinks connected 482 times, mostly with power punches. Larry Holmes scored 320

> times against Ali, and 125 of those punches landed in the ninth and tenth rounds when Ali was most vulnerable and Holmes was throwing everything he had.

Eig devotes a great deal of time and space to statistics compiled recently by CompuBox that show Ali was a different fighter after his exile from boxing than before. But then he goes off the rails, writing that "the percentage of punches landed [by a boxer] compared to the percentage of punches landed by opponents [is] the most telling of all boxing statistics."

By this measure, summarizing statistics compiled by CompuBox after a review of available fight footage for Ali's entire ring career, Eig states, "Ali failed to rank among history's top heavyweights. By these statistical measures, the man who called himself The Greatest was below average for much of his career."

This use of these statistics brings to mind the old axiom regarding the difference between wisdom and knowledge. Knowledge is knowing that a tomato is a fruit. Wisdom is not putting a tomato in fruit salad.

As more information about Muhammad Ali becomes available, Ali is ripe for reinterpretation. Eig offers readers new details but no new interpretations that expand what we know about, or cause us to rethink, Ali's importance.

In some ways, the most serious omission here is Eig's disinclination to discuss the final twenty years of Ali's life in a more than superficial way. These decades cry out for interpretation. What did Ali mean to the world over the past twenty years? Is there still an Ali message that resonates? In memory, can Ali be a force for positive change? Is there a way to harness the extraordinary outpouring of love that was seen around the world when Ali died?

In 2006, eighty percent of the marketing rights to Ali's name, likeness, and image were sold to CKX for $50 million. These rights were subsequently transferred to Authentic Brands Group. This transaction and its implications (including the "sanitization" of Ali's image for economic gain) are barely mentioned in Eig's book.

Lonnie Ali played an enormous role as Muhammad's wife in overseeing the day-to-day details of living, supervising Ali's health care, managing his finances, and crafting his image over the final thirty years of his life.

One can agree or disagree with some of the things Lonnie did. But her presence was at the core of Muhammad's life; his life was better because she was in it; and her input is largely ignored by Eig.

Nor does Eig acknowledge Laila Ali's boxing career, the fact that several of Ali's daughters have married white men, or that one of Ali's grandsons was bar mitzvahed.

Other choices are equally strange.

Howard Bingham was Ali's best, truest, most loyal friend for more than fifty years. No one was closer to Muhammad than Howard was during the whole of that time. Yet Eig introduces readers to Bingham when he meets Cassius Clay in 1962 and, thereafter, largely ignores him. Other members of Ali's entourage aren't mentioned at all. By contrast, while the importance of Bingham in Ali's life is downplayed, the role of Gene Kilroy (who feuded with Bingham and was one of Eig's significant sources) is overblown.

But let's cut to the chase.

Ali, as portrayed by Eig, isn't a nice man.

Eig's Ali is not just a womanizer but a vain, inveterate whoremonger who was physically abusive to two of his four wives. He's characterized again and again as having an indiscriminate, selfish, ravenous sexual appetite and verges on being a sexual predator.

Some of Eig's material is accurate. Some of it is based on rumor and unreliable sources.

I like Khalilah Ali. I think she's a good woman who was thrust into difficult circumstances and the harshest spotlight imaginable when, at age seventeen, she married Ali. In February 2016, I conducted a six-hour interview with Khalilah for a documentary that aired on television in the United Kingdom. At that time, I also reviewed an unpublished manuscript that Khalilah had written.

Much of what Khalilah said to me and wrote was compelling and had the ring of truth. Some of what she said was "headline material," but otherwise unsubstantiated, and conflicted with what I understood the facts of a particular situation to be.

Eig recounts an incident that supposedly occurred sometime around 1970, when, in his words, "Wilma Rudolph, Ali's Olympic teammate, [came] to the Ali's house in New Jersey asking for money to support a child that Rudolph claimed belonged to Ali. Ali admitted the affair with Rudolph, but told Belinda he didn't believe the child was his."

It's a matter of record that eighteen-year-old Cassius Clay—along with just about every other male athlete on the 1960 United States Olympic team—had a crush on Wilma Rudolph. It's possible that, years later, Ali and Rudolph engaged in a sexual relationship. But Wilma was a woman of exceptional dignity and grace. It's unlikely that she would have appeared at the Ali's home as described by Eig. The fact that she died of brain cancer in 1994 and is not here to speak for herself makes the allegation ugly.

Looking at the end notes to *Ali: A Life*, one sees that the sole source for the Wilma Rudolph story is Khalilah Ali. One might add that Khalilah gets her comeuppance in the unsubstantiated rumor category when Veronica Porche (Ali's third wife) suggests to Eig that Khalilah might have tried to poison her.

Eig makes clear his belief that, while Ali was married to Veronica, he was having sexual relations with Lonnie Williams, who would become his fourth wife.

There's also an extensive recounting of the children that Ali fathered out of wedlock and references to affairs with girls who allegedly were as young as twelve. Some of this has long been a matter of record. Some of it is of questionable veracity. And after a while, it seems like overkill.

Waxing eloquent about Ali's sexual proclivities, Eig states, "Black women, white women, young women, old women, Hollywood actresses, chambermaids: Ali didn't discriminate."

I don't think that's accurate. More specifically, I don't think there were white women.

When Cassius Clay was thirteen years old, a fourteen-year-old African American named Emmett Till was brutally murdered in Mississippi after allegedly making flirtatious remarks to a white woman. Cassius Clay Sr talked about the murder incessantly in the weeks that followed, and it made an impression on Cassius Jr on a primal level: Don't fool around with white women. If you do, bad things will happen.

Later, that message was augmented by black pride.

During my years with Ali, I developed what I considered to be an easy-to-use, reliable lie detector test. By that time in Muhammad's life, he'd become deeply religious. He was doing his best to live his life in accord with what he believed to be the teachings of Islam. Whenever Ali said something I doubted, I'd ask him to "swear to Allah" that it was true. Many a fable (such as the falsehood that young Cassius Clay threw his Olympic gold medal in the Ohio River) was recanted pursuant to the "swear to Allah" standard.

Ali swore to Allah that he never had sexual relations with a white woman.

Further with regard to the issue of white women, Eig writes, "Everyone close to the fighter knew his proclivities."

Well . . .

Lloyd Wells was the primary procurer of women in Ali's training camp (although he had considerable help from others). Wells told me, "Ali was never involved with a white woman. Never, never, never! I'm a guy that tells it like it is, and I don't think Ali ever had sex with a white woman. He had all sorts of opportunities. They'd throw themselves at him, some big names, too. I saw them. But I never saw Ali date a white woman, and I'm sure he never had sex with a white woman. That's just not the way it was. And I'd know if he had because, on that score, when it came to women, I was closer to him than anyone. I was the one he talked with. I was the one he came to before and after."

Howard Bingham, as earlier noted, was as close to Ali as anyone on earth. Speaking of Ali and women, Bingham acknowledged, "His habits were bad. When we met in 1962, he looked at girls a lot but didn't touch. Maybe he'd flirt a little. But even if someone was interested, which a lot of them were, it didn't go beyond talking. Then Sonji turned him on and, after they split up, there were a lot of women. You know, most men have to wine 'em and dine 'em. But all Ali had to do was look at a woman and she'd melt. He got an awful lot of encouragement. But I don't think there was ever a white woman. Some people have written, and some women have bragged, that I'm wrong about that. But I know Ali as well as anyone, and I don't think there ever was a white woman."

And a final thought . . .

There was a lot about Jonathan Eig's work that impressed me as I read *Ali: A Life*. But I never felt comfortable with what I was reading. Then, as I neared the end of the book, I realized what was troubling me most.

Eig fails to communicate how deeply spiritual Ali was in his later years. And he fails to understand what a genuinely nice man Ali was.

In reading *Ali: A Life*, I didn't see the word "love" attached much to Ali as a human quality. But Ali was a loving man who, in many ways, taught the world to love.

*There was a time when the heavyweight champion was one of the most famous and admired men in America regardless of who wore the crown.*

# Jess Willard

Jess Willard's ring career was defined by two fights: an April 5, 1915, victory over Jack Johnson in Havana, when he fulfilled his destiny as a "great white hope," and a brutal knockout defeat at the hands of Jack Dempsey on July 4, 1919, that heralded the dawn of a new era in sports.

"Jack Johnson and Jack Dempsey," Arly Allen writes, "are remembered as great American heroes. But like an old book between two elaborate bookends, Willard is now forgotten."

*Jess Willard: Heavyweight Champion of the World*, published by McFarland & Company, is Allen's attempt to remedy that oversight.

Willard was born in Kansas on December 29, 1881. His father died before Jess was born, leaving a widow with three sons—ages eleven, nine, and six—and a fourth on the way. Jess's early years were spent in Pottawatomie County. He quit school at age twelve and found work herding cattle and breaking wild horses. Much of his later life was spent in California.

Willard was twenty-eight years old when he walked into a boxing gym for the first time. He stood six feet, six inches tall, weighed roughly 230 pounds, and had never seen a professional fight. Years later, when asked how he got into boxing, he answered, "I never had any thought of it until Johnson beat Jeffries in Reno."

Willard's first professional bout was contested on February 15, 1911, in Sapulpa, Oklahoma, and ended in a disqualification loss when he threw his opponent to the canvas. The *Daily Oklahoman* wrote of that fight, "Willard behaved in a most ignorant manner in the ring. He probably knew less about what he should do than any boxer that ever stepped inside the ropes."

More significantly, as Allen writes, "Most men, when they get involved in boxing, have been involved in fights and violence during their childhood which prepared them for the rigors of the ring. Boxing was often their best alternative to prison. Jess Willard was different. His strength was prodigious, but his temper was mild. Willard did not like to fight. Most of his opponents enjoyed boxing and were happy to destroy their opponents in the ring. Willard did not and often said that, if his opponent was not hurting him, he saw no reason to hurt his opponent."

Allen then notes, "Willard's exceptional size made few men want to fight him. His non-aggressive style led to boring fights. His temperamental habits made him a manager's nightmare. His physical ability carried him to victory. [And] his mental attitude left him vulnerable to defeat."

On August 22, 1913, in Willard's twenty-first professional bout, his attitude toward boxing grew even more ambivalent when he knocked out a 1-and-2 opponent named Bull Young (who he'd knocked out twice before in previous fights). Young lapsed into unconsciousness and died the next day. In the months that followed, Willard was charged with manslaughter but was acquitted.

Willard was thirty-three years old and weighed 238 pounds when he fought Jack Johnson. Papa Jack, well past his prime by then, was four years older and entered the ring at a career high of 225 pounds, an indication that he wasn't in the best of shape.

After Willard beat Johnson, writer Damon Runyon told one-time lawman Bat Masterson (who served as timekeeper for John L. Sullivan's fights against Jake Kilrain and James Corbett), "Jess Willard can't fight a lick."

"No, he can't," Masterson answered. "But who's going to beat him?"

For a while, no one had a chance. Willard simply refused to fight.

He had emerged from his victory over Johnson as one of the most famous and admired men in America. But the fight had failed financially, and Willard needed money badly. So he moved quickly to the vaudeville circuit, followed by appearances in "Wild West" shows, where he made as much as $6,000 a week. He fought only once during the next fifty-one months, surviving that encounter with an unimpressive "newspaper decision" over Frank Moran.

Meanwhile, Willard was squandering his popularity. Not only didn't he like fighting, he was, as Allen recounts, "totally unprepared for the reception that awaited him [after he defeated Johnson]. Before the fight, he was just an ordinary man, taller than most but nothing special. But because he had won, he became a famous celebrity. Willard did not know how to handle his fame. As champion, he always felt uncomfortable around crowds. He was not a great people person. He did not delight in the adulation of his fans and tried to avoid it as much as he could."

Willard was thirty-seven years old and weighed 243 pounds when he fought Jack Dempsey in Toledo, Ohio. Dempsey was thirteen years younger and weighed fifty-six pounds less. The temperature was 110 degrees when the bout began at 4:09 p.m. The fight was scheduled for twelve rounds. Dempsey brutalized Willard, who failed to answer the bell for the fourth round.

Forty-six months after losing his championship, Willard returned to the ring at age forty-one and knocked out Floyd Johnson at Yankee Stadium in eleven rounds. Two months after that, on July 12, 1923, he fought Luis Firpo at Boyles 30 Acres in New Jersey and was knocked out in the eighth round in front of an estimated one hundred thousand fans, the largest crowd to witness a prizefight up until that time.

That was Willard's last fight. His final ring record stands at 22 wins, 5 losses, and 1 draw with 20 knockouts and 3 KOs by.

It's hard to separate fact from fiction when reconstructing long-ago boxing history, but Allen does a pretty good job of it. His book is extensively researched. There's some interesting material on the crowning of Luther McCarty as the "white heavyweight champion of the world" in 1913 and McCarty's death in the ring later that year.

There's also a lot of material on Willard's business ventures (most of which failed) and other outside-the-ring activities.

"I believe Jess was a square dealer," Jess Stone (a longtime friend of Willard's) said. "But I don't believe he thought anybody else was. That made him a tough person to do business with."

It also led to Willard being a magnet for breach of contract lawsuits and other complaints.

There are times when Allen's fondness for Willard calls the objectivity of his writing into question. Allen persuasively assembles the evidence that supports the legitimacy of Willard's knockout victory over Jack Johnson. Less credibly, he litigates the case for Willard being done in by injustice in his bout against Jack Dempsey.

Allen raises the dubious claim that Dempsey's gloves were loaded, points to fouls that Dempsey committed during the fight, and argues that

Dempsey should have been disqualified for leaving the ring after round one when he thought the fight was over.

"Willard was robbed of his title in the Dempsey fight," Allen states. "That is established."

Not really.

As Allen ultimately concedes, there's no sound probative evidence that Dempsey's gloves were loaded.

Dempsey fought within the rules as they were widely interpreted and enforced at that time.

And Dempsey leaving the ring after round one actually worked to Willard's advantage because it gave Jess more time to recover from the brutal punishment that he absorbed in the first stanza.

Here, Willard's own thoughts are instructive.

"That story about a body blow is all wrong," Willard said of the Dempsey fight. "There may have been a few landed after I was dazed by the first left hook to my jaw, but they didn't affect me any. That left hook landed clean on the point of my jaw. From that time on, I didn't know whether I was in the ring or in a cornfield. That was the blow that started me on defeat. I was virtually knocked out before I had started. I felt physically able to continue [when the fight was finally stopped]. But my head wasn't clear and my eye was closed, and I realized it would have been useless for me to attempt to box while half-blinded."

*Jess Willard* by Arly Allen is the most thorough biography of its subject to date. It's fitting to give the final word to Willard himself, who once said, "I am no believer in violence. In bringing up my kids, I say, 'What's the use of spanking them just because they make noise? If you spank them, they only make more noise.'"

*I was fortunate to experience Canelo Alvarez vs. Gennady Golovkin from the perspective of being inside Canelo's dressing room in the hours before and after the fight.*

# Canelo Alvarez vs. Gennady Golovkin: Great Expectations

Sports have international appeal. Fans want to see the best athletes in the world compete against one another regardless of where they come from.

Roger Federer, Rafael Nadal, and Novak Djokovic have thrilled tennis fans around the globe. Rory McIlroy has a huge following in golf. NBA stars Giannis Antetokounmpo, Kristaps Porzingis, Manu Gianobili, and Pau Gasol are favorites in the American arenas where they ply their trade.

The most anticipated boxing match fought in the United States in 2017 was contested between fighters from Kazakhstan and Mexico.

Gennady Golovkin was born in Kazakhstan in 1982. After compiling a reported 345-and-5 amateur record and winning a silver medal at the 2004 Athens Olympics, he turned pro and won his first thirty-seven professional bouts, scoring thirty-three knockouts in the process and claiming the WBC, WBA, and IBF 160-pound titles. He moved to California three years ago.

Golovkin's opponents are unpleasantly surprised by his power when he hits them. Carlos Acevedo recently wrote, "Trying to out-finesse Golovkin is like being one of the truck drivers in the film *Wages of Fear*, who must transport loads of nitroglycerin across rugged terrain. Every rut in the road, every hairpin turn, every sudden brake amounts to potential catastrophe."

The one important component that Golovkin's resume lacks is a victory over an elite boxer in his prime.

Saul "Canelo" Alvarez began boxing professionally in 2005 at age fifteen and compiled a 49–1–1 (34 KOs) record en route to becoming one of boxing's biggest stars.

The "Canelo" moniker is a marketing tool.

"A lot of family members and friends, they call me 'Saul,'" Alvarez said during an August 8 media conference call. "Sometimes they call me 'guero.' Sometimes they'll slip and they'll say 'Canelo.' It doesn't matter to me. I accept it. That's become natural for me. But mainly, close friends and family refer to me as 'Saul.'"

Golden Boy president Eric Gomez and director of publicity Ramiro Gonzalez went to Guadalajara to meet with Alvarez before signing him to a promotional contract seven years ago.

"The first thing that struck me was how quiet and reserved and mature he was for his age," Gomez recalls. "Then we started working with him. And Canelo has never disappointed us. He's very responsible. He always takes care of business. In a drinking culture, he doesn't drink. He's a true professional."

"He's very respectful," Gonzalez adds. "A little guarded with the media and in public. He a private person and is quiet with people he doesn't know. He's stubborn, persistent, a hard worker, and a perfectionist."

Alvarez has been in the spotlight since he was an adolescent. The weight of great expectations has been on his shoulders for a long time. Now twenty-seven, he has defeated some of boxing's biggest names; most notably, Shane Mosley and Miguel Cotto. But they were naturally smaller men and past their prime when he beat them. Victories over Erislandy Lara and Austin Trout also stand out on his resume.

Canelo takes questions from the media in English but answers in Spanish. He has a two-year lease on a house in San Diego, where he lives for much of the year, and spends the rest of his time in his hometown of Guadalajara. He was a star before his boxing skills warranted it but kept working to get better.

He's much more than a fighter with red hair.

"My job, and I'm very fortunate, is to box," Alvarez said in 2016. "I train hard and I give the best of me. I'm not trying to tap into my market. It's just something very fortunate that I've been able to have in my career. I don't like to talk trash just to sell fights. I train hard and do my talking in the ring. I want people to respect me and to follow my fights, not because of what I say but what I do."

The one significant blemish on Canelo's record is a September 14, 2013, loss by decision to Floyd Mayweather. At age twenty-three, he wasn't ready for Mayweather. And the bout was fought at a 152-pound catchweight that wasn't right for him.

But Alvarez didn't just lose to Mayweather. He lost quietly. He looked confused (because he was) and didn't fight with the intensity that was expected of him.

"I was very young," Canelo says of that outing. "I don't take it as a defeat. I take it as an experience."

On November 11, 2015, Alvarez decisioned Miguel Cotto at a 155-pound catchweight to claim the WBC middleweight throne. He defended the title successfully against Amir Khan and Liam Smith at a similar weight limit before fighting a non-title bout against Julio Cesar Chavez Jr, at a contract limit of 164.5 pounds.

Meanwhile, Golovkin was collecting belts while fighting at 160 pounds, and it was getting harder to justify Canelo's claim to the middleweight crown.

An athlete should be praised for wanting to give his optimum performance every time out. No fighter should be forced to fight above or below his own best weight class. No one criticized Usain Bolt for not proving his dominance on the track by running 400-meters at the Olympics.

But Canelo was holding on to the WBC middleweight title while refusing to fight Golovkin (the mandatory WBC challenger) at 160 pounds. Eventually, the WBC forced the issue and Canelo vacated his throne.

"Canelo wanted to fight Golovkin at 160 pounds a long time ago," Eric Gomez said one day before the bout finally took place. "But Oscar, Chepo, and Eddy [promoter Oscar De La Hoya and Canelo's trainers, Chepo and Eddy Reynoso] felt it was too soon. It was the same thing before Canelo fought Mayweather. Back then, Canelo wanted the fight. Oscar, Chepo, and Eddy didn't. They felt it was too soon and at the wrong weight, but they bowed to Canelo's wishes. This time, Canelo listened when they told him a year ago that it was too soon for Golovkin, that he should wait until he grew to where his best weight was 160. They told him, 'Look what happened in the Mayweather fight. Now listen to us.'"

In spring 2017, Team Alvarez decided their man was ready. Canelo–Golovkin would be contested on September 16, 2017, at the T-Mobile Arena in Las Vegas at the middleweight limit of 160 pounds. The purse split heavily favored Alvarez. Golovkin would be obligated to fight an immediate rematch on prearranged terms if he won. Gennady would also be required to enter the ring first because, in De La Hoya's words, "Canelo is the lineal champion and the star of the show."

The bout was announced on May 6. Moments after Canelo scored a whitewash decision over Chavez Jr, Golovkin walked to the ring for the first of many pre-fight promotional encounters, and Alvarez told him, "I've never feared anyone. When I was born, fear was gone. I never got my share of fear."

"Good luck," Golovkin said.

"Luck is for mediocre people," Canelo countered.

Later, Alvarez would complain, "After this fight, they'll say there's another guy I'm avoiding."

Tickets were priced from $300 to $5,000 and soon sold out.

"We're ready for this fight," Alvarez proclaimed during an August 8 media conference call. "We asked for it. This is what we wanted. Anything can happen in boxing at any time, more so when both fighters have punching power. We both have the power to win by knockout. Whatever it takes to win the fight, that's what I'm going to do. I'm going to give all of me."

"He respects me, and I respect him," Golovkin acknowledged. "This is boxing. Every day is difficult and dangerous."

"It's going to be a chess match at the beginning," Abel Sanchez (Golovkin's trainer) posited. "Then, once you get past that point where they see what each other is doing, they're going to go at each other. I think both guys are going to hurt each other and may go down. It's going to be difficult for us, and we're looking forward to the challenge."

"That's a fight I'll actually buy tickets for and go to myself," UFC president Dana White said.

Technically, Golovkin's WBC, WBA, and IBF belts were on the line, as were Alvarez's *Ring* and "lineal" titles. But Canelo remained angry that the WBC had pressured him to fight Golovkin before he was ready to do so.

When asked about the world sanctioning bodies during the New York leg of the kickoff press tour, Eric Gomez diplomatically told the media, "We absolutely intend on fighting for the WBA and IBF. We haven't decided on the WBC."

Canelo quickly disagreed, saying, "No, I'm not fighting for the WBC."

In response, WBC president Mauricio Sulaiman later decreed, "It is a matter for the boxer. Golovkin will defend his title. We will sanction the fight and the winner will be the champion of the WBC. If anyone wants to resign or not accept the title, that decision is beyond our organization. The rules are clear. A boxer can vacate. And if that's the case, then the title will remain vacant."

There was a resounding buzz in the media center at the MGM Grand in Las Vegas during fight week.

A sport can't thrive if it relies exclusively on big events to satisfy its fans. A handful of big fights won't remedy boxing's problems.

Still, Canelo–Golovkin was special. Hardened scribes who've seen it all were genuinely looking forward to the fight. Expectations ran high. This was more than a big event. It was a big fight, important in terms of boxing history and likely to be both competitive and entertaining.

Every champion wants to be part of a fight for the ages. Elite athletes thrive on the biggest stage possible. Within that milieu, both fighters exuded quiet confidence like the calm in the eye of a hurricane.

Golovkin had never been involved in a fight of this magnitude before, but this was what he wanted. Big fight, big stage, big money, big historical importance.

"Gennady has been a little frustrated the last couple years that he hasn't had that marquee name step up and want to fight him," Abel Sanchez noted. "But he's happy that it's finally here. He has a sparkle in his eye."

"I am excited, waiting for fight," Golovkin said just prior to the final pre-fight press conference. "It's like you're going to meet with your new girlfriend. Is huge history fight."

Canelo responded in kind, saying, "I know it's going to be a tough fight, and that's what I'm ready for. I want to make it clear that I'm better than him. I'm writing my history now."

It promised to be a career-defining fight for each man and the biggest challenge that either had ever faced. Both men are big punchers. Each has a granite chin. Golovkin likes to force his opponent to the ropes. Canelo likes to counter off them. Each fighter knew that more than a few liver shots would be aimed in his direction.

No stone was left unturned in searching for clues as to the outcome. Six years earlier, Alvarez and Golovkin sparred with each other at Gennady's training camp in Big Bear, California. Asked about that session, Golovkin responded, "I knew him, big prospect from Golden Boy. I just remember a couple of rounds. I help him and he help me, just boxing, not true fight, sparring, not like very hard sparring. I remember he's a little bit young. His speed is good. His power for 154 is okay, not for 160. Different power, different time. That's a long time ago. This is different story right now, different weight, different age. Right now, last couple of fights, he has power. He has more experience. He's bigger, stronger. He's better."

"I was able to pick up some things," Canelo said. "But you can't really compare a sparring session to a fight. And we're different fighters now."

Alvarez had better-schooled opponents on his ring ledger than Golovkin did although, as earlier noted, many of them were smaller men past their prime. Also, his hands are faster than Golovkin's. The assumption was that Canelo would counterpunch against Gennady and pick his spots.

Alvarez's partisans also pointed to Golovkin's most recent outing, when he struggled against Danny Jacobs, as a source of hope. The counter-argument to that was, even in their prime, all great fighters have struggled against certain opponents. And Canelo's style is very different from Jacobs's.

Golovkin is now thirty-five. Alvarez is twenty-seven. "Gennady's age will catch up to him some day," Abel Sanchez conceded. "But it won't be in this fight."

Still, one wondered whether, against Alvarez, Golovkin might tire enough to make him vulnerable.

"GGG is not a boxer," Bernard Hopkins (an equity participant in Golden Boy) stated. "He has some boxing skills but he's essentially a stalker. He's going to be who he's been until it doesn't work for him. So he'll go after Canelo. Canelo can frustrate GGG. What I see happening is Canelo out-boxing him over twelve rounds. Once Golovkin shoots his load and realizes he has to go to Plan A, B, C, and D, we'll see if he knows his ABCs."

"We respect Golovkin's power," Eddy Reynoso said. "We know what his power is, and we have to be wary of that. But I truly believe Canelo is a more complete fighter, a more intelligent fighter."

Canelo is certainly a stronger, more complete fighter now than he was when he fought Mayweather. But Golovkin presented a completely different set of challenges.

Golovkin comes forward, attacking, attacking. He prefers non-stop engagement to more measured forms of combat. He'll trade punches all night if his opponent is willing. In theory, that leaves him vulnerable to counterpunches. But his opponents to date have found it difficult to put that theory into practice.

"I don't think we'll have to lure Canelo into a firefight," Abel Sanchez hypothesized. "I think that's in his nature as a fighter. But Canelo doesn't have Gennady's power. You can teach punching technique. You can't teach power. Gennady has power. Gennady will hit Canelo harder than Canelo has ever been hit."

"Canelo says he dreams about a knockout victory every night," a reporter told Golovkin just before the final pre-fight press conference.

"Yes," Gennady responded. "But he is dreaming."

Then Golovkin added what everyone knew.

"Is not an easy fight for him. Is not an easy fight for me."

Which fighter would dictate the pace of the fight and impose his fight plan on the other? There was no way to know. Golovkin had opened as a 3-to-2 betting favorite. By fight day, the odds had dropped to 7-to-5.

"My heart is with Canelo one hundred percent," Eric Gomez said. "And I think he'll win. But these are two great fighters, and this is boxing. Canelo can lose, and he can lose badly. Or he can win and look great."

"If you put a gun to my head," Larry Merchant offered, "I'd pick Golovkin. But if you put a gun to some other part of my body, I'd pick Canelo. That's how close it is."

"I am supporting Gennady because he is my friend," Sergey Kovalev noted. "But any prediction is no good."

For Golovkin, winning would be validation. For Canelo, winning would make him a legend.

★ ★ ★

Canelo Alvarez entered dressing room #7 at the T-Mobile Arena on Saturday, September 16, at 5:02 p.m. The partition that normally separates rooms 7 and 8 had been moved aside, creating a space roughly twenty yards long and twenty feet wide. Five black leather armchairs, a black leather sofa, and fourteen cushioned folding chairs were spread around the floor.

The walls were gray with fuchsia trim. The carpet was maroon and black. Four huge Golden Boy backdrops had been strategically hung from poles around the room so that one of them would be visible from every camera angle. Two large Mexican flags and a large flat-screen television monitor were on separate walls.

The ceilings were high, with recessed lighting. The room was big enough for a pick-up basketball game.

Alvarez was wearing a cobalt-blue tracksuit with gold lettering and white trim that matched the trunks and robe he would wear later in the night. The words on the back of his jacket read "Never Feared Anyone." The other members of his sixteen-man team, which included his father and four of his brothers, were similarly dressed.

When a fighter reaches star status, his dressing room reflects his own personal rhythm. Ricky Hatton's dressing room was a madhouse from the moment he walked in the door. There was booming music. Hatton never stopped dancing, throwing punches, and bouncing around, except when his hands were being taped. Bernard Hopkins, by contrast, would engage in quiet conversation until the end stages of preparation, when he morphed into Executioner mode.

Alvarez likes a low-key, quiet atmosphere in the hours before a fight. Reggae music would play softly in the background for the next few hours and the conversation would be limited.

Canelo sat on the sofa. A dozen members of his team took chairs around the room. Chepo Reynoso unpacked the corner equipment and put it next to Canelo's trunks, groin protector, shoes, and robe on one of four long tables that stretched along the wall adjacent to the door.

Chepo is the patriarch of Team Alvarez. He's the one who began the process of molding Canelo into a fighter when the thirteen-year-old boy walked into a gym in Guadalajara fourteen years ago and a journey to manhood began.

Later, the people around Canelo realized that, someday, he might be great.

Chepo still oversees Alvarez's training. His son, Eddy, does the hands-on work. Four years ago, after Canelo lost to Floyd Mayweather, a lot of people told him it was time to move away from the Reynosos. They could just as easily have told him to change his parents.

"This is beyond boxing," Canelo says of the Reynosos. "I met them when I was thirteen years old. They are my family."

Chepo has the face of a man who has seen the hard side of life. It's a face that says, even if life breaks your heart, it doesn't have to break you. And it's a kind face.

"I'm a happy man," Chepo said during fight week. "I've been married to my love for forty-three years."

Before leaving the hotel on fight night, Chepo gathered everyone on Team Alvarez together for a short prayer: "God, please, let no one be badly hurt. If we win, we win. It is in your hands."

MGM Grand president Richard Sturm came into Canelo's dressing room with several sponsor representatives. Canelo rose from the sofa, shook hands with each of them, and sat down again. Then he took out his smartphone, checked for messages, and began texting.

Times and pre-fight rituals have changed. It's hard to imagine Rocky Marciano texting in his dressing room before a fight.

When Canelo had finished texting, he leaned back on the sofa, arms folded across his chest. There were more well-wishers and sponsor representatives, each of whom wanted a handshake and smartphone photo. Chepo looked on with an air of resignation. Golden Boy matchmaker Robert Diaz orchestrated the procession well. The visitors were soon gone.

Eddy Reynoso took a seat to Canelo's left. For the most part, they sat silently, engaging in only sporadic conversation. Other members of the entourage sat or stood quietly in a large semi-circle with Canelo as the focal point.

Alvarez turned his attention to the TV monitor on the wall. The first televised undercard fight of the evening was underway. Occasionally, he rested his forearms on his thighs or raised his left hand to stroke his chin.

HBO production coordinator Tami Cotel entered with Max Kellerman for a brief pre-fight interview. After they left, Canelo lay down on the floor, put two rolled-up towels beneath his head, folded his hands across his chest, and closed his eyes.

The room was quiet except for the soft music in the background. Canelo opened his eyes from time to time, looked briefly at the TV monitor, and closed his eyes again. His face seemed to radiate the vulnerability of a boy. It's a young face for someone who's twenty-seven years old and has engaged in more than fifty professional fights over the course of twelve years.

In two hours, the eyes of the world would be upon him as he engaged in brutal combat.

Golden Boy president Eric Gomez came in, circled the room, and shook hands with everyone. He was followed by Bob Bennett (executive director of the Nevada State Athletic Commission), who entered with Nevada governor Brian Sandoval and referee Kenny Bayless.

Bayless gave the fighter his pre-fight instructions. When he was done, Chepo requested that the referee warn Golovkin about hitting behind the head and to be vigilant about the infraction during the fight.

"Please, from the first time you see it, address it."

Bayless promised that he would.

Canelo put on his trunks, stood up, stretched while pacing around the room, yawned, and went back to watching the TV monitor.

It was hard to imagine that, in a little more than an hour, this quiet, almost-passive young man would transform into an instrument of destruction.

Victor Espinoza, who won horseracing's triple crown onboard American Pharaoh two years ago, came in and wished Alvarez well.

At 6:45, Canelo dropped to the floor and did twenty push-ups followed by a series of stomach crunches, his first exercise of the evening. Then he asked that his hands be taped.

An inspector was dispatched to Golovkin's dressing room to summon the customary witness. A minute later, he returned and reported, "Abel Sanchez says he was told the taping would be at seven o'clock. He won't be here until seven."

NSAC chief inspector Francisco Soto, who was assigned to Canelo's dressing room, wasn't pleased.

"Tell him we start in two minutes whether he's here or not."

Sanchez arrived.

Eddy began taping Canelo's left hand.

A thin layer of gauze. Tape. More gauze.

"You can't do that," Sanchez protested. "It's stacking."

"It's done by everybody and his mother," Soto said.

"I won't allow it," Sanchez persisted. "I'll file a protest."

The taping continued with a second layer of tape.

"You can't do that," Sanchez said again.

"Abel," Soto warned, "you have to stop or send someone else over here."

At 7:12, the taping was done. Sanchez left. He was not a happy camper.

"There are a lot of things that aren't specifically forbidden by the rules," Abel said after the fight. "But you aren't allowed to do them because they're wrong. Stacking is illegal. Just because some people get away with it doesn't make it right."

Canelo's family and the members of his entourage who wouldn't be in his corner left the room. Canelo hugged each of them as they departed. Then he put on his protective cup and trunks. Eddy Reynoso applied Vaseline to his face, arms, and legs.

Canelo began shadow-boxing to rhythmic clapping from the members of his team who were left.

The mood was changing. There was an undercurrent of nervous energy. Part of the price a fighter pays for competing is that he can be beaten up.

Canelo paced back and forth.

Abel Sanchez returned at 7:40. Chepo gloved Canelo up, left hand first.

When that task was done, Eddy held up a round black leather cushion with both hands and moved it from position to position as Canelo punched. That was followed by Eddy swinging two yellow Styrofoam tubes in Canelo's direction as the fighter parried or evaded them by bobbing and weaving.

There was a minute of traditional padwork.

"We can teach him," Eddy has said. "But in the ring, he has to make his own decisions."

HBO production coordinator Tami Cotel returned and announced, "Six minutes until your opponent walks."

Oscar De La Hoya and Bernard Hopkins entered and wished Alvarez well.

Canelo had been in his dressing room for three hours. There had been relatively little exertion. But he was ready.

★ ★ ★

It had been agreed that Golovkin would be introduced last but walk to the ring first. The partisan crowd of 22,358 let out a near-deafening roar as Canelo made his way down the aisle. They were there for what they hoped would be the dawn of a new era in boxing.

Michael Buffer introduced the fighters. Excitement inside the arena was at a fever pitch.

The fighters fought cautiously in the opening rounds, each one showing respect for the other's power. Golovkin advanced behind an aggressive jab. Canelo had the faster hands and seemed to land the cleaner punches. But Gennady kept stalking his man, landing more often than his counterpart.

Rounds four through nine belonged largely to Golovkin, who took control of the fight. He increased his output of power punches while Alvarez circled away and fought off the ropes, shaking his head when Gennady landed and also when Gennady missed. What Canelo didn't do was land enough effective punches of his own and make Golovkin pay for his misses.

Canelo is a counterpuncher. But as a general rule, he's quick to exchange when an opponent wants to. Here, more often than not, he didn't.

"Gennady will go out and do what he does best," Abel Sanchez had said before the fight. And Canelo will have to adapt to it."

Now, whatever Alvarez did, Golovkin moved inexorably forward. Even when Canelo landed solidly, Gennady walked through the blows.

There were outbursts of furious action that sent the crowd into a frenzy. Neither fighter went to the body as often as might have been expected. Afterward, Sanchez would explain, "Canelo's movement and quicker hands made going to the body difficult. He counters well. A couple of times, I asked Gennady to go to the body a bit more, but he didn't feel the opportunities were there."

Still, Golovkin was fighting confidently. And Alvarez seemed to be fading in the face of his adversary's power.

The action was intense from beginning to end. There was no margin for error. A fight isn't like Microsoft Word. A fighter can't simply click "command-Z" to undo a mistake.

Then, remarkably, Canelo turned the tide.

A fighter doesn't win fights by taking big punches. But if he can take big punches, it can keep him in the fight.

Alvarez took Golovkin's punches better than anyone else had before. Gennady is accustomed to seeing opponents crumble as he grinds them down. Canelo didn't crumble. He came back strong.

In round ten, Alvarez launched his most effective sustained assault of the fight. Now it was Golovkin's turn to take punches and fight back hard. But he was no longer in control.

Heart, courage, stamina, skill. Each man showed it all. They were warriors in the finest tradition of boxing and fought hard until the end. It was superb fight.

Some of the rounds were difficult to score. The consensus at ringside was that Golovkin had done enough in the middle rounds to win. Then Michael Buffer announced the scoring of the judges.

Boxing fans have a sense of justice. Adelaide Byrd's tally was the first that Buffer read: 118–110 for Alvarez. That was greeted with disbelief from the crowd, as though Buffer had incorrectly read the score.

Dave Moretti was next: 115–113 for Golovkin.

And finally, Don Trella: 114–114, a draw.

Several days after the fight, Abel Sanchez told this writer, "I scored it seven rounds to five for Gennady. I can't argue with a draw."

But Adelaide Byrd's 118–110 scorecard cast a pall over the proceedings. If she had scored the bout 115–113 for Alvarez, the result would still have been a draw, but the decision would have smelled better.

Hall of Fame sportswriter Red Smith was fond of saying, "If you want to know who won a fight, just ask a nine-year-old kid who watched it."

A nine-year-old kid would have known that Byrd's scorecard was a travesty. Promoters and fighters have objected to her erratic judging in the past, but the Nevada State Athletic Commission continues to assign her to important fights.

In this instance, NSAC executive director Bob Bennett acknowledged that Byrd's scorecard was "a little wide." That's like saying that, after Hurricane Harvey, Houston got "a little wet." Thereafter, Bennett backtracked and acknowledged, "In any business, sometimes you have a bad day. It happens, I'm not going to put her right back in. She'll still be in the business, but she needs to catch her breath. Unfortunately, she didn't do well."

Millions of dollars and fighters' careers hang on a judge's judgment. Things happen in boxing that aren't expected to happen. And things happen that shouldn't happen. There's a difference.

After the fight, Canelo sat in a black leather chair in a corner of his dressing room with a disconsolate look on his face. He thought he'd won and was bitterly disappointed.

Eddy and Chepo Reynoso sat on either side of him. Several toddlers who had no idea what had happened an hour earlier were asleep in their mothers' arms or scurrying around the room.

"The judges think he punches like a monster," Alvarez said. "So when his punches landed, he got more credit for them that I got for mine. My punches were just as hard as his, harder."

Still, the lumps and bruises on Canelo's face bore witness to the fact that he'd been in the ring with his equal as a fighter.

Eric Gomez entered the room. "Nobody lost here tonight," he reminded the assemblage.

Each fighter kept the titles he'd had when the evening began. A rematch on Cinco De Mayo 2018 would be lovely.

In recent years, it has been lamented that a fighting spirit is no longer prerequisite to being a star in boxing. Gennady Golovkin and Canelo Alvarez each evidenced a fighting spirit. Their battle was a celebration of boxing.

*When there's a high-profile matchup in boxing, I usually write after the fight. This piece on Floyd Mayweather vs. Conor McGregor, written four weeks in advance, was an exception to that rule.*

# Mayweather–McGregor: The Dark Underside of the Sting

## Part One

Hall of Fame matchmaker Bruce Trampler was reminiscing recently about a meeting with Al Haymon that took place at Top Rank years ago. Floyd Mayweather was still a Top Rank fighter. Haymon was Mayweather's advisor.

"Al came in to discuss Floyd's next fight with Bob [Arum]," Trampler recalled. "They were going to meet in Bob's office. Al was early. He had a few minutes to kill, so he stopped by my office. And I remember very clearly, Al said to me, 'I'm going to be talking with Bob about a fight for Floyd. Bob will probably call you in at some point for your opinion. I'd appreciate it if you didn't mention Antonio Margarito as a prospective opponent.'"

"That was the formula," Trampler continued. "Al and Floyd were ducking a guy who, at that time, would have been a very dangerous opponent. They knew how to minimize risk versus reward, which, if you're a fighter or a fighter's manager, isn't necessarily a bad thing to do."

On August 26, 2017, at T-Mobile Arena in Las Vegas, Floyd Mayweather will face Conor McGregor in a boxing match that shapes up as offering the greatest high-reward to low-risk ratio in the history of sports.

We live in an age when spectacle is often valued more highly than substance. Mayweather–McGregor fits that billing.

Mayweather has fashioned a 49–0 (26 KOs) record as a professional boxer and is universally regarded as one of the best fighters of his time. McGregor has a 21–3 record as a mixed martial arts combatant and has never boxed in a recognized amateur tournament or as a pro.

The fight will be contested at 154 pounds and is scheduled for twelve rounds or less, with emphasis on the less. To ensure that McGregor doesn't revert to MMA tactics, the bout contracts contain a substantial penalty for "extreme fouls."

The public ticket sale began on July 24, with list prices ranging from $500 to $10,000. It's unclear how many tickets were actually made available to the general public.

The pay-per-view price is $99.95 for HDTV and $89.95 for standard transmission. There will be an aggressive anti-piracy effort by the promotion. A confidentiality clause precludes both camps from disclosing revenue splits and other financial details of the promotion.

Mayweather–McGregor will likely be the second-highest-grossing event in the history of boxing. It's "trash sports." But as event, it will be huge.

"People can downplay it and call it whatever they want," Mayweather Promotions CEO Leonard Ellerbe said in New York on July 13. "This is big."

British boxing writer Tris Dixon put the matter in further perspective, writing: "Mayweather–McGregor might not make sense to you. It does not need to. It needs to generate interest across different age groups, across different demographics, tap into a wide audience, and build on a storyline that has already generated considerable global interest. Floyd knows how to play this game better than anyone, and you shouldn't hate the player but the game that enables it. You might not like it, but that's business. That's show business. And ultimately, that's boxing."

Dixon is right. Don't blame the fighters. Is there a boxer on the planet who would turn down the opportunity to fight a novice opponent for $100 million? I doubt it. If someone offered me tens of millions of dollars to embarrass myself by singing badly at Carnegie Hall, I'd do it.

That said, no amount of pre-fight promotion can void that fact that Mayweather will be boxing a guy who doesn't know how. If Mayweather–McGregor were to go twelve rounds, Floyd would win fifteen of them. The fight has no more credibility as a sports competition than the 2008 WWE spectacle of Mayweather vs. Big Show.

Anyone who pays to watch Mayweather–McGregor because they think it will be a competitive sporting event has a ludicrously wrong idea of what combat sports are about.

McGregor isn't a boxer. He's a mixed martial artist with lesser boxing skills than most good club fighters have. He might not even be the most skilled combatant that mixed martial arts has to offer. Let's not forget, Conor has been beaten three times, including a loss by submission seventeen months ago to Nate Diaz (who had an 18-and-10 record). When they met in a rematch five months later, the best McGregor could do was eke out a 48–47, 48–47, 47–47 majority decision.

In an effort to propagate the notion that Mayweather–McGregor will be a competitive fight, the promotion has relied on a series of myths.

Myth 1: McGregor has a solid amateur background in boxing.

Rebuttal: McGregor reportedly (the operative word is "reportedly") won a novice (the operative word is "novice") tournament in Ireland when he was a boy. But no hard facts have been presented in support of this contention. And even if it were true, it would be irrelevant. McGregor will be the least-skilled opponent that Mayweather has fought in his fifty-bout professional boxing career.

Myth 2: McGregor knows how Mayweather boxes, but Floyd will be unable to prepare properly for Conor because Floyd doesn't know how Conor will box.

Rebuttal: Mayweather doesn't know how McGregor will box because Conor doesn't know how to box.

Myth 3: Mayweather has trouble fighting southpaws, and McGregor is a southpaw.

Rebuttal: Mayweather has trouble with southpaws? Really? Maybe Clayton Kershaw or Madison Bumgarner can fight Floyd next. And by the way, Manny Pacquiao was a southpaw.

Myth 4: Mayweather, at age forty, is getting old. McGregor, at twenty-nine, is in his prime.

Rebuttal: Is Mayweather aging as a fighter? Yes. But he's still a professional boxer. And McGregor isn't. Any professional golfer on the PGA Seniors Tour would trounce Oscar De La Hoya (a relatively young man and pretty good golfer) over eighteen holes. Why? Because they're professional golfers and Oscar isn't.

Myth 5: Mayweather–McGregor is similar in principle to the 1976 boxer-wrestler matchup between Muhammad Ali and Antonio Inoki, which was a competitive fight.

Rebuttal: Parallels to Ali–Inoki are fallacious. Ali–Inoki wasn't a boxing match. If it had been, Ali would have knocked Inoki out whenever he wanted to. Inoki was allowed to wrestle and spent the entire fifteen rounds crab-walking around the ring on his rear end, trying to kick Ali in the legs.

Myth 6: Mayweather–McGregor is a classic matchup between a "boxer" and a "puncher." McGregor has a "puncher's chance."

Rebuttal: Actually, Mayweather punches harder than McGregor. By and large, mixed martial artists don't hit as hard as boxers do because their weight is distributed differently. If a mixed martial artist sets himself to punch like a boxer, he's vulnerable to kicks. And learning to punch like a boxer can't be achieved in a few months of training. Also, the "knockout power" in McGregor's fists has been sheathed in four-ounce gloves. Against Mayweather, his blows will be cushioned by eight ounces on each hand.

In today's world, if something is said again and again and pushed out over social media, people who want to believe it will believe it no matter how absurd it is. Show Mayweather and McGregor standing face to face often enough, talk enough about how it will be a competitive fight, and people who don't understand boxing (which includes much of the mainstream media) will think there's a chance that it will be competitive.

Anyone who thinks that Conor McGregor has a realistic chance to beat Floyd Mayweather in a boxing match is living in a universe of "alternative facts."

People can con their way through a lot of things in today's world, but not through a professional fight.

It's not hard to imagine how Mayweather–McGregor will play out. Mayweather will stuff a few stiff jabs in McGregor's face. Jabs that a world-class boxer would be used to but will be the sharpest punches that McGregor has been hit with in his life. Then Floyd will dance around. At some point, McGregor will start posturing and shouting things along the lines of, "Stand and fight like a man, you [expletive deleted]." And Floyd will knock him out when he wants to.

McGregor has never fought more than five rounds before (yeah, I know; UFC rounds are longer). If Mayweather chooses to not knock McGregor out, Conor is likely to collapse from exhaustion.

If I'm wrong, I'll eat my words. But I don't think there will be a need for that.

Hey, McGregor isn't even used to wearing shoes in combat.

Mayweather–McGregor is the sporting equivalent of an eating contest between a python and a bunny rabbit, or entering one of Budweiser's Clydesdale horses in the Kentucky Derby. It's Roy Jones going one-on-one in basketball against Stephen Curry.

The people who say Mayweather–McGregor will be competitive make the point that boxing and MMA both involve punching people. I'm unimpressed. The marathon and the hundred-meter dash both involve running. But the most accomplished marathon runner in the world wouldn't stand a chance against an elite sprinter in a 100-meter dash. And vice versa in a marathon. The shotput and javelin both involve throwing things as far as possible. But the best javelin thrower in the world wouldn't be competitive in a field of elite shotputters. Could the best ping-pong player in the world beat Roger Federer at Wimbledon? Of course, not. Why not? Because they're different sports.

As Laila Ali said on ESPN last month, "You've got a UFC fighter, who has no boxing experience, fighting one of the best fighters in the world. So if you buy the fight, don't be pissed if it ends too fast or it wasn't competitive. I'm going to be asking, 'What did you expect?' If you think it's going to be a good fight, then you're stupid and you get what you deserve."

So much for Mayweather–McGregor as a sporting event. But as the promotion has evolved, it has come to represent much more than a prizefight. There has been a dark underside to it all.

## Part Two

As a general rule, Michael Buffer steers clear of controversy. He has strong opinions on a wide range of subjects, including politics. But the greatest ring announcer in boxing history understands that his success is based in part on the fact that fans view him as impartial and evenhanded. So when Buffer has something critical to say, it's generally confined to a close circle of friends.

On July 12, 2017, Buffer pushed the envelope of this self-imposed limitation a bit. Following a media tour event that day in Toronto to promote Floyd Mayweather vs. Conor McGregor, Buffer sent an e-mail to Bob Bennett (executive director of the Nevada State Athletic Commission). Mayweather–McGregor will be contested in Las Vegas on August 26.

The e-mail, which is accessible under the Nevada Open Records Act, recounted Buffer having just watched an online stream of the Toronto event. It expressed dismay at the conduct of the participants, which Buffer termed "quite disgusting and disgraceful" and "degrading and insulting to the spirit of sportsmanship." Buffer then urged the Nevada State Athletic Commission to take steps now and in the future to make it clear that conduct like this "does not represent the values of the NSAC and will not be condoned at any time" because it "reflects on the values of the commission, the community of the promotion, and the state."

On the two days that followed, when the media tour was in New York and London, the conduct got worse.

Mayweather–McGregor is a personality-driven spectacle. For many, McGregor's most redeeming personal quality is that he's not Mayweather. And vice versa. On the media tour, there were times when the two men resembled actors in a bad porn film.

Tim Freeman of the *Daily Beast* described the proceedings as "a spectacularly debasing scramble to the bottom of the barrel" and "a whacked-out circus of two apparently straight men touring the world in ridiculous outfits, screaming demented insults at each other to promote a boxing match."

Mayweather and McGregor hadn't met prior their four-city media tour. Their union was not cordial. "It gets worse every city we go to," UFC president Dana White said. "In each city, they seem to hate each other more."

Some of the dialogue was standard fare.

"He will be unconscious inside four rounds," McGregor declared. "The movement, the power, the ferociousness; he has not experienced this. He's not gonna be able to keep me off him. He's too small. I'm gonna have my way."

"We know Mr. Tap Out likes to quit," Mayweather responded, referencing McGregor's prior MMA losses. "I'm guaranteeing you this. You're going out on your face or on your back. So which way do you want to go?"

Then there was the matter of the tax liens that the Internal Revenue Service has filed against Mayweather, claiming that "Money" owes lots of it to the federal government: $22,200,000 for tax year 2015 and $7,200,000 for 2010.

"He's in a dire situation," McGregor chortled. "The reason he has accepted this fight to come out of retirement is because he has to."

Typical promotional banter. But things quickly crossed over the line between decent and indecent.

The tour was designed to attract attention from the mainstream media and also to energize each fighter's fan base. To accomplish these ends, Mayweather and McGregor engaged in racist, misogynist, homophobic, profanity-ridden tirades throughout the tour. Each day was uglier than the day before.

Tens of thousands of fans (the overwhelming majority of them pro-McGregor) attended the proceedings and became part of the show.

At the Los Angeles tour event, McGregor wore what would otherwise have been a conservative tailored suit. But the pinstripes read "fuck you." In Toronto, Conor led fans in chanting, "Fuck the Mayweathers!" and referenced an adult club called The Girl Collection that Mayweather recently opened in Las Vegas. He also called Showtime Sports executive vice president and general manager Stephen Espinoza a "little fucking weasel" and a "fucking bitch."

By the time the promotional tour reached Barclays Center in Brooklyn, any semblance of decorum was gone. The event at Barclays started ninety minutes late, reportedly because Mayweather was jewelry shopping in New York's diamond district. There were flashing lights, loud music, and 13,165 screaming fans in attendance.

McGregor was shirtless, wearing a white fur coat with a serpent on the back, gaudy pants that looked as though they'd been fashioned from psychedelic draperies, and sunglasses.

Mayweather entered with an Irish flag draped over his shoulders and later threw it to the ground.

McGregor ranted for slightly more than five minutes in his opening statement, calling Mayweather a "fucking little squirt" and saying that Floyd could "suck this dick."

In Los Angeles and Toronto, McGregor had told Mayweather to, "Dance for me, boy." That had engendered criticism, which McGregor spoke to in New York.

"Let's address the race [issue]," McGregor told the crowd at Barclays Center. "A lot of the media seem to be saying I'm against black people.

That's absolutely fucking ridiculous. Do they not know I'm half-black? Yeah. I'm half-black, from the belly button down. And just to show that that's squashed, here's a little present for my beautiful, black female fans."

Then McGregor began thrusting his pelvis back and forth with his microphone strategically placed to simulate sexual intercourse.

At each stop, Mayweather sank as low as McGregor. In London, he called McGregor a "faggot."

Why sanitize and camouflage it? Put it out there in all its glory.

All four press conferences were posted online in their entirety by the promotion.

How offensive were they? Boxing is fond of punch counts. Here's a different kind of count.

McGregor started relatively tamely at the Los Angeles media conference, limiting himself to saying "fuck" and derivations thereof seven times and "shit" four times. Mayweather equaled him with seven "fucks," adding four "bitches," and two "shits."

In Toronto, McGregor "outfucked" Mayweather by a 21-to-17 margin, but Floyd had an 8-to-5 edge in "bitches." Conor also said "shit" four times and "pussy" twice.

In Brooklyn, McGregor uttered "fuck" five times, adding "cunt," "shit," and "bitch" for good measure. Floyd utilized "fuck" and "bitch" equally (nine times each), throwing in "shit" and "pussy" for good measure. Each man also called the other a "ho" twice.

In London, McGregor "outfucked" Mayweather 21 to 11 and called Floyd "a stupid baldy twat." Floyd had a narrow 10-to-9 edge in "bitches" and unfurled the more varied vocabulary, spewing forth three "shits," two "hoes," and two "pussies." There was also Floyd's "faggot" utterance.

All of this was regarded as effective marketing by the promotion. On August 26, McGregor is likely to be reduced to the role of a trash-talking punching bag. But he'll make tens of millions of dollars.

As for Mayweather, this fight fits perfectly with his legacy and finances. Floyd has generated extraordinary pay-per-view numbers for fights against Manny Pacquiao, Canelo Alvarez, and Oscar De La Hoya. But his most recent outing against Andre Berto in 2015 fell flat, engendering roughly five hundred thousand buys. That would be a strong showing for most fighters. But it was Mayweather's lowest pay-per-view total since he fought Carlos Baldomir eleven years ago. In other words, the public seemed to be tiring of Floyd. He needs a dance partner.

McGregor is the perfect dance partner.

Meanwhile, Mayweather–McGregor represents a difficult balancing act for UFC and Dana White.

UFC is used to calling the shots. It's not calling them here. Mayweather–McGregor isn't a UFC event. Conor is fighting Floyd pursuant to what is essentially a provision of services agreement. Mayweather Promotions is promoting the fight and Showtime (not UFC) will produce the telecast.

People can like or dislike MMA. But White is almost universally admired for being a credible advocate for fans. Unlike many promoters, he keeps it real.

Mayweather–McGregor has forced White to straddle the line between reality and salesmanship. At times, he has been candid:

- "It's the fight that everybody wanted. We're delivering it. Now when I go out and start talking to people, they want me to defend the fight. I didn't make this fight. The fans made this fight. It is what it is."
- "Conor wanted to do this fight, so we're doing it for him. Whatever happens happens." "I hope it's a good fight. If the fight sucks, it's bad."
- "Listen, he's a fighter, not a boxer."

But other times, White has been more salesman than honest analyst:

- "Floyd Mayweather's going to fight at 154 pounds against a monster. Conor McGregor is huge. Wait till they meet face to face for the first time and square off and people see the difference in the size between them."
- "When Conor McGregor touches people, they go to sleep."
- "The great thing about fights is, you never know who's going to win."
- "I stopped doubting Conor McGregor a long time ago."

UFC has avoided branding Mayweather–McGregor as a UFC venture. But the fight risks taking the UFC brand into the gutter. There have been times during the promotion when White has looked uncomfortable and embarrassed to be there.

For Floyd, Mayweather–McGregor is a one-time money grab. The same holds true for Conor, who might retire after the bout (costing UFC its flagship fighter).

UFC has to view the bout in a long-term context. One assumes that it has a plan in place to deal with the fallout that's likely to follow.

The State of Nevada loves the fight.

After approving Mayweather–McGregor, the Nevada State Athletic Commission will be hard-pressed to turn down any fight ever again on grounds that it's not competitive. Unless, of course, the commission's explanation for approving Mayweather–McGregor is, "A fight doesn't have to be competitive if it generates enough money."

But that has always been the standard in Nevada.

Last year, the Nevada State Athletic Commission ordered McGregor to perform twenty-five hours of community service after Conor acted out inappropriately at a press conference in advance of his August 2016 rematch against Nate Diaz. To fulfill the requirement, McGregor spoke with children in Dublin about physical and verbal bullying. How does that square with his performance on the recent Mayweather–McGregor media tour?

Showtime, at least in the short term, also comes out a winner.

Things might have been a bit unpleasant for Stephen Espinoza, who has been cast in the role of corporate villain by McGregor and his fans. Millions of viewers watched the media tour events on Facebook and other platforms. For some McGregor partisans, Espinoza immediately became an object of derision, scorn, and even hate.

One day after the promotional tour ended, a Google search for "weasel" with the requirement that the posting include "Espinoza" yielded 147,000 results. Espinoza had previously laughed off the "weasel" appellation, saying, "At the range of insults, it's certainly at the low end." But one person with knowledge of the situation says that Showtime took the step of providing Espinoza with extra personal security when the media tour reached London.

Over the years, Showtime and HBO have both enabled Mayweather's anti-social conduct, particularly with regard to his treatment of women. But after Manny Pacquiao uttered homophobic remarks last year, HBO repudiated them in a statement that read, "We felt it important to leave no uncertainty about our position on Mr. Pacquiao's recent comments toward the LGBTQ community. We consider them insensitive, offensive and deplorable."

Showtime has been institutionally silent so far with regard to the misogyny, racism, and homophobia that marked the Mayweather–McGregor promotion. The network has increased its visibility and stands to make money, both directly from its share of pay-per-view revenue and indirectly by increasing its subscriber base as a consequence of the fight. But its silence is a sad commentary on the relationship between entertainment and responsible television.

Whether or not fans who buy the Mayweather–McGregor pay-per-view are satisfied will depend, obviously, on the flow of the fight and what their expectations are.

Some people will watch Mayweather–McGregor because they think Conor has a good chance to win. They don't know they're being hustled. Others will buy it because they look forward to seeing McGregor get his comeuppance. A third group will buy in because the fight is a happening and they're enjoying the ride.

"Times have changed," Mayweather Promotions CEO Leonard Ellerbe said in Brooklyn in defense of the fight. "You've got to get away from the way things were done before. Don't get mad at us because we found a way to take this to a whole new level. We're giving the fans exactly what they want."

When Mayweather–McGregor is over, will the people who paid $99.95 to buy it feel satisfied or ripped off ? And will anyone involved in the promotion care?

A warning to would-be buyers who think that the pre-fight spectacle has been great fun. You're likely to find that the actual fight is less entertaining than the hoopla you've enjoyed so far.

## Part Three

Floyd Mayweather and Conor McGregor aren't responsible for the welfare of boxing. There are organizations that are charged with that mission. Still, it's appropriate to ask whether Mayweather–McGregor is good or bad for the sweet science.

Some people believe that Mayweather–McGregor is good for boxing because it will bring casual viewers to the sport. But so did the 2015 fight between Mayweather and Manny Pacquiao. And what casual viewers saw that night turned them off.

Also, no matter how the storyline in Mayweather–McGregor plays out, the fight epitomizes the sad condition that boxing is in today.

There's a certain purity to signature sporting events in that they feature the best competing against the best. Professional basketball would be in a sorry state if a team comprised of successful rap artists could play the Golden State Warriors and engender better television ratings than the NBA Championship Finals. The fact that a substantial segment of the public is supporting Mayweather–McGregor with its dollars in the belief that it's the best entertainment that boxing has to offer confirms that boxing is in a bad place.

If the lords of boxing did their job properly, Mayweather–McGregor would be a sideshow, not a major event. But they haven't done their job properly. Instead, by flooding the market with more than one hundred "world champions" and too often denying fans the fights they want to see, they've created an environment in which Mayweather–McGregor became possible.

Andreas Hale put the matter in perspective when he wrote: "If you are one of those people who think that this spectacle hurts boxing, then you are overlooking everything from terrible matchmaking and the existence of sanctioning bodies to horrible judging that has marred the sport. This fight absolutely cannot add to that. The only way this fight can actually hurt boxing is if McGregor were to knock Mayweather out. Rest assured, boxing will be in the same state it was before and after Mayweather–McGregor, for better or worse."

Similarly, writing for *The Queensberry Rules*, Brent Hedke observed, "There's always going to be bad decisions. There's always going to be horrible broadcasting. There's always going to be some form of corruption. There's always going to be psychotically inaccurate rankings. There's always going to be boring fights. But what there's maybe not always going to be is an audience. It seems like having two guys punch each other in the face and pointing a camera at it would be impossible to fuck up. But here we are."

However, there are issues surrounding Mayweather–McGregor that go far beyond boxing.

The Mayweather–McGregor media tour was toxic and added to a poison that has been spreading throughout the United States. It was all there. The devaluation of women, racism, homophobia, the use of personal attacks and obscenities instead of rational dialogue.

Dana White called Mayweather and McGregor "two of the best shit-talkers in both sports" and sought to justify their conduct.

"It's funny when people say they've taken this thing too far," White opined. "This is a fight, not a croquet game. This part of the deal; the reality is what's going on here is just as much of the fight as the fight itself, the mental warfare game. What this is all about is trying to get in each other's heads. That's why you've seen this thing escalate to where we are now."

Oh, I understand it now.

So if LeBron James called Stephen Curry a "faggot" before the NBA Championship Finals last year. And Kevin Love, after saying he was "half-black, from the belly button down," simulated sexual orgasm with a hand-held microphone between his legs as "a little present for my beautiful black female fans." And Draymon Greene responded by calling Kyrie Irving, a "cunt," a "bitch," and a "ho." . . . NBA commissioner Adam Silver would say, "This is basketball, not a croquet game. This is part of the deal."

I don't think so.

The establishment (Showtime, Las Vegas, corporate sponsors) and pay-per-view buyers around the world are coming together to reward these expressions of bigotry and prejudice with two of the largest paychecks in the history of sports.

Writing in *Sports Illustrated*, Charles Pierce called the promotion a "glorified cholera outbreak" and "festival of fools." He then condemned the "racism, sexism, and homophobia" at the core of the promotion and placed it in the context of 2017, noting, "It is a fearful dangerous time. And while there is never a good time for a prizefight that seeks to turn that dread and unease into a big payday, it's especially not that time now."

Sarah Spain expressed similar thoughts on ESPNW.com: "As their exchanges get uglier and more offensive, it's time to check back in with ourselves. Are these the kind of people deserving of our attention, admiration, and time? If we give celebs like them a pass on homophobia, misogyny and bigotry, how many others will feel entitled to express their own hate?"

One of the most eloquent critiques came from Tim Freeman of the *Daily Beast*, who weighed in on Mayweather calling McGregor a faggot:

> To give his ugly litany proper context 'Punk. You faggot. You ho.' There it is. Loud. Like a bullet. A knife. Threatening. I'm ready for 'It's only pre-match hype.' It's all pantomime. This happens in every big boxing match. None of them mean it. This is just boxers trash talking.' . . . Don't bother. We can all hear how Mayweather says, and means, 'faggot.' He means 'faggot' when faggot means 'gay,' when 'gay' means 'less of a man than me' who should be scared of me when I shout 'faggot' at him, and know his lower disgusting place. The ultimate, demasculinizing insult. That kind of 'faggot.' Mayweather said 'faggot' just the way gay men and men assumed to be gay have heard 'faggot' shouted, said, whispered, spat at them for centuries.
>
> If this all sounds a little dramatic and you've never been called a 'faggot,' here's a primer. You never know when it's coming. You might be at school. You might be in a restroom. You might be going to lunch. You might be leaving a bar or club. You may be with friends. You may be on a bus or train. At night. During the day. But every time, it scythes the air. And you think: Now? You may not be out as gay. You may be coming out. You may not even be gay. But the threat is suddenly there. This is 'faggot' as the bigots with their fists, guns, weapons, and whatever else they have to injure and degrade gay people intend it to be heard. And ironically, as Mayweather said this as a prelude to beating another man up, it often comes with the threat of a fist or worse. The word can even be carved into both your arms—'Die Fag,' to be precise—by your attackers. Perhaps Mayweather thinks that sounds pretty cool.

The genie is now out of the bottle. We might hear statements later on to the effect of, "Oh, we were just doing this to build interest in the fight" . . . "One of my closest business associates is gay" . . . "I love women and black people" . . . "I apologize if I offended anyone."

That won't eliminate the damage that has been done so far and is being done every day by this toxic promotion. It's a metaphor for some of the worst impulses of our time.

And there's another important point to make.

During the media tour, McGregor taunted Mayweather for not being able to read at an adult level. He taunted Mayweather for owing millions of dollars in back taxes. He was crude, belligerent, and insulting. But McGregor did not mention the fact that Mayweather was convicted on multiple occasions and served sixty-three days in jail for being physically abusive to women.

Let's make that point again so you don't miss it.

With all the insults and profanity and bigotry and prejudice that were hurled back and forth, McGregor didn't reference the fact that Mayweather was criminally convicted on three occasions and spent time in jail for physically abusing women.

Why not?

Because to do so might have led to closer mainstream media scrutiny of the underside of Mayweather–McGregor. It might push some potential pay-per-view buyers, corporate sponsors, and others away and cost the promotion dollars.

Racism, misogyny, and homophobia might be good for business to a point. But reminding people that hate speech sometimes translates into action could pose problems.

It would be interesting to know if one or more clauses in the many contracts that govern Mayweather–McGregor preclude McGregor, Showtime personnel, and others from referencing Mayweather's criminal convictions for being physically abusive to women.

We're living in a time of hate-filled rhetoric and an assault on human rights. The gains made in recent decades by women, people of color, and the LGBT community are under attack.

Somewhere, as you read this, men who think that Floyd Mayweather and Conor McGregor are really cool role models are abusing women. The abuse will psychologically scar some of the women for life. Maybe one of the abusers will kill his victim. Similar abuse is playing out against victims because of their race and sexual orientation.

This is not a time to glorify and financially reward people who demean others by calling them "bitch," "ho," "boy," "cunt," and "faggot." Every person who buys or otherwise supports the Mayweather–McGregor pay-per-view is doing just that.

## Postfight: Mayweather–McGregor in a Nutshell

The announced crowd of 14,623 was well short of T-Mobile Arena's capacity for boxing. But as of this writing, it appears as though Mayweather–McGregor will be wildly successful in terms of pay-per-view buys.

The fight itself continued the false narrative that had been spun regarding the ability of mixed martial artists to compete at the highest levels of boxing.

Mayweather fought the first part of the fight like a man who didn't want the matchup to look like travesty. He did virtually none of the things that made him great and landed a total of three jabs through the first five rounds. By contrast, in the first five rounds against Manny Pacquiao (who, like McGregor, is a southpaw), Mayweather landed twenty-two jabs.

McGregor wasn't the whirlwind of activity that he'd promised he would be. Conor fought a cautious, conservative fight and looked like a man who was trying simply to survive. Then he got tired.

In round nine, Mayweather stepped up the pace. He was pummeling McGregor around the ring in round ten when referee Robert Byrd stopped the fight.

Give McGregor credit for being a fighter. Don't give him credit for being a top-echelon boxer, because he isn't.

As for the overall nature of the promotion . . .

When Kobe Bryant called a referee a "faggot," the NBA didn't post a video of it to market the league. It fined Bryant $100,000. Major League Baseball suspended Matt Joyce for two games after he directed a similar slur at a fan during a game.

If a Showtime employee tweeted that someone was a "faggot" or sent an email that contained racist remarks or demeaned women the way that Mayweather and McGregor did throughout the promotion, the employee, presumably, would be fired.

Showtime sanctioned misogynist, racist, homophobic conduct throughout the promotion of Mayweather–McGregor and posted videos of it—videos that engendered millions of hits—as a marketing tool.

Not good.

# Curiosities

*A lot of fighters have tried their hand at singing. Tony Middleton made the transition early on.*

# Tony Middleton: From Fighting to Singing

The sports heroes and the music of our youth have a particularly evocative hold on us as we grow older.

Recently, I was watching the Willows—one of the quintessential 1950s doo-wop groups—on YouTube. They were performing at a revival concert in the late-1990s, singing their signature song: "Church Bells May Ring." I wanted to know more about their lead singer, Tony Middleton. So I Googled him.

And this came up: "As a teenager, he was working toward becoming a Golden Gloves boxer."

That piqued my interest. A week later, I was sitting opposite Middleton at a diner on the east side of Manhattan.

Middleton was born in Richmond, Virginia, in 1934 and moved to New York with his mother in the mid-1940s.

"I used to fight in the streets all the time," he says. "I didn't look for fights. They just happened. Guys would bother me after school. Or something else would happen. That's the way things were. There was always somebody fighting. I was good on the street. I picked up some moves. I had fast hands. Guys would say, 'Nobody can beat Tony.'"

When Middleton was sixteen, he began to explore boxing more seriously and started training in the basement of the Salem Crescent Church in Harlem. For the uninitiated, in 1934, the year Middleton was born, a thirteen-year old named Walker Smith Jr began training in the same basement under the tutelage of George Gainford, who coached the Salem Crescent Athletic Club boxing team. Smith was later known to the world as Sugar Ray Robinson.

"I could fight," Middleton recalls. "But I could sing, too. There was a group called the Dovers. Someone told them, 'This guy can sing.' They asked me to join them, and I did. I couldn't fight and sing at the same time, so I put fighting aside. I could have been a professional boxer. I really believe that. I was good at singing and boxing, but there are no regrets. The only thing I felt bad about was, after I quit boxing, I gave my equipment to a guy named Curtis. I don't remember his last name. He died. His sister came and told me, 'He's gone. It's your fault.' I felt bad, but I didn't see it that way."

Middleton joined the Dovers in 1952. The group soon changed its name to the 5 Willows and, after one of its members left, to the Willows. "Church Bells May Ring," which Middleton wrote and sang lead on, was released in 1956 and reached number fourteen on the *Billboard* charts. It would have gone higher. But many radio stations in the 1950s wouldn't play rock and roll sung by black recording artists, choosing to play white "cover" versions instead. An all-white group called The Diamonds recorded "Church Bells May Ring" for those who preferred the old order.

Middleton left the Willows in 1957 to pursue a solo career. He worked with numerous world-class performers and had significant roles in several major theatrical productions. Movers and shakers like Quincy Jones sought him out. He also sang with later incarnations of the Platters, the Crests, and several other groups from the Golden Age of Rock and Roll. Trivia buffs might be aware that, when Middleton was on Broadway in the musical, *Purlie*, one of the chorus singers was Morgan Freeman. Decades later, the Willows reunited and toured throughout the 1980s. There were occasional concerts until 2009. Middleton is their only surviving member.

Meanwhile, "Church Bells May Ring" is the equivalent of a world championship in boxing. It's there forever. Middleton's place in history is secure. It can never be taken away from him. And he can look back on a lifetime of extraordinary memories.

"Malcolm X used to preach on the street on a soapbox under my window," Middleton reminisces. "I spent time with James Baldwin at a bar called Juniors in the Alvin Hotel and got to know Lena Horne. I ran with a lot of big people and liked being around, but I never made it my business to hang in their lives. I never played the game to stick with them. One time, I was playing a club called Dionysus and Frank Sinatra came in for the show. Another time, I was at the Rainbow Room to hear Duke Ellington and he stopped the show to introduce me. You remember things like that."

There are also memories of boxing.

"I had a drink with Joe Louis at Wells's Restaurant on 132nd Street and Seventh Avenue [in Harlem]. Just the two of us, talking at one o'clock in the afternoon at the bar. And I had a conversation with Rocky Marciano at the Copa one night when Sam Cooke was playing there. Rocky told me he didn't want to fight Joe Louis. He said knocking Joe out felt like beating up his own father.

"I liked Ali," Middleton continues. "But I was skeptical about him in a lot of ways. When Ali and Joe Frazier fought, I was rooting for Joe. Joe was my man. We were together from time to time."

Asked about Frazier's singing, Middleton responds diplomatically, "Joe had a rough voice, but he sang with enthusiasm. And he had a good band."

Then Middleton's thoughts turned to boxing today.

"I watch boxing on TV now," he says. "But most of the fighters get in the ring without knowing what they're doing. They're not trained the way they used to be, and they don't give what they should give. The last really great fighter I saw was Sugar Ray Leonard. He was the best since Sugar Ray Robinson, better than Ali."

Singers, like fighters (and the rest of us), get old. At eighty-three, Tony Middleton can't hit the high notes the way he once did. But he still has an active career guided by his manager, Phyllis Cortese. And whatever else is on his calendar, he sings every Sunday at noon at the Kitano Hotel at 66 Park Avenue in New York, where he has been a fixture for ten years.

On a recent Sunday, accompanied by a bass player and pianist, Middleton sang a dozen songs at the Kitano's "jazz brunch." He began by introducing himself to the audience: "I'm Tony Middleton. I'm Kate Middleton's uncle."

That got a laugh. A dozen timeless standards followed.

Middleton's voice is still strong. He has style. His timing is impeccable. And he puts his emotions into the lyrics, telling a story with each song.

When Middleton sings "Almost Like Being in Love," one gets the feeling that he's remembering a special person and there have probably been more than a few special ladies in his life. When he sings "All of Me," the audience knows that he has been hurt after falling in love.

Jazz, blues, ballads. Middleton does it all.

"He has a sexy voice," the attractive blonde sitting next to me said.

"There's probably two thousand songs I can sing," Middleton noted afterward. "But I can't do them all in one show."

One advantage to singing over fighting is that practitioners can do it longer. Tony Middleton has been singing professionally for sixty-five years. He has lived a long, full life. And he's still living it.

"Making people smile is happiness to me," Middleton says. "I love singing. When I'm on stage, the audience belongs to me and I can make them happy. What I always wanted out of life was to have a place to live, pay the rent, be happy, and leave something for my children. I live in a house now [in suburban New York]. It has a yard. I own it. It's nice to own something. I plan on being around for a long time. My mother is 106 years old and still here, God bless her. So get used to me. I am the way I am. Always have been, always will be."

*When I spoke with Seanie Monaghan for this article, Seanie told me, "I was at a bar that James Moore owns the other night. There was James, John Duddy, Matthew Macklin, Michael Conlan, Seamus McDonough, and myself. All of us fighters. I was looking at the faces, thinking, 'We all have scars.'"*

## I Fell on My Face

Earlier this year, I fell on my face. I was running to catch a bus with a shopping bag in each hand. There was a raised section of sidewalk that I didn't see. The tip of my shoe caught the edge of the sidewalk and I went down.

I knew I was falling. I tried to put my arms in front of me to break the fall but couldn't let go of the bags fast enough.

BOOM! ! !

My head was spinning.

I could have beaten the count if I was a fighter. But the referee would have stopped the fight.

I knew I was hurt. The question was, how badly.

I ran my hand across my face. No blood.

I did a quick cognitive test, asking myself questions that I'd heard ring doctors ask fighters after they'd been knocked out. Not the simple, "Do you know where you are?" But the more sophisticated, "Recite the months of the year backward. What's your telephone number?" I asked myself the results of a basketball game I'd watched the night before.

The right side of my face was throbbing.

So that's what it feels like to get knocked out by the punch you don't see.

Soon, there was a discolored lump high on my cheekbone. The odds were good that I'd have a black eye. There was an abrasion above the edge of my right eyebrow that wasn't bleeding but would turn into a scab. The right side of my upper lip was discolored and swollen, and there was another abrasion above my lip.

I was "lucky." There were no broken bones or other structural damage. I didn't have headaches (symptomatic of a brain bleed) afterward. It took a while to fully heal.

In the days that followed, the people who saw me were kind. To the best of my knowledge, no one tweeted, "It's about time someone punched Hauser in the face." But the experience was a reminder that, every time a fighter enters the ring, he's facing a skilled adversary who's trying to disfigure his face.

Most of us seek immediate medical aid if we're damaged. Certainly, we don't keep doing what we were doing. After I fell, I didn't get up and run as fast as I could to catch the next bus. But fighters keep fighting. They ask for more.

Light-heavyweight contender Seanie Monaghan takes it for granted that, each time he fights, there will be damage to his face.

"It's the price we pay," Monaghan says. "You just don't want to pay a price where something like your eye is functioning differently for the rest of your life. But if you're thinking about things like that too much, you shouldn't be a fighter."

"The worst damage I had," Monaghan continues, "was when I fought Elvir Muriqi at Barclays Center [on June 14, 2014]. He head-butted me, and it felt like someone slammed a bowling ball into my face. My orbital bone was broken in two places. It broke my nose and severed a tendon. I needed internal and external stitches, and they had to reattach the tendon I use to lift my eyelid. When I woke up the morning after the fight, the pillow was stuck to my face because of all the blood."

Last year, Monaghan was putting his son to bed. Sammy was four years old at the time.

"You never lost a fight, right?" Sammy said.

"Nope."

"Except that one fight," Sammy corrected.

"Which fight?"

Sammy pointed to the scar from the Muriqi fight

"No. I won that one, too."

"Sammy got a big smile on his face," Seanie remembers. "He stared straight up at the ceiling, and I could see the wheels in his head turning. He was thinking, 'Wow. You can get hurt that bad and still win.' That was a good message for him. No matter how tough life is, you can still win."

Former world champion Paulie Malignaggi had his share of bruises and worse. Now retired, Malignaggi says, "One of the things I hated most was losing a fight and having to get on a plane the next day and everyone is staring at you. If you win, you can say. 'Yeah, I won.' The bruising and swelling is like a badge of honor. If you lost, you're self-conscious about it; especially if people don't know you're a fighter and look at you like, 'That punk got beaten up.'"

In 2006, Malignaggi fought a heroic battle against Miguel Cotto. His right eye socket was broken in the second round. His jaw was horribly swollen. But he persevered, winning four rounds on two of the judges' scorecards and five on the third.

"I had to wait a week for the swelling to go down before they performed the surgery," Malignaggi recalls. "For a long time, I couldn't do things I wanted to do. Not just in boxing, but in the rest of my life, too. Italy won the World Cup that year. I spent a lot of time that summer watching soccer on television."

"When you're young," Paulie says, "it's win at all costs. During a fight, you don't care about the damage. In the Cotto fight, I kept trying to win for every second of every round regardless of the consequences. I don't think I could have done that when I was older. You think about getting hurt more when you're older. The damage adds up. It takes longer to heal. Your face changes. You start to look like a fighter. You want to finish your career healthy, which you're not thinking about when you're young."

Former heavyweight Vinny Maddalone wasn't known for his defense.

"I got cut in most of my fights," Maddalone says. "I needed hundreds of stitches. During a fight, it feels like you're getting hit with a baseball bat. You don't think about the damage while the fight is going on. But afterward, a lot of times, I felt the hurt in my head for a couple of days. The first few days after a fight, the way your face looks gets worse. Then the bruises go from purple to green to yellow to the way you looked before. The bruises never bothered me. I never cared about what other people thought. That was where I earned my stripes. I knew where the bruises came from. If you play football and your uniform isn't dirty, you didn't play."

Micky Ward, whose career highlights include a bloody ring trilogy against Arturo Gatti, has similar thoughts.

"It's weird," Ward says. "You know there's blood during the fight. You know you're getting hit. But you don't think about it. After I fought

Arturo the first time, I went back to my room and went to bed. Around three o'clock, I woke up to take a pee. I went into the bathroom, saw my face in the mirror, and said, 'Oh, Jesus. I should have moved my head more.'"

Chuck Wepner is boxing's patron saint of damaged faces. He fought professionally for fourteen years against the likes of Sonny Liston, George Foreman, and Ernie Terrell. On March 24, 1975, "the Bayonne Bleeder" (as Wepner was known) lasted nineteen seconds short of fifteen rounds against Muhammad Ali. Wepner's courage that night inspired an out-of-work actor named Sylvester Stallone to write a screenplay entitled *Rocky.*

"A lot of the damage to my face came from the way I fought," Wepner says, stating the obvious. "I'd take two or three punches to land one. Al Braverman [who trained and managed Wepner] used to say. 'Three steps forward and two back.' But I liked to take five steps forward."

"I got 328 stitches over my eyes," Wepner continues. "I think that's an alltime world record. One time, I needed fifty-one stitches inside my mouth. I got seventy-something stitches after I fought Sonny Liston. Barney Felix refereed that fight. They stopped it on cuts and because I couldn't see. Barney asked me, 'How many fingers do I have up?' And I answered, 'How many guesses do I get?' The morning after is when the pain catches up to you. You feel like hell. But if you won, the way you look doesn't bother you that much."

Meanwhile, it's worth noting that, when I fell on the sidewalk, I'd been on the way to have lunch with my thirty-year-old niece.

"It doesn't look so bad," Jessica assured me when she surveyed the damage. "It makes you look kind of rugged."

Or like a guy who fell on his face.

*Some thoughts on the light side of boxing.*

# Fistic Nuggets

What was it like to be Muhammad Ali?

For starters, "this-couldn't-possibly-be-happening" moments were common. Like the time Ali walked out of his home in Berrien Springs, Michigan, and found a real, live, enormous, honest-to-goodness elephant in the back yard.

That doesn't happen to most people. But it happened to Ali. Let me explain.

When I was researching and writing *Muhammad Ali: His Life and Times* almost thirty years ago, Muhammad and Lonnie Ali lived on an eighty-eight-acre farm in Berrien Springs, Michigan. Half of their property was leased to a flower nursery. The other half, which the nursery operators maintained for the Alis, included a comfortable house and nicely kept grounds.

I traveled to Berrien Springs on numerous occasions while I was working on the book. One of these trips coincided with Bill Burke having some fun.

Burke was a longtime player in Los Angeles politics and, in the late 1980s, president of the Los Angeles Marathon. He was also friends with Ali's closest friend, Howard Bingham.

Lonnie Ali was outside when the elephant arrived.

"I remember that a moving truck brought the elephant," Lonnie reminisced when we compared memories recently. "And I kept saying, I didn't order any furniture, so why was a big moving truck coming through the gate?"

Then an elephant emerged from the truck with its keeper. Lonnie went into the house and told Muhammad, "I think you better come outside."

Actually, the elephant wasn't Muhammad's to keep. After an hour, the keeper loaded it back onto the truck and off they went. Meanwhile, Ali was surprised that an elephant was in his back yard, although not as surprised as the average person might be. He asked if he could pat the elephant, and the keeper said yes. Then the keeper offered Ali the opportunity to climb on top of the elephant and go for a ride, but Muhammad declined. As did I.

It's also worth noting that, at dinner that night, Ali observed, "It's a good thing they didn't send a lion. It might have eaten the dog."

* * *

The recent heavyweight championship fight between Anthony Joshua and Wladimir Klitschko brought back memories of my first in-depth conversation with the Klitschko brothers.

I don't recall precisely when it was. I do know that, by then, the Klitschkos had begun to have an impact on boxing, although not to the extent that they would in later years. There was still some confusion among boxing fans as to which one was Vitali and which was Wladimir.

Bernd Boente, the Klitschkos' manager, set up the meeting. We had breakfast at a hotel in midtown Manhattan. The conversation began with boxing but shifted soon to other subjects.

The Klitschkos have lived for much of their lives in Ukraine. Their father, a Soviet Air Force colonel, was actively involved in the clean-up after the 1986 nuclear power plant disaster at Chernobyl. Years later, cancer believed to have been caused by exposure to radiation claimed his life.

I had co-authored a book about Chernobyl that was translated into Ukrainian and Russian. That was my first bond with the Klitschkos. Then our conversation turned to Pythagoras.

Pythagoras was born in Greece around 570 BC and is best known as the mathematician whose teachings led to formulation of the Pythagorean theorem used to calculate the length of the hypotenuse in a right triangle ($A^2 + B^2 = C^2$). But he was also a philosopher and founder of the Pythagorean brotherhood, which espoused self-discipline, self-analysis, and belief in an eternal soul. His teachings later influenced Plato and Aristotle.

Vitali and Wladimir have incorporated certain principles of Pythagorean philosophy into their daily lives.

The conversation lasted for two hours. At the end, Vitali told me, "There are not many boxing writers that we can discuss Pythagorean philosophy with."

"And there are not many boxers that I can discuss Pythagorean philosophy with," I countered.

★ ★ ★

One of the nicest things about being on site in Las Vegas for Canelo Alvarez vs. Gennady Golovkin was the opportunity to spend time with Hall of Fame promoter Don Chargin.

Russell Peltz, another member of that exclusive club, says fondly, "Don is the only guy I look up to as a promoter. His word is good. He's as astute an analyst of boxing as any promoter I've ever known. He's made great fights his entire career. I've never heard anyone say anything bad about Don. In boxing, that makes him unique."

Three days before Canelo–Golovkin, Chargin was reminiscing about an incident at the Arco Arena in Sacramento that occurred twenty-two years ago.

Don and his wife Lorraine were promoting a fight card headlined by Lennox Lewis vs. Lionel Butler and Michael Moorer vs. Melvin Foster. Lorraine, as was her custom, was overseeing the fighter-media entrance. Don was on the arena floor when the head usher approached him.

"There's a problem downstairs," the usher reported.

The "problem" was Don King, who had arrived with an entourage of ten and was demanding that he and his party be admitted free of charge. Lorraine was willing to let King in for free as a courtesy to another promoter. But there was no way the rest of his group was getting past her unless they bought tickets.

"It's pretty heated," the usher said. "Lorraine and King are going at it jaw to jaw."

"She can handle it," Chargin said.

Then Don thought better of it and headed downstairs.

"Are you worried about Lorraine?" the usher inquired.

"No," Chargin answered. "I'm worried about what she might do to King."

While in Las Vegas, Chargin spoke of that long-ago night.

"By the time I got there," he recalled, "King had given up and bought tickets for his entire entourage. The next time I saw him was when I was inducted into the Hall of Fame in Canastota. He came over to me with a kind of relieved look on his face and said, 'I want you to know. I just saw Lorraine. We're okay now.'"

★ ★ ★

Another familiar face in the media center at the MGM Grand in Las Vegas in the days leading up to Canelo–Golovkin belonged to Kelly Pavlik.

Pavlik was in town to promote *The Punchline*, a podcast he hosts with James Dominguez. He's thirty-five years old now, the same age as Golovkin. But Kelly's fighting days are long behind him.

"This reminds me of when I fought Jermain Taylor here nine years ago," Pavlik told me one day before the fight. "I'm like, oh man, this was my title. They say the middleweights are boxing's glamour division. And I'm part of that lineage. I was that person. That's kind of cool."

Pavlik went through some hard times after peaking in the ring. "When you're a champion," he noted in Las Vegas, "everyone wants to be your friend. I don't have as many friends as I had before. But I have the same number of real friends."

Does he miss fighting?

"I miss it and I don't miss it," Kelly answered. "I'd go back and do it over if I could be young again. But what I like now is, I don't have to worry about making weight. I can walk around during fight week, eat cookies, and drink water."

★ ★ ★

Go to YouTube. Type in "Al Bernstein–Kenny Davidsen."

Does that guy with the beard singing "You Make Me Feel So Young" look familiar?

Boxing fans are used to seeing Al Bernstein behind a microphone. Usually, he's commentating on a fight. This time, he's singing.

When Bernstein was young, he took voice lessons. In his late teens and twenties, he sang old standards in Chicago nightclubs. Then he set music aside to concentrate on boxing.

In 1987, the powers that be at Caesars Palace in Las Vegas let Bernstein sing in one of their lounges for three nights in conjunction with Marvin Hagler vs. Sugar Ray Leonard. Several years later, Al put together a show called "The Boxing Party" where he sang a half-dozen songs interspersed with boxing patter and video clips of fights.

"Then I stopped singing," Bernstein says. "But I missed it. So not long ago, I decided to sing again."

Kenny Davidsen is a singer and pianist who performs at the Tuscany Hotel and Casino in Las Vegas every Friday night with a different co-host each week. On March 31, 2017, Bernstein joined him.

"There's nothing about doing boxing on television that makes me nervous," Bernstein acknowledges. "Getting up and singing in front of a bunch of people makes me nervous. But I love singing old standards and the stories they tell. There's no larger plan, no agenda. I did it for fun, and I had fun. I don't have grand illusions about what the future might bring. But I'd love to do it again."

It's not Frank Sinatra. But it is Al Bernstein.

★ ★ ★

Michael Buffer has lost count of how many feature films he has been in. His best guess is around twenty. That includes three appearances in Sylvester Stallone's *Rocky* franchise.

Most of the time, Buffer plays himself. On occasion, he steps out of character, as was the case in Adam Sandler's *Don't Mess with the Zohan,* when Michael was featured as the villainous corporate magnate Grant Walbridge.

Now Buffer has what, for him, is the role of a lifetime. He has been cast as the Ringmaster in director Tim Burton's remake of the 1941 Walt Disney animated classic, *Dumbo.*

The remake stars Colin Farrell, Eva Green, Michael Keaton, Danny DeVito, and Alan Arkin. Buffer was on set in London for four days this past September. To take full advantage of his bona fides, the script was fashioned so that Dumbo is introduced to the circus audience with the cry of "Let's get ready for Dumbo!!!"

Principal photography is now complete. The time-consuming addition of elaborate special effects means that the film won't be released until early 2019.

"I've had some great moments in TV and movies," Buffer said recently as he reflected on his thespian career. "Playing myself on *The Simpsons* was one of them. But being in *Dumbo* has enormous sentimental meaning for me. I remember seeing *Dumbo* in a theater when I was a kid and loving it. I took my own children to see it in the 1970s. I bought the VHS when that came out and then the DVD. To be part of the remake with so many brilliant creative people is special for me."

★ ★ ★

Seth Abraham was reminiscing recently about an incident that occurred in the 1980s when he was president of HBO Sports and working to build the network's boxing program.

Abraham met in his office at HBO with professional wrestling entrepreneur Vince McMahon as a courtesy to Caesars, which was hosting Worldwide Wrestling Federation events as well as big fights at that time. McMahon wanted HBO to televise pro wrestling and made his pitch. Abraham turned him down.

"I told Vince it would damage our boxing brand," Abraham recalled. "I explained that boxing already had trouble maintaining its credibility and that pairing it on HBO with a scripted sport that had prearranged outcomes wouldn't work. Then things got ugly. Vince became abusive. I asked him to leave. He wouldn't. And I threatened to call security, which finally prompted him to go."

Fast-forward to 2003. Abraham, who had left HBO to become president of Madison Square Garden, was asked by MSG officials to approve McMahon's induction into the Madison Square Garden Walk of Fame.

McMahon's credentials for induction were substantial. The WWF, known by then as Worldwide Wrestling Entertainment, had promoted *WrestleMania* at the Garden every year since 1985. McMahon's own father had been inducted into what was previously known as the Madison Square Garden Hall of Fame.

When asked about inducting the junior McMahon, Abraham replied, "Absolutely."

"I called Vince and invited him to my office at the Garden," Abraham told this writer. "Vince came, not knowing what to expect. His jaw dropped when I gave him the news. Then he got teary. He mentioned my throwing him out of my office years before and said he couldn't believe I was part of giving him this honor. And I told him, 'Vince, it ain't the HBO Hall of Fame.'"

★ ★ ★

How deeply ingrained is Don King in popular American culture? Promoter Richard Schaefer recounts a moment that answers that question.

Years ago, Schaefer took his two sons to Party City to buy them costumes for Halloween. There were costumes for heroes like Superman and Batman, monsters like Frankenstein. And nestled among them, Don King.

"I don't know if Don was supposed to be a hero or a scary monster," Schaefer acknowledges. "But it brought a smile to my face. There was a Don King wig, an American flag, and some plastic bling. My boys chose other costumes. And I bought a Don King costume for myself."

"When I put it on," Schaefer notes in closing, "am I a superhero or a super-villain? You can make an argument for both."

★ ★ ★

Three Things You'll Never Read on a Boxing Website:

1. Al Haymon signs contract for tell-all biography.
2. I'd like Al Haymon to come up to the podium and say a few words.
3. Al Haymon is hanging out in the media center.

★ ★ ★

Michael Buffer readily acknowledges that a lot of people helped him get to where he is in boxing today. One of them was a man named Jody Berry.

Berry was born in Kentucky in 1936 and was a successful amateur boxer in the pre-Cassius-Clay era. Then he embarked upon a career as a nightclub singer, the highlight of which was opening on occasion for Ella Fitzgerald.

Buffer met Berry after working a fight for Dan Goossen in the 1980s at the Reseda Country Club in California.

"We were in a cocktail lounge after the fights," Buffer recalls. "In those days, I'd say 'let's get ready to rumble' and go right into 'ten rounds of boxing' or whatever came next without a break. Jody was a showman. He knew timing. He said to me, 'Michael, after you say let's get ready to rumble, shut the fuck up.'"

"What do you mean?" Buffer asked.

"People want to react," Berry explained. "Give them time to voice their enthusiasm."

"So I tried it," Buffer says. "And you know the rest. It's interesting how you can be doing something that's working well, and then you get a little tip on how to make it better, and there it goes. Jody died of cancer about ten years ago. I'll always be indebted to him."

★ ★ ★

And another Don King moment . . .

Over the years, Roy Langbord has been involved in the acquisition of fights by multiple television networks and counseled a wide range of boxing luminaries. Recently, Langbord was reminiscing about a dinner he shared with Don King at Piero's Italian Cuisine in Las Vegas years ago.

"When I got to the restaurant," Langbord recalled, "Don was sitting at a table with two women he'd just met. They gave every appearance of being hookers. One of them was in her late thirties or early forties. The other was in her twenties. The older woman was acting as a sort of pimp. She kept talking about the charms of the younger woman and saying things like, 'She can make you feel so good. The two of you could have so much fun together.'

"Don kept agreeing with what the older woman said," Langbord continued. "He seemed interested. It was an expensive dinner. Don paid the bill and tipped generously, as he always does."

And then?

"Don told his driver to take the women wherever they wanted to go and went back to his hotel alone. I asked why he'd spent so much time with them if he wasn't interested. And Don told me, 'Sometimes, I just like to watch a good hustler do their job.'"

*It has become a tradition, as a reminder that there's a world outside of boxing, to include a bonus piece in each year's collection of boxing articles published by the University of Arkansas Press. The essay below was written for the Columbia College alumni magazine to commemorate the fiftieth reunion of the Class of 1967.*

# Reflections on a Fiftieth Reunion

My first impression on arriving at Columbia was that the campus was magnificent.

Butler Library and Low Library gave it an aura of historical elegance. Fourteen massive columns rose to the Butler facade where eight names were chiseled in stone: "Homer . Herodotus . Sophocles . Plato . Aristotle . Demosthenes . Cicero . Virgil." Low Library was just as inspiring with a facade that told of Columbia's founding as King's College in 1754.

The grounds were beautifully kept with a lot of green and very pretty flowers.

Freshman orientation began in Wollman Auditorium (the centerpiece of Ferris Booth Hall) and lasted for eleven days. The orientation booklet advised, "Freshmen are reminded that coat and tie is required dress for every event listed in this program except athletic field day."

There were no female students at the college then, so Wollman would take on added importance over the next four years as the site of social mixers.

John F. Kennedy was assassinated on November 22, 1963, two months after the Class of 1967 arrived on campus. The first bulletin of shots being fired in Dallas came while I was listening to the radio in my dorm room. I went downstairs to the TV room in the basement and watched until Walter Cronkite told us that the president had died.

Two and a half months later, the Beatles invaded America and the TV room was jammed with students watching John Lennon, Paul McCartney, George Harrison, and Ringo Starr on *The Ed Sullivan Show*. Sixteen days after that, Cassius Clay upset Sonny Liston to claim the heavyweight championship of the world.

Regardless of what the calendar says, those three months were when "the sixties" began.

Some of what I was taught in the classroom at Columbia seemed useless to me then and remains useless to this day. But courses in Contemporary Civilization and Humanities started me on a journey of analytical thinking that has served me well over the years.

I fell in love for the first time when I was in college, in keeping with the third of Shakespeare's seven ages of man: "And then the lover, sighing like a furnace with a woeful ballad made to his mistress's eyebrow." (*As You Like It*, Act II, Scene 7)

Given the existence of the war in Vietnam, I hoped to avoid Shakespeare's fourth age: "A soldier, full of strange oaths and bearded like the pard."

The war in Vietnam, the civil rights movement, and Lyndon Johnson's effort to build a Great Society were hallmarks of our college years. It would have been considered ludicrous then to suggest that, fifty years later, we'd be enmeshed in a national debate over whether children should be taught evolution or creationism in school. But it was equally improbable that the United States would elect an African American president or that gay marriage would become law.

One day before we graduated from college, the Six-Day War broke out in the Middle East. None of us could have known then the extent to which religious hatred would endanger the world in our lifetime. But over the years, I've reflected often on something that Warner Schilling said on the final day of a course he taught in American foreign policy: "The past was far more confused, the present is far more complex, and the future is far more contingent than we care to realize."

I did some things that I'm proud of during my college years and others that I wish I hadn't done because I can see now that they were foolish and hurtful.

I've pursued separate careers as an attorney and author. The political debate at Columbia helped shape my thinking in ways that led to my writing *Missing*, which served as the basis for the Costa-Gavras film about United States involvement in the 1973 Chilean military coup. Later, another touchstone of my Columbia years moved full circle when I became Muhammad Ali's official biographer.

We're now closer to the end than the beginning of Jaques's Shakespearean soliloquy: "The sixth age shifts into the lean and slipper'd pantaloon with spectacles on nose and pouch on side."

And we're uncomfortably near the seventh age: "Last scene of all that ends this strange eventful history is second childishness and mere oblivion, sans teeth, sans eyes, sans taste, sans everything."

Those of us who make our way to Morningside Heights this spring for our fiftieth anniversary reunion will step into a world where memory and reality intermingle.

The V&T Pizzeria and Tom's Restaurant (made famous in later years by *Seinfeld*) still exist. The West End and Gold Rail are long gone. Almost half of today's 4,600 undergraduate students (there were 2,800 in our day) are women.

Butler Library and Low Library have retained their grandeur. Many of the reading rooms in Butler have been reconfigured. But the polished floors, interior artwork, and first-floor college library look remarkably similar to what we saw fifty years ago.

Ferris Booth Hall was torn down at the close of the last millennium and replaced by Alfred Lerner Hall. Wollman Auditorium is no more. Freshman orientation now begins in Roone Arledge Auditorium. There's a carpeted lounge in the basement of the dormitory where the TV room used to be. But no television. The communications revolution has rendered that need obsolete.

The students look very young. They're the same age that we were a half-century ago. In their eyes, we're old.

Some campus landmarks look as they did decades ago. One can stand at the bottom of the steps in front of Hamilton Hall, gaze upward at the statue of Alexander Hamilton, and see what we saw during our college years. Hamilton was a son of Columbia centuries before Lin-Manuel Miranda discovered him.

The plaza in front of Low Library overlooking College Walk also looks the same. I remember throwing a frisbee there with an agile, very pretty, young woman. She died from ALS ten years ago. When the disease was in its final stages, I sent her a card quoting Shakespeare's 104th sonnet:

To me, fair friend, you never can be old,
For as you were, when first your eye I ey'd,
Such seems your beauty still.

As Columbia graduates, we moved on with our lives long ago. But as classmates, we're held together by a common bond. We shared the same world when we were young.

# Issues and Answers

*Over the years, Don King and Bob Arum have been bitter rivals. But their relationship has been marked by respect.*

*"There has never been a better salesman in boxing than Don King," Arum has acknowledged. "I worked my tail off as a promoter because I had such a measuring stick, a bar to reach. Don made me a better a promoter than I would have been, and I think I made Don a better promoter than he would have been."*

# Don King and Bob Arum in Perspective

Don King turned eighty-six on August 20, 2017. Bob Arum is four months younger.

Arum is still a force in boxing, although the calendar suggests that he's nearing the end of a long, impressive run.

For King, the clock struck midnight in the first decade of the new millennium insofar as the promotion of big fights is concerned. After years of glory, his carriage has turned into a pumpkin.

King and Arum have dominated boxing for much of the past fifty years and shaped the business as we know it today. There hasn't been a time since the mid-1960s when one or both of them wasn't significantly influencing the sport. They've thrived in the jungle that is boxing and been its most important promoters since Tex Rickard died eighty-eight years ago.

Rickard was boxing's first modern promoter and, arguably, the greatest boxing promoter who ever lived. More than anyone else, he was responsible for creating the Golden Age of Boxing. His promotions included Jack Johnson vs. James Jeffries, Joe Gans vs. Battling Nelson, Jack Dempsey vs. Jess Willard, and Dempsey's later fights against George Carpentier, Luis Firpo, and Gene Tunney.

Rickard gave the public what it wanted and promoted in every sense of the word. He didn't get a site fee from a casino and a license fee from a television network. His revenue came primarily from the sale of tickets.

At times, he built his own arena (in Reno for Johnson–Jeffries, in Toledo for Willard–Dempsey, and in Jersey City for Dempsey–Carpentier). He set the standard by which future boxing promoters would be judged.

Two years after Rickard died, Bob Arum was born in the Crown Heights section of Brooklyn. The son of an Orthodox Jewish accountant, Arum graduated from New York University in 1953 and Harvard Law School in 1956. Six years later, he was working as an attorney in the tax division of the United States Attorney's Office in Manhattan when Floyd Patterson defended his heavyweight title against Sonny Liston. Arum was given the assignment of impounding revenue from the fight's closed-circuit television outlets. He had never seen a fight before. But he could count, and the numbers impressed him.

Arum left government service in 1965 and was introduced to Muhammad Ali by football great Jim Brown. In 1966, he formed a company called Main Bouts to promote Ali's fights. The other equity participants in Main Bouts were Herbert Muhammad (Ali's manager), John Ali (chief aide to Nation of Islam leader Elijah Muhammad), Lester Malitz (an expert in the area of closed-circuit telecasts), and Brown. Their first promotion was Ali vs. George Chuvalo in Toronto on March 29, 1966.

After Ali was stripped of his title for refusing induction into the United States Army, Arum set up a second corporation called Sports Action and promoted a world elimination tournament to crown a new heavyweight champion. Top Rank (his current promotional company) was incorporated in the early 1970s.

As of April 1, 2017, Arum had promoted more than two thousand fight cards. These cards were contested in 215 American cities located in 42 different states and in 92 foreign cities located in 26 countries. Breaking these numbers down further, Arum, as of April 1, 2017, had promoted 596 world title fights, 127 shows on HBO, 30 on Showtime, 48 pay-per-view cards, and 27 closed-circuit telecasts.

These are staggering numbers.

Don King came out of a very different environment than Arum. He was born in the underside of Cleveland, Ohio. When King was nine, his father was killed in an industrial accident. Don, his sister, and four brothers were raised by their mother.

Over time, King became one of the largest illegal-numbers racketeers in Cleveland. He fatally shot one man and beat another to death. The first killing was ruled justifiable homicide as a matter of self-defense. The second landed King in prison after a jury convicted him of murder, a finding later reduced to manslaughter.

Released from prison in 1971, King made his way into boxing and soon realized that the sweet science was an environment in which people made their own laws. He began as a manager and moved quickly to promoting. In 1974, he was brought into the George Foreman vs. Ken Norton championship bout by Video Techniques, the closed-circuit firm promoting the fight.

"I was their token nigger," King later recalled. "A black face to deal with the blacks."

Thereafter, working with Video Techniques and the Hemdale Corporation, King journeyed to Zaire and persuaded president Mobutu Sese Seko to part with ten million dollars of his nation's scarce foreign currency to cover the fighters' purses for Muhammad Ali vs. George Foreman, "The Rumble in the Jungle."

Ultimately, King gained control over the heavyweight division as no one else ever has. At one point during Larry Holmes's championship reign, King had promotional ties to Holmes and eleven of the top twelve ranked World Boxing Council challengers. Later, King had promotional control over Mike Tyson, which he leveraged to extend his power.

There was a time when King could lay claim to having promoted seven of the ten largest pay-per-view fights in history (as gauged by total buys) and twelve of the top twenty highest-grossing live boxing gates in the history of Nevada. He has promoted Ali, Tyson, Foreman, Holmes, Joe Frazier, Evander Holyfield, Ray Leonard, Roberto Duran, Julio Cesar Chavez, Felix Trinidad, Roy Jones, and dozens of other Hall of Fame fighters.

It's easy to praise King and Arum, and easy to criticize them. They're similar in some ways and radically different in others.

"King forgives but he doesn't forget," Jerry Izenberg (the dean of American sportswriters) says. "Arum does neither. A lot more people respect them than like them."

Both men are too complex for simple caricature. They're brilliant and demanding, focused and driven, indefatigable and imaginative, admired in some circles and disliked in others. They're not ordinary people. Each man enjoys the process and is a survivor.

Ethical standards aren't known for being high among boxing promoters or within the industry as a whole. Decades ago, Jimmy Cannon labeled boxing "the red-light district of professional sports." The sweet science had reputation issues long before King and Arum got involved. As John Schulian noted, "Charles Darwin would have loved the fight racket." The Marquis of Queensberry's rules apply only to what goes on inside the ring.

Reflecting on the respective careers of King and Arum, Izenberg recently opined, "Neither one has a moral edge over the other where boxing is concerned. It's like a discussion about the Bible. It depends on which side you're on and which sin you're talking about."

Both men have had questionable relationships with sanctioning body officials and state athletic commission officials over the years.

Each can tell a lie now and then. King boldly proclaimed, "The boxing business is predicated on lies." Arum will be followed to the grave by his utterance, "Yesterday I was lying. Today I'm telling the truth."

Arum made an accommodation with the apartheid government in South Africa and sent fighters to Sun City (a resort located within the unrecognized state of Bophuthatswana) in circumvention of the international sporting boycott that saw South Africa banned from the Olympics from 1964 until the 1992 games. King responded by calling Arum "the Master of Apartheid" (as well as the "Prince of Eviality" and "Wizard of Trickeration").

Then King sent one of his own fighters, Greg Page, to fight in South Africa. That led Arthur Ashe and Harry Belafonte to begin the process of removing King from the executive committee of Artists and Athletes Against Apartheid. King resigned from the organization before the removal could be implemented.

Ferdie Pacheco once advised, "Think of Don King as a sledgehammer and Bob Arum as a stiletto."

"One's black and one's white," British promoter Mickey Duff offered. "That's the only difference."

But there are significant differences other than race, starting with King's persona.

King has the physical presence and vitality of a man far younger than his eighty-six years. His large, bulky frame (he stands six feet, two inches tall and has weighed as much as 280 pounds), trademark hair, ostentatious bling, booming voice, and high-pitched laugh suggest a force of nature.

He's loud, flamboyant, sometimes vulgar, and has a smile that brightens a room more effectively than theatrical lighting.

Unlike Arum, who stays largely in the background, King thrives on attention. His carnival barker's style has made it appear at times as though he's the ringmaster for all of boxing. He takes joy, not just satisfaction, in promoting. His ego is on display for the whole world to see. He's a brand unto himself and his own monument. His greatest accomplishment is the creation of Don King.

No one who meets Don King forgets him. With the exception of Muhammad Ali, no one in boxing has had more charisma. For decades, King has sold the fights and himself. His presence adds a buzz and entertainment value to a promotion. Even today, casual fans assume that, if King is involved, a fight is big.

"Don King," promoter Lou DiBella acknowledges, "is the only person in the world who can promote a fight by force of personality."

King became larger than boxing. Over the years, he has met with Nelson Mandela, Mikhail Gorbachev, Leonid Brezhnev, Vladimir Putin, Pope John Paul II, Pope Benedict XVI, Tony Blair, Fidel Castro, Ferdinand Marcos, and eight presidents of the United States. Also, as he recites, "most of the people who have been president of a country in Africa, some Chinese heads of state, every president of Mexico for thirty years, that woman who's chancellor of Germany, and more senators, governors, and mayors than you can count."

Even today, long removed from his glory years, King is one of the most recognizable people in the world. His face is more familiar than that of any active fighter. He has stamped his persona on boxing more visibly than all but a handful of legendary champions.

Arum could walk down any street unnoticed. Wherever King goes, he's encapsulated in a bubble of public attention. Everyone from high-ranking corporate executives to day laborers stop and stare. People in boxing are asked all the time, "Do you know Don King?" One is rarely asked, "Do you know Bob Arum?"

Any discussion of King's accomplishments has to include the issue of race.

America dealt King the race card, and he played it brilliantly. "I'm a black man from the ghetto, an ex-convict," he proudly proclaimed. "I came out of the penitentiary to rewrite history."

When King got into boxing, black men weren't sports entrepreneurs. For the most part, they still aren't. King gave African Americans a feeling of empowerment. For many, he was an inspiration. He walked into rooms filled with white guys from Harvard Business School who thought they were smarter than he was and forced them to treat him as an equal. Eventually, many of them were forced to concede that King played the game better than they did.

Race was a potent weapon in King's battle to sign black fighters. His appeal to them was personal: "I love you. I love your momma. I come from the same place that you come from."

Richie Giachetti, who trained Larry Holmes and worked extensively with King, observed, "The man's greatest asset is that he was born black, because the fighters are black. He knows them. He knows how to rile them, how to sweet-talk them. He'll say and do whatever it takes to win them over."

"Don doesn't get fighters to sign with him just by offering them a lot of money," legendary trainer Emanuel Steward added. "He signs them by getting inside their heads."

It's not easy to put big fights together. Anyone who questions that assertion should ask how many truly big fights Al Haymon has put together on behalf of Premier Boxing Champions with hundreds of millions of dollars in his warchest. The answer is, none.

King made big fights; fights that the public wanted to see. He was the driving force behind "The Rumble in the Jungle" and "The Thrilla in Manila." Historic co-promotions like Larry Holmes vs. Gerry Cooney and Felix Trinidad vs. Oscar De La Hoya bore his imprint. His showmanship put 132,247 fans in seats for Julio Cesar Chavez vs. Greg Haugen in Azteca Stadium in Mexico City.

At times, King promoted pay-per-view extravaganzas with four legitimate world championship fights on the card. He took an unknown female fighter—Christy Martin—and got her on the cover of *Sports Illustrated*.

Seth Abraham (former president of Time Warner Sports and the architect of HBO's boxing program) says, "There were times when Don's promotions seemed like they were from another planet. Bob's promotions were carried out on a very high level, but they tended to be conventional. If you took a Don King fight and gave it to Arum, Bob might increase the gross a bit. If you took a Bob Arum fight and gave it to King, it became a more important cultural event. Don was incredibly creative in making his fights bigger than just a boxing match and infusing them with sociological importance. Look at how he turned Ali–Foreman into one of the major cultural events of the 1970s by taking the fight to Zaire."

But King also added to the negativity in boxing. He came from the school of "whatever it takes" and played by the rules of the street. Everyone he dealt with was a target to be hustled. "Looking for fair play from Don King," British sportswriter Hugh McIlvanney wrote, "is like asking a wolverine to use a napkin."

King could talk faster and shout louder than anyone else. He had ready cash and used it to his advantage. The image of King luring heavyweight champion Hasim Rahman away from promoter Cedric Kushner with a duffel bag filled with $400,000 in cash endures to this day.

Long ago, Lou DiBella declared, "I wouldn't flip a two-headed coin with Don King if I had heads."

King's alliance with WBC president Jose Sulaiman was toxic for boxing. It raised the corruption of boxing's world sanctioning organizations to a new level. And there were other misdeeds, such as the promotion in the late-1970s of tournaments on ABC, replete with rigged ratings that smeared the entire sport and tarnished *The Ring* (which was complicit in the phony ratings) in the process.

Ultimately, King's image was irreparably damaged by the near-universal recognition that he was financially exploiting the fighters he promoted.

Like most business people, boxing promoters profit by taking in as much money as possible and paying out as little money as possible A boxing promoter does not have a fiduciary duty to the fighter.

That said, King raised the exploitation of fighters to a new level. As former HBO boxing analyst Larry Merchant notes, "Neither King or Arum qualifies as a choirboy. Each one probably did as many bad things as the other insofar as boxing is concerned. But when Arum signed a contract with a fighter, the fighter got what he signed for. The number might not have been fair, but at least the fighter got it. And when King signed a contract with a fighter, that was just the starting point for a new round of negotiations. Unless a contract ran in King's favor, a contract was just a piece of paper with some writing on it."

"Don King has made a lot of fighters rich," Larry Holmes (a cornerstone of King's power) declared. "And Don King has made a lot of fighters poor."

Jay Larkin, who ran Showtime's boxing program for years, had his own take on the subject. "Imagine Don King without his false teeth," Larkin posited. "Then consider Don's character."

Arum, like King, made many big fights happen at the right time. He has thrived by being ahead of the curve when it comes to the business of boxing. Like a good fighter, he has made adjustments as time goes by.

Seth Abraham worked with Arum for years and says, "There's no question in my mind that Bob is the most advanced thinker ever in the marriage of television and boxing. Don operated largely in the present. Bob was always thinking down the road."

Arum says that his essential strength as a promoter is his ability as an administrator. His companies have always had a strong infrastructure. He surrounds himself with competent people, likes organization, and wants his office to operate like clockwork.

By contrast, much of what happened around King was unplanned. Ten years ago, Alan Hopper (then King's director of public relations) acknowledged, "Working for Don is crazy. He keeps no schedule. Everything is subject to change. He does what he wants to do when he wants to do it. He might call up and say, 'We're having a press conference in China in two days,' and he expects you to get it done. I never know what will happen when I go to work in the morning."

Building a boxing superstar is a long, arduous task. Over the years, nobody has done it better than Arum. King tended to excel with already made fighters. His modus operandi was, "You build the fighter, and then I'll take him away from you." Arum builds fighters from scratch pursuant to longterm plans that look years into the future.

Oscar De La Hoya was Arum's promotional masterpiece. Arum promoted De La Hoya's first thirty-seven fights. Arum also built the careers of Miguel Cotto (forty-one fights), Floyd Mayweather Jr (thirty-five fights), and Marvin Hagler (twenty fights late in Hagler's journey). Manny Pacquiao was a star when he signed with Top Rank, but Arum lifted him higher.

Arum didn't invent any new technologies (such as closed circuit, pay-per-view, the Internet, social media). But he has used them well.

When ESPN was launched in 1979, it was far from the colossus that it is today. Lumberjacking and replays of Australian rules football were common fare. *Top Rank Boxing* on ESPN debuted on April 10, 1980, and continued for fifteen years. The series guaranteed regularly scheduled programming fifty-two weeks a year and enabled boxing to hold onto a fan base that had been dwindling since the demise of *Gillette Friday Night Fights*.

Arum's deal with ESPN established basic cable as a significant new outlet for boxing programming. In 1981 he moved a step further, contracting for Marvin Hagler to appear three times on HBO. It was the first multi-fight contract ever for an elite fighter to appear on a premium cable television network.

Arum also championed boxing's lighter weight classes. In part, that was out of necessity. By the early 1980s, the number of good heavyweights was dwindling, and King had a stranglehold on the heavyweight division.

One can argue that it was a no-brainer to build lucrative championship fights around Ray Leonard, Marvin Hagler, Roberto Duran, and Thomas Hearns. Ditto for Aaron Pryor and Alexis Arguello. But Arum took 108-pound Michael Carbajal out of the 1988 Olympics and promoted him to a million-dollar purse in a matchup against Umberto Gonzalez. Boxing's two biggest stars in recent years—Floyd Mayweather and Manny Pacquiao— have been "small" fighters.

Also, before and more than any other major promoter, Arum understood the wisdom in targeting the Hispanic market.

Not all of Arum's ventures reflected well on the sweet science. The demeaning Muhammad Ali vs. Antonio Inoki (boxer vs. wrestler) competition comes quickly to mind. But it was Arum who sold the world on the possibilities inherent in a comeback by a washed-up, overweight, hamburger-eating heavyweight who hadn't fought in ten years.

When George Foreman returned the ring in 1987, his comeback was mocked as a Quixotic quest. Big George's early opponents (Steve Zouski, Charles Hostetter, Bobby Crabtree, Tim Anderson, Rocky Sekorski, Tom Trimm, and Guido Trane) did little to dispel that notion. But in 1994, Foreman knocked out Michael Moorer to reclaim the heavyweight championship of the world.

Arum is still a force in boxing. His current roster of fighters is headed by Terence Crawford, Vasyl Lomachenko, and Manny Pacquiao (who still has some earning power left in him).

King has been humbled in recent years. Control of the heavyweight championship in the person of Ali, Holmes, Tyson, and their brethren was his most valuable asset. He played that leverage to the hilt. But after King took Tyson to Showtime in the mid-1990s, HBO made a decision to license fewer fights from him. Then King lost Tyson, and Showtime also moved away from him.

King managed to thrive for a while with lighter-weight fighters like Felix Trinidad and Julio Cesar Chavez. But the power dynamic was shifting against him. Network executives found other promoters easier to deal with. What had worked in the past no longer worked as well as it had before. King had enough money and enough trappings from the glory years that he chose not to adapt. The times changed. Unlike Arum, King didn't change with them. His stable of fighters today consists of a few fringe contenders.

"That makes me sad," says Don Elbaum, who began teaching King the nuances of promoting more than four decades ago. "Don was the Ringling Brothers, Barnum & Bailey of boxing. They just closed down the circus, and Don is closing down, too. I'll miss them both."

Most professional sports are structured so, in many respects, a win for one is a win for all. Tiger Woods's dominance in golf meant higher TV license fees and greater income streams that benefited his competitors on the PGA Tour. Tom Brady and LeBron James generate a lot of money for themselves and more for their respective leagues' coffers. A rising tide lifts all boats.

Not so in boxing. There's virtually no cooperation among rivals, no sense that anyone is part of a larger whole. Each promoter is an island unto himself, as are most fighters.

Within that framework, what will the legacies of King and Arum be?

"Tex Rickard left boxing better off than when he found it," historian Mike Silver answers. "You can't say that about King and Arum. They exploited boxing and, particularly in King's case, brought boxing down to their level. They helped drive the process that has led to boxing having more than one hundred so-called world champions at any given point in time."

A gentler view might be that greatness in a promoter is measured by four criteria:

1. Did the promoter promote big fights that the public wanted to see? For decades, King and Arum did.
2. Did the promoter match fighters in a way that helped them grow as ring craftsmen and build the fighters as commercial attractions? Here, Arum has the upper hand, but King was no slouch.
3. Longevity: Arum has been a force in boxing since the 1960s. King was a dominant player for more than thirty years.
4. Did the promoter take boxing to a new level? For both King and Arum, for better and for worse, the answer is "yes."

Arum, more than anyone else, brought the business of boxing into today's era. King had an enormous impact in shaping the public perception of boxing.

Just as Muhammad Ali was at his most important in the 1960s when he was a revolutionary force, King was at his most dynamic and important in the 1970s when, fresh out of prison, he redefined himself and boxing. With his extraordinary personal gifts, he could have been a great man. Instead, he settled for being a rich man and an icon.

"Culturally, what did King represent?" asks historian Randy Roberts. "Well, as King himself was fond of saying, 'Only in America!' Only in America could a loud flamboyant black man, recently released from prison, where he'd served three years for beating a man to death while he was one of the largest numbers racketeers in Cleveland, take over an industry that was ingrained in the fabric of America, become famous virtually overnight, and make tens if not hundreds of millions of dollars in the process."

"King and Arum were Ali and Frazier," Jerry Izenberg proclaims. "They fought each other with everything they had and made each other better."

*Keith Thurman vs. Danny Garcia shaped up as everything a fight should be. But there was a problem.*

# Angel Garcia and the New York State Athletic Commission

At a January 18, 2017, press conference at Barclays Center to announce the March 4 championship bout between Keith Thurman and Danny Garcia, Angel Garcia (who trains his son) called Keith Thurman a "nigger" (or "nigga" or both).

Angel Garcia is a provocateur with a well-deserved reputation for unacceptable public conduct. Sooner or later, most of his son's fights have an unpleasant pre-fight moment as a consequence of Angel crossing over a line. Here, he repeated the epithet several times as part of an incendiary rant and also had a few choice words for "motherfucking immigrants [who] come from another country." Another member of Team Garcia called Thurman a "faggot."

There's a line that separates decency from indecency, and Angel Garcia crossed it. That afternoon, he fit the stereotype of a hate-filled bigot. The press conference could have turned physical if Thurman weren't the person he is. But Keith took the high road, labeling Garcia's rant "unnecessary" and "a form of ignorance" before adding, "I can go that route too, but I don't have to and I'd rather not. I'm above that."

In a properly run sport, Garcia would face serious consequences for his outburst. Imagine how NBA Commissioner Adam Silver would react if a coach spoke like that at a press conference, or if New York Knicks owner James Dolan said of former Knick power forward Charles Oakley (with whom Dolan is feuding), "Fuck that nigger."

Garcia's views are antithetical to the core beliefs professed by DiBella Entertainment (which is promoting the fight), Barclays Center (where the bout will take place), and CBS (which will televise the contest in conjunction with Showtime).

One day after the press conference, Showtime executive vice president Stephen Espinoza condemned Garcia's outburst, saying, "The remarks were reprehensible and have no place at this event, or anywhere else for that matter." That followed a statement from Lou DiBella, who tweeted, "N-words, homophobic epithets, and anti-immigrant rhetoric have no place at a boxing press conference (or anywhere else)."

But DiBella then evinced less wisdom, announcing that, to avoid future problems, no member of either fighter's team would be allowed on the dais at the final pre-fight press conference. That will deprive Angel Garcia of a microphone to use in disseminating his poison. But it was the wrong response because it treats Dan Birmingham (the thoroughly decent man who trains Thurman) as Angel's equivalent in terms of disgraceful public conduct.

Meanwhile, CBS is still planning to televise the fight, with or without Angel Garcia in his son's corner. Lou DiBella will still promote it. Barclays Center will still host it. And boxing fans will come out in force because Thurman–Garcia shapes up as a very good fight. Any sanction against Angel Garcia will have to come from the New York State Athletic Commission, which has regulatory authority over the bout.

Angel Garcia is not currently under the jurisdiction of the NYSAC. His previous license to work as a trainer in New York expired last year. However, Section 207.1 of the commission rules and regulations states that no person shall act as a trainer or second in a professional boxing or mixed martial arts competition unless he or she has a valid license issued by the commission.

In other words, Garcia will have to be licensed by the commission before he can work his son's corner on fight night. Under the law, a license to work as a trainer on fight night is a privilege, not a right.

On January 20, the NYSAC issued a statement that read, "The New York State Athletic Commission does not in any way condone or excuse Mr. Garcia's words and actions. Angel Garcia is not a licensee of the Commission and therefore is not subject to its jurisdiction at this time. In the event Mr. Garcia pursues a license with the State Athletic Commission, this incident and all relevant information will be reviewed and this matter would be revisited in that context."

Sources say that, thereafter, the NYSAC communicated indirectly with Garcia, told him that a final decision on licensing wouldn't be made until fight week, and suggested that, if he avoided further incidents, the license would be granted.

On February 21, a spokesperson for the New York Department of State (which oversees the NYSAC) told this writer that NYSAC personnel had "been in contact with Mr. Garcia and his camp regarding this matter," that commission personnel would meet with Angel Garcia shortly to discuss his request for a license, and that "the matter will be resolved before the March 4 bout."

Meanwhile, Danny Garcia hasn't helped matters. Commenting at the kickoff press conference on his father's bigoted rant, Danny told the media, "That's how he is. I can't change him. I just sit back and laugh."

Except Angel's rant wasn't funny. Good people have an obligation to rebut bigotry and prejudice. At the very least, Danny should have disassociated himself from his father's diatribe. Instead, he took an opposite tack. Following a February 15 media workout, Danny publicly challenged the NYSAC's authority by threatening to pull out of the March 4 bout if his father were denied a license to work his corner during the fight.

"I won't fight," Danny said. "Nope. What got us here is teamwork. And I know, if they wanna do that, then it's just something personal. You know what I mean? Who's gonna work the corner? A ghost?"

Most likely, that's an idle threat. Pulling out of the fight would expose Danny to lawsuits that could bankrupt him. And to return to the NBA for a moment; suppose Golden State Warriors coach Steve Kerr called LeBron James a "nigger" (or "nigga") and several of the Warriors said they wouldn't show up for a game against the Cleveland Cavaliers if Kerr were suspended. Does anyone on the planet think that Adam Silver would roll over and play dead?

That said, the New York State Athletic Commission has shown in the past that it sometimes administers one set of rules for the powerful and another set of rules for everyone else.

So . . . what can and should the commission do?

Article 41, Section 1007 of the New York General Business Law requires that all trainers and seconds in combat sports competitions be licensed by the NYSAC and further provides, "The commission shall establish by rule and regulation licensing standards for all licensees."

Section 207.7 of the NYSAC rules and regulations enumerates these standards, which include demonstration "to the satisfaction of the commission" that the applicant is knowledgeable with regard to the commission's rules and regulations, understands the fundamentals of training, and evinces "general fitness" and "trustworthiness."

Other than the terms "general fitness" and "trustworthiness," there's nothing there that's remotely relevant to Angel Garcia's remarks.

Article 41, Section 1014 of the New York General Business Law states, "The commission shall promulgate regulations governing the conduct of authorized professional combative sports that . . . (4) establish responsibilities of all licensees before, during, and after an event; (5) define unsportsmanlike practices."

Last summer, the NYSAC revised its rules and regulations. But it did nothing to address what constitutes unsportsmanlike conduct, other than to define the use of illegal performance-enhancing drugs and certain fouls committed during competition as "unsportsmanlike conduct."

In other words; we're in uncharted territory.

One point of view regarding Angel Garcia can be expressed as follows: The New York State Athletic Commission can issue all the lofty press releases it wants. But if New York governor Andrew Cuomo's handpicked commissioners license a man who spreads hate by spewing racial epithets and attacking "motherfucking immigrants," then the governor and his commissioners are enabling hate. Donald Sterling was forced to divest himself of his ownership stake in the Los Angeles Clippers because he objected to his mistress bringing people of color to NBA games. Is it too much to ask that Angel Garcia be required to sit out for one fight?"

But . . . And this is a big but . . .

The NBA is a private enterprise. The New York State Athletic Commission is a government entity. Thus, there must be a constitutionally permissible basis for the NYSAC's decisions regarding who it licenses and refuses to license in conjunction with fights.

Let's assume for a moment that it was Danny Garcia (rather than his father) who uttered the venomous remarks. Should Danny be licensed to fight?

Floyd Mayweather called Manny Pacquiao a "sushi-eating faggot." Pacquiao called gay people "worse than animals" and posted a Biblical verse on Instagram that, in his view, endorsed gay people being "put to death." Bernard Hopkins ripped a Puerto Rican flag from Felix Trinidad's hand and threw it on the ground at a press conference in

San Juan to promote their 2001 Madison Square Garden middleweight championship bout.

Suppose a fighter refuses to stand for the National Anthem?

Denying a license can be a slippery slope, particularly when one recalls that Muhammad Ali was denied a license to fight because he refused induction into the United States Army at the height of the war in Vietnam. Ultimately, Ali vs. Oscar Bentvena and Ali–Frazier I were allowed to proceed at Madison Square Garden because a federal judge sitting in New York ruled that the New York State Athletic Commission's refusal to grant Ali a license to fight was a denial of Ali's right to "equal protection" under the Constitution.

The issue here is whether the government should be in the business of making judgments about and punishing speech, however reprehensible that speech might be. We wouldn't trust Donald Trump with the power to decide this issue. Should we trust Ndidi Massay, John Signorile, and Edwin Torres (the three sitting NYSAC commissioners)?

However, there's one more factor to consider. Not all speech is protected from government interference. The most commonly cited example of this is the illegality of falsely shouting "fire" in a crowded theater, because doing so presents a clear and present danger to public safety.

The NYSAC has to weigh the possibility that Angel Garcia's presence in his son's corner on fight night will constitute an increased danger to public safety.

Ethnic tensions contributed to the July 11, 1996, riot at Madison Square Garden that erupted after Andrew Golota was disqualified for repeated low blows inflicted on Riddick Bowe and one of Bowe's seconds (manager Rock Newman) assaulted Golota.

Many of the fans at Barclays Center on March 4 will know the history of Angel Garcia's bigoted rant. Will that lead to added tension between diverse ethnic groups attending the fight? Maybe not. But Danny Garcia didn't help matters when he declared last week, "I don't like Thurman. The bad blood will run on March 4th."

Boxing is an emotional sport. Emotions always run high on fight night, particularly in a fighter's corner.

Angel Garcia can be calm and rational. And in the next minute, without provocation or warning, he can explode. We don't know what Angel is going to do on fight night because Angel doesn't know. He might conduct himself in exemplary fashion. He might be erratic. Left to his own devices, he might decide to walk to the ring wearing a red Donald Trump "Make America Great Again" baseball cap. Under normal circumstances, that would be protected speech. But given the circumstances that presently exist, it would increase tensions outside the ring.

What will Angel do during the fight if Danny is getting beaten up? What if something else goes wrong during the bout? Remember, Danny isn't just any fighter. Danny is Angel's son. And Angel has shown that impulse control isn't his strong point.

If the NYSAC thinks there's a danger that Angel Garcia will go off the rails on fight night, it's not enough to warn him not to. Remember, a license to work as a trainer is a privilege, not a right.

Moreover, it's troubling that Angel Garcia has yet to apologize publicly for his comments. At this point, such an apology might be a matter of convenience rather than heartfelt. But a refusal to apologize and retract would speak to Angel's mindset and increase the likelihood of problems on fight night.

Important principles sometimes conflict with one another. The Angel Garcia conundrum involves issues of (1) free speech; (2) the desire to rebut open expressions of bigotry and prejudice; and (3) the need to minimize the possibility of conduct that could endanger NYSAC personnel, members of the boxing community, and the general public. Where the lines should be drawn is subject to debate. But lines have to be drawn.

*Instead of giving CT-scans to fighters, maybe boxing should administer CT-scans to state athletic commission personnel who allow certain things to happen.*

# Trouble at the Arkansas State Athletic Commission

## Part One

On Wednesday, November 22, 2017, Association of Boxing Commissions president Mike Mazzulli sent a letter to Arkansas Governor Asa Hutchinson. In the letter, Mazzulli advised the governor that the Arkansas State Athletic Commission is engaging in conduct that the ABC believes constitutes "an egregious disregard for health and safety standards" and "appears to be a direct violation of Federal Law."

Mazzulli's concern traces directly to a fight card that was contested in Arkansas on November 11. On that day, Mazzulli's letter declares, "The State of Arkansas Athletic Commission knowingly allowed an HIV positive fighter to engage in a bout."

Making matters more troubling, as Mazzulli's letter points out, the boxer in question was denied a license in the State of Florida due to a positive HIV test in July. Thereafter, he was placed on the national suspension list maintained pursuant to federal law under the auspices of the ABC.

Worse still, as Mazzulli's letter recounts, "Both the Florida Commission and I notified Arkansas through the Department of Health [which oversees the Arkansas State Athletic Commission] of the HIV positive status of a boxer but he was allowed to fight anyway. Since Arkansas had actual knowledge of the HIV positive result, the fighter should not have been allowed to engage in a bout and, under Federal Law, the action of Florida denying a license for medical reasons should have been honored."

"This situation," Mazzulli's letter to the governor concludes, "is one of the most serious we have seen in many years. Hence we feel compelled to bring this matter to your attention."

Copies of the letter were sent to Arkansas Attorney General Leslie Rutledge and a half dozen personnel at the Arkansas Department of Health.

The Arkansas State Athletic Commission website has a "mission statement" that proclaims, "The Arkansas State Athletic Commission is committed to maintaining the health, safety and welfare of the participants and the public as they are involved in the combative sports regulated by the Commission."

But in truth, Arkansas trifles with fighter safety. Under ASAC rules and regulations, the commission isn't even required to conduct blood tests. There is a question on the Arkansas fighter license application form that reads, "Have you ever tested positive (even if a 2nd test was negative) for HIV or Hepatitis or Staph infection. If yes, please describe, including dates and name of doctor or medical provider." The application also includes a HIPPA release.

While the administration of a blood test is discretionary under Arkansas law, the commission's regulations provide, "A positive test for the presence of infectious diseases shall result in an immediate suspension of the licensee's license."

The fighter in question is not being named in this article so that he can be the one to tell family members and others of his situation should he choose to do so. Suffice it to say for the moment that he has had a long association with at least one well-connected person in Arkansas boxing. He fought on November 11 and won his bout. There's no indication that the opponent was advised of the situation so that he could make an informed decision as to whether to participate in the bout. Nor is it publicly known at this time whether the physician who cleared the boxer to fight was informed of the boxer's HIV positive status.

An HIV-positive test result doesn't necessarily mean that a person has AIDS. And false positive test results have been known to exist. But the fighter in question is still on national suspension because of the findings in Florida. And the Arkansas commission can't claim ignorance of the situation. As Mazzulli told this writer, "Multiple people at the Arkansas State Athletic Commission and Arkansas Department of Health were notified by the ABC, and the fight was still allowed to take place. We have not heard from them since the fight, either."

Also, the facts suggest that a possible cover-up of wrongdoing might now be taking place. As Mazzulli's letter to Governor Hutchinson states, "Eleven days later, the bout still has not been reported to the Boxing Registries, which is in violation of the Federal Muhammad Ali Act requiring that results be reported to the ABC official record keepers within 48 hours."

A telephone call by this writer to the Arkansas State Athletic Commission was answered by a voice message that advised, "Office hours are by appointment only." A return call was requested. To date, no one from the commission has called back.

Meanwhile, Greg Sirb (the Pennsylvania State Athletic Commission executive director who has worked with Mazzulli on this issue) has his own take on the matter.

"Arkansas," Sirb states, "should stop all boxing and other combat sports immediately and should not allow them to resume until the state has regulations and policies in place that ensure the effective testing for and handling of situations involving infectious diseases."

## Part Two

On Thanksgiving Day, November 23, this writer reported that the Arkansas State Athletic Commission had allowed a fighter to compete in Arkansas after being advised by the Association of Boxing Commissions and the State of Florida that the fighter had tested HIV positive. The information in the report came primarily from a November 22, 2017, letter sent by Association of Boxing Commissions president Mike Mazzulli to Arkansas Governor Asa Hutchinson.

Mazzulli's letter advised the governor that the Arkansas State Athletic Commission was engaging in conduct that amounted to "an egregious disregard for health and safety standards" and appeared to be "a direct violation of Federal Law." Mazzulli concluded with the observation, "This situation is one of the most serious we have seen in many years. Hence we feel compelled to bring this matter to your attention."

There are three primary blood-borne infections of concern to the medical community: hepatitis B, hepatitis C, and HIV.

HIV is a virus, not a moral failing.

In my previous report, the fighter in question was not named out of respect for his privacy and to give him the opportunity to tell family members and others of his situation should he choose to do so. But the fact that he fought after being told he was HIV positive and recently told this writer that he plans to fight again is troubling to me. More significantly, Mazzulli's letter to Governor Hutchinson is a public document, and there is now more than enough information publicly available for anyone with internet access to identify the fighter.

Kiun Evans is twenty-four years old and resides in Little Rock, Arkansas. He was the 2011 Arkansas Golden Gloves 123-pound champion and turned pro in 2012.

Evans's attorney, Robert Holitik of Little Rock, told this writer late tonight (November 28), "We don't know that the man in question is my client. He is unaware of any failed test in Florida. He has not been advised of any failed test. It's my understanding that he has tested negative multiple times. Our hope is that, when the facts come out, we'll see that there was no failed test for my client."

Evans won his first twelve professional bouts. Then he stepped up the level of opposition and lost three fights in a row. As of July 2017, his record stood at 13 wins, 3 losses, and 1 draw with 8 knockouts. All of his defeats were by KO.

Then Evans applied for a license to fight in Florida. His application was rejected. A July 14, 2017, entry on Fight Fax reads, "Unable to obtain license—Contact Florida Commission."

Ozell Nelson (who trained Jermain Taylor in the amateur ranks and for much of Taylor's pro career) trained Evans as an amateur and pro. Nelson told this writer today that he was working with Evans in anticipation of the Florida fight (which was scheduled for July 7 in Tampa) when Evans told him the bout was off because he'd just learned he had lymphoma.

"Then," Nelson recounts, "he called me a week before the Arkansas fight and said he was fighting again but was training himself. And I said okay. I didn't know anything about HIV. I thought he had cancer."

Ruben De Jesus is director of operations for All Star Boxing, which promoted the Florida card. De Jesus steers clear of mentioning "HIV" and Evans by name when discussing the situation. But he told this writer, "When I submitted him for lab work, he came back positive, I felt bad for the kid, so I went ahead and paid to have him retested just to make sure it wasn't a false positive. The results were the same, and I notified Frank Gentile [of the Florida State Athletic Commission] that the kid has bad labs because I knew he would attempt to fight."

Damian Walton was Evans's adviser. When Evans told Walton that he wanted to fight again, Walton advised him orally and in writing that he would no longer represent him.

"The agreement was near an end," Walton says. "And we decided to discontinue the relationship. I sent him an email, he sent me an email back, and we parted on good terms. He's a nice young man, and I hope the best for him."

That brings us to Arkansas.

The administration of blood tests for fighters is discretionary under Arkansas law, although the Arkansas State Athletic Commission's regulations provide, "A positive test for the presence of infectious diseases shall result in an immediate suspension of the licensee's license."

Robert Brech (general counsel for the Arkansas Department of Health which oversees the Arkansas State Athletic Commission) told this writer, "Initially, the ABC didn't advise us which fighter was involved. So after we were notified of a potential problem by the ABC, we asked for and received bloodwork on each fighter. We got the test results from the promoter. In each instance, the results we were given indicated that the fighter had tested negative for HIV."

The Arkansas State Athletic Commission lists Richard Wright as the promoter and matchmaker for the November 11 fight card.

Then, earlier today, Brech advised this writer, "Late last night [November 27], we determined that the blood test for the fighter in question was falsified. Someone created a false document using a previous blood sample and previous test result and it was sent to the commission."

As noted above, Brech says that the test results were given to the Arkansas State Athletic Commission by the promoter. The provenance of the "false document" itself is unknown at the present time.

Are criminal charges possible?

"That's a good question," Brech answers. "We're not a prosecutorial agency. But there are statutes in Arkansas that cover knowingly filing false documents with a government agency and exposing someone else to HIV. The matter is under further investigation at this time."

The boxing media deals primarily with fight cards in states that host bigtime boxing. We forget sometimes how seamy small club shows can be.

There were four bouts on the November 11 fight card in question, which was contested at the Boys and Girls Club in Camden, Arkansas.

A fighter identified as fifty-year-old, 247-pound Donald Caples was knocked out in the second round by a forty-year-old fighter named Maurenzo Smith. *Boxrec.com* states that Caples weighed 151 pounds for a February 13, 2016, bout and that he began his career at 116 pounds. It would appear as though either Caples recently developed an eating disorder or identity fraud was involved.

In other supporting bouts, forty-year-old Starr Johnson (5–28–1, 23 KOs by) knocked out Andrew Hartley (2–28, 27 KOs by) and Demario Moore (pro debut) knocked out Raymond Johnson (0–4, 4 KOs by).

Kiun Evans's opponent was Terrance Roy (11–53, 43 KOs by), who has won two of his last thirty-seven fights. Evans weighed in at 130 pounds. Roy weighed in 118. Roy was knocked down six times before the fight was stopped in the fifth round.

The focus here should be on the performance of the Arkansas State Athletic Commission, not Kiun Evans. The Arkansas Department of Health has entrusted the regulation of boxing to a group of men and women who, collectively, don't seem to be doing the job properly.

As for Evans, he appears to need good medical treatment so he can live a long productive life, not more fights. As Damian Wright says, "He's a guy who wanted to fight to feed his family. He's not particularly sophisticated. He's a nice young man. He might not have fully understood what's involved here. He told me he was unaware that he had been suspended in Florida and that a doctor had told him he was cleared to fight. I said, 'Okay, good luck.'"

*I've criticized the World Boxing Council on many occasions. But the WBC was on the side of the angels on this one.*

# Congratulations to the WBC and VADA

The much-anticipated November 4, 2017, WBC heavyweight title fight between Deontay Wilder and Luis Ortiz appears to be off.

A urine sample taken from Ortiz during a random drug test conducted by the Voluntary Anti-Doping Association on September 22—two days after Wilder–Ortiz was formally announced—has tested positive for banned substances. More specifically, Ortiz's "A" sample tested positive for chlorothiazide and hydrochlorothiazide, banned diuretics that are sometimes used to treat high blood pressure but are also used to mask performance-enhancing drugs.

The test was administered by VADA as part of the WBC Clean Boxing Program.

Ortiz previously tested positive for illegal drug use after a first-round knockout of Lateef Kayode in 2014. In that instance, a urine sample taken from Ortiz by the Nevada State Athletic Commission prior to the bout tested positive afterward for the banned anabolic steroid nandrolone. Ortiz was fined by the NSAC and suspended for eight months.

Ortiz also raised eyebrows on April 14, 2017, when he pulled out of a fight against Derric Rossy scheduled for April 22 at Barclay's Center, claiming that he had suffered a thumb injury while sparring on April 12. This injury was revealed shortly after Ortiz was advised that the New York State Athletic Commission had instructed him to be available for a random drug test because, as stated in the NYSAC directive, "Mr. Ortiz has previously tested positive for PEDs."

Copies of the VADA report regarding Ortiz's most recent positive test result were sent on September 28 to the Ortiz camp, the WBC, promoter Lou DiBella, Kim Sumbler (executive director of the New York State Athletic Commission), and Mike Mazzuli (president of the Association of Boxing Commissions).

VADA was founded by Dr. Margaret Goodman, who serves as its president and receives no compensation for her service to the organization.

The WBC Clean Boxing Program was inaugurated under the leadership of WBC president Mauricio Sulaiman. It requires all WBC champions and fighters ranked by the WBC in the top fifteen of any weight division to submit to random PED testing by VADA at any time. The WBC underwrites the direct cost of these tests.

Ortiz's positive test result will hurt the WBC financially in the short run. A substantial sanctioning fee for Wilder–Ortiz has been lost. Also, it's likely that some fighters who are "dirty" will avoid the sanctioning body for fear of being caught. However, clean fighters may well be more comfortable fighting for a WBC belt because of the increased likelihood that their opponents will also be clean.

Over the years, VADA has tested several hundred boxers, roughly five percent of whom have tested positive for the presence of a banned substance. In addition to Ortiz, fighters who tested positive include, most notably, Alexander Povetkin, Andre Berto, Lamont Peterson, Lucas Browne, and Brandon Rios.

VADA testing isn't perfect. Given the random nature of drug testing and the sophistication of PED cheaters today, some WBC fighters might be dirty. But there's a better chance that WBC fighters are clean than there is for the fighters who compete under the auspices of any other world sanctioning body.

The United States Anti-Doping Agency (USADA) has also tested hundreds of professional boxers for performance-enhancing drugs. However, according to public statements by USADA, only one of these tests has resulted in a positive finding of an illegal substance in a fighter's system.

On October 20, 2012, Erik Morales fought Danny Garcia at Barclays Center in Brooklyn. Two days before that bout, Halestorm Sports reported that Morales had tested positive for a banned substance. Thereafter, the New York State Athletic Commission acknowledged that, prior to the revelation on Halestorm Sports, the NYSAC had not been notified of the positive test by USADA. Garcia–Morales was allowed to proceed, which was a black eye for boxing.

At present, the Ortiz camp is claiming that Ortiz took the banned diuretics to combat high blood pressure. There are multiple problems with this explanation: (1) Ortiz failed to previously state on required forms that he has high blood pressure; (2) Ortiz neither applied for nor received a therapeutic use exemption for the banned diuretics; and (3) there's an issue as to whether a fighter with blood pressure so high that it that requires the use of chlorothiazide and hydrochlorothiazide should be allowed to fight.

Meanwhile, congratulations to the WBC and VADA for their honest efforts to make a dangerous sport fairer and safer.

### Five Days Later

The World Boxing Council took another step forward on October 4, when WBC president Mauricio Sulaiman announced that the organization had withdrawn its sanction of the scheduled November 4 heavyweight championship fight between Deontay Wilder and Luis Ortiz.

The WBC's action came in the aftermath of a positive test result on a urine sample taken from Ortiz during a random drug test conducted by the Voluntary Anti-Doping Association on September 22. Ortiz's "A" sample tested positive for chlorothiazide and hydrochlorothiazide, banned diuretics that are sometimes used to treat high blood pressure but are also used to mask performance-enhancing drugs. The test was administered by VADA as part of the WBC Clean Boxing Program.

The Ortiz camp claims that Ortiz took the banned diuretics to combat high blood pressure. On October 2, it issued a press release headlined "Breaking News" followed by the title, "Victor Conte Reveals the Truth on Luis Ortiz Positive Test."

The release then referenced a video posted by Conte on YouTube and stated, "Sports scientist Victor Conte reveals in detail why he believes undefeated heavyweight contender Luis Ortiz is innocent in regard to his recent positive drug test. An expert in the field of scientific nutrition, Conte feels Ortiz was negligent in [not] declaring his blood pressure medicine but also believes there is no evidence of intent to cheat. Conte's position is that the WBC heavyweight championship fight between Deontay Wilder and Luis Ortiz, should move forward without delay."

"Unless you have strong evidence of intent to cheat," the release quoted Conte as saying, "then you don't have a case. Let the fight go on."

Thereafter, Conte told this writer that Mario Serrano (Ortiz's publicist) had sent him the VADA letter and lab reports for review but that he was not paid for his work. "I don't know all the answers," Conte said. "I just want to make sure we ask the right questions." In a later exchange, Conte clarified that he made the video at the request of a third party, not Serrano.

Conte also acknowledged to this writer that, at the time he made the video, he was unaware that the doctor who the Ortiz camp claims wrote the prescription for the banned diuretics has a checkered past.

Richard Allen Hill is a Fort Lauderdale, Florida, physician. A June 27, 2005, press release issued by the United States Attorney for the Southern District of Florida reveals that Dr. Hill was sentenced to twenty-one months in prison for financial misconduct related to the wholesale distribution of prescription drugs.

Just as troubling, the *Palm Beach Post* reported in 2016 that at least six women had complained to the authorities that Hill sexually molested them during medical examinations. As part of a plea deal, Hill pled "no contest" to five misdemeanor battery charges.

After Wilder–Ortiz was placed in jeopardy, Wilder called Ortiz a "fucking liar, a motherfucker," and just about everything else he could think of. Then Deontay indicated that he was not necessarily averse to the fight going forward as planned.

On October 3, Sulaiman addressed Wilder's desire to proceed with the fight and declared, "That's a fighter. A fighter has a heart and a desire. But there's no compromising safety. If it is not safe for him, if it is not safe for Ortiz, we will never be part of something like that."

This afternoon, the WBC took the next step in the adjudicative process when Sulaiman announced, "The WBC has concluded the process according to its Clean Boxing Program protocol in the adverse finding of Luis Ortiz. An official ruling has been sent to the corresponding parties. The WBC has withdrawn its sanction of the Deontay Wilder vs. Ortiz fight, and Wilder will fight next his mandatory fight against Bermane Stiverne."

*Author's Note:* As 2017 neared an end, there were disquieting signs that the WBC might be moving away from its commitment to VADA and clean sport. More on that in the year to come.

*"A sensible human being," Walter Lippmann wrote, "always learns more from his opponents than from his fervent supporters."*

# A Reporter Faces the Issue: To Stand or Kneel

What began as a protest against the inappropriate use of force by a minority of police officers against people of color and the inadequate response of the criminal justice system to these incidents is turning into something more.

On August 26, 2016, San Francisco 49ers quarterback Colin Kaepernick sat while the national anthem was played prior to a preseason game against the Green Bay Packers. Kaepernick later modified his protest by kneeling on one knee instead of sitting while the anthem was played. His protest has been emulated by other athletes in other sports at all levels of competition.

Thirteen months later, Donald Trump got into the act. At a September 22, 2017, campaign rally in Alabama, Trump declared, "Wouldn't you love to see one of these NFL owners, when somebody disrespects our flag, to say, 'Get that son of a bitch off the field right now. Out! He's fired. He's fired!' The only thing you could do better is, if you see it, even if it's one player, leave the stadium. I guarantee things will stop. Things will stop. Just pick up and leave. Pick up and leave."

A Twitter storm from Trump followed.

> September 23: "If a player wants the privilege of making millions of dollars in the NFL or other leagues, he or she should not be allowed to disrespect our Great American Flag (or Country) and should stand for the National Anthem. If not, YOU'RE FIRED. Find something else to do!"
>
> September 24: "If NFL fans refuse to go to games until players stop disrespecting our Flag & Country, you will see change take place fast. Fire or suspend!"

> September 24: "NFL attendance and ratings are WAY DOWN. Boring games yes, but many stay away because they love our country. League should back U.S."

> September 24: "Courageous Patriots have fought and died for our great American Flag—we MUST honor and respect it! MAKE AMERICA GREAT AGAIN!"

> September 25: "Many people booed the players who kneeled yesterday (which was a small percentage of total). These are fans who demand respect for our Flag!"

> September 30: "Very important that NFL players STAND tomorrow, and always, for the playing of our National Anthem. Respect our Flag and our Country!"

Then, on Sunday, October 8, in a move that was choreographed as carefully as the dropping of balloons at a political convention, vice president Mike Pence walked out of a game between the Colts and 49ers in Indianapolis because several players knelt during the playing of the national anthem. This came after Pence had tweeted, "I stand with @POTUS Trump, I stand with our soldiers, and I will always stand for our Flag and our National Anthem."

Thereafter, Dallas Cowboys owner Jerry Jones poured more fuel on the fire, warning his players, "If you do not honor and stand for the flag in the way that a lot of our fans feel that you should, then you won't play."

Here I should note that I haven't heard Jones complain about fans who start shouting halfway through the anthem. Does it bother him when, around the time the anthem gets to "rockets' red glare," fans are screaming, "Go, Cowboys! Fucking go!"

For NFL players who choose to kneel, the primary issue is still the inappropriate use of police force and other matters of concern to the minority community.

Trump, on the other hand, is seeking to frame the issue in terms of whether the players support country, flag, and American troops who are fighting overseas. His comments bring to mind the thoughts of Samuel Johnson, who proclaimed, "Patriotism is the last refuge of a scoundrel."

Still, Trump's message resonates with his base, particularly among those of his supporters who don't like black people and see the protest as being driven by ungrateful African Americans who don't appreciate the opportunity they've been "given" to play in the NFL.

At this point, I should make clear my feelings toward Donald Trump. I think he's a crude, vulgar, mentally unstable narcissist with fascist tendencies. I love this country as much as he does, probably more. I have enormous respect for the democratic institutions that have made America great. I don't need lessons in patriotism from a man who says that the neo-Nazis and torch-carrying white supremacists who marched in Charlottesville, Virginia, included "some very fine people."

When the kneeldowns began last year, I didn't think the tactic was well-chosen. I agreed with Jim Brown (one of the greatest football players ever and an outspoken civil rights activist), who said, "I would not challenge our flag. I would not do anything that has to do with [dis]respecting the flag or the national anthem. I don't think it's appropriate."

Like Brown, I believe that we need more unifying symbols in this country, not fewer. And the national anthem, like the flag, has the potential to be one of these symbols.

As for the effectiveness of the protest, I felt then—and still feel—that the chosen means of protest allows people like Donald Trump to frame the debate on their terms and avoid confronting the underlying issues. Rather than reject what the American flag stands for, we should be challenging people to live up to the ideals that the flag is supposed to represent.

As for whether NFL players have a First Amendment right and other basis to protest in this manner, we're looking at issues of law, power, and the difference between right and wrong.

You can't work for McDonald's and say "Heil Hitler" each time you give a hamburger to a customer. At least, I hope you can't.

If the NBA can fine Kobe Bryant for calling a fan a "faggot" and force Donald Sterling to sell the Los Angeles Clippers because of his racist remarks, I assume there are circumstances under which a sports league can legally penalize players for "disrespecting the American flag."

But suppose Jerry Jones says to Dallas Cowboys fans, "If you don't respect the anthem, you can't come into my home." Can Jones terminate the season-ticket licenses of fans who refuse to stand?

And what about the media? I write about boxing and attend roughly two dozen fight cards each year. Should I stand or kneel when the anthem is played?

Let's start with the understanding that the media is credentialed to report on the story, not be the story. Writers who sit in the press section aren't athletes.

Nor are we there as fans. We have advantages and opportunities that fans don't have. In return, there are limitations on our conduct. For example, it's inappropriate to openly root for or verbally denigrate an athlete from the press section.

Virtually all media credentials, regardless of the sport, state on the back that the credential can be revoked for disorderly conduct or other offenses. Suppose someone wears an American-flag lapel pin in the press section? No problem, right? A Black Lives Matter button? Seems okay. An ISIS-flag lapel pin or a swastika armband?

We're in the press section to report on the event, not to make a political statement.

The private sector can't discriminate in most instances on the basis of race, religion, age, or sexual orientation. If Jerry Jones announced that he was banning people of color, Jews, Muslims, and members of the LGBTQ community from the press section, he'd be violating the law. But the private sector is allowed to limit free speech in ways that the government can't.

Want an example? ESPN disciplined Curt Schilling (to the delight of the political left) and Jemele Hill (to the delight of the political right) for expressing their political views on social media.

The sports editors at three major newspapers offer differing views as to whether reporters on assignment at a sports event should be required to stand when the national anthem is played.

*New York Times* sports editor Jason Stallman says that the *Times* doesn't have a policy governing the issue and that it's left to the conscience of each reporter. Asked what he anticipates the position of the *Times* would be if a reporter's credential were revoked because he or she chose to not stand for the anthem, Stallman declined comment because "it's a hypothetical question."

Like the *Times*, the *Boston Globe* doesn't have a policy that's specific to the national anthem. But *Globe* sports editor Joseph Sullivan, says, "We do have a policy for reporters that has been in place for more than a decade. Our reporters are not allowed to take a public stance on elections or other political issues. They have to remain neutral. In this instance, I think that would mean standing. The reader comes first. If you're a reporter for the *Globe*, your job on this given day is to report on the game. You have to put your feelings aside."

But *Los Angeles Times* sports editor Angel Rodriguez has a different perspective.

"The *LA Times* does not have a policy on it," Rodriguez states. "And it has never really come up here. If we needed a policy, mine would be, I would leave it up to the individual to make a decision to stand or not for the anthem. If they had a political reason to not stand, I'd be fine with them sitting. If they wanted that time to sit and tweet, then I'd ask them to be respectful and stand.

"My parents are Cuban and fled Fidel Castro and his revolution in the sixties over restrictions on personal freedoms," Rodriguez continues. "So individual rights are important to me as they've had a direct impact in my life. My father was a political prisoner who was viewed as a counter-revolutionary because his views were different than what that government imposed on its people. I am always fearful whenever a government looks to restrict individual choice. If one of my reporters decided they did not want to stand for the anthem because of political reasons, I would support them one hundred percent. It is why my parents are in this country. I will stand and honor the anthem and the flag because this country has given me opportunities I would never have in Cuba. But I realize my experiences may be different than others."

And suppose Jerry Jones or another owner refused to credential writers who knelt when the anthem was played?

"If we were denied a credential over this," Rodriguez answers, "then we'd raise it to the league/promoters/whoever and complain and hope to resolve it through negotiations. We'd involve the Associated Press Sports Editors group and rally support from that organization and other media outlets. If that doesn't resolve it, then I'll be damned if I'd send another *LA Times* reporter to cover their event."

Some things are more important than sports.

There's a time-honored tradition in America of non-violent civil disobedience to achieve social justice. The civil rights movement succeeded because tens of thousands of foot soldiers braved much more than the loss of a day's pay or being deprived of a press credential to achieve a desired goal.

Responsible media are already under assault by the Trump Administration. If Trump continues to force the issue, there may well come a time when standing for the national anthem is interpreted, not as a statement of respect for cherished American values but as a symbol of support for Donald Trump. If that time comes, I'll kneel.

Kneeling under these circumstances would not be disrespectful to the American flag. It would be a statement of belief in what our country can and should be. In the words of Clarence Darrow, "True patriotism hates injustice in its own land more than anywhere else."

And a final thought: I'd like to see athletes who are kneeling for the national anthem also go out and register people to vote.

*As a contrast to "Fistic Nuggets," these "Notes" are on the serious side.*

# Fistic Notes

Earlier this year, IBF heavyweight champion Anthony Joshua was in Dubai as a tourist. As Joshua later explained, "One of my best friends is a Muslim, and we went to the mosque. It was afternoon prayer, so I asked him to pray for me ahead of the Klitschko fight. He asked me to join in, and I joined in, and someone took a picture. I took it from Instagram and posted it."

Accompanying the photo, which Joshua posted on his own Twitter and Instagram accounts, the fighter wrote, "Besides luck, hard work & talent, Prayer is a solid foundation. It was nice to join my brother as he led through afternoon prayer."

Joshua is not a Muslim. He has said in the past that he doesn't follow the teachings of any one religion but has an interest in faith. After posting the photo, he was on the receiving end of a torrent of cyberabuse. In response, Joshua said, "One of my idols in the boxing industry [Muhammad Ali] is Muslim. I didn't think it would have the backlash. Religion is supposed to be a positive thing. It's a shame it had that backlash, but I can't control how people think. As long as my intentions are pure, that's what counts."

Joshua's experience brought back memories of my own visits to mosques with Muhammad Ali.

My parents were Jewish, but I was raised with values that have a secular foundation. I consider myself more spiritual than religious. Prayer, in my view, isn't about asking the Creator to make my wishes come true. True prayer, to my way of thinking, is a moment of reflection about oneself and asking, "Am I doing all that I can do to become a better person? Am I using this precious gift of life in a way that justifies what has been given to me?"

There have been times when I've walked into a church and sat alone in a pew to contemplate these questions in a spiritual setting. I've also done it in temples, in natural surroundings . . . And in mosques with Ali.

The first time I went to a mosque with Ali was in Chicago. Before the service began, Muhammad told me, "When we say our Islamic prayers, you can say your Jewish prayers. Only don't say them out loud because it might offend someone."

On another occasion, we were at my apartment in New York and visited a mosque a block from where I live for a Friday morning service. The hundreds of people there were enthralled by Ali's presence. Then we went back to my apartment for lunch and Muhammad told me, "I thought about inviting everyone back here for lunch, but I figured you wouldn't like that."

My most memorable visit to a mosque with Ali took place in 1991 at the Grand Mosque in Jakarta, Indonesia. Word spread that Ali was there, and a crowd estimated by authorities at two hundred thousand surrounded the mosque. When the service was over, a vehicular military escort was necessary to transport Muhammad through the throng back to our hotel.

The world needs more interfaith attendance at religious services, not less.

★ ★ ★

Charles Caleb Colton was an English clergyman who published a popular collection of aphorisms in the early 1800s. The best known of his sayings is "Imitation is the sincerest flattery."

There are times when imitation is also a trademark violation.

Michael Buffer has elevated the craft of ring announcing to a level that boxing has never seen before. He's known the world over for his trademark (and trademarked) phrase, "Let's get ready to rumble."

Joe Martinez is a ring announcer who works frequently for Golden Boy. When Martinez announces fights, he often employs the same voice inflection, cadence, and style of delivery as Buffer. It's not subtle. A recent main event introduction by Martinez was highlighted by, "And now, ladies and gentlemen. The judges are ready. The fighters are ready. The world is ready. Make some noise if you are ready."

Sound familiar?

Trademark protection is a complex area of the law. Buffer trademarked "Let's get ready to rumble" and various spinoffs of the phrase years ago. United States Patent and Trademark Office records show that Martinez tried to trademark the phrase "Are you ready?" in English, but his application was rejected. Buffer has the trademark on that. Martinez then successfully filed a trademark application for "Stan listos" without a question mark. "Estan listos" can be translated to "They are ready" or "Are you ready?" depending on whether there's a question mark at the end. Martinez also successfully filed for trademark registration for "the judges are ready," "the fighters are ready," and "let the world know you are ready!"

Numerous cease-and-desist letters have been written back and forth over the years.

I spoke with Martinez recently while he was on the road in Iowa.

"My wife and I sold our home six months ago and have a full-time ministry now," Martinez told me. "We bought a mobile home and travel around the country, preaching the glory of God. We homeschool our kids. We feel very strongly that we have to be the light in this dark world. God has called us to do great things."

Asked about the similarity between his ring announcing and Buffer's, Martinez answered, "It's funny you say that. I don't see it that way. I like to think I was doing it this way before he was. I started ring announcing in 2000 and said what I said because I thought it was the thing to do. I'm not trying to imitate anybody or use similar phrases. I have my trademarks and Michael has his. But of course, he's Michael Buffer. So he can say he said something in the bathroom thirty years ago and people will give him credit for it."

Buffer, of course, has been ready and rumbling since the mid-1980s. And Jake Gutierrez offers further insight into the situation.

Gutierrez has been the public-address announcer for the UNLV Lady Rebels basketball team for twenty-nine years. Arena Football, soccer, boxing, and several other sports are also on his resume. Recently, he added public-address duties for the NBA Summer League in Las Vegas to his portfolio.

Gutierrez recalls being one of roughly thirty candidates who auditioned to become Golden Boy's regular ring announcer when the job opened up years ago.

"I drove from Las Vegas to Los Angeles," Gutierrez recalls. "We got up in a ring, one at a time. There was a script we could read off of or we could do our own thing. Joe got up and—I remember it very clearly—it was like he was doing everything possible to sound like Michael. His choice of words, his delivery. Near the end, Joe actually said 'let's get ready to rumble' as close as he could to the way Michael says it. Some of the people I was sitting with were like, 'What is this?' I just shrugged my shoulders."

"I learned a long time ago not to copy people," Gutierrez continues. "I learn from them, but that's different from copying. Michael is at the top. He and Jimmy Lennon have both been kind in giving me pointers along the way. But you have to be your own person."

Meanwhile, Mark Kalmansohn (a Los Angeles attorney who represents Buffer's trademark interests) says of Martinez, "It's like trying to play Whac-A-Mole. We shut one thing down and then he pops up again."

★ ★ ★

Dreams die hard for fighters. One of the saddest moments in a boxer's life is when he realizes that he'll never be a world champion. Whether he's young or old, it's a painful awakening.

Don Elbaum has been a promoter, manager, matchmaker, and just about everything else in boxing for longer than many Social Security recipients have been alive.

Elbaum was seven years old when he went to his first pro fight. "Willie Pep," he remembers. "It was magic. That's what I was going to be."

And then?

"I had my first amateur fight when I was thirteen years old," Elbaum reminisces. "I weighed 126 pounds. The opponent was sixteen and weighed 140, but a lot of his weight was in his stomach. He was out of shape and had a huge belly. I got in the ring and I was terrified. The other guy kept coming forward, throwing punches. And I ran. I didn't dance. It wasn't side-to-side movement. I ran backwards as fast as I could to get as far away from him as I could. The entire first round, I didn't throw a punch. Second round, same thing. My cornerman, a guy named Frankie Schwartz, was screaming at me. 'Throw the right hand!' So finally, I stopped, closed my eyes, and threw a right hand as hard as I could. It hit him flush in the belly. There was a loud 'Oooooh!' The other guy doubled over and threw up. So they stopped the fight and gave me a knockout."

So far, so good.

"I won my first fifteen fights," Elbaum continues. "I could box. I had a good chin. I was beating tough guys. And I was a dreamer. I had my dreams. All fighters do. Fight number sixteen was in Erie, Pennsylvania. I was fighting a guy who was just out of the Marines and on the verge of beating the crap out of me. I was doing all right until he stunned me with a left hook and followed with a right hand that landed on the top of my head. Then he screamed. He'd broken his hand on my head, so they stopped it. That was my second knockout."

The saga continues.

"So now I'm 16 and 0," Elbaum recalls. "And I'm more sure than ever that, someday, I'll be a world champion. I didn't think it. I knew it. My next fight, I lost a decision at a tournament in Chicago. I felt bad. But hey, it happens. By the time I was nineteen, my record was 40 and 7. But the fights I'd lost were to fighters who were bigger than me, older than me, more experienced than me. There was always a reason for losing."

Then something bad happened.

"I lost three fights in a row," Elbaum recounts. "And I realized I'd never be a world champion. It was like a death sentence. I was devastated. I'd thought my destiny was to be like Willie Pep. Now my dream was dead, and it was like the world had come to an end."

★ ★ ★

Don Elbaum, like Zelig, surfaces from time to time in proximity to a wide range of players. So let's travel back in time to the early 1970s.

"I was promoting fight cards in Buffalo and living in the Statler Hotel or the Sheraton, I forget which," Elbaum recalls. "There was a fantastic deli called Harvey's attached to the hotel that had great corned beef sandwiches. One day, the deli owner said to me, 'Don, let me sell tickets for your fights.' I told him okay, and he did it for four or five shows. He could sell; he was good. And once he started selling tickets for me, I never had to pay for a corned beef sandwich."

"Anyway," Elbaum continues, "time goes by. I move to New York. And one day, there's a story in the newspaper that Harvey is now in Manhattan and has started a film company. I called his office and left a message congratulating him. His secretary called me back and said Harvey was thrilled to hear from me and would be in touch shortly. And that was it. I never heard from him again."

Why is that bit of Americana relevant today?

"Harvey" was Harvey Weinstein, the Academy-Award-winning film producer who has recently been outed as a bullying sexual predator.

"I liked Harvey," Elbaum says. "The guy I'm reading about now isn't the guy I thought I knew. But I guess I was wrong. What he did disgusts me."

★ ★ ★

Boxing writers, like most fans, develop a fondness for certain fighters. What separates us from the average fan is that we sometimes also develop personal relationships with the fighters we're covering.

I was at Seanie Monaghan's pro debut on May 21, 2010. It was at Capitale in New York on the undercard of a dreadful mismatch between Shannon Briggs and Dominique Alexander. Seanie was fighting a guy named Simeon Trigueno, who would finish his ring career at 0 and 4 with 3 KOs by. Promoter Joe DeGuardia was protecting Monaghan (as Bob Arum would later) because Seanie was a ticket-seller. Being a contrarian sort who's inclined to root for the underdog when I don't know either fighter, I was rooting for Trigueno. Seanie knocked him out in the first round.

Several years later, I spent three hours talking one-on-one with Seanie for an article I was writing. And I came away thinking, "This is a great guy."

Every time Monaghan has fought since then, my heart has been in his gloves.

"You need a mean streak to be a fighter," Seanie once told me. "But it's not just fighters. There are rich people who've never thrown a punch in their life who are just as mean and cruel as any fighter. Sometimes they're worse. It just comes out in different ways. Outside the ring, I try to be as nice as person as I can be."

On July 15, 2017, Seanie suffered the first loss of his pro career when he was knocked out in the second round of a fight at Nassau Coliseum by Marcus Browne. I watched on television, and it hurt to watch.

Seanie suffered more physical damage in some of his victories than he did in the Browne fight. But the loss to Browne exacted an enormous price. Serious economic consequences will follow. There's also an emotional low that comes with losing.

Writing in *Intimate Warfare*, Dennis Taylor and John Raspanti summed up the emotional turmoil that accompanies a fighter's first loss: "Gone is the fighter's own mindset of invincibility. Suddenly, he has a chink in his armor that wasn't there before. He is forced to relinquish the illusion that he is unbeatable, that he will always find a way to overcome and prevail. Now he knows better. He will always know better. A record that is blemished just once won't turn the fighter into a non-entity. But an unspoken probationary period descends like a threatening storm cloud. The ledge overlooking oblivion becomes a bit more precarious, feeling like it could crumble beneath the fighter's feet at any moment."

Monaghan can look back on what he has accomplished over the past seven years in boxing and in his personal life with pride. But the odds that he'll make life-changing money from boxing in the future just got longer.

★ ★ ★

I was going through some old files recently and came across several thoughts that Emanuel Steward shared with me that I'd never used in articles. Now is as good a time as any to relate them:

- "There are no standards for being a trainer anymore. Just throw a towel over your shoulder and say you're a trainer. It's like being a writer for a boxing website. Anyone can do it."
- "I was watching a fight the other night, and the trainer kept telling his fighter to double-up on the jab. I wanted holler, 'How can he double up on the jab when he can't land the first one?'"
- "In the dressing room before a fight, you can ask your fighter if he feels good. But he'll always tell you 'yes.' So unless you know your fighter very well, you don't know if he's feeling good or not."

Emanuel died five years ago. The day it happened, Larry Merchant told me, "I haven't been this sad since my father died."

Emanuel Steward was important to boxing. A lot of people miss him.

★ ★ ★

On June 16, 2017, WBC president Mauricio Sulaiman said that the WBC might bestow its Diamond Belt on the winner of the August 16 Floyd Mayweather vs. Conor McGregor spectacle. That raises an interesting possibility.

In order to fight for a WBC championship, or if a fighter is ranked by the WBC in its top fifteen in any weight division, the fighter must be registered in the WBC Clean Boxing Program and submit to year-round performance-enhancing drug testing by the Voluntary Anti-Doping Agency.

Mayweather has studiously avoided VADA testing, preferring to be tested by the more compliant United States Anti-Doping Agency.

If the WBC requires Mayweather and McGregor to submit to VADA testing, it would reaffirm the sanctioning body's commitment to clean sport. But that's unlikely to happen. Either Mayweather and McGregor will decline the WBC's offer. Or propelled by a desire to be part of Mayweather–McGregor, the WBC will find a way to negate its Clean Boxing Program's VADA requirement. Sulaiman hinted at that possibility on July 19, when he said that neither Mayweather nor McGregor is currently ranked by the WBC and, if they fight for the Diamond Belt, it would be regarded as a commemorative trophy, not a championship.

The WBC's Clean Boxing Program is the most promising of boxing's current anti-PED initiatives. It would be a shame if Mauricio Sulaiman were to undermine it for the sake of participating in one fight.

★ ★ ★

Jim Thomas is best known to boxing fans as the attorney who guided Evander Holyfield through the glory years of Evander's career. But Thomas has a history of his own as a participant in combat sports. In his words, "I spent 1/365th of one year as a professional regulated full-contact kickboxer."

Thomas grew up poor, earned a scholarship to college and law school at William and Mary, and was a reasonably good athlete. Along the way, he spent seven years training as a karate kickboxer. The high point of his career was a three-week stint in Japan when he won sixty-three out of sixty-three amateur bouts under Japanese karate rules, which allow full contact to the body but not the head. That led his sensei (teacher/trainer) Hiroshi Hamada (who—again in Thomas's words—had "a go-out-on-your shield warrior spirit") to enter Jim in a professional bout.

"It was for five hundred dollars," Thomas recalls. "That was like food for a year when I was in law school."

The bout was contested in 1975 in Williamsburg, Virginia, where the twenty-three-year-old Thomas was in his final year of law school. The contract weight was 175 pounds. Jim's chief second was Jeff Smith (a friend who later became a seven-time Professional Karate Association world light-heavyweight champion).

And, oh yes . . . The opponent was Jerry Rhome, who would become a full-contact karate kickboxing U.S. heavyweight champion.

"I knew I was overmatched going in," Thomas recounts. "Rhome was so far above me. In the first round, I was like a Chihuahua chasing after a German shepherd. Rome was just getting in work. Then, in the second round, he got tired of it and landed a left punch to the head followed by a right punch to the head. I ducked under the right, which brought my head within perfect range of a left round kick that landed on flush the bridge of my nose. It was one of the few times that people saw a guy go down and actually hit head-first on the canvas."

"I could see the crowd," Thomas continues. "They were waving but I couldn't hear them. The sound came on at the count of six. I got up and did what I'd seen fighters do on television; pounded my gloves together and said, 'I'm okay.' The referee said the fight could continue, and Jeff threw in the towel."

"I was upset with Jeff," Thomas recalls. "Jeff said, 'Explain to me what you thought you were going to do to Jerry if the fight went on.' I told him to go screw himself, although in less polite terms than that. And Jeff told me, 'Look, you were already knocked out once, and you'll have a headache for twenty-four to forty-eight hours. If I'd let it go on and you got knocked out again, which would have happened, you'd have a headache for the next six weeks. You're in law school, right?'

"Yes," Thomas answered.

"And you're one of the top students in your class?"

"Yes."

"How well will you do in law school if you can't think?"

Two hours later, Thomas, Smith, and Rhome were having beers together at a local bar.

And there's an epilogue to the story. Years later, Thomas was the head of litigation for Long Aldridge & Norman (a major law firm in Atlanta). It was there that he met Holyfield for the first time. Evander was in Jim's office for a get-acquainted session, and Jim mentioned that he'd once fought Rhome (who by then had served briefly as one of Evander's sparring partners). That led to an expression of disbelief. So Jim took a scrapbook off the shelf and showed Holyfield a photo of his squaring off against Rhome at the start of their fight.

"Look at that," Evander exclaimed.

"Don't get too excited," Thomas cautioned. "It doesn't end well."

Then Jim turned to the final photo.

"It doesn't matter how it ended," Holyfield told Thomas. "You got in there and fought this guy. I never thought I'd know a lawyer who got in there and did what I do."

★ ★ ★

Misrepresentations and forgeries are common in the sports collectibles market. Within that environment, many buyers rely on Professional Sports Authenticator and PSA/DNA for authentication.

PSA focuses on authenticating and grading sports cards and other trading cards. PSA/DNA focuses on authenticating autographs and the overall memorabilia market. According to the PSA website, the two companies "have processed over 20 million cards and collectibles with a cumulative declared value of over a billion dollars."

The PSA/DNA website states that PSA/DNA was founded by PSA in 1998 "in response to widespread counterfeiting, forgery, and piracy of autographed collectibles." The website further states, "PSA/DNA is the world's leading third-party authentication service for autographs and memorabilia," and adds, "PSA/DNA experts conduct ink analysis, structure analysis, object evaluation, and side-by-side comparisons. Experts may also use a video spectral comparator to further evaluate the autograph."

Impressive. Right?

Wrong.

A photograph listed for sale on eBay as of this writing is described as follows: "Michael Dokes Authentic Autographed Signed 16x20 Photo . . . This is a 16x20 Photo that has been hand signed by Michael Dokes. It has been authenticated by PSA/DNA and comes with their sticker and matching certificate of authenticity."

Confirming the authenticity of Michael Dokes's signature, the PSA/DNA website states:

> "PSA/DNA Certification Verification #T14814—It is the opinion of PSA/DNA Authentication Services that the signature(s) listed below is/are genuine. According to the Certification Database, this item is defined as follows:
> Item: Photograph
> Primary subject: Michael Dokes
> Result/Grade: Authentic.

Now we come to the problem.

The "authentic autographed photo that has been hand signed by Michael Dokes" and "authenticated by PSA/DNA and comes with their sticker and matching certificate of authenticity" isn't a photo of Michael Dokes signed by Michael Dokes. It's a photograph of Michael Grant signed by Michael Grant.

★ ★ ★

Daniel Mendoza earned recognition as champion of England when he defeated Bill Warr in 1794. He's widely regarded as pugilism's first "scientific" boxer and was also boxing's first Jewish champion. He learned Hebrew as a boy, was bar mitzvahed at age thirteen, and is said to have been the first Jew that King George III ever spoke with.

Mendoza authored both a personal memoir and a treatise on boxing. In each instance, the writing now seems dated. That's to be expected since Mendoza's championship reign coincided with the presidency of George Washington.

But some thoughts are eternal. Thus, it's worth repeating one of Mendoza's observations: "A knowledge of the art of pugilism can never be acquired by theory alone."

Those of us who sit on the easy side of the ropes should remember that pearl of wisdom.

★ ★ ★

Nine years ago, I wrote an article entitled "*BoxRec.com*: Boxing's Indispensable Website." I praised John Sheppard, the indefatigable Brit who has maintained the site as a gift to the boxing community since its inception in 2000. And I quoted numerous boxing aficionados, among them:

- Matchmaker Bruce Trampler: "Short of actually being at a fight, they're the best source of information out there. I have my own computerized records, and I'm on *BoxRec* at least a dozen times a day. We take it for granted, but everyone in boxing would miss it if it was gone."
- Historian Mike Silver: "*BoxRec.com* is a dream come true. It's one of the greatest gifts to boxing fans and boxing historians in the history of the world. Years ago, you needed a whole shelf of *Ring* record books to track the records of fighters. Now anyone can do it in seconds for free. Every time I write about boxing, I want to thank them."
- Promoter Lou DiBella: "Anyone in boxing who says he doesn't use *BoxRec* is either a complete imbecile or lying."

Virtually everyone who follows the sweet science, from the most powerful denizens of the boxing world to casual fans, uses *BoxRec.com*. John Sheppard still works fulltime on the site, as he has since 2005. He recently hired his first fulltime employee, a computer programmer who works from home "so I'm not so stressed anymore." The site has almost two hundred editors located around the world, none of whom are paid. The result is a database that's unparalleled in the history of boxing.

*BoxRec.com* has data on more than 55,000 referees, judges, managers, promoters, matchmakers, supervisors, and other "non-fighters." But its core content consists of more than 2,050,000 bouts that have been entered into its database. That includes roughly 23,000 active (having fought within the past 365 days) and 622,000 nonactive fighters. These numbers keep growing as new fights take place and more old ones are recorded.

And there's a feature unique to *BoxRec.com* that makes it the clear industry favorite. Anyone who views a fighter's record can also see the complete record of that fighter's opponents, his opponents' opponents, and so on down the line.

One change from recent years is that *BoxRec.com* has now been embraced by, and is an official registry for, the Association of Boxing Commissions. That makes life easier for Sheppard because, in his words, "Even the most recalcitrant states now send us results."

On a typical day, *BoxRec.com* has 116,000 visitors who view 700,000 pages. These are impressive numbers that translate into 3,596,000 visitors who view 21,700,000 pages per month. Roughly 27 percent of this traffic comes from the United States and 25 percent from the United Kingdom.

Converting *BoxRec.com* to a pay site would mean a big payout for Sheppard. But nine years ago, he told this writer, "I've always lived within my means. I've never needed a lot of money to be happy. That's not why I started the site. That's not what it's all about. I don't want *BoxRec* to ever become a closed shop."

To this day, Sheppard maintains that view, saying, "It's never going to happen. Not on my watch."

Three years ago, the Boxing Writers Association of America honored Sheppard with the James A. Farley Award for Honesty and Integrity. He deserves that recognition and any other accolades that come his way.

★ ★ ★

There are times when the New York State Athletic Commission ill-advisedly tampers with standard practice. That was evident at Barclays Center on January 14, 2017.

Recently enacted NYSAC medical protocols call for ring doctors to stand on the ring apron and observe both fighters during all breaks between rounds. If a doctor wants to examine a fighter from inside the ring, the doctor asks the referee to call a time out.

This led to multiple occasions on January 14 (in the co-featured bouts and also on the undercard), when a boxer was examined, and the action was put on hold, to the dismay of the crowd and the opposing fighter.

Does this practice contribute to safeguarding the health and safety of fighters?

Dr. Margaret Goodman (former chief ringside physician and chairperson of the medical advisory board for the Nevada State Athletic Commission) is a neurologist and one of the foremost advocates for fighter safety in the United States. She's also president of the Voluntary Anti-Doping Association, which oversees the most credible performance-enhancing-drug testing in boxing today.

Dr. Goodman has this to say about New York's new medical protocols:

"First, as far as standing on the ring apron is concerned, that's more for show than anything else. If you need to get in there, get in there. As far as extending the one-minute break between rounds; I understand the need to safeguard the fighter. But in my opinion, that one minute should only be extended in extreme circumstances. Otherwise, you're interfering with the flow of the fight and possibly changing the outcome of the fight."

"Also," Dr. Goodman continues, "I have safety concerns with the New York procedure because you're giving the damaged fighter extra time to recover and exposing him to second impact syndrome. In most situations an experienced ring doctor should be able to do what he or she has to do within the one minute that's allotted. Except in rare situations, a talented ring doctor doesn't need the extra time. They have some very good ring doctors in New York, but they're operating within a flawed system."

★ ★ ★

Not long ago, I was talking with Freddie Roach about Muhammad Ali, and the conversation turned to Roach's own physical condition.

Roach suffers from Parkinson's syndrome, which is characterized by various symptoms including, in Roach's case, visible tremors. Most likely, his condition was caused by taking too many blows to the head during his career as a boxer.

"I never thought ever in my life about being injured in a fight," Roach said. "It never crossed my mind once. There was a time when Eddie Futch [Roach's trainer] told me that I was starting to get hit too much; it's time that I give it up. I was upset with Eddie at that point. I got a little mad. I said, 'Well, you're pretty old. Why don't you retire? I can still do this.' I fought five more fights and I lost four of the five. Then I humbly went to Eddie and asked him if I could be his assistant trainer and have a job. That changed my whole life from being a washed-up fighter to being something in life."

"I became aware of the health issues about two years after I retired," Roach continued. "I was running with Virgil Hill up in Reno. It was a very nice place for conditioning, running, horses and so forth. I was watching a horse as we ran and I hit a hole and broke my leg. When I came out of the cast, I developed a dropped foot and then the tremors started coming. I remember the first time someone asked me about the tremors. It was a girlfriend. She said, 'Are you saying no or are you just shaking again?' I said, 'What do you mean, shaking again?' She goes, 'You shake all the time.' Then I met a couple doctors and they took me to the Mayo Clinic and they diagnosed me with Parkinson's about six months later."

* * *

*Chuck* is the latest in a string of recent biopics about professional boxers. "Once upon a time," it begins, "I was the heavyweight champion of New Jersey. Hoboken had Sinatra. Bayonne had Chuck Wepner."

Liev Schreiber plays Wepner. That presents a challenge, since Wepner is a huge hulking man and Schreiber lacks Wepner's physicality, but he's credible in the role. Elizabeth Moss gives a virtuoso performance as Wepner's long-suffering first wife, Phyllis. Ron Perlman is suitably obnoxious as Wepner's manager, Al Braverman. Naomi Watts is enticing as the woman who becomes wife number two, Linda Wepner.

*Chuck* focuses on Wepner's fifteenth-round knockout loss to Muhammad Ali, the *Rocky* franchise that grew out of his inspirational effort that night, and the then-sordid underside of Wepner's character. Among other transgressions, the highlighted character flaws include profligate womanizing and a love affair with cocaine that led to a twenty-six-month stint in prison for cocaine distribution. It's an unvarnished warts-and-all portrait of Wepner.

*Raging Bull* set the standard to which all boxing biopics (and many other films) aspire. Years ago, Vikki LaMotta told me about sitting next to Jake at the premiere of *Raging Bull* in New York.

"When the movie ended," Vikki recounted, "the audience seemed stunned. Jake was sitting directly beside me. For a long time, he was silent."

"Jake, did you like it?"

"I don't know," he said finally. "I could see this movie ten times and not know what to think. DeNiro is great. He's really me. But I see that man on screen. I know I've done all those things, and I don't like that person. He's a bad man, and I know it's me."

So how does the real-life Chuck Wepner feel about Liev Schreiber's portrayal of him in *Chuck*?

"I know it's not complimentary," Wepner acknowledges. "But it doesn't bother me. I wasn't always good. There were times when I was bad. It's who I was."

"This whole experience has been very gratifying for me," Wepner continues. "It's a major movie with two of the biggest stars in the world. It's a good movie, and I have a piece of it, so I'll make some money. And as far as me as a fighter, I know I wasn't great. I was a tough guy who could take a punch. That's what the movie shows me to be."

The fight scenes in *Chuck* are reasonably realistic, which is more than can be said of the fight scenes in many boxing movies today. The 1970s are nicely recreated. At one point in the film, Linda says to Chuck, "There's more to you than meets the eye, Chuck Wepner. Not much. But enough."

The same can be said of this movie. It's an enjoyable ride.

★ ★ ★

## Words of Wisdom from Fighters

Art Aragon (boxing's original "Golden Boy"): "When you quit the ring, if you're a big success, you're only a few thousand dollars in debt and only a little bit brain-damaged."

Jorge Arce: "People want to see fighters fighting, not dancing. They want to see blood. I give them blood; I love that. If it gets on me, I get more motivated and excited."

Earnie Shavers: "Thank God, I was a puncher. I had no fear. I believed in myself and thought I could knock out the world. The only time I remember a little fear was when I fought Roy 'Tiger' Williams. I'd been promised a shot at Ali if I beat him, so I took the fight. But I knew it would be tough. Right before I went to the ring, I looked at some pictures of my little girls and said to myself, 'This is what you're fighting for.' I wore Williams down and knocked him out in the tenth round. After that, I feared no man."

Alexis Arguello (on being counted out in his second fight against Aaron Pryor): "It's hard to accept, but it's good to accept. I did it with grace and just accepted that the guy beat me. Even though I did my best, in the tenth round I accepted it right there. I said, 'This is too much. I won't take it. I'll just sit down and watch Richard Steele count to ten.'"

Johnny Nelson: "In boxing, if you're a fighter, it's all about you. It's the chance to be completely selfish and not have to explain why you're being completely selfish."

Roger Mayweather: "Do I have injuries from boxing? To be honest, I don't know. If you've had that many fights, somewhere along the line, something happens. I just don't know what the fuck it was. But that's the risk of doing it. I took my chances."

★ ★ ★

When John Duddy retired from boxing in 2011, the popular Irish middleweight decided to try his hand at acting.

"I always liked storytelling," Duddy explains. "When I was growing up, we had a family movie night at home once a week when we watched a movie on the VCR. The first movie I saw in a theater was *The Empire Strikes Back*. My mother took me, and I loved it. It was like seeing my dreams on the screen or my playing with my toys come to life on the screen. Movies are incredible. Wherever you are in your life, they can take you away to another world."

Since leaving the sweet science, Duddy has had roles in a half-dozen films and several plays. He also helped Robert DeNiro prepare for the fight scenes in *Grudge Match*, which led to John landing a bit part as Ken Buchanan in *Hands of Stone*. But Duddy's most significant film role to date is in *Emerald City*, which had its American premiere in New York on March 26, 2017.

*Emerald City* is a simply made, moving film about a crew of Irish construction workers in New York. To say that it was made on a small budget would be overstating the case.

"Not many people believed we could make the movie," Duddy says. "But Colin Broderick [who wrote, directed, co-produced, and stars in *Emerald City*] made it happen. Each character has his own story. None of them is as happy as you'd want them to be. For most of them, their lives are work, drink, bed. But they get on with their lives."

"Working on the movie was an incredible experience," Duddy continues. "Watching people put it all together on a shoestring budget. Working with young producers, a young director, the other actors, the technical people, everyone dedicated to their art. The friendships I've made working on this movie will last forever."

As for the future, Duddy says, "No one knows where any of us who worked on *Emerald City* will go in our lives. I'm still with The Padded Wagon [a moving company in New York]. I lift things up, carry them someplace, and put them down again. They're great about my work schedule being flexible. Whenever there's an audition, a rehearsal, a performance, they let me off."

"If Grainne [John's wife, who had a small role in *Emerald City*] and I can live our lives as actors, that would be great. Right now, just like I did with boxing, we're starting at the bottom and trying to work our way to the top. To make it in acting, you have to have talent. You have to be dedicated. You have to be dependable. And you need the breaks. But one way or another, I'll always do this. Acting is amazing to me. You read something. You think you have it in your mind. Then you work on it with other people, you learn from each other, and it grows into something else. I love it."

★ ★ ★

Rosie Perez has enjoyed a storied career as an actress and been a prominent supporter of progressive social causes. She's also a fervent fight fan.

Looking back on her many years as a fan, Perez recently recalled, "I did not have an emotional attachment to a fight until Wilfred Benitez fought Sugar Ray Leonard. Years later, when I met Leonard, I quivered. It was at the Boxing Hall of Fame in Nevada. Ray goes, 'Are you shaking?' I said, 'Yeah.' He goes, 'Why?' I said, 'Because I'm meeting Sugar Ray Leonard, the guy who defeated Wilfred Benitez.' He looked at me and he goes, 'Who are you?' And I said, 'I cried that Wilfred lost. But I felt guilty because I really wanted you to win and I felt like I was betraying my heritage because Wilfred is a Puerto Rican.'"

Ray Leonard has his own memories of fighting Benitez. And he remembers his conversation with Perez. In fact . . .

"I vividly remember that conversation with Rosie," Leonard says. "I got teary eyed because I saw the honesty in her eyes."

★ ★ ★

Pennsylvania State Athletic Commission executive director Greg Sirb is on the short list of administrators who have a full understanding of how to regulate boxing. Sirb is passionate about the sweet science and recently directed his passion toward the State of Montana.

Section 6303(a) of the federal Professional Boxing Safety Act provides that no person may promote or participate in a professional boxing match held in a state that does not have a boxing commission unless the match is supervised by a boxing commission from another state and subjected to the regulatory guidelines published by the Association of Boxing Commissions as well as any other professional boxing regulations and requirements promulgated by the supervising state.

"Montana started putting a commission together about a year ago," Sirb says. "But it's not up and running yet. Montana does not have a working commission in any sense that I'm aware of."

Under federal law, the Association of Boxing Commissions is supposed to notify the state attorney general in any state where an illegal fight card takes place. Sirb has written to Attorney General Tim Fox at the Montana Department of Justice on numerous occasions to voice his concern.

Most recently, on March 8, 2017, Sirb wrote, "I am inquiring about the professional boxing matches that have occurred in Montana over the past sixteen months. Since Montana does not have a working Athletic Commission to regulate these events, the Professional Boxing Safety Act of 1996 takes effect. This law specifically states that, if the state where the boxing is to be held does not have a commission, the event must be supervised by another state commission. This is federal law. Your state has had at least five pro boxing events where there was no Commission to supervise—a direct violation of federal law. It is only a matter of time before some boxer gets hurt."

Sirb's March 8 letter to Fox specifically referenced a fight card that was scheduled to take place at the Shrine Auditorium in Billings, Montana, on March 25.

Seven fights were contested on the March 25 card in Billings. The main event saw local favorite Duran Caferro (15–1), who has fought one fighter with a winning record in his entire career, take on Cheyenne Zeigler (3–12), who'd lost his seven most recent fights by knockout. Caferro knocked Zeigler out in the third round.

In the featured undercard bout, Eric Hempstead (5–0, 5 KOs) fought for what was described as the "vacant Montana State Heavyweight Title." Hempstead's previous five opponents have a career total of one win among them. His adversary on March 25, Warren Brocky, fit that profile. Brocky entered the bout with an 0–2 record, both of his losses coming by knockout. Hempstead knocked Brocky out in the first round.

The fights in Billings were promoted by Silver Wolf Fight Promotions, which is run by thirty-nine-year-old Jon Jay Mount. Adding to the questionable nature of the proceedings, Mount fought on the card and knocked out 0-and-4 Andrew Howk in the third stanza.

"It's an outrage," Sirb says. "Montana has had a least five illegal cards that I know of. Who referees? Who judges? Who's performing medicals on the fighters?"

Eric Sell is communications director for the Montana Department of Justice. On March 23, Sell told this writer, "There is a boxing commission as defined by federal law under the Montana Department of Labor and Industry, but I don't know what they're doing."

Sell referred further questions to Derek Sherlock (a supervisor for the Licensing Bureau in the Business Standards Division of the Montana Department of Labor and Industry). Sherlock did not return telephone calls regarding the matter.

Meanwhile, it's worth noting that the Montana Annotated Code provides that the Montana Department of Labor "may appoint a representative to act specifically on behalf of the department" at boxing events.

Montana law further states that "the representative may be a volunteer" and that "the department may accept private donations for the costs of administering the boxing program."

Finally, a doctor need not be present at ringside for fights in Montana. A "licensed physician assistant" or "licensed advanced practice registered nurse" will suffice.

And it's not just Montana.

Michigan has a proud boxing tradition. Joe Louis lived in Detroit. Thomas Hearns came out of the famed Kronk Gym in Detroit and fought thirty-four times in Michigan.

"Michigan now sends one inspector to each show," Sirb states. "One inspector. That's their entire staff on site. There's no way you can properly regulate a fight card with one inspector. And in Michigan, the promoter now assigns the referees, judges, and doctors. The only limitation is that the referees, judges, and doctors have to be licensed by the Michigan commission."

"That satisfies the Ali Act because technically there's still a state commission in Michigan," Sirb notes. "But it's a disgrace. It's ripe for abuse when a promoter chooses the referee and judges for a fight. And it adds to the dangers facing a fighter when the promoter is choosing the doctors."

★ ★ ★

The dictionary defines "empathy" as "the ability to understand and share the feelings of another."

It's remarkable how little empathy most boxing fans feel for fighters. We're happy when our guy wins and disappointed when he loses; emotions that we experience in varying degree depending on how much we care about a particular fight to begin with. We're more likely to be drawn into the elation of the winner than the pathos of the loser, perhaps because that's what the television cameras are inclined to focus on. As a general rule, television gives sports fans more close-ups of the agony of defeat in the eyes of basketball players sitting on the bench as the clock ticks down that it does of a defeated fighter sitting on his stool after a loss.

So the next time you watch a fight, here's something to remember. These aren't wind-up toys or Rock 'Em Sock 'Em Robots. They aren't computer-game figures on a monitor. These are real live people. A losing fighter hasn't just lost a sports competition. His career and his earning potential have been damaged. And oftentimes, he has been beaten up.

To repeat: Beaten up. Try it sometime and see how you like it.

So don't feel sorry for yourself the next time your guy loses. Feel sorry for the fighter.

★ ★ ★

The New York State Athletic Commission remains adrift in matters large and small.

The commission website is so out of date (as of September 9, 2017) that Eric Bentley is still listed as director of boxing with an accompanying biographical sketch, although Bentley left the commission in early May. Similarly, Kim Sumbler is listed as MMA project coordinator, although Sumbler became NYSAC executive director months ago.

So many NYSAC deputy commissioners are now assigned to each fight card at taxpayer expense that one might wonder if each deputy commissioner is responsible for monitoring a different ring rope.

More troubling, the Department of State (which oversees the NYSAC) has adopted a "circle the wagons" mentality that interferes with the lawful flow of information and the implementation of progressive reforms.

On June 23, 2017, the Department of State refused to honor a Freedom of Information Law request for a May 23, 2017, letter sent by New York State inspector general Catherine Leahy Scott to secretary of state Rossana Rosado on grounds that the letter contained "privileged" information within the meaning of the law.

On August 30, 2017, the Inspector General's office released the same letter to this writer pursuant to an identical Freedom of Information Law request.

The May 23 letter from the Inspector General stated that former NYSAC athletic activities assistant Mario Mercado had been "forced to resign in or about February 2015 due, in part, to his having used his state-issued credit card for a personal expense," but was then rehired by the NYSAC as a per diem deputy commissioner. Leahy Scott's letter concluded that Mercado's appointment as a deputy commissioner should be "reconsidered."

★ ★ ★

Sports can lead to a loss of objectivity. That's particularly true when it comes to scoring a fight.

Lou DiBella is one of the most knowledgeable boxing people I know. Over the years, we've watched countless fights together. Our scorecards are almost always similar. Except when Lou has a significant vested interest in one of the fighters. In those instances, without fail, Lou's scorecard is more heavily weighted toward his guy than mine is.

People in a fighter's camp tend to view fights through rose-colored glasses. Almost always, their scorecards are more heavily weighted toward their fighter than the judges' scorecards and consensus media scoring. I can count on one hand the times when the opposite was true.

This phenomenon extends far beyond boxing. Jim Harbaugh isn't the only football coach who goes into conniptions and rages against the inequities of life when a penalty call goes against his team. We've come to expect similar behavior from most coaches and athletes.

That leaves open the question of whether the people involved with a fighter are oblivious to the fact that they're scoring a fight badly or refuse to acknowledge their bias. Probably, it's a bit of both. It also leads me to recall a moment that highlights the respect I had for former WBC 140-pound champion Billy Costello, who died of cancer six years ago.

In 1999, at age forty-three, Costello made an ill-advised return to the ring to fight 40-year-old Juan LaPorte on a "legends" card in North Carolina. Billy won a split decision in a bout that most observers thought should have been scored the other way.

"To be honest with you," Costello said during a post-fight interview, "I think a draw would have been fairer."

★ ★ ★

Over the years, thousands of participants and observers have tried to explain why boxing is important. ESPN commentator Teddy Atlas recently put his imprint on the subject in a conversation with this writer.

"It's real simple what it is about boxing more than any other sport that sends shockwaves, that gets people's attention," Atlas said. "It's that, in a world where life is often unfair, on one given night if it means enough to you, if you have trained yourself hard enough, if you are determined enough, if it's inside of you; you are going to go in that ring no matter where you came from, no matter what you didn't have growing up, no matter who your parents were, no matter what your ethnicity was, your religion, anything, no matter how poor you were; you can get in that ring and you can make things right on one given night. If you want to be champion bad enough, you can be the best in the world. You can even the playing field in an unfair world. That's magic. That makes this sport special."

★ ★ ★

A video review of ESPN's Vasyl Lomachenko vs. Guillermo Rigondeaux telecast reveals that Anatoly Lomachenko (Vasyl's father and chief second) wore either an earbud or a hearing aid in the corner during the fight. Both are legal. But should an earbud be?

Boxers, like all athletes, are always looking for an edge. The classic example of this dates to Muhammad Ali's 1977 fight against Earnie Shavers at Madison Square Garden.

NBC, which televised the bout, was allowed by the New York State Athletic Commission to see and tell viewers at home the judges' scores after each round. Angelo Dundee, who trained Ali, arranged for a Baltimore matchmaker named Eddie Hrica to watch the broadcast on television in the arena and relay the scoring to Dundee via hand signals as it was announced. After twelve rounds, Angelo knew that, under the round system in effect in New York, Ali was leading 8 to 4 on two judges' cards and 8–3–1 on the third. That dictated his strategy for the final three rounds.

Suppose a TV telecast picks up a fighter telling his trainer, "I think my hand is broken" or "my ribs hurt."

Knowledge is power.

Earbuds shouldn't be allowed in the corner during fights. The trainers aren't listening to Ella Fitzgerald.

★ ★ ★

Veteran sportswriter Robert Lipsyte has covered his share of fights over the decades, starting with Cassius Clay vs. Sonny Liston in Miami

Beach on February 25, 1964. Reflecting on those years, Lipsyte recently observed, "One thing about covering boxing was that, if it was a major fight, you got to spend a few days in the training camp of the fighters, talking to them, talking to their handlers. And in the course of those days, it was very hard not to become emotionally invested with the fighters. In some cases, I loved every moment of the coverage until the bell for the first round. Then these two guys, who I had come to like in the last month, were now trying to give each other brain damage."

★ ★ ★

The State of New York has agreed to pay $22,000,000 to Magomed Abdusalamov and his family following almost four years of litigation in the New York State Court of Claims.

Abdusalamov suffered grievous injuries and irreversible brain damage in a fight against Mike Perez at Madison Square Garden on November 2, 2013. Subsequent investigations, including a thirty-two-month probe by the New York State Inspector General's office, found the New York State Athletic Commission at fault.

More specifically, the Inspector General's report declared, "Many Athletic Commission practices, policies and procedures were either non-existent or deficient, specifically those relating to post-bout medical care, tactical emergency plans and communication, and training." The Inspector General also found a lack of appropriate engagement and oversight by Athletic Commission commissioners and its chair.

The settlement was agreed to during the week of July 10, 2017, but was not announced until September 8 because it required the pro forma signing of an order by Jeanette Rodriguez-Morick, the New York State Court of Claims judge overseeing the case. It's unclear why it took the judge two months to sign the order. However, the delay made it more difficult for the Abdusalamov family (which has been living on loans) to repay the loans and fund annuities in a timely manner.

Paul Edelstein, the lead attorney for Magomed and his family, had initiated the proceeding in the Court of Claims because, as a state entity, the New York State Athletic Commission is statutorily immune to suit in the regular courts and can be sued only in the Court of Claims.

On March 26, 2014, Edelstein filed a separate lawsuit in New York State Supreme Court against five commission doctors (Barry Jordan, Anthony Curreri, Osric King, Gerard Varlotta, and Avery Browne), Matt Farrago (the NYSAC inspector assigned to Abdusalamov's dressing room), Benjy Esteves (who refereed the fight), K2 Promotions (which promoted the bout), and Madison Square Garden.

The $22,000,000 settlement releases only the New York State entities and two individuals who were classified as direct employees of the state (Barry Jordan and Matt Farrago). The case against Esteves as well as doctors Curreri, King, and Varlotta will proceed in New York State Supreme Court. Edelstein previously offered to settle with the doctors for an amount equal to the limits of their individual insurance policies (a total of $6,000,000). But that offer was rejected.

K2 Promotions, Madison Square Garden, and Avery Browne were dismissed as defendants in the Supreme Court case at an earlier date.

The $22,000,000 to be paid in settlement is more than all but a handful of boxers have earned in an entire ring career. The number reflects both the nature of the injuries suffered by Abdusalamov and the inexcusable manner in which his medical care was mishandled by the New York State Athletic Commission.

* * *

A note on the photograph of Evander Holyfield that graces the cover of this book.

Wojtek Urbanek was born in Poland in 1975. He came to the United States in 2012 and is now global creative director for Springer Nature, which publishes *Nature*, *Scientific American*, and several other prestigious magazines.

He's a brilliant photographer in his own right.

The photo in question was taken on September 6, 2017. Holyfield was in New York on business for Real Deal Sports & Entertainment, his recently formed promotional company. Wojtek brought his equipment to Evander's room at the Crowne Plaza Hotel near JFK Airport.

"Evander opened the door," Wojtek recalls. "And I was like, 'Omigod! It's really Evander Holyfield."

While Urbanek set up his equipment, Holyfield fiddled with his iPad. Then Evander hit a button and the Commodores started playing.

"If I only knew how to sing," Evander said wistfully.

Then, at Wojtek's request, Holyfield took off the white T-shirt he was wearing.

"I only shot for a few minutes," Urbanek remembers. "I felt I should honor his time. At one point, I asked him to hold his hands in prayer. And Evander started praying. He looked very peaceful. Then I asked for a staredown and his face became dangerous. I think he was a little angry, actually, that I interrupted his prayer."

Holyfield is often referred to as one of boxing's quintessential warriors. Wojtek's photograph captures this essence. Evander was fifty-four years old when the photo was taken. He's at rest in a hotel room, not fighting. But this is what opponents saw when they entered the ring to do battle against him. Hands clasped in prayer, he looks very much like a wrathful god.

★ ★ ★

I've always been a collector. When I was a kid, I collected baseball cards and comic books. Eventually, my mother gave the comic books to a local children's hospital and I sold the baseball cards for a fraction of what they're worth today. That's life. If everyone kept their old treasures, they'd be less rare and, hence, less valuable.

Still, over the years, I've amassed some pretty good collectibles. I have documents signed by every president of the United States except for the current White House occupant. My favorite is a handwritten legal brief penned by Abraham Lincoln in 1855.

England is well represented in my collection in the form of a cut signature from Queen Victoria and a note signed by Charles Dickens in 1862 on stationery from his Gad's Hill Place home.

There's a lot of sports memorabilia, most notably, boxing. I have an enormous amount of Muhammad Ali memorabilia and dozens of uncut tickets from major fights.

My favorite ticket is from the September 7, 1892, bout at the Olympic Club in New Orleans, when James J. Corbett wrested the heavyweight championship from John L. Sullivan. The most valuable of my tickets would have gained admission to the July 3, 1905, contest when Marvin Hart claimed the heavyweight throne by knocking out James Root.

I have uncut tickets from eleven fights where a new heavyweight champion was crowned. (Corbett, Hart, Jack Dempsey, Gene Tunney, Joe Louis, Rocky Marciano, Ingemar Johansson, Sonny Liston, Mike Tyson, Evander Holyfield, and Riddick Bowe). Also, an uncut ticket from the night of October 4, 1940, (when Sugar Ray Robinson made his pro debut at Madison Square Garden on the undercard of Henry Armstrong vs. Fritzie Zivic) and the September 3, 1906, confrontation between Battling Nelson and Joe Gans in Goldfield, Nevada.

The July 4, 1910, "great white hope" fight between Jack Johnson and Jim Jeffries is in my collection, as are the two confrontations between Joe Louis and Max Schmeling. Not to mention oddities like a Christmas card signed by both Don King and Bob Arum. How many of those do you think are around?

But one piece has a special place in my heart.

In the mid-1980s, I authored a book about the sweet science entitled *The Black Lights*. The book explored the sport and business of boxing through the prism of WBC 140-pound champion Billy Costello. After it was published, I asked Billy to inscribe it for me. He wrote, "To Tom, a great friend and pal, the best always, Bill Costello."

Thus, a new pursuit was born.

That was in 1985. Since then, I've brought the book to numerous boxing-related events and asked world champions to sign it. My criteria are simple. The signer must have held a recognized world title. Currently the WBC, WBA, IBF, and WBO merit inclusion. To date, 188 champions have signed my copy of *The Black Lights*. Some simply wrote their name. Others inscribed longer messages.

The signees include alltime greats like Muhammad Ali, Joe Frazier, George Foreman, Larry Holmes, Archie Moore, Gene Fullmer, Carmen Basilio, Emile Griffith, Jake LaMotta, Joey Maxim, Reuben Olivares, and Willie Pep.

Also, modern superstars like Mike Tyson, Lennox Lewis, Evander Holyfield, Vitali Klitschko, Wladimir Klitschko, Sugar Ray Leonard, Roberto Duran, Marvelous Marvin Hagler, Thomas Hearns, Julio Cesar Chavez, Alexis Arguello, Pernell Whitaker, Roy Jones, and Manny

Pacquiao. Plus the likes of Marco Antonio Barrera, Erik Morales, Juan Manuel Marquez, Joe Calzaghe, Bernard Hopkins, Felix Trinidad, Miguel Cotto, and Oscar De La Hoya.

Thirty-nine heavyweight champions (Jersey Joe Walcott, Floyd Patterson, and Ingemar Johansson among them) signed the book. The fact that I wrote a book that has been signed by thirty-nine heavyweight champions is pretty cool. The fact that we live in an era when boxing is so fragmented that I've been able to meet thirty-nine heavyweight champions isn't.

★ ★ ★

The New York State Athletic Commission lost a valuable asset when Keith Sullivan resigned as a deputy commissioner on November 13, 2017. Sullivan joined the NYSAC in 2012. A lawyer by trade, he brought an understanding of the sport and business of boxing as well as his legal acumen to the commission. He knows who the players are, both at the commission and in the boxing community at large.

Before joining the NYSAC, Sullivan represented Joey Gamache in a lawsuit against the commission that stemmed from irregularities at the weigh-in prior to the fighter's February 26, 2000, bout against Arturo Gatti at Madison Square Garden. Gamache was brutally knocked out in that bout and suffered a career-ending brain bleed.

In the past, Sullivan has also represented fighters in contractual matters. His decision to leave his per diem position with the NYSAC was spurred in part by the desire to become more involved in boxing as a practicing attorney.

Sullivan is widely respected within the boxing community. The NYSAC's loss is a potential gain for fighters and anyone else who's looking for an honest, competent lawyer with knowledge of boxing.

★ ★ ★

As Miguel Cotto's illustrious ring career comes to an end, it's appropriate to acknowledge a special friendship.

Miguel and Bryan Perez met in 2002. Bryan was recording a demo show for what he hoped would be a new boxing program. Miguel was his first interview. Over the next five years, they grew closer. They've been together on a fulltime basis since 2007 as business associates and friends.

Bryan is rarely in the spotlight. He's not one of those guys who push and shove to be on camera and walk around on fight night shouting, "You da man." His official title is vice president of operations for Cotto Promotions. But he's much more than that.

Let Miguel tell the tale:

> Bryan and I see each other every day. I spend more time with Bryan than with anybody else, including my wife. Bryan wants me to be safe and happy. There have been many times when he could take advantage of a situation to do for himself. But he never does. Always, he thinks about me first and putting me in a safe place in business and every other way. Many times, he takes better care of me than he takes of himself.
>
> Being with Bryan makes me feel comfortable and secure. Around him, I can be me. And Bryan is my conscience. He makes me a better Miguel. When I was young, I had a lot of trouble in my marriage. Bryan spoke to me brother to brother and helped me to understand certain things. He taught me to do things better for me, for my wife, for my whole family.
>
> My time in boxing is ending now, but Bryan will always be with me. If we went together into a war, Bryan would put my life ahead of his own. I really believe that. This is love, man love as a true brother and friend. And I would do for Bryan what he does for me.

★ ★ ★

Jake LaMotta, who died on September 19, 2017, left a mixed legacy. He was good fighter but a shabby human being who was physically abusive to more than one of his six wives.

That said, LaMotta understood boxing. So he knew how much about the sweet science he didn't know.

"There are times," LaMotta acknowledged, "when boxing makes you stop and realize that it will always have the ability to surprise you. You try to read a fight, imagine how it will go based on your knowledge and experience. And then something else happens to blow your mind."

★ ★ ★

The dialogue over racial prejudice in the United States has gotten uglier the past few months. Let me add an experience I had years ago to the discussion.

I had a friend who was in my home with his wife on a number of occasions. They were African American. I live in a highrise apartment building in a residential neighborhood on the west side of Manhattan. One evening after dinner, I went down to the street with my friend, his wife, and another guest to help them into a taxi for the ride back to their hotel.

A taxi was coming toward us. The "on duty" light was on and there were no passengers in the back seat. I stepped off the curb and flagged the driver down. He blinked his lights in acknowledgement. The taxi slowed. Then the driver saw that I was with two black men and a black woman, assumed the taxi was for them (which it was), and drove off.

The three people left standing at the curb were Muhammad Ali, Lonnie Ali, and Ali's closest friend, Howard Bingham.

*Again and again, The Bittersweet Science makes the point: Longterm physical damage to fighters isn't just possible or likely. It's nearly inevitable.*

## The Bittersweet Science

*The Bittersweet Science* (edited by Carlo Rotella and Michael Ezra, University of Chicago Press) is a collection of fifteen essays about the sport and business of boxing by contemporary writers. Some of the pieces have been previously published. Others were written exclusively for this book. As with any anthology, some entries are better than others. Ten of the pieces merit particular praise. Listed alphabetically by author, they were written by Robert Anasi, Brin-Jonathan Butler, Donovan Craig, Charles Farrell, Rafael Garcia, Gordon Marino, Hamilton Nolan, Carlo Rotella, Sam Sheridan, and Carl Weingarten.

In an introduction to *The Bittersweet Science*, Rotella and Ezra write, "The more you know about boxing, the more you discover that you never truly know what's going on. No matter how many layers of meaning you peel away, there will always be others beneath them."

In that regard, the essays go beyond what the editors call "the usual sports-page concern with winners, losers, and athletic drama." They cover a wide swath of boxing territory, from the opinionated Charles Farrell writing unapologetically about fixing fights to Brin-Jonathan Butler's in-depth exploration of Roy Jones Jr's psyche. There are dramatic accounts of ring action at the professional and amateur levels and a look at long-ago ring history.

The book also serves the purpose of introducing boxing fans to some good writers they might not know. One of these scribes is Rafael Garcia.

"The truth is," Garcia writes, "there's no purity in boxing. Not all we see is real, and we'll never see it all."

"Seen from a distance," Garcia continues "boxing is a deceptively simple spectacle: two men beating on each other until cunning, physical prowess, or a combination thereof produces a winner. Many who watch boxing never move past their romantic notion of the sport, constantly framing what they see in terms of concepts such as courage, valor, honor, and pride. Yet these same notions are hammered into irrelevance by forces significantly more pressing to the fighters and the suits promoting and managing them; namely money, power, and influence."

Viewing boxing through the prism of the first fight between Miguel Cotto and Antonio Margarito, Garcia observes, "You can't just jump to the end of a fight and skip everything that happens in between. To do that would be to miss everything that makes boxing boxing. More than in any other sport, how and why one fighter wins and the other loses is of the utmost importance and can have massive consequences for each one's future."

Garcia's description of round seven of Margarito's now-tarnished victory over Cotto is particularly good writing:

> It was either brutal or thrilling to watch, depending on whom you were rooting for or what side of your brain was calling the shots. It was at this moment that what had been billed as a fight became a rite as there was little question from that point on as to who was the stronger fighter causing the damage and who was the one getting hurt. Cotto kept fighting, of course, after the turn of the tide in round seven. But for the rest of the night, Margarito's most significant enemy was no longer Miguel Cotto but the timekeeper. The contest was decided in that brutal round. As Margarito walked back to his corner at the end of the seventh, his face and torso and back splattered with Cotto's fresh blood, he nodded to the fans celebrating at ringside. It was clear that thereafter all Margarito had to do was keep hacking and chopping away at Cotto, keep grinding him down and keep hammering him with those heavy fists until Cotto couldn't take it anymore. Then, at some point, Cotto would stop fighting and that would be it. That's exactly the path the contest took. Cotto went from sharpshooter to prey, just as Margarito went from lumbering target to heartless hitman.

Garcia then asks the question, "What does it say about us that we're willing participants—and paying customers—in this sort of blood spectacle in which someone as hurt and helpless as Cotto was for a large part of the contest had to endure so much physical punishment from a man who was obviously going to defeat him that night. The question is not novel in any way, but that doesn't take away from its sting. Fans of boxing have tried to deal with it for a long time, and all of us who enjoy the sport have learned that a corollary of our love for it is that we have to make peace with more than a few ugly truths."

Finally, Garcia notes, "There are times when boxing matches resemble more a bullfight than they do a sports contest, when only a deus ex machina will do in changing the outcome. Bullfights are all about the journey and not the destination. The inevitable outcome is that of a bull lying dead even though there are many ways to arrive at that outcome."

Charles Farrell, a former fight manager, also sees boxing as a hard sport.

In "Why I Fixed Fights," Farrell begins with the premise that "no sport is romanticized more than boxing." But the truth of the matter as he sees it is, "Boxers are born poor and they usually die poor. For their short spell in the business, they inhabit a place in its professional hierarchy that all but guarantees they'll remain poor even during their active careers."

Getting to the heart of his subject, Farrell writes, "Why did I fix fights? I fixed fights because it was the smart thing to do." He then recounts setting up a fight for Leon Spinks in the dying years of Neon Leon's ring career against a novice named John Carlo, who was making his pro debut. Farrell engaged in all manner of chicanery, including the creation of a fictitious 13-and-2 record for Carlo. But he ruefully acknowledges, "I failed to take the one step needed to guarantee the result. I didn't fix the fight."

Carlo knocked Spinks out in the first round.

"In the real world," Farrell concludes, "boxers and their managers prearranging the outcome of fights, working collusively against a hostile system, makes sense. Fixing fights, even at the expense of the public, isn't just good business. It's a survival strategy for the disenfranchised class in boxing: the fighters themselves."

Sam Sheridan, another largely unknown voice, weighs in with an essay entitled "What Boxing Is For." Among the thoughts Sheridan shares are:

- "Not all men are created equal in boxing, and we know it."
- "Professional boxing is about money. If it's about anything else, you probably shouldn't be doing it."
- "Fighting is a little like losing your virginity. Before you do it, there

is a lot of speculation, a lot of anxiety, some wild flights of imagination. Then you start doing it and you find, 'Oh, this is fighting. I'm still me.' You aren't transformed into something else. It's not some dark door you pass through. The world is still the world."

- "[Watching a fight] has to be live. Tape it and watch it later, and it's like reading about a fine wine versus drinking it. It has to be happening in the moment. We're all discovering it together, the tick of seconds, the real-time surge of real wonder in the crowd."

A sampling of other worthwhile thoughts in *The Bittersweet Science* include:

- Gordon Marino: "It's as though the crowd gets its red badge of courage with the fighter's blood."
- Donovan Craig: "Usually a street fight is over so quickly that you don't have time to appreciate it. In a boxing match, you have time to appreciate what's going on."
- Brin-Jonathan Butler: "If you're looking for happy endings for your heroes, boxing remains one of the worst places in America to look."

*The Bittersweet Science* is a good book.

*H. C. Witwer viewed the boxing world with a jaundiced eye. Many of its denizens, he wrote, were "shy the intelligence to be a first-class crook."*

# The Leather Pushers

Eight years ago, my good friend Dave Wolf died. Dave was known to boxing fans as the manager of Ray Mancini and Donny Lalonde. Basketball fans knew him as the author of *Foul: The Connie Hawkins Story*, one of the best books ever written about the city game. Soon after Dave's death, his daughter and brother invited me to his apartment and told me to take as many books about boxing from Dave's collection as I'd like. Otherwise, they'd be sold for pennies on the dollar to The Strand.

Many of the rooms in my apartment are lined with floor-to-ceiling bookshelves. I have 4,500 books arranged by subject matter and author. Almost five hundred of them are about boxing. I took forty or so of Dave's books and added them to my collection. Since then, I've read some for pleasure and others for reference purposes. Recently, I took Dave's copy of *The Leather Pushers* by H. C. Witwer off the shelf.

Witwer was born in 1890 and died of liver failure at the much-too-young age of thirty-nine. He wrote novels, short stories, and film shorts. *The Leather Pushers* was published in 1920. Putting that date in perspective, Jack Dempsey had been heavyweight champion of the world for one year. Joe Louis was six years old. Rocky Marciano had yet to be born.

Dave told me once that *The Leather Pushers* was among his favorite books when he was a teenager. Reading it, I understood why. The story is told in the first person by an unnamed narrator, a likable rogue who manages a young heavyweight prospect named Kane Halliday a. k. a. Kid Roberts. It's pulp fiction with a plot and ring action that are melodramatic to the point of being unbelievable. But Witwer had a wonderful way with words and conveyed the essence of boxing in a manner that encouraged the reader to suspend disbelief.

*The Leather Pushers* loses some of its luster in the second half but is still an entertaining read. Boxing is referenced as "the manly art of aggravated assault." After a hard first round, a fighter comes out of his corner for round two "as fresh as a daisy but not as good looking." A conniving fight manager named Dummy Carney "could dive into a haystack and emerge with ten dollars worth of needles."

A boxer's ring assault is likened to "a billion tons of coal going down a tin chute into an empty cellar." A left to the pit of a fighter's stomach doubles him up "like a match stick in its last glow." A manager tells his fighter, "I don't blame you for wanting to make money. There's a certain time in our lives when all of us get that feeling, usually during the first seventy-five years."

Witwer's narrator observes that boxing is "a game which packs more tricks than Houdini ever seen." Talking about one of his fighters, he acknowledges, "Sending Bearcat Reed into a ring with this rough Loughlin person was like entering an armless wonder in a bowling tourney. If Loughlin was trying, my battler wouldn't have a chance if they let him climb through the ropes with an ax in each hand. But for a guarantee of a thousand fish, I would let Bearcat Reed box five starving lions and a couple of irritated wildcats in the middle of the jungle."

He also notes, "The nearest I ever been to college was the time I went up to New Haven to go behind Young Evans when he fought K. O. Hines. I passed Yale on the way to the clubhouse."

Recounting a walk down the aisle to the ring for a fight, Witwer's narrator recalls, "They had a rule against smoking; and the smoke on that trip to the battleground was so thick, we got all the sensations of a fireman. The yell which went up from them lunatics all around us was one continuous roar in which it was impossible to pick out any words. Nothing but plain sound, that's all. This here demonstration wasn't [for either fighter]. It was caused by the same thing which makes lions in the zoo bellow when the keepers start in with the meat."

And there are grim moments: "McCabe fell with a crash, his face hitting first. He was still there at 'ten.' He was still there half an hour later when the crowd had milled out of the clubhouse. He was still there two hours after that when another kind of boxer—the undertaker—come to take him and his broken neck away. It was an unfortunate accident, pure and simple. The same kind of an accident as sunrise is."

And there are thoughts that are as true today as when Witwer wrote them a century ago:

- "Oughta be able and can do is different in boxing."
- "It's a real treat to watch the master ring artist at work. He can do with a pair of four-ounce gloves what the average guy might accomplish with a baseball bat and an ax."
- "Ring records all the way down from the time Battlin' David knocked out One Round Goliath is studded with the names of gluttons for punishment. Their favorite punch is delivered with some part of their battered face to the point of the other guy's glove, and they seldom if ever miss. They'll always be in demand because the difference between the modern prize-fight fan and the cuckoos which used to sit around Nero and holler for the gladiators to quit stalling and knife each other has stopped at the matter of dress."
- "No matter how nifty he is with his hands, a fighter without absolute confidence in his ability to weather whatever unexpected hurricane of smashing wallops he may run into is a fighter with no good reason for remaining in a tough game. The faint-hearted bird is no good when he's hurt. The real fighter is no good till he's hurt. The clever but weak-spirited boxer is usually a world beater among the tramps and a tramp among the world beaters. But confidence is a heady drink. Too much is as dangerous to success as too little. You want to dilute it a bit with a little respect for the other guy's chances. Allow leeway for the unreckoned break, the bolt from the blue, the chance that you might slip on the banana peel Fate or be flattened by the thunderbolt Chance."
- "There's probably no other competition in the world, sporting or otherwise, which draws a human gathering as miscellaneous and interesting as a prize-fight crowd. While waiting for the gladiators to enter the bull pen the next time you go to a mill, sit back and look around at the customers. You'll find every trade, art, gift, science, business, profession, sex, and color represented. Bankers and bricklayers, doctors and dock hands, millionaires and mechanics, accountants and actors, jostle, kid, and argue each other purple in the face over the merits of their respective favorites."
- "Pan the fight game all you want. Call it brutal, disgusting, crooked, sordid, anything you please. But don't say you can't get a kick out of it."

As a writer, I love the idea that, a hundred years from now, someone might come across a book I wrote and spend a day with it. If they do, I hope they enjoy it.

Meanwhile, thank you, H. C. Witwer; and thank you, Dave.

*More on boxing's literary tradition.*

# Literary Notes

Arthur Conan Doyle is known throughout the world as the creator of Sherlock Holmes, the most famous detective of all time. Less known is the fact that Doyle, a doctor by trade, was a boxing enthusiast.

Holmes first appeared in print in 1887, when Doyle was twenty-eight years old. A decade later, Doyle authored a fifteen-thousand-word novella entitled *The Croxley Master: A Great Tale of the Prize Ring.*

*The Croxley Master* tells the story of Robert Montgomery, a young medical student with a background in amateur boxing, who enters the prize ring out of desperation to compete for a 100-pound purse that he needs to finance the final year of his medical education. Montgomery's opponent is a miner from the Croxley pit and a seasoned veteran of ring wars known as *The Master of Croxley.*

Doyle describes Montgomery's first sighting of his opponent on the day of the fight as follows:

> The prize-fighter had come out from his curtain, a squat formidable figure, monstrous in chest and arms, limping slightly on his distorted leg. His skin had none of the freshness and clearness of Montgomery's, but was dusky and mottled with one huge mole amid the mat of tangled black hair which thatched his mighty breast. His huge shoulders and great arms with brown sledge-hammer fists would have fitted the heaviest man that ever threw his cap into a ring. But his loins and legs were slight in proportion. Montgomery, on the other hand, was as symmetrical as a Greek statue. It would be an encounter between a man who was specially fitted for one sport and one who was equally capable of any.

The fight, scheduled for twenty three-minute rounds, is dramatically told.

Doyle's hero fights through adversity of the worst kind:

"Montgomery," the narrative reads, "sprang wildly forward and, the next instant, was lying half senseless with his neck nearly broken. The whole round had been a long conspiracy to tempt him within reach of one of those terrible right-hand uppercuts for which the Master was famous. When Montgomery sprang in so hotly, he had exposed himself to such a blow as neither flesh nor blood could stand. Whizzing up from below with a rigid arm which put the Master's eleven stone into its force, it struck him under the jaw. He whirled half round and fell, a helpless and half-paralyzed mass. A vague groan and murmur, too excited for words, rose from the great audience. With open mouths and staring eyes, they gazed at the twitching and quivering figure. The timekeeper called the seconds. If ten of them passed before Montgomery rose to his feet, the fight was ended. As if in a dream—a terrible nightmare—the student could hear the voice of the timekeeper. 'Three-four-five.' He got up on his hand. 'Six-seven.' He was on his knee, sick, swimming, faint, but resolute to rise. 'Eight.' He was up, and the Master was on him like a tiger, lashing savagely at him with both hands."

But Montgomery rallies to turn the tide.

"It was a magnificent blow, straight, clean, crisp, with the force of the loins and the back behind it. And it landed where he had meant it to—upon the exact point of that blue-grained chin. Flesh and blood could not stand such a blow in such a place. Neither valour nor hardihood can save the man to whom it comes. The Master fell backwards, flat, prostrate, striking the ground with so simultaneous a clap that it was like a shutter falling from a wall. A yell broke from the crowded benches as the giant went down. He lay upon his back, his knees a little drawn up, his huge chest panting. He twitched and shook, but could not move. His feet pawed convulsively once or twice. It was no use. He was done. 'Eight—nine—ten!' said the timekeeper. And the roar of a thousand voices with a deafening clap like the broadside of a ship told that the Master of Croxley was the Master no more. Montgomery stood half dazed, looking down at the huge, prostrate figure. He could hardly realize that it was indeed all over."

Doyle wrote those words more than a century ago. As I read them recently, I was struck by the fact that they could have been written about a boxing match contested today. That shows how little the essence of boxing has changed over the ages.

★ ★ ★

The written history of Muhammad Ali is on ongoing construction. *Sting Like a Bee* by Leigh Montville (Doubleday) is the latest building block in that process.

*Sting Like a Bee* focuses on the five years from February 17, 1966, when Ali was reclassified 1-A (eligible for military service) by his draft board in Louisville, through June 28, 1971, when the United States Supreme Court unanimously reversed his conviction for refusing induction into the United States Army.

These years included the pre-exile period when Ali was at the peak of his powers as a fighter and fought seven times in less than twelve months through his March 8, 1971, loss to Joe Frazier.

"For a stretch of time," Montville writes, "1966 through 1971, the most turbulent divided stretch of the nation's history outside of the Civil War, Muhammad Ali was discussed as much as anyone on the planet."

That might seem like an outlandish statement. But those who lived through the era can attest to its truth.

Montville paints a portrait of Ali as a gifted, charismatic, talented, determined, sometimes confused young man, often courageous, occasionally fearful, intellectually limited in some ways, insightful in others.

"Pretty much illiterate," Montville recounts, "he was supremely good-looking and supremely verbal at a time when television invaded everywhere and these qualities became more important. He was part boob, part rube, part precocious genius, somewhat honorable, and could be really funny. He stumbled into his situation, said he didn't want to go to war because of his religion, put one foot in front of the other, and came out the other end a hero."

Readers of Montville's earlier work, such as his biographies of Ted Williams and Babe Ruth, are familiar with his writing style. There are few flourishes. That said, *Sting Like a Bee* has several particularly well-crafted passages, such as the one in which Montville describes Ernie Terrell on the eve of the fight in which Ali savaged him to shouts of "What's my name!"

> Ali made it sound like he was the first black man who ever lived, the first to fight through injustice. Uncle Tom? Terrell said he would compare hard roads to the Astrodome with this guy any day of the publicity week. He grew up in Inverness, Mississippi, one of ten children. His parents were sharecroppers. His father got a factory job in Chicago when Terrell was in his teens, so everyone headed to the cold north. He was a professional boxer two years before he graduated from Farragut High School. There were no press conferences when the first contract was signed. He never had the carefully planned list of opponents. His style was bang and hold, bang and hold, hit with the left and grind around the ring. He was a defensive fighter, a neutralizer. He had no dazzling speed, no shuffle. He was a survivor. His record was an honest 39–4, and he hadn't been beaten in five years.

Montville also gives readers an intriguing portrait of Hayden Covington, the larger-than-life attorney who oversaw much of the early draft-related legal work on Ali's behalf (and later resigned over unpaid legal fees).

Similarly, Lawrence Grauman, the hearing examiner whose recommendation to the Kentucky Appeals Board that Ali be granted conscientious objector status was ignored, is well portrayed.

And thank you to Montville for debunking the oft-repeated notion that it was Ali who originated the phrase "No Viet Cong ever called me nigger." The credit for that properly goes to Stokely Carmichael.

Montville has conducted serious research into the legal maneuvering and legal issues surrounding Muhammad Ali and the draft and brought the source material together in a way that makes it more easily accessed and more fully understood. That's a valuable service.

★ ★ ★

Max Baer reigned as heavyweight champion for one day shy of a year during the seven-year interregnum between Gene Tunney and Joe Louis. John Jarrett tells his story in *Max Baer: Clown Prince of Boxing* (Pitch Publishing). The book isn't up to the standard that Jarrett set two years ago with *Dempsey and the Wild Bull.* But it does have some entertaining moments.

Baer fashioned a 66–13 (51 KOs, 3 KOs by) career ledger. He was a showman and a womanizer, kind-hearted and erratic, with a potent right hand. "I don't like to fight," he once said. "I never did, except when I'm hurt. Then I want to get in there and hurt back."

Baer's career was defined by four consecutive fights contested within the span of twenty-seven months.

On June 8, 1933, he knocked out former heavyweight champion Max Schmeling in the tenth round of a brutal back-and-forth encounter. After the bout, Baer observed, "I was pretty rough in there. But say, a fight's a fight, isn't it?"

After beating Schmeling, Baer took advantage of his good looks and outgoing personality to land a starring role in the Hollywood film *The Prizefighter and The Lady*. It was soon apparent that he preferred vaudeville, acting in motion pictures, and womanizing to fighting. But on June 14, 1934, he returned to the ring to challenge Primo Carnera, who had knocked out Jack Sharkey to claim the heavyweight crown.

Baer had the good fortune to challenge the mob-controlled Carnera in an honest fight. Before the bout, the challenger promised. "That's one that will be so good, I wish I was out in the audience watching myself." In a sloppy, free-swinging affair, he knocked the Italian giant down an implausible twelve times en route to an eleventh-round stoppage.

"Carnera didn't look bad," sportswriter Joe Williams declared afterward. "He looked terrible."

Baer looked just as terrible 364 days later when he made his first and only title defense, coming in undermotivated and out of shape to lose a decision to James Braddock in one of the worst heavyweight championship fights ever.

Interviewed after his defeat, Baer told Tommy Manning of NBC radio, "I'm glad and really happy to see Jimmy happy. He'll appreciate it more than I did. After all, he's got a family and he's married. Of course, I might have a family around the country too, but I don't know it."

Baer chose unwisely for his comeback fight after losing to Braddock. Three months later, on September 24, 1935, he stepped into the ring before an estimated 95,000 fans at Yankee Stadium to face an undefeated young heavyweight named Joe Louis.

Louis knocked him out in four rounds. Baer could have gotten up after his final trip to the canvas but didn't.

"Sure I quit," he acknowledged afterward. "He hit me eighteen times while I was going down the last time. If anybody wants to see the execution of Max Baer, he's got to pay more than twenty-five bucks for a ringside seat."

Baer died of a heart attack in 1959 at age fifty. Damon Runyon summed up nicely when he wrote, "There have been many greater fighters than Max Baer, but never a greater showman."

★ ★ ★

For more than a century, the heavyweight champion of the world was sports royalty. But unlike many kings, whose authority is bestowed as an accident of birth, these men derived their authority first through conquest and then from the consent of the governed.

*The Boxing Kings: When American Heavyweights Ruled the World* by Paul Beston (Rowman & Littlefield) is a history of the heavyweight championship in America from the 1880s through the end of the twentieth century.

The heavyweight title, Beston writes, was once "a defining property in sports" and American champions were "symbols of national might." But "boxing lost its narrative in America. The rise of competitive sports as a commercial industry, a story in which boxing was integral, eventually left the sport trailing badly behind."

Beston places special emphasis on seven champions who held what he calls "a defining place in our culture": John L. Sullivan, Jack Johnson,

Jack Dempsey, Joe Louis, Rocky Marciano, Muhammad Ali, and Mike Tyson. He then examines these seven and their brethren in the context of their times and with appreciation for boxing's "capacity to absorb such varieties of human character."

The lineage begins with John L. Sullivan.

"Sullivan," Beston writes, "came along with no precedents for the role he was about to play, which was to become the George Washington of boxing and America's first sports superstar. In 1882, the year Sullivan won the heavyweight championship, the idea of professional sports was in its infancy. Professional baseball was just coming into existence. The National League had been founded six years earlier. American football was barely a flicker in the eye of Yale's Walter Camp. Basketball had not yet been invented."

Thereafter, Beston continues, "The evolution of the heavyweight championship from an underground quasi-mythical title to a commercial property was part of a social revolution, one in which working-class passions would create a new popular culture in America."

No sporting event in history has matched the social significance of Jack Johnson vs. James Jeffries, the second encounter between Joe Louis and Max Schmeling, and the first Ali–Frazier fight.

Beston acknowledges Johnson's greatness as a fighter, his prominence in American social history, and the oppressive racial climate in which he lived. But citing Papa Jack's personal flaws, he posits that "the long cycle of redefinition has produced a heroic image that is almost as misleading as the original racist caricature."

Of Jack Dempsey, Beston observes, "So many people wanted to see his fights that special arenas were built to accommodate them."

Then, after Gene Tunney (Dempsey's conqueror) retired, Max Schmeling, Jack Sharkey, Primo Carnera, Max Baer, and James Braddock, arrived sequentially on the scene. That paved the way for Joe Louis. In Beston's words, "Five uninspiring heavyweight champions plus Depression economics made the public more receptive to breaking the color line."

Ultimately, Rocky Marciano filled the void in the public imagination left when Louis retired.

Muhammad Ali was the next man to be enshrined in heavyweight boxing's pantheon of gods.

"Ali, Frazier, and Foreman made an unequaled heavyweight trio," Beston declares. "It was as if Jack Dempsey, Joe Louis, and Rocky Marciano had all competed during the same era." But Beston goes on to write, "Before Ali, the title had made smaller men into bigger men. After him, the title seemed somehow smaller."

That trend continued with Mike Tyson, who Beston calls "the final towering figure" in the American heavyweight lineage. Writing of the years after Tyson was deposed, Beston states, "For most of the public, the term 'heavyweight champion' still signified one man: Tyson. As with Ali, his non-possession of the title seemed incidental, a nettlesome technicality. Tyson's global fame made his possession, or non-possession, of the official title virtually irrelevant."

Beston writes well. There's a nice flow to the book. He has done a lot of research, and it shows. The major fights are nicely recounted.

He also does a pretty good job of separating allegorical anecdotes from reality. For example, there's a tale that many writers (including yours truly) have told of Franklin Roosevelt inviting Joe Louis to the White House in 1938, squeezing Louis's biceps, and saying, "Joe, we need muscles like yours to beat Germany."

"The 1938 meeting," Beston writes, "never happened. Louis did have a friendly visit with FDR a few years earlier."

But there are places where Beston falls short. Some of his errors are niggling misstatements of fact. He writes that the three Patterson-Johansson fights represented the first time that "two men fought three times for the heavyweight title." Ezzard Charles vs. Jersey Joe Walcott counters that notion. Similarly, Beston states that Axel Schulz (who challenged George Foreman in 1995) was "the first German to fight for the crown since Max Schmeling." People who remember Muhammad Ali vs. Karl Mildenberger would dispute that claim.

More seriously, there are instances where Beston seems to have relied on promotional hype rather than accurate reports. For example, he writes that Larry Holmes and Gerry Cooney had a "50–50 money split" with each fighter being promised $10 million for their 1982 encounter. In reality, Cooney's purse was $8.5 million, and Holmes received significantly less.

There are also unsourced statements of questionable veracity, such as the claim that "eight doctors confirmed a torn tendon" in Sonny Liston's shoulder after his loss to Cassius Clay.

That said, *The Boxing Kings* is a good book. Beston condenses a great deal of history into 313 pages and does it well.

★ ★ ★

There was a time when boxing fans relied on newspapers for the timeliest recounting of big fights. That changed in the 1920s with the mass commercialization of radio. Then, in the 1940s, television began the process of supplanting radio.

Frederick V. Romano tells the tale in *The Golden Age of Boxing on Radio and Television* (Carrel Books).

The first boxing match transmitted by radio was an experimental broadcast of the April 11, 1921, encounter between Johnny Dundee and Johnny Ray. Twelve weeks later, Jack Dempsey's July 2, 1921, championship defense against Georges Carpentier was heard by an estimated three hundred thousand listeners.

By the mid-1920s, radio had advanced from being a curiosity to a fixture in American homes. Fifteen million people heard Graham McNamee's call when Gene Tunney dethroned Jack Dempsey on September 23, 1926, to seize the heavyweight crown.

The preeminent blow-by-blow commentators of the radio era were McNamee, Ted Husing, Clem McCarthy, Sam Taub, and Don Dunphy.

Nat Fleisher, the founding editor of *The Ring*, took a turn behind the microphone for a May 7, 1926, bout between Sammy Baker and Larry Estridge at Madison Square Garden. But the broadcast did not go well. Stuart Hawkins, a boxing columnist for the *New York Herald*, described Fleischer's effort as "the most woefully inadequate, utterly colorless, and consistently exasperating broadcast that has ever disappointed eastern listeners."

The high point of the marriage between boxing and radio was Joe Louis's first-round knockout of Max Schmeling on June 22, 1938. NBC carried the bout on 146 stations throughout the United States, and it was transmitted in multiple languages around the world. Clem McCarthy called the blow-by-blow in what was arguably the most important sports broadcast of all time.

The golden age of boxing on radio, by Romano's reckoning, lasted into the twilight of Joe Louis's heavyweight reign. By then, it was clear that television was the wave of the future.

Early boxing telecasts were primitive compared to what fans see today. Benny Leonard had boxed an exhibition on television in 1931. But as noted in the *New York Herald Tribune*, the picture quality was such that the fighters "seemed to be struggling through a severe blizzard."

The first major televised boxing match was a June 1, 1939, encounter at Yankee Stadium between Max Baer and Lou Nova. Here too, the grainy black-and-white images were far from satisfying.

The first heavyweight championship fight seen live on home television was the June 19, 1946, rematch between Joe Louis and Billy Conn. Romano calls that "the start of the modern era of boxing and commercial TV," but adds, "At this juncture, the live gate was still overwhelmingly the most important source of revenue."

The numbers support this contention. The live gate for fights at Madison Square Garden in 1947 was $2.2 million. By comparison, the radio and television revenue streams for those fights were $220,000 and $100,000 respectively.

By the early 1950s, boxing was ubiquitous on television. Not only was it a national sport, it was the perfect sport for the tiny black-and-white TV screens of that era. The action was contested in a small, enclosed area with only two competitors for the camera to follow and no hard-to-see balls flying through the air.

The Gillette Safety Razor Company took the lead in sponsoring boxing on television with weekly telecasts under the banner of *The Gillette Cavalcade of Sports*.

Don Dunphy transitioned successfully from radio to television, where he was joined by Chris Schenkel as the two preeminent TV blow-by-blow commentators of that era.

But the seeds of destruction were being sown. Other sports rose in popularity. TV technology advanced to accommodate them. United States Senate hearings chaired by Estes Kefauver lay bare the influence of organized crime on boxing. Then, on March 24, 1962, Benny Paret was beaten to death by Emile Griffith.

Boxing and tragedy walk hand in hand. In 1947, a national radio audience had listened as Sugar Ray Robinson bludgeoned Jimmy Doyle into unconsciousness. Doyle, age twenty-two, was taken from the ring on a stretcher and died one day later. There had been similar tragedies in minor televised bouts. But Griffith–Paret was a major championship fight witnessed by millions on national television.

Sponsors grew wary of the sweet science. In 1964, regularly scheduled national telecasts ended, marking the end of what Romano calls "boxing's golden age of television."

Romano deserves credit for having undertaken an enormous amount of research. His book contains an extensive recounting of the not-so-behind-the-scenes machinations of James Norris, the International Boxing Club, the mob-linked Managers Guild, Franky Carbo, Blinky Palermo, and their brethren. There's also a recounting of the technology behind radio and television boxing broadcasts and an exploration of radio and television contractual arrangements.

On the downside, there are places where Romano's recounting goes on for too long, as if he's determined to include everything he learned rather than edit down. And the writing is a bit dry. Historic milestones like the Dempsey–Tunney and Louis–Schmeling fights are treated with little drama.

That said, *The Golden Age of Boxing on Radio and Television* is a valuable resource for those interested in the subject.

★ ★ ★

On March 5, 2016, unbeaten Australian heavyweight Lucas Browne journeyed to Grozny (the capital of the Chechen Republic) to fight Ruslan Chagaev. Chagaev was the WBA "regular" world heavyweight champion and a favorite of Chechen strongman, President Ramzan Kadyrov, who attended the fight. Trailing badly on the judges' scorecards, Browne knocked Chagaev out in the tenth round. *The World Champion That Never Was: The Story of Lucas Browne* by Graham Clark (Hardie Grant Books) is the story of that fight.

Let's start with some caveats. Clark was a member of Browne's team in Grozny, so his objectivity might be questioned. Also, Chagaev–Browne wasn't a real-world championship fight. But sanctioning-body belts, no matter how bogus they might be, are important to fighters.

Clark has an easy-to-read writing style. He describes Grozny as a beehive swarming with Chechen rebels, a spawning ground for Islamic extremists, and a safe harbor for the Russian mob.

The climactic fight is well told. Chagaev dominated in the early going. Browne was badly cut, lost a tooth, and endured a stream of damaging body blows. Round six, when Chagaev dropped Browne and had him in trouble, was three minutes fifteen seconds long. Round seven, when Browne turned the tide and staggered Chagaev, was forty-four seconds short.

The battle ended in round ten, when referee Stanley Christodoulou wrapped his arms around a defenseless Chagaev to protect him from further harm. At that point, there was significant concern for Browne's safety. Rather than celebrate in the ring, Team Browne retreated to the dressing room as quickly as possible.

Sadly, Browne never got his championship belt. After the fight, he was told that it would be sent to him within two weeks. But a post-fight urinalysis by the Voluntary Anti-Doping Association revealed traces of clenbuterol in his system.

Clenbuterol, a banned drug, is used primarily to help athletes lose weight. That made no sense in Browne's situation, since a 250-pound heavyweight has no need to make weight. Also, all VADA testing of Browne prior to the fight was negative insofar as illegal performance-enhancing drugs were concerned. That lent credence to the theory that Browne was a "clean" athlete and that either he had inadvertently eaten contaminated meat or his food had been deliberately laced with clenbuterol.

However, the rules of the game are clear. Athletes are responsible for what goes into their system. Browne was stripped of his title and suspended by the WBA for six months.

"Now," Clark writes, "it was almost as if the fight had never happened. The achievement had been wiped from the records, the glory had been tarnished, and the story had been retold with the hero cast as the villain."

Then an even more troubling eventuality occurred. In November 2016, a random test sample taken from Browne by VADA pursuant to the WBC Clean Boxing Program tested positive for ostarine (a banned drug that produces effects similar to anabolic steroids).

That leaves Clark to acknowledge, "As with the previous positive result, Browne was unable to explain the finding. This time, sabotage or eating contaminated foods could be immediately dismissed. All notions of a wronged fighter seeking redemption had been blown away. The sporting public hardens its heart very quickly to a man who fumbles his second chance."

★ ★ ★

James Lawton calls boxing "the world's oldest and most embattled sport." *A Ringside Affair: Boxing's Last Golden Age* (Bloomsbury Publishing) recounts his sojourn through the sweet science as lead sportswriter for the *Independent* and *Daily Express* in London.

Lawton's remembrance begins with what he calls "the first significant fight" he covered, the 1977 matchup between a fading Muhammad Ali and Earnie Shavers.

Ali, Lawton writes, "was so much more than a fabled sportsman. He was a touchstone for the possibilities of life, for the rewards of courage. He had no rival in his genius for touching people."

After Ali–Shavers, Madison Square Garden matchmaker Teddy Brenner said sadly, "I never thought I'd live to see the day when Muhammad Ali's greatest asset was his ability to take a punch."

Three years later, Lawton was at ringside to witness Ali's destruction by Larry Holmes. "It wasn't that Ali didn't fight," he writes. "The problem was much more fundamental. He couldn't fight. He had become disabled."

Recollections of Larry Holmes, Mike Tyson, Buster Douglas, Evander Holyfield, Riddick Bowe, and Lennox Lewis follow.

One of the most poignant passages in *A Ringside Affair* concerns Eddie Futch recalling how he decided to train Bowe, the fighter who ultimately broke his heart.

"I loved what I had seen of his talent," Futch observed. "For a big man, he moved beautifully. He had the balance and the grace of a real fighter, and that was exciting. You can go a long time in boxing without seeing such qualities leaping out at you. But it doesn't mean anything if the guy deep down doesn't really want to fight."

Lawton also re-creates the glorious round-robin combat amongst Sugar Ray Leonard, Thomas Hearns, Marvin Hagler, and Roberto Duran.

"Any lover of the fights," he writes, "the real ones that forced men into every resource at their disposal and reminded all who watched them why this was the most ancient and durable of sports, would surely say, 'You gave us your best.'"

Of Leonard–Hearns, Lawton notes, "Leonard was accused of impertinence when he took the appellation 'Sugar.' It was, some said, an affront to the achievements of a man still regarded by many as the greatest pound-for-pound fighter of all time. But not any more."

Outraged by the judges' decision in Hagler–Leonard, Lawton declares, "Some fights are never over, whatever the ringside adjudication. They go on down through the years, harboring old regrets, spawning fresh anger."

But Lawton concedes that a poor fight plan that saw Hagler switch from southpaw to an orthodox stance in the early rounds contributed to The Marvelous One's loss ("He resembled someone running through his keyring, confused that a familiar lock refused to open"). And he acknowledges that, from Leonard's point of view, "A knockout was not the point of the exercise. He had gone to beat Hagler within the rules of boxing. He had seen and exploited the way to reduce him with his speed and flair and ineffable self-belief. He hadn't gone to floor Hagler but to scale him down, to say that his own talent was of a different and superior kind."

Hagler–Hearns is deftly described with an observation from Budd Schulberg: "I never thought I'd see anything so intense outside of war."

Of Roberto Duran, Lawton says simply, "He might have come not from the raw and volatile streets of Panama City but from a separate planet devoted exclusively to waging war."

There's very little in *A Ringside Affair* that knowledgeable readers don't already know. But the familiar is well-told. The big fights are nicely recounted. And there's a thoughtful digression in the form of a chapter about Pat Putnam, the award-winning writer for *Sports Illustrated*, who wove a false narrative about years spent as a prisoner of war in Korea when, in fact, he hadn't served in the military at all.

*For far too long, the New York State Athletic Commission has been a comedy of errors courting a tragedy.*

# Keystone Cops at the New York State Athletic Commission

In the early days of silent film, Americans were entertained by the exploits of a group of incompetent policemen known as "The Keystone Cops." The Keystone Cops had very little idea what they were doing but expended a great deal of energy running around in an uncoordinated manner, screwing things up.

There are times when the New York State Athletic Commission resembles the Keystone Cops.

In a series of investigative articles in 2016, I cataloged the problems that plague the commission. Many of the concerns expressed in these articles were confirmed in a report issued by the Inspector General of the State of New York. All of them were viewed against the backdrop of the horrific injuries suffered by Magomed Abdusalamov in a November 2, 2013, fight at Madison Square Garden.

Referencing the sloppy procedures and practices ingrained at the NYSAC that led to the Abdusalamov tragedy, I observed, "A motorist can run a red light ten times without adverse consequences. Then, one day, there's a truck."

The NYSAC is still running red lights with regard to fighter safety.

Let's start with a given. There are some dedicated, hardworking, public servants who work for the New York State Athletic Commission. One of them is acting executive director Tony Giardina, who has been thrust into a position he didn't seek or want. Giardina assumed his present position in August 2016 out of loyalty to New York governor Andrew Cuomo. While with the NYSAC, he has played by the rules of his profession. Unfortunately, these rules sometimes place a premium on political considerations.

Recent fight cards in New York have revealed a commission that's continuing to spiral downward. There has been significant improvement in some medical protocols. But overall, the NYSAC has been undermined by poor performance on the part of too many commission personnel. In the most dangerous of these situations, a fighter was allowed to fight without undergoing the mandatory fight-night physical examination.

Moreover, not only is the commission endangering the lives of fighters, some of its own personnel now feel endangered by the erratic behavior of other NYSAC personnel.

Further contributing to the problems, NYSAC director of boxing Eric Bentley will leave the commission on April 21, 2017, for a job in the private sector. Bentley was one of the few commission employees who understood the sport and business of boxing and tried to do his job without giving in to the political forces that have weakened the commission. He was also on the short list of NYSAC employees who spoke openly and honestly with investigators from the Inspector General's office regarding problems at the commission.

The March 17, 2017, St. Patrick's Day fight card at Madison Square Garden headlined by Michael Conlan vs. Tim Ibarra exemplified the problems facing the NYSAC.

New York requires that all fighters be examined by a commission doctor on fight night prior to entering the ring. In the past, an NYSAC doctor would come to the dressing room and conduct this examination. Current procedures call for the commission inspector assigned to a fighter to bring the fighter to a designated area for examination. This examination is crucial to protecting the health and safety of the fighter.

On March 17, Jean Seme was assigned to work as an inspector with Jhovany Collado, a fighter with a 4–11–2 (1 KO) record who was in the fourth bout of the evening. Seme failed to take his fighter to the mandatory pre-fight physical examination. Then, when deputy commissioner Anthony Careccia visited the dressing room prior to the fight and asked if the pre-fight physical examination had been conducted, Seme misstated the facts and told him "yes."

The consequences that could have followed from this breach of protocol were potentially devastating. Suppose Collado had developed a medical problem subsequent to the previous day's physical examination and was seriously injured during the fight?

Collado lost a unanimous six-round decision. Later that evening, when the oversight was discovered, Seme was terminated as an inspector.

With better procedures, the error would have been discovered before Collado fought, not after.

But that's not the end of the story. Multiple sources say that Seme waited in the Theater at Madison Square Garden where the fights were held and confronted Giardina, Bentley, MMA project coordinator Kim Sumbler, and athletic activities assistant Matt Delaglio as they left the arena and demanded to "see the commissioners." Giardina told Seme that any complaint he might have should be directed to the Department of State's Human Resources Department. Seme is said to have responded, "You fucked me good." Soon after, Sumbler passed Seme on the street and heard him shouting into his cell phone, "These motherfuckers can't do that. I'll kill them all." The matter was referred to the state police, who, sources say, visited Seme to discuss the incident.

The following week, Seme filed a complaint with the Human Resources Department, claiming that Giardina had discriminated against him because he's black and that his termination was, at least in part, an act of retaliation against him because he'd filed earlier discrimination complaints against two other commission employees. The earlier complaints had been dismissed after an investigation into the allegations led to a finding that they were unfounded.

The NYSAC has also been put on notice that three other commission employees have exhibited what was perceived by one or more co-workers as unusually aggressive, hostile behavior. In one of these situations, John Signorile (an NYSAC commissioner since 2013) filed a formal complaint with Human Resources, stating that he'd been physically threatened by Deputy Commissioner Mario Mercado prior to a December 31, 2016, World Series of Fighting card at Madison Square Garden and that Mercado put his hands on Signorile in an aggressive threatening manner. Human Resources found "no cause" to take action against Mercado. Signorile has filed a second complaint with the New York State Inspector General's office.

Meanwhile, one night after the March 17 show at Madison Square Garden, the sweet science returned to the Mecca of Boxing. And again, there was regulatory chaos.

The co-featured bouts on March 18 were Gennady Golovkin vs. Danny Jacobs and Roman Gonzalev vs. Srisaket Sor Rungvisai. At the pre-fight rules meeting, John Hornewer (a lawyer for K2, which was promoting the event) asked when a championship fight would become official in the event the fight was stopped because of an accidental foul.

The Unified Rules of Boxing promulgated by the Association of Boxing Commissions and adopted by the State of New York specifically provide that a fight will go to the scorecards in the event of a stoppage "after four rounds have occurred."

The commission representative mistakenly stated that the fight would not become official "until the bell for round five rings."

There's a difference. And given the dangerous cut sustained by Gonzalez early in his fight against Rungvisai, that difference could have been crucial.

Also, the Golovkin–Jacobs weigh-in was conducted at the unusually early hour of nine o'clock on Friday morning (more than thirty-eight hours before the bell for round one) because the New York State Athletic Commission felt it would be difficult to handle an early-afternoon weigh-in on the same day that it was overseeing the 7:00 p.m. Conlan–Ibarra fight card.

Golovkin vs. Jacobs was for the WBC, WBA, and IBF 160-pound titles. At the official weigh-in on Friday morning, Golovkin weighed in at 159.6 pounds and Jacobs at 159.8.

The IBF has a mandatory morning weigh-in on the day of its championship fights that limits middleweights to 170 pounds. After this second weigh-in, a fighter can put on as much additional weight as he wants. When the Golovkin camp agreed to the 9:00 p.m. Friday weigh-in, it did so in the belief that Jacobs would have to weigh-in at 170 pounds or less on Saturday morning. But Jacobs failed to appear at the fight-day weigh-in. The NYSAC could have forced a fight-day weigh-in of Jacobs because it was in the contracts for the fight. But it chose to not do so.

Then a more serious weight problem occurred. One day before the April 8 UFC 210 card at Keybank Arena in Buffalo, Daniel Cormier weighed in.

Cormier was slated to fight Anthony Johnson in a cruiserweight title bout that was the main event on a thirteen-bout card. The UFC cruiserweight limit is 205 pounds. Cormier stripped naked and, with two defenders of public decency holding a towel in front of him to shield his genitals, weighed in at 206.2 pounds.

Then things got crazy.

Literally 143 seconds later, Cormier returned to the scale and weighed in at 205 pounds.

How did Cormier lose 1.2 pounds in 143 seconds?

He didn't. Video evidence shows that, on the second weigh-in attempt, Cormier was holding onto the towel and pressing downward, an age-old con used by amateur wrestlers in poorly-regulated competitions to make weight.

Thereafter, an article on *Deadspin* referred to "bureaucratic shenanigans." *MMA Weekly* referenced a "weigh-in debacle." Writing for *ESPN.com*, Brett Okamoto observed, "Cormier clearly pushed down on the towel, which would presumably offset his weight slightly." Brian Campbell of *CBS Sports.com* noted that, by using the towel, Cormier "likely shifted his body weight just enough to affect the scale."

The following night, Cormier won by submission over Johnson in the second round.

The NYSAC's handling of a scheduled UFC 210 bout between Cynthia Calvillo and Pearl Gonzalez was also farcical.

The NYSAC Medical Manual states, "Due to the concern over rupture, boxers who have breast implants are not eligible to box in New York."

Gonzalez disclosed in writing that she has breast implants when she applied to the commission for her license weeks in advance of the fight. Then, at the weigh-in, she was told that her fight was off. But after UFC officials voiced their displeasure, the commission reversed itself based on the sophistry that its medical manual refers to boxers, not MMA contestants.

Apparently the people running the NYSAC think that getting punched in the breast by a gloved fist is more dangerous than getting punched, kneed, and kicked in the breast by a trained mixed martial artist.

Meanwhile, Gonzalez was displeased that the NYSAC had announced to the world that she has breast implants. "At the end of the day, it's out," she said. "There's nothing I can do about it. I'm not going to dwell about it. I don't think I wanted the world to know about my surgery and to be talked about like this."

The UFC 210 co-main event—Gegard Mousasa vs. Chris Weidman—also posed problems.

The Unified Rules for Mixed Martial Arts—which New York purports to adhere to—provide that it's illegal to kick or knee a downed opponent in the head. A fighter is considered down when he, or she, has both hands on the canvas. Mousasa delivered a knee to Weidman's head while Weidman was on the canvas. Referee Dan Miragliotta ruled the knee illegal and gave Weidman five minutes to recover. Then Miragliotta consulted with NYSAC officials at ringside, who viewed a video replay and told him that the knee was legal because Weidman was not "down." At that point, instead of the fight continuing, Mousasa was declared the winner. However, the use of video review as a tool in making in-fight decisions is not allowable under New York law.

Writing for *Bleacher Report*, Scott Harris declared, "The co-main event of UFC 210 was marred by controversy and ineptitude on the part of the New York State Athletic Commission officials in attendance. No one seemed to know what was going on. No one seemed to fully understand the rule about strikes to downed opponents or how it was supposed to be applied. It was a messy situation that harmed everyone involved, and it was an unfortunate end to a bout that was shaping up to be a great contest."

Matthew Ryder of *Bleacher Report* added, "What it does illuminate is a degree of concern surrounding the New York State Athletic Commission and its capacity to regulate MMA to an adequate standard. It's apparent the NYSAC is as much a kangaroo court as it is a governing body."

UFC agreed to promote five shows within one year in the State of New York as part of a package of quid pro quos that led to the legalization of mixed martial arts in New York. The last of these five shows will take place at the Nassau Coliseum on July 22. After that, who knows?

The list of embarrassing—and potentially dangerous—problems that have undermined the New York State Athletic Commission in recent months goes on.

Last year, the NYSAC made a good decision when it relieved referees of the responsibility for picking up the judges' scorecards between rounds. That decision was made to enable the referee to more closely observe the fighters and communicate with the ring doctors during these sixty-second periods.

Fast forward to January 14, 2017, when James DeGale and Badou Jack fought to a draw in their 168-pound title-unification bout at Barclays Center. There were several instances during the fight when DeGale lost his mouthpiece and the referee waited until long after a lull in the action to have the mouthpiece put back in. At the post-fight press conference, Jack told the media that the referee had threatened to disqualify DeGale for repeatedly losing his mouthpiece.

But the reason DeGale kept losing his mouthpiece was that the dental bridge had been knocked out of his mouth early in the fight. He was not purposely spitting out his mouthpiece or losing it due to negligence. That being the case, the ring doctor in DeGale's corner should have been aware of the situation and communicated the information to the referee.

In the fifth bout on the March 17 card at Madison Square Garden, Brazilian Olympic gold medalist Robson Conceicao made short work of Aaron Hollis, stopping him in the second round. Following the stoppage, the NYSAC inspectors and ring doctor assigned to Hollis's corner let him stand there even though he was obviously on shaky legs. It was left to an inspector in Conceicao's corner to bring Conceicao's stool across the ring and place it Hollis's corner, enabling a grateful Hollis to sit.

The lead inspector assigned to Hollis said afterward that she thought the ring doctor was supposed to put the stool in the ring if it was necessary. The ring doctor said he thought the stool was necessary if there was a knockout but not a TKO.

Meanwhile, the New York State Athletic Commission (which is trying to justify its budget while presiding over the elimination of club fights and ruination of small promoters in New York because of ill-considered insurance requirements) is over-staffing big fights at taxpayer expense.

Greg Sirb (executive director of the Pennsylvania State Athletic Commission) says that, for its biggest events, the Pennsylvania commission has twenty-five to thirty people on site. Bob Bennett, who oversees the Nevada commission, says that, for a big card (e.g. ten fights including three twelve-round championship fights), the NSAC has up to forty-five people on site.

By contrast, the New York State Athletic Commission had more than sixty people on site for the January 14 (DeGale–Jack) and March 4 (Thurman–Garcia) boxing cards at Barclays Center and the March 18 (Golovkin–Jacobs) boxing card at Madison Square Garden.

More than sixty NYSAC personnel were also assigned to work the ten-bout February 11, 2017, UFC 208 card at Barclays Center in Brooklyn.

Were all these employees (most of whom are paid on a per diem basis) necessary? Let's look at the numbers. Roughly twenty fewer NYSAC personnel were assigned to UFC 210 on April 8 in Buffalo.

One might divine from these numbers that assignments are made (and taxpayer dollars are unnecessarily spent on transportation, hotel, meals and salary) so some NYSAC personnel can travel from upstate New York to New York City and have a good time. After all, if more than sixty NYSAC employees are necessary to properly regulate a ten-fight card in Brooklyn, shouldn't the same number be necessary to properly regulate a thirteen-fight card in Buffalo?

And by the way . . . Isn't it time that the New York State Athletic Commission stopped wasting taxpayer dollars by "regulating" professional wrestling? In February 2017, Anthony Bazzoffi was named deputy director of upstate athletics. According to an NYSAC memorandum, Bazzoffi 's responsibilities include, among other things, "overseeing all activity regarding professional wrestling." The NYSAC could just as appropriately regulate theatrical performances on Broadway.

There have been several welcome additions to the New York State Athletic Commission in recent months. In that regard, newly appointed deputy commissioners Ed Kunkle and Tom Aceto come to mind.

But Kim Sumbler, who was installed last year as MMA project coordinator, has failed to coordinate.

Jim Leary (who developed considerable expertise in recent years while serving as counsel to the NYSAC) is moving on to another assignment.

And the departure of Eric Bentley is a body blow to the commission. Bentley will go to work for Evander Holyfield's new promotional company (Evander Holyfield Real Deal Promotions), where he's expected to oversee boxing-related activity on a daily basis. Bentley was one of the few bright spots at a commission that has institutionalized mediocrity in the appointment and assignment of personnel and is laden with political appointees of limited ability who know next to nothing about the sport and business of boxing.

How can the problems be fixed?

It starts at the top. Under New York law, the NYSAC is supposed to be overseen by five commissioners. At present, there are three commissioners, two of whom are serving as holdover appointees pursuant to terms that have expired. This means that New York governor Andrew Cuomo has four seats to fill.

In autumn 2016, multiple people were told that the governor would announce his choices to fill the four commissioner seats by the end of the year. Then they were told that the governor was holding the positions as bargaining chips for use in negotiating with state legislators. It's now expected that the nominees for the commissioner positions will be named and voted upon before the state legislature adjourns at the end of June 2017.

It's essential that Governor Cuomo appoint qualified men and women with a history of excellence and a working knowledge of combat sports to these positions. If history is any guide, he won't.

Interim NYSAC chairperson Ndidi Massay (who has been serving on a per diem basis since July 2016) is said to be lobbying for the chair on a permanent fulltime basis now that the state legislature has decided to retain the six-figure salary for the position. The chaos at the commission that has accompanied Ms. Massay's stewardship to date speaks for itself.

Acting executive director Tony Giardina has said that he would like to leave the commission in the not-too-distant future. In replacing Giardina, the powers that be should keep in mind that administrative ability is just one prerequisite. Here too, a working knowledge of combat sports is required.

The New York State Athletic Commission isn't unique among government agencies in New York or elsewhere. We live in an age when not enough qualified people opt for government service. Too often, political considerations take precedence over good performance. But what's particularly troubling here is that lives are at stake. The Keystone Cops were funny. No one will be laughing if a fighter is killed or damaged for life.

Tragedies happen in boxing, sometimes even when everyone does their job properly. What's happening now at the New York State Athletic Commission makes a tragedy inevitable.

*There will always be tragedies in boxing. That grim reality is ingrained in the nature of the sport. But lax oversight makes it more likely that a tragedy will happen.*

# The NYSAC is Still Courting Disaster

As the parties involved work to settle the various legal claims arising out of the horrific injuries suffered by Magomed Abdusalamov at Madison Square Garden on November 2, 2013, the New York State Athletic Commission is still playing Russian roulette with fighter safety.

Medical procedures and protocols have improved since the Abdusalamov tragedy. But there are still instances where the NYSAC is turning a blind eye toward the health and safety of fighters.

On April 14, 2016, governor Andrew Cuomo's office issued a press release heralding the return of mixed martial arts to New York. In part, the press release read, "Mixed martial arts contests will be supervised either directly by the New York State Athletic Commission or by a sanctioning entity approved by the Commission."

On August 31, 2016, Jim Leary (counsel for the NYSAC at that time) elaborated on this third-party supervision of MMA, saying that it would apply only to certain amateur cards. In response, promoter Lou DiBella noted, "Right now, you have a situation where some small promoters are putting on MMA shows using unknown fighters, paying them under the table, and calling them amateur shows. That way, they can get around the state insurance regulations and a whole lot more."

Is this situation a cause for concern? Absolutely.

The case of Gabriella Gulfin is in point. Gulfin is listed by Tapology.com as having had five MMA fights dating back to March 14, 2015, when she was placed on indefinite medical suspension by the New Jersey State Athletic Control Board after being knocked out by a punch on an amateur MMA card in Rahway. In mid-July 2017, the Pennsylvania State Athletic Commission (which regulates both amateur and professional MMA bouts) refused to license Gulfin for an August 19 MMA card in Pennsylvania.

"I won't touch her unless she gets off medical suspension in New Jersey," Greg Sirb (executive director of the Pennsylvania State Athletic Commission) told this writer.

Here's the problem. While on medical suspension, Gulfin has fought four times on unregulated "amateur" MMA cards in New York. These fights were contested in 2016, on July 18 and July 30 in Astoria, September 24 in Corona, and December 16 in Westbury.

So much for the high priority that the New York State Athletic Commission places on the health and safety of fighters.

On July 5, 2017, it was announced that NYSAC acting executive director Tony Giardina (who had served in that role since August 31, 2016) was leaving the commission to become one of three commissioners on the New York State Tax Appeals Tribunal.

Giardina leaves a mixed legacy. To his credit, he worked to improve medical procedures and protocols at the NYSAC. But by his own admission, he knew little about combat sports. And he helped lock in a system where political considerations take priority over performance, and employees who perform in mediocre fashion are given as much responsibility (sometimes more) as employees who are competent. He had an opportunity to change the culture at the NYSAC for the better and failed to do so.

Too many commission employees seem more concerned with moving into position to get their faces on television on fight night than in doing their job.

MMA project coordinator Kim Sumbler has succeeded Giardina as interim executive director and is likely to be given the job on a fulltime basis. Sources say that, with Giardina's departure, political directives are likely to be funneled to the NYSAC through Brendan Fitzgerald (first deputy secretary of state at the New York State Department of State).

Sumbler is entitled to a grace period to show what she can do in the job. Meanwhile, the best procedures and protocols in the world are of limited value if they're not properly implemented.

On May 13, 2017, the NYSAC held a training seminar for inspectors that focused on handwraps and the taking of urine samples. There was a time when trainers like Emanuel Steward were brought in to lecture commission personnel on handwraps. This year, recently appointed deputy commissioner Tony Careccia did the job. Dr. Louis Rotkowitz gave the lecture on the collection of urine samples and was corrected by Dr. Angela Gagliardi when he confused a woman's urethra with a woman's vagina.

More recently, on July 29, 2017, Sebastian Heiland fought Jermall Charlo at Barclays Center in Brooklyn.

Heiland is a southpaw. That means he plants his left foot to throw punches. Shortly before the fight, a commission employee (deputy commissioner Robert Orlando) noticed that Heiland's left knee was heavily taped, which is a violation of NYSAC rules. The matter was brought to Kim Sumbler's attention, and the Heiland camp was ordered to remove the tape.

In round one, Heiland's footwork, to be polite, was "awkward." Commentating for Showtime, Paulie Malignaggi observed, "It's strange footwork. It's like his legs are too straight." In round two, Malignaggi added, "It's almost like his knees aren't bending at all."

Midway through the second stanza, Heiland's knee gave way and he slipped. As he was falling to the canvas, Charlo landed a solid right uppercut. The punch was legal since Heiland was not yet on the canvas. Referee Benjy Esteves, who had seen the slip but apparently not the uppercut, waved off the knockdown. Then, realizing that Heiland was hurt, he picked up the count at "five."

Put the puzzle pieces together. The commission had reason to believe before the fight began that Heiland's left knee was injured. He was obviously having trouble moving and planting his left foot to punch. He was being pounded around the ring like a one-legged punching bag. But Benjy Esteves, who also refereed Magomed Abdusalamov vs. Mike Perez and Arturo Gatti's brutal beatdown Joey Gamache (two bouts that resulted in brain bleeds), let Heiland take a beating for two more rounds.

Things were worse in round three. Showtime blow-by-blow commentator Mauro Ranallo noted, "There appears to be something wrong with [Heiland's] left leg, although the doctors are allowing him to continue."

"It's weird," Malignaggi responded. "I don't know if he came into the fight like this. It's so strange. There's something wrong with this guy's leg."

"There's no question about that," veteran Showtime analyst Al Bernstein said.

The fight ended in round four when Heiland was knocked down again and his knee couldn't support his weight anymore.

Where was the New York State Athletic Commission inspector assigned to Heiland's dressing room when Sebastian's knee was being illegally taped? What sort of pre-fight physicals did the NYSAC medical staff administer to Heiland at the weigh-in and in the dressing room prior to the fight? What did NYSAC commissioner Ndidi Massay, who was sitting in the first row at ringside during the fight, think she was watching?

Suppose Heiland had suffered a subdural hematoma as a consequence of the beating he endured against Charlo? The New York State Athletic Commission would be right back where it was with Magomed Abdusalamov.

Let's repeat that point so no one misses it. Suppose Sebastian Heiland suffered a subdural hematoma after being pounded in the head again and again by Jermall Charlo? The result could have been a tragedy on the order of Magomed Abdusalamov.

Meanwhile, the NYSAC is in turmoil at the commissioner level.

Legislation enacted in April 2016 increased the number of NYSAC commissioners from three to five. However, at present, there are only three commissioners: Ndidi Massay, John Signorile, and Edwin Torres. Massay's term runs through January 1, 2019. Torres's term expired on January 1, 2014. Signorile's term expired on January 1, 2015. Both Signorile and Torres have been serving on a holdover basis.

It's not often that more than one NYSAC commissioner attends a commission seminar or fight card in New York. Too often, there are none.

On June 30, 2017, Michelle Nicoli-Rosales (Andrew Cuomo's deputy director of communications for economic development) confirmed that the governor had nominated three new NYSAC commissioners subject to approval by the State Senate. The nominees are (1) Dr. Philip Stieg, a New York City neurosurgeon; (2) Dr. James Vosswinkel, an East Setauket critical care surgeon; and (3) Donald Patterson, a Buffalo resident who has been involved with amateur boxing. None of the three has extensive experience in the world of professional combat sports. Moreover, the new commissioners can't be confirmed until the state legislature returns to Albany, most likely after January 1, 2018.

So the New York State Athletic Commission keeps lurching along.

The commission's July 11 open meeting was instructive. It began with a review of revised medical protocols formulated by the NYSAC's Medical Advisory Board under the leadership of Dr. Nitin Sethi.

Sethi, who is widely respected within the boxing community, presented the revised protocols to the commissioners. But the protocols are in a lengthy document that hadn't been sent to the commissioners until the previous night. It appeared as though none of the commissioners had read the revised protocols, let alone reflected on them.

The commissioners approved the revised protocols. But the discussion that preceded their vote did little to build confidence in the commission.

There was a discussion of whether fighters who are colorblind should be allowed to fight because, it was theorized, they might have trouble distinguishing between the red and blue corners. Sethi explained that colorblindness in and of itself should not disqualify a fighter from fighting.

In the past, fighters with breast implants have been barred from fighting in New York. But that policy was undermined when the NYSAC bowed to pressure and reinterpreted the rule, saying it applied only to boxing, not MMA. This allowed a fighter with breast implants to compete on a UFC card in Buffalo on April 8.

At the July 11 NYSAC meeting, it was announced that the Medical Advisory Board had determined that a ruptured breast implant is not life-threatening. Henceforth, breast implants will be allowed in all combat sports competitions in New York as long as the combatant signs a form acknowledging and accepting the risk of a rupture. In addition, there was discussion of the difference between saline and silicone breast implants (saline is safer) and how large an implant has to be in order to pose a health risk in the event of rupture.

The commissioners also agreed to consider a suggestion that the ring doctor be allowed to interrupt a fight in the middle of a round to determine if a fighter is concussed. As John McEnroe once raged, "You cannot be serious!"

Finally, John Signorile complained that the NYSAC had yet to ban flag poles from the ring and that this represents a safety hazard because, if there's a confrontation between the fighters' camps during the introductions, someone could use a flag pole as a weapon.

Commissioner Signorile also said that the conference room was too sterile, and it would be a more inspiring setting within which to conduct business if there were New York State and American flags at the end of the room.

A word to the wise: Don't put the flags in the NYSAC meeting room on poles. Someone might use them as weapons.

*Dick Gregory died four days after Donald Trump equated white supremacists and Nazi sympathizers with human rights advocates.*

# Dick Gregory and Muhammad Ali

Dick Gregory, who broke down color barriers in white nightclubs as a comedian in the 1960s, died on August 19, 2017, at age eighty-four.

Like Muhammad Ali, Gregory understood the meaning of sacrifice. Ali sacrificed the world heavyweight championship and risked going to jail for five years to stand up for his religious beliefs. Gregory, after reaching remarkable heights as an entertainer, walked away from a lucrative career as one of the most successful stand-up comics in America to pursue a lifelong passion as an advocate for social justice.

Gregory came to prominence as the civil rights movement was moving into high gear. His performances were notable for his commentary on black-white relations and a penchant for confronting racism with barbed humor:

- "I sat in at a lunch counter for nine months. When they finally integrated, they didn't have what I wanted."
- "When I was a little boy, I told my mama, 'Mama, I don't believe in Santa Claus. You know damn well there ain't no white man coming in our neighborhood after dark.'"
- "I was in a restaurant in Mississippi that was just forced to integrate. Three white boys came over to me and said, 'Boy, we're giving you fair warning. Anything you do to that chicken, we're gonna do to you.' So I put down my knife and fork; I picked up that chicken; and I kissed it."

Gregory ran for president as a protest candidate in 1968. Then he turned away from standup comedy to become a fulltime political and social activist. He opposed the war in Vietnam, championed the fight against world hunger, and became a forceful advocate for good nutritional habits.

Speaking about the way he chose to live his life, he later said, "The movement gave me a turtle philosophy. I am the turtle. Hard on the outside, soft on the inside, and willing to stick my neck out. That's what it's about."

Gregory wasn't always wise. As the years went by, he was given to bizarre conspiracy theories. But he continued to employ comedy as a self-described "social satirist" to confront stereotypes, combat the establishment, and flat-out make people laugh.

A video of Gregory at a February 23, 2008, symposium on The State of the Black Union at the New Orleans Morial Convention Center tells the tale:

- "I thanked the white dude from Walmart for my cousin. This past Christmas, they had prices so low, he didn't have to shoplift."
- "I heard it's these rednecked uneducated pot-bellied crackers that are creating the problem. And I asked myself, 'Since when does that type of white boy determine public policy?' My problem is with the president of Harvard, Yale, MIT, and the major corporations."
- "They accused Kobe Bryant of raping a white woman, and he went home and bought his wife a four-million-dollar diamond ring. Let me tell you something. If a white woman accused me of raping her and I go home and give my wife a four-million-dollar diamond ring, she'll go get two more white women."

I saw Gregory perform onstage in the 1960s. In 1989, I met him.

I was researching a biography of Muhammad Ali that eventually would be entitled *Muhammad Ali: His Life and Times*. Part of my research included interviewing political figures and social activists who had interacted with Ali.

Jimmy Carter, Gerald Ford, Andrew Young, Julian Bond, Ted Kennedy, Bill Bradley, Ramsey Clark, and others were on my list. I met with Gregory at a Holiday Inn near the Hudson River on the west side of Manhattan.

Gregory was a good athlete. He'd gone to college on a track scholarship. So he knew what it meant to be athletically gifted and understood what it took to be great.

We talked for three hours. Part of our time together was devoted to Ali's career in boxing. But that wasn't what interested Gregory. Some of the thoughts he shared with me that day follow:

- "There were a lot of us against the war in our way. But nobody heard us because we didn't command the worldwide attention that Ali enjoyed. Then he stood up and said, 'War is wrong; people get killed in wars.' And when he did that, he didn't embarrass the United States. He embarrassed armies all over the world. Had he used his energies differently, had he supported war, this planet would be an even more violent place than it is today. But instead, he taught love."

- "There are men who will let themselves down and play with their children in the privacy of their own living room. They become silly. They become children with their own children, but nobody else ever sees it. Ali was like that with the whole world."
- "He was what God meant people to be. Loving, kind, generous, good. His whole life was a prayer for peace, justice, and human dignity. He gave so much and never asked for anything back. People didn't know where he came from. They didn't know where he was going. But they knew he was there. And when he entered people's lives, he made them feel good. Right then, not next week, not tomorrow. Being in his presence was like entering a warm room on a bitter-cold winter night."
- "We live in a society where we claim we don't want our children to drink. Even drinkers say they don't want their children to drink. But when the World Series, the basketball championships, any great athletic competition is over, there's always champagne. Little kids see their heroes pumping champagne, guzzling champagne, pouring champagne on each other's heads. And until Ali, you never heard praise to God. He was the first great athlete to show the world the importance of prayer. After his fights, right in the ring, the whole world got to see the spiritual Ali. When they put that television microphone in front of him, the first thing Ali always did was give thanks to God. Then the interview could begin."
- "I don't know of anyone who's had as great an impact on people as Ali. Not just black people, not just Muslims. This great monument of a human being is loved all over the world. There's no person on this planet who's had the same effect as Ali. He got our attention. He made us listen. And then he grew within people who weren't even aware that he was there. Whatever the universal God force meant for him to do, it's out of the bottle and it isn't ever going back. Ali is inside all of us now. And because of him, no future generation will ever be the same."
- "If people from outer space came to Earth and we had to give them one representative of our species to show them our physical prowess,

our spirituality, our decency, our warmth, our kindness, our humor, and most of all, our capacity to love—it would be Ali."

- "If I wanted to teach a little grandchild of mine about the universe, I'd go and get Muhammad Ali's story and say, "Here is what happened to the universe. One day, something went from nothing to BOOMMMM. The big bang. And it keeps getting bigger. If you wanted to do a movie to depict Ali, it would just be a small light getting bigger and bigger and bigger and bigger. That was Ali in a sea of darkness."
- "Ali lived a lot of lives for a lot of people. And he was able to tell white folks for us to go to hell."

Wherever Dick Gregory's spirit is now, I doubt that it's resting in peace. More likely, he's happily advocating for a higher cause.